CALVIN O. SCHRAG
AND THE TASK
OF PHILOSOPHY AFTER
POSTMODERNITY

D1527279

Northwestern University
Studies in Phenomenology
and
Existential Philosophy

CALVIN O. SCHRAG AND THE TASK OF PHILOSOPHY AFTER POSTMODERNITY

Edited by
Martin Beck Matuštík and
William L. McBride

Northwestern University Press
Evanston, Illinois

Northwestern University Press
Evanston, Illinois 60208–4210

Copyright © 2002 by Northwestern University Press.
Published 2002. All rights reserved.

Printed in the United States of America

10 9 8 7 6 5 4 3 2 1

ISBN 0–8101-1874–2 (cloth)
ISBN 0–8101-1875–0 (paper)

Library of Congress Cataloging-in-Publication Data

Calvin O. Schrag and the task of philosophy after postmodernity / edited by
Martin Beck Matuštík and William L. McBride
    p. cm.—(Northwestern University studies in phenomenology and existential
philosophy)
    Includes bibliographical references.
    ISBN 0-8101-1874-2 (alk. paper)—ISBN 0-8101-1875-0 (pbk. : alk. paper)
    1. Schrag, Calvin O. I. Schrag, Calvin O. II. Matuštík, Martin Joseph, 1957– III.
McBride, William Leon. IV. Northwestern University studies in phenomenology
& existential philosophy.
B945.S3264 C35 2002
191—dc21   2001006689

Contents

Introduction

William L. McBride and Martin Beck Matuštík

The present volume is a tribute to Calvin Orville Schrag, both the person and the philosopher. Few widely known academic figures are as universally liked by colleagues as he is: This is a simple fact. It is therefore regrettable that space constraints forced us to confine our invitations to the relative handful of contributors to this volume, for we know that there are many other distinguished philosophers who would have been just as pleased to have been invited, and happy to contribute, as were those whose tributes to him are to be found here. Only one among all of those whom we invited, a longtime associate of Cal's, declined, and that was for reasons of severely deteriorating health.

Calvin Schrag is a very modest individual, not at all given to self-publicizing. Nevertheless, to say that he is "widely known," particularly but by no means exclusively among philosophers with a twentieth-century Continental European bent, is no exaggeration. We have had the frequent experience, for example, of traveling to conferences abroad and making new acquaintances who, when we happen to mention his name in conversation, immediately express pleasure and/or envy at learning that he and we are at the same university, Purdue.

A short biographical sketch is in order. Born the son of a minister in South Dakota, into a Mennonite farming community with a long history of migration from the German-speaking part of Switzerland to Germany to Russia under Catherine the Great, and then eventually to the United States, Calvin Schrag received his first higher education at Bethel College in Kansas. He then proceeded to Yale Divinity School, where he received his B.D. in 1953, and went on in 1957 to earn his doctorate in philosophy at Harvard. While he was at Harvard, his strong interdisciplinary background and evident talent made him the perfect choice to be teaching assistant to the newly appointed university professor, Paul Tillich, an appointment which was to become the source of many anecdotes in later years. At the same time he was also affected, probably in intellectually more significant ways than by Tillich, by his association with long-time Harvard philosophy professor John Wild, the individual who was no doubt the single most important driving force behind the great expansion of interest in Continental European thought among American philosophers in the ensuing decade. Wild was to leave Harvard for Northwestern, in large part as a protest against what he considered the untenable narrowing of Harvard's philosophical horizons by analytically oriented zealots, three years after Schrag did. The latter, meanwhile, came directly from Harvard to Purdue, which was then just beginning to develop a philosophy department (at first, only one section within a joint department of government, history, and philosophy!) that would attempt to define itself, over the next four decades and beyond, by an openness to diversity of philosophical tendencies—eclectic in, at least so it has always been hoped, the best sense of that word.

Calvin Schrag has, more than any other single individual, been the gentle guiding spirit behind this department's commitment to philosophical tolerance along with excellence. He has held three visiting appointments—at the University of Illinois and at Northwestern University for a year each, and at Indiana University for one semester—but otherwise, although widely traveled, he has kept Purdue as his home base since his arrival in 1957. The university, generally better known until comparatively recently for its programs in engineering and agriculture, honored him by making him George Ade Distinguished Professor of Philosophy in 1982, the first named chair in its School of Liberal Arts (then known as "Humanities, Social Science, and Education"). He has served, at various times, as chair of the university senate and faculty representative to the board of trustees, part-time administrator in the dean's office, acting department head, and so forth, but above all he is known within the institution for his unstinting commitment to graduate, postgraduate, and undergraduate education. For example, he cofounded the joint Ph.D. programs in both English and Philosophy and Philosophy and Communication, directed two Summer Seminars and a Summer Institute for college teachers under the auspices of the National Endowment for the Humanities, and has served as principal adviser for dozens of doctoral dissertations and as a member of several hundred additional dissertation committees, many of them of an interdisciplinary nature, besides. Through his students, between whom and himself the relationship is always one of mutual respect, his influence has extended literally worldwide. Moreover, by serving at different times in such various capacities as executive secretary of the Society for Phenomenology and Existential Philosophy, member of the executive committee of the

Eastern Division of the American Philosophical Association, secretary-general of the International Society for Phenomenology and the Human Sciences, and longtime coeditor of the journal *Man and World* (now renamed, in accordance with current sensibilities and at his own unrelenting insistence, as the *Continental Philosophy Review*), he has made many additional contributions to the national and global philosophy communities.

But Calvin Schrag's broadest influence has, of course, been exerted through his numerous publications, which are the focal points of a number of the contributions in the present volume. His first two books, *Existence and Freedom: Towards an Ontology of Human Finitude* (1961), which had its origin as his doctoral dissertation at Harvard, and *Experience and Being: Prolegomena to a Future Ontology* (1969), were in fact published by the same publishers as is this volume, Northwestern University Press. *Existence and Freedom* was designed above all to show that important ontological claims had been and were being made by philosophers in the existentialist tradition from Kierkegaard through Heidegger and beyond, and what some of them were. The next book took *experience* as its focus and urged readers to move beyond the traditional Western metaphysics in which its author himself was/is so well versed. In *Radical Reflection and the Origin of the Human Sciences* (1980), an award-winning work, he began to pay greater attention to other humanistic disciplines besides philosophy, as the subtitle indicates, and critically to analyze postmodern structuralist thinkers such as Barthes and Foucault. His subsequent books, all of which are alluded to and discussed by contributors to this volume, and numerous articles continue the dialogue between the already revolutionary tradition of existential phenomenology and the newer tendencies in Continental European and (some) American philosophical thought. As we shall discuss briefly below, *Communicative Praxis and the Space of Subjectivity* (1986) involves a dialogue with poststructuralist "deconstruction," particularly the thought of Jacques Derrida, while *The Resources of Rationality: A Response to the Postmodern Challenge* (1992) introduces the notion of transversal rationality as a way of responding to radical attacks on the notions of theory, meaning, and value and engages the thought of Jürgen Habermas and Jean-Francois Lyotard. Postmodernism has engaged in radically questioning many traditional concepts, such as, for example, the very notion of the *self*. Sympathetic to, but not entirely persuaded by, such questioning, Schrag's role is typically that of a mediator, as suggested by the title of a collection of a few of his essays, *Philosophical Papers: Betwixt and Between* (1994)—but a very creative, original mediator, as is made clear by the several extended analyses of his most recently published monograph, *The Self after Postmodernity* (1997), which the present volume includes.

Among Schrag's most significant and original philosophical achievements, then, are the figures, now well known and widely referenced, of *transversal rationality,* the *self after postmodernity,* the *fourth cultural value sphere,* and *communicative praxis.* While this ordering of the four figures is conceptual and, as we shall see later, represents the major divisions of this book, we shall restrict ourselves here to a brief glance at them as they emerge chronologically in Schrag's work.

a. *Communicative praxis.* In his seminal volume, *Communicative Praxis and the Space of Subjectivity,* Schrag initiates a dialogue with Jürgen Habermas and Jacques Derrida, thereby intervening in an important way in late twentieth-century philosophy, communication studies, critical literary theory, and critical social theory. He moves from affirming Derrida's deconstruction of speculatively metaphysical and foundationalist ways of doing philosophy to his own recovery of an open space for human discursive and nondiscursive social praxis. Schrag's yes-and-no to deconstruction allows him to develop a unique version of hermeneutics, whereby he brings Habermas's theory of communicative action into a broader conversation with Hans-Georg Gadamer's theory of interpretation and Paul Ricoeur's notion of narrative identity. Along with Derrida (as well as Richard Rorty), Schrag objects to the quasi-transcendental requirements set by Habermas's conception of communications rationality (i.e., a context-transcending notion of rationality with a formal structure of universal validity claims to truth, rightness, and sincerity). Yet he does not, as a consequence, simply embrace a limitless play of narrative and textual difference, or a deconstructive deferral of meaning. Rather, he corrects Habermas's universalist, formal, and regulative ideal of communicative community with something at once more robust and existentially situated, concrete and historically embedded—communicative praxis. In the open space of communicative praxis, the events of speaking and hearing, acting and undergoing, *implicate* us not as some "what" but rather as "who" we always already are in practices of communication.

b. *Transversal rationality.* Schrag's existentially rich notion of communication—as a practice that is embodied, intersubjective, and historical—complements and, indeed, improves on Habermas's linguistic-communication turn in philosophy. Only concretely situated communicative interactions, with rationality running across (i.e., transversally, not above) the situations of actors and their cultures and times and histories, can inform us about human life-worlds without philosophically sterilizing their plural loci. We wish to suggest that, against Habermas's admirably sober but ultimately inadequate ideal of communicative interaction, Schrag endorses a certain *postmodern* notion of the death of the Subject (human being and author) and a certain conception of an end of history and of grand narratives. These endorsements situate Schrag among the postmoderns—for example, with Jean-François Lyotard, Derrida, or Michel Foucault (even as the latter two protest against being subsumed under Lyotard's label of "postmodernism")—and on the other side of Habermas, who will have no truck with postmodernity and all its works. This is not to say that Habermas relies on a grand philosophy of history or on a philosophy of the Subject. But it is to claim that his communicative ideal retains assurances of enlightenment and radical democracy which today, given the disasters that these assurances have failed to forestall in the twentieth century, betray worrisome, uncritical blind spots. Indeed, Schrag's agreements with the postmoderns also serve as the basis of his "Response to the Postmodern Challenge" (the subtitle of *The Resources of Rationality*). Transversal reason is neither universally valid for all social times and historical places nor paralogical, that is, irretrievably lost in contexts of particular times and places. Schrag's agreements with the postmoderns are thus of a critical sort. His nod to postmodern disenchantments echoes Horkheimer and Adorno's *Dialectic of Enlightenment* (1944) and Husserl's "Crisis" lectures from 1935, both of which represent early critiques of modernity that still aspire to be situated within modernity. Schrag resonates both with the early Frankfurt School and with the late Foucault's turn to an ethic of reciprocity. And he anticipates Derrida's more recent defense of a new enlightenment, now aligned with Marx against the New World Order—the one remaining and not yet deconstructed grand narrative.

    c. *The self after postmodernity.* By elaborating on the distinction between the narrative self and the existential self, Schrag takes a more receptive position in contrast to Habermas's more hostile engagements with postmodernists, thereby introducing his own recent notion of the self after postmodernity. Schrag's conceptions of critical hermeneutics and existential selfhood are implicated within the figure of communicative praxis. To speak of an *implicature* is appropriate here, insofar as the space of critical communicative praxis is not something to be owned and yet it is something existentially concrete. Schrag's notion of self is reminiscent of what Kierkegaard, with a keen modern sensibility, called the salutary forms of dying to all immediacy of self-ownership. To absolutize one's own existential or historical standpoint would, like wanting to exercise absolutely the infinite possibilities of one's freedom, amount to despair. But despairing would at the same time lead to giving up one's freedom once the will has been found to be something merely finite, situated, historical, all-too-human. Both the figure of an absolute self and that of the nostalgic "death of the self" are forms of being in despair; abstract modernist universalism and antirationalist postmodernity, in their extreme caricatures of the self, encourage such despair. In this dual sense Schrag's self comes, thus, equally after a certain modernity and a certain postmodernity, while learning in dialogue from both.

    d. *The fourth cultural value sphere.* Schrag first writes about his insight that there may be a distinct, untheorized cultural value sphere in his groundbreaking opening essay for the volume, *Kierkegaard in Post/Modernity,* edited by Matuštík and Westphal (1995). Schrag's contention that there is such a sphere, and that it is the fourth one, depends on first enumerating the three established spheres of culture agreed upon by Kant, Hegel, Weber, and Habermas—science, morality and law, and art or aesthetics—and then going beyond these three. These modern thinkers contend that the disenchantments of modernity have brought about a situation whereby Western culture, once unified by metaphysics or tradition, has become dirempted into separate spheres of professional competence with no available route of reunification other than Weber's gods and demons, or the iron cage of unfree, anomic modern life, or Habermas's disconsolate democratic rationality. Schrag insists on the important role of a fourth, critical cultural sphere. This is the sphere of *religion after the death of God* (or, in Tillich's earlier formulation, a God beyond the God of theism). Kant had intimations of this fourth sphere in his work on religion within the limits of reason alone. But it is Lévinas's notion of radical alterity, Kierkegaard's distinction between religiousness A and B in his *Concluding Unscientific Postscript,* and Derrida's development of the notion of gift that have preoccupied Schrag's thoughts during the most recent years of his illustrious career. We find him not only devoting his final graduate seminar at Purdue (spring 2000) to these very topics but also daring to write another book, which he (unwisely, in our opinion) calls his last. It will be an expansion of his 1995 essay on Kierkegaard.

    Given the chronology of the four figures as we have described them emerging in Schrag's life work, what are some of their significant overlapping features?

    Schrag's corrective and complement to critical theory displays his own unique critical-phenomenological origins. Those beginnings, conjoined with the linguistics-communication turn, gave birth to his sui generis praxis philosophy. It should be noted that his innovations have taken place within the fields of communication studies, hermeneutics, and philosophy, and in dialogue with critical theory and postmodernism, and that they occurred both quite some time after the early Marcuse and the later Sartre attempted to conjoin existential phenomenology with Marxism and quite apart from the preoccupations that inspired the Yugoslav Praxis philosophers from the 1960s to the 1980s and that at one point inspired Habermas as well. If one hears echoes of Marx in Schrag's Kierkegaard, or if one discerns a critique of the patriarchal and racist elements within modern rationality in Schrag's defense of an open space for communicative praxis, one is not mistaken. These orientations are present in his writings, and they are intended. Hence one finds some of Schrag's most innovative graduate students—for example, Ramsey Eric Ramsey, a recent graduate of Purdue's joint philosophy and communication Ph.D. program, author of *The Long Path to Nearness,* with a foreword by Schrag (1998)—accentuating the critical and political dimensions of Schrag's communicative praxis. Or one finds his former Purdue colleague, Lewis R. Gordon, stressing the antiracist dimensions of Schrag's new humanism, with its conception of the self on the other side of Heidegger's and Derrida's critiques of humanism. Or one finds the former Purdue visiting scholar, Patricia Huntington, exploring the work of Julia Kristeva in one of Schrag's recent graduate seminars and bringing out, in her review essay (in vol. 21 of *Human Studies* [1998]) of *The Self after Postmodernity,* Schrag's pivotal contributions to contemporary feminist theory.

If we accept the idea that Schrag's in-between position on the cusp of post/modernity is the appropriate creative move to make, then there *is* a significant place for both transversal rationality and the fourth sphere of culture. Both conceptions, as developed by Schrag, invite us to consider the need to foster a postcultural or postnational or postsecular attitude. Let us suppose, moreover, that Schrag is right in maintaining that a distinct cultural dimension or existential attitude is needed to help us suspend and be suspicious of our conventional beliefs (including our conventional "religious" cultures). If he is right, then such diverse but ultimately related notions as those of the wholly other than this unjust world (Lévinas and the early Frankfurt School), of existential pathos (a nonspecific, generic pathos of an ethico-religious sort, Kierkegaard's religiousness A), of a messianic gift (as intimated by Derrida), or of a Messianic "now-time" (Benjamin) become welcome complements to any future critique of ideology. Such complementary dimensions would be there to protect us from cultural and politico-economic imperialism. We witness Schrag, at what may well be the climax of his intellectual journey up to now, not only returning to his first philosophical love, Kierkegaard, but also joining with those other thinkers on the cutting edge (Caputo, Marion, Westphal, etc.) who, somewhat against the current, advocate some kind of God-talk under the conditions of post/modernity. And yet, we should add, he makes this return not by withdrawing from the world of communicative praxis and of struggles for justice, but as a critical theorist and a praxis philosopher contributing to those struggles. Schrag bequeaths to us an untimely timeliness of that hope which inspires anew in every generation its radical reflections on the situation of the present age.

For anyone familiar with *American Phenomenology* (the title of a volume coedited by Schrag and Eugene Kaelin in 1989), it will be evident that the present tribute to him features contributions from some of this field's most distinguished luminaries. It will also become clear, from the texts, that all of the contributors deal here with themes central to his own philosophical concerns; indeed all refer, in varying degrees ranging from occasional references to focused critical studies, to his own salient "interventions" into the dialogue of late twentieth-century thought, the period that has aptly, though sometimes confusedly, been characterized as "postmodernity" or, perhaps even a little more aptly at the very end of one millennium and the beginning of the next, as postmodernity's aftermath. In various ways, all of the contributors appear to us either to address directly or to try to illustrate, some with more optimism than others but all with great seriousness, the question of philosophy's role and responsibility ("task") in this new era. Hence our choice of title.

It further occurred to us that the four Schragean figures which we have singled out above could serve very well as organizing principles for this volume. Accordingly, we have thought to divide it into five parts, the first part containing a single overview of the "task" and of Schrag's contributions to it, the other parts grouping articles which focus primarily on each of the four figures in their conceptual order. Gary B. Madison's essay, "Bringing Philosophy into the Twenty-First Century: Calvin Schrag and the Phenomenological Movement," is the overview; it is written from the perspective of a resolute defender of the phenomenological tradition, viewed as a bulwark of rationality against relativistic, particularistic, and antisubjectivist challenges. It is the "reconfiguration" of this tradition that Schrag has accomplished through his introduction of such figures as transversal rationality, according to Madison, that will enable it to survive into the next millennium.

Accordingly, essays in Part 2 of this volume pursue and report some of the adventures, good and bad, of transversal rationality. In his study of the person who has often been labeled the "father" of modern philosophy, " 'Where Are You Standing . . . ?': Descartes and the Question of Historicity," Robert C. Scharff employs a question posed by Schrag in a seminar three and a half decades ago, a question challenging the very possibility of a "view from Nowhere," in order himself to challenge

once-standard assumptions about "Cartesian rationality" in the thought
of Descartes himself. In "'Catch Me If You Can': Foucault on the Repressive Hypothesis," Sandra Bartky brings us back into the era of postmodernity to raise significant doubts about Foucault's dismissive account
of repression and dismissive treatments of earlier theorists of psychoanalysis, relying in part on her own lived experiences as an adolescent and
on Schragean concerns about Foucauldian rational relativism. Hwa Yol
Jung's "Transversality and Geophilosophy in the Age of Globalization"
brings Chinese philosophical insights together with Schragean and other
contemporary Western perspectives in an effort to confront present-
day ecological degradation in an ethical way. The ethical aspect of phenomenology's approach to the life-world is rendered even more explicit
in Edward S. Casey's "The Ethics of the Glance." Finally, Bruce Wilshire's
timely and sobering paper, "Decentered Subjectivity, Transversal Rationality, and Genocide" makes extensive use of two of the four Schragean
figures upon which we have focused in order to try to make some head-
way into understanding how the so-called rational animal can do the
terrible things that he/she all too often does.

Wilshire's treatment of the problem of subjectivity in conjunction
with that of rationality provides a segue to Part 3, on the self after postmodernity. Completing the segue from its further side, Fred Dallmayr's
"Transversal Liaisons: Calvin Schrag on Selfhood" begins with an extended summary of Schrag's views on the self—showing, among other
things, their intimate connection with his views on rationality—and goes
on to express a few reservations about them and to suggest their applicability to notions of a global community. Bernard P. Dauenhauer, in
"Schrag and the Self," critically analyzes three aspects of the Schragean
self, to wit, its connections with discourse, action, and community, and
explores some of its affinities with and differences from the philosophies of self held by a number of other thinkers, from Kierkegaard to
Ricoeur. He says at one point that he has deliberately chosen to omit
discussion of the relationship of the Schragean self to *transcendence*. It
is precisely on this latter issue that Linda Bell, in "Calvin Hears a Who:
Calvin O. Schrag and Postmodern Selves," takes a certain critical distance
from Schrag's views while otherwise expressing her appreciation for his
work, both on a theoretical and on a personal level: What he taught
furnished her with tools, she says at the outset, for fighting the sexism
that was so rampant in the climate of academic philosophy during her
early graduate years. Then Martin C. Dillon, sharing some of Bell's reservations about transcendence but applying them to a rather different set
of issues, offers a strong critique of "Romantic Love" in his chapter with
that title.

In Part 4 of this volume, Calvin Schrag's explorations of transcendence in relation to the self, as they have issued in his positive appraisal of the fourth cultural value sphere to which we have alluded, are themselves given a more positive reception. Merold Westphal argues in "Transcendence, Heteronomy, and the Birth of the Responsible Self" that it is only by retaining a religious dimension that genuine ethical responsibility is made possible. John D. Caputo's "In Search of a Sacred Anarchy: An Experiment in Danish Deconstruction" employs intellectual tools borrowed from Schrag, together with Kierkegaard's idea of the name of God as a *task* and Jacques Derrida's key trope of *différance*, to advance a conception of religion as "scandalous" and "disruptive"—disruptive to, inter alia, contemporary philosophy.

Part 5 of our volume, on communicative praxis, begins with a meditation of not altogether different provenance from that of Caputo, Michael J. Hyde's "The Interruptive Nature of the Call of Conscience: Rethinking Heidegger on the Question of Rhetoric." Himself a professor of communication rather than of philosophy eo nomine, Hyde juxtaposes Heidegger's notion with Schrag's and others' philosophies of communication in order to explore the possibility of an ethically "fitting response" (another favorite Schragean expression) to this call—a response of a kind made with greater success by Schrag, he suggests in conclusion, than by Heidegger. Focusing more on writing than on speech, David Crownfield's "Structure, Deconstruction, and the Future of Meaning" analyzes recent developments in the philosophy of language, particularly Derrida's, situating some of the by now very familiar Schragean tropes in the context of these discussions. Lenore Langsdorf, writing "In Defense of Poiesis: The Performance of Self in Communicative Praxis," juxtaposes Schrag's work on the topic with important elements of the Aristotelian tradition in order to argue the case that communicative praxis ought to be reconceived as a kind of *making* and not simply as a kind of doing. And in conclusion Victor Kestenbaum, a professor of both philosophy and education, in his "The Professions, the Humanities, and Transfiguration," draws on some recent writings in that field as well as on a number of Schrag's works, particularly a short article on liberal learning and *Communicative Praxis and the Space of Subjectivity*, to delineate an attractive, "transfigured" notion of education in the humanities which would be true, he suggests, to the Socratic/Schragean spirit.

On April 1, 2000, an all-day symposium took place in West Lafayette to celebrate Calvin Schrag. All but two of the contributors to this volume (John D. Caputo and Edward S. Casey) were able to attend and to summarize their papers, half in the morning and half in the afternoon. At the end of each of the two sessions, the guest of honor offered comments, part anecdotal and part analytic, on both the individuals and their contributions. These were, of course, at once entertaining and highly insightful, and we thought that it would make a fitting and especially valuable conclusion to this book if we could prevail upon their author to prepare a shortened version of them for us. To our great delight, he acceded to our request. Some of the anecdotes, to be sure, have been elided for reasons of space and of the difference of genres, and Professor Schrag has wisely chosen to adhere to the alphabetical order of the authors' last names in the version published here; nevertheless, the flavor of the original occasion has been preserved to a considerable extent, and it has even been enhanced by the addition of references to the two absent contributors.

Our highest hope is that readers will exit this volume with greater appreciation, first, of all the contributors, second, of philosophy's new millennial tasks, and, third and above all, of Calvin Schrag as thinker and as human being. In the last analysis, this book should be regarded as a milestone, not as a conclusion. For, as another prominent contemporary American phenomenologist, Don Ihde, wrote, along with his reminiscences, on the occasion of the celebration: "Although seventy seems young for retirement, I fully expect his momentum and interests will continue and we will be reading more Schrag for a long time to come."

CALVIN O. SCHRAG
AND THE TASK
OF PHILOSOPHY AFTER
POSTMODERNITY

PART 1

AN OVERVIEW

Bringing Philosophy into the Twenty-First Century: Calvin Schrag and the Phenomenological Movement

Gary B. Madison

> Precisely through our finitude, the particularity of our being,
> which is evident even in the variety of languages, the infinite
> dialogue is opened in the direction of the truth that we are.
>
> —*Hans-Georg Gadamer*, Philosophical Hermeneutics

Phenomenology-at-the-End-of-Metaphysics

The year 2000 marks the one hundredth anniversary of the phenomenological movement.[1] What are its chances of surviving into the new millennium? There are of course those who would have us believe that phenomenology already died a quiet death with the arrival on the philosophical (Parisian) scene, beginning in the 1960s, of "poststructuralist" modes of thinking. Nothing could be further from the truth, however. The onward march of history has seen to it that, today, some of the more "deconstructive" (or "destructionist") forms of poststructuralism have, in their own place of origin, been displaced by a renewed interest in the "classics" of phenomenology.[2] *C'est un fait, la phénoménologie vit, toujours.* It is therefore fully appropriate that we should inquire into how it stands with phenomenology at the turn of the twenty-first century. What are some of the resources and insights that the ongoing phenomenological movement might bring to bear on the intellectual challenges that are sure to confront the human life-world in the unsettling, globalizing times that lie ahead? Oddly enough, this is an issue that Charles Scott, one of America's foremost Continentalists, fails to consider in an important survey of Continental philosophy at the turn of the century.[3] It is therefore to address this oversight that, in this chapter, I focus my attention on the work of Calvin O. Schrag. I know of few other philosophers who have more pointedly demonstrated the relevance of a renewed phenomenology to the tasks that confront the philosophical enterprise as we enter into a new century and a new (let us hope) postmetaphysical millennium.

Perhaps the greatest task confronting philosophy at the end of a very tumultuous century and the beginning of another, very uncertain one is that of demonstrating that the much-heralded "end of philosophy" has itself finally come to an end. The last third of the twentieth century was replete with proclamations of various monumental endings and deaths: not only the End of Philosophy but also the End of History and, of course, the Death of the Subject (the "author," "man"). These were troubling times for philosophy, a gloomy and despondent time when we were told that the phenomenon "Auschwitz" signals nothing less than the bankruptcy of Reason itself. During these years advocates of "localism" and "particularity" were widely to be heard denouncing the claim to universality on the part of reason—a claim so passionately defended by the late Husserl—as nothing more than a supremely hegemonic form of "Eurocentrism."[4] Their criticisms were misplaced (as I hope to show in what follows with the case of Schrag in mind), but at least the doomsayers were logical. For if, as the antiphilosophical "culturalists" maintain, reason cannot legitimately lay claim to universal validity and everything is "relative" or "ethnocentric," then indeed philosophy has reached its end, since the (historical) essence of philosophy *is* its claim to universality. Then indeed the 2,500-year-old history of philosophy (and the 100-year-old history of phenomenology) has run its course, and philosophy's age-old dream of instituting social reason on a universal scale (what Kant referred to as "perpetual peace") is now over, *ausgetraumt,* as Husserl would have said.

But is it really over? Why is it that so many oppressed peoples throughout the world continue to place their profoundest hopes in reason, in, that is to say, that quintessentially philosophical idea (or Idea), the idea of *universal human rights?*[5] It is of course true that, as postmodernists of a "deconstructive" bent have untiringly insisted, all forms of metaphysical "essentialism" and "foundationalism" are intellectually bankrupt. The notion of universal human rights cannot, as we now know, be (philosophically) justified by appealing to the supposed existence of

a universal (univocal or invariant) human "nature."[6] Does this mean,
however, that ordinary people are hopelessly naive when they attempt to
justify their local, emancipatory praxis by an appeal to universal, philosophical values? I rather doubt it. In any event, there is no reason, philosophically and phenomenologically speaking, why the "end of metaphysics" should spell the end of philosophy itself. There is no good reason
why "getting over" metaphysics (as Heidegger would say) should ne-
cessitate renouncing philosophy's universalist vocation. What Merleau-
Ponty said of his antiphilosophical predecessors (Marx, Nietzsche) applies equally well to his poststructuralist successors: "The negation of
metaphysics cannot take the place of philosophy."[7] Philosophy has always
demonstrated an amazing ability to regenerate itself, as has phenomenology. The history of the phenomenological movement is in fact nothing
other than the history of the attempts on the part of each succeeding
phenomenologist to purge phenomenology of the residual and unjus-
tified metaphysical presuppositions associated with the "philosophy of
consciousness" or the "metaphysics of presence"—so as better to enable
it to lay hold of the "things themselves."[8] The work of Calvin Schrag is a
perfect case in point. Not only was Schrag greatly instrumental in introducing classical phenomenology to America, he has also, over the course
of a philosophical lifetime, never faltered in his attempts aimed at a *reconstruction* of phenomenology (reconstructing phenomenology is what
constructing phenomenology has itself always been about). Speaking of
the resilience of Continental philosophy in general, Charles Scott writes:
"The life of thought, its vitality and creativity, requires a process of moving
beyond itself, a critique of the ideals that hold it in place, a displacement
of its own way of viewing and valuing things."[9] In what follows I shall focus
on some of the ways in which Schrag has attempted to "displace" some of
the inherited topoi of phenomenology—and, in so doing, has positioned
the phenomenological movement to "move beyond itself," regenerated
and renewed, into the twenty-first century.

A Phenomenology of Experience and Worldly Being

With the publication in 1961 of his first book, *Existence and Freedom*,
Schrag was among the first to initiate a serious discussion of what in
those days was commonly referred to as "Phenomenology and Existentialism." In this book he dealt with Kierkegaard and Heidegger and what
he called the "existence-problem." His main preoccupation was (and is)
with Kierkegaard.[10] With regard to Heidegger he has more recently (and

8

GARY B. MADISONGARY B. MADISON

quite rightly) said that Heidegger's own development, which led away from existence to "Being," "occasions some pesky and persistent second thought."[11] Such pesky and persistent second thought is precisely what propelled Gadamer, a student of both Husserl and Heidegger, on his own way to phenomenological hermeneutics, and it is also what enabled Schrag to avoid the trap, fatal to so many others, of following Heidegger down the garden path into a nebulous *Seinsmystik*—and an equally nebulous mode of discourse, one so lamentably common in the latter part of the twentieth century on the part of the "Continentalists" of various persuasions who seem to believe that renouncing the Cartesian quest for certainty requires giving up on the Cartesian virtue of clarity. This is where Schrag, as a phenomenologist, tacked true. Schrag, much to his credit, never gave up on clear thinking and on clear speaking, and he always set his bearings, not by the latest in passing fads, but by *die Sache selbst*. Like Gadamer—who said that he "bypassed" Heidegger's Being-problematic and was concerned only "with what is feasible, what is possible, what is correct, here and now"—Schrag likewise focused his attention on actuality, on "experience" (in the phenomenological, existential sense of the term).[12] Accordingly, in his *Experience and Being* (1969) he sought to outline a phenomenology of the structure and dynamics of experience.

"Experience" is, to be sure, a very problematic notion, as the deconstructionists have made us more than aware ("experience" tends generally to be [mis]understood in terms of the metaphysics of presence or the metaphysics of identity). With this realization in mind, Schrag saw that the reconstruction of phenomenology necessitated a decisive overcoming of the "transcendentalism" inherent still in classical phenomenology. "Transcendental inquiry," he wrote, "still moves about within an epistemological space. An elucidation of the polysemy of experience, I soon realized, required a more radical rupture of the epistemological paradigm, inviting a move to the hermeneutical space of discourse and action."[13] This move is precisely what he has sought to accomplish in incremental steps over the past many years, from *Radical Reflection and the Origin of the Human Sciences* (1980) through *Communicative Praxis and the Space of Subjectivity* (1986), *The Resources of Rationality: A Response to the Postmodern Challenge* (1992), and, most recently, *The Self after Postmodernity* (1997). In these various works Schrag has explored different aspects of what he calls a "non-epistemological, hermeneutical space" and has addressed various multidisciplinary issues having to do with discourse, action, textuality, rhetoric, communication, and the role of the human sciences.[14] As this list of topics indicates, Schrag's work is broad and multifaceted. I would like to concentrate on the philosophical significance (as I see it) of Schrag's work as it has evolved over the years in response to new challenges and developments on the wider cultural scene.

Linguisticality and Subjectivity

In the latter part of the twentieth century, the issue of language not only moved to the forefront of philosophical concern, it tended also to eclipse the earlier phenomenological concern with "subjectivity." Indeed, there was no lack of writers proclaiming that the centrality of language entailed the death of the "subject." The things that phenomenologists used to think they were talking about when talking about them—"things" such as the world or the self—are nothing more, we were told, than "significative effects" of language, mere simulacra, as it were. According to Roland Barthes, the subject, or the "I," is nothing but "the instance of saying I"; the subject, he said, is "empty outside the very enunciation which defines it."[15] According to the New Nietzscheans, the world is nothing but a "sign-world," a mere semiological construct, a free-floating signifier signifying only itself. Schrag's work is noteworthy in that it meticulously avoids facile overgeneralizations of this sort.[16] Language is all important (it is what makes humans—the speaking animals—human), but it is not everything (notwithstanding the fact that, as Gadamer said, "Being that can be understood is language"). Although, as a good phenomenologist, Schrag resolutely rejects what Derrida called the "metaphysics of presence," he has nevertheless always been careful not to fall prey to the nihilistic excesses of a hyperstructuralism" ("*Il n'y a pas de hors-texte*"), a "semiological reductionism" (as Martin C. Dillon has called it) which reduces everything to a Dionysian free play (*jeu*) of words.[17] Schrag does not assert, for instance, that because, from a purely linguistic (Saussurian) point of view, there are only differences in a language, everything is therefore, *überhaupt*, pure, unrestrained *différance*. Schrag's general endeavor in this regard is well summed up in the title *Communicative Praxis and the Space of Subjectivity:* What he has sought to do is to carve out a space for a renewed conception of subjectivity in the wider field of communicative praxis. In other words, Schrag has resisted the temptation to sever language from the (experiential, praxial) domain of its effective realization.

One of the central arguments of *Communicative Praxis* was indeed directed against what Schrag called "a widespread misdirection in contemporary philosophy" which he characterized thus: "This misdirection has to do with an excessive and self-limiting preoccupation with discourse and discursive practices." A misdirection of this sort lands us

GARY B. MADISON

in "a crisis-situation of linguistic closure."[18] In opposition to this sort of self-debilitating move on the part of much current philosophizing, Schrag has worked against "the progressive isolation of discourse from nondiscursive human action and from the fabric of world-oriented experience more generally," and he has done so by emphasizing what he has called "the amalgam of discourse and action."[19] Sensitive to the legitimate demands of both linguistics and praxis philosophy, of both semiotics and pragmatics, Schrag has stressed the interrelatedness, indeed, the inseparability, of language, experience, and action.

The target of his critique in this matter was not only Derrida, whom Schrag accuses of "pantextuality," of allowing referential discourse to "collapse under its own weight in the rhapsodic play of metaphor," but also Paul Ricoeur, who, as Schrag saw it, overextends the "model of the text" (to use Ricoeur's expression) or, as Schrag put it, "the metaphorics of textuality."[20] Even though his criticism of Ricoeur was perhaps excessive, as I have suggested elsewhere, the point Schrag was attempting to make is well worth making. As phenomenologists have often had to do, Schrag was battling on two fronts simultaneously: in this instance, against those who ignore the essential linguisticality of human experience as well as those who, contrariwise, reduce everything to language.[21] Schrag's point was that "discourse and action within the dynamics of communicative praxis are nonreducible twin halves of an undivided history. The texture of communicative praxis is reducible neither to the textuality of discourse nor to the tissues of human action."[22] As illustrated so well by Schrag's own philosophical practice, phenomenology, in its adherence to the fullness of lived experience or to what Gabriel Marcel called "the concrete," has always been strenuously opposed to all forms of crude reductionism—as much to, for instance, biologistic materialism and the artificialism of "cognitive science" as to the semioticism of the poststructuralists.

What Schrag was above all interested in is what might properly be called the "performativity" of language. Action (like experience), considered on its own, apart from language, is mute and unintelligible; language, considered on its own, in a purely structuralist sort of way, is meaningless. Discourse, or more precisely, discursive praxis, transcends this artificial and untenable opposition; discourse is "the concrete amalgamation of speech and language within a social practice."[23] With his focus fixed solidly on communicative praxis (i.e., language *and* action), Schrag was able to do justice to the "*event-character* of discourse and narration," thereby transcending the intrinsic limitations of the semiotic model (language viewed as a static, closed-in-upon-itself system of diacritically defined signifiers) in such a way as to lead to "a space *outside* the text."[24] It is simply not the case (phenomenologically speaking) that there is nothing outside the text ("there is indeed something outside the text").[25] This "outside" is not, to be sure, the "in-itself" reality so dear to naive objectivism, the so-called external world of the moderns; it is what phenomenologists have all along called the "life-world," the world of lived experience. It is a "hermeneutical" world, one which is inescapably bound up with language and in which "interpretation goes all the way down and all the way back."[26] The world that humans inhabit is, as Wallace Stevens said, a world of words to the end.

It is in this world (and in it alone, never in any "inner space") that we encounter the *self* or *subject* that various hyperstructuralist postmoderns believe died a while back along with the onto-theological god of metaphysics. Man, we were told by these "prophets of extremity," is "an invention of recent date," destined to be "erased, like a face drawn in sand at the edge of the sea."[27] In the manner of an earlier midwesterner, Schrag reminds us that reports from Europe as to the death of man, of the author, have been greatly exaggerated. There is, as Schrag reminds us, "life after [the] death of the subject, the life of a new subjectivity, opening new horizons for a possible reclamation of humanism."[28] The truth of the matter is that the subject has not died but has, rather (thanks to ongoing work in phenomenology) finally discovered his or her true home, which is also the home of meaning.[29] This "home" is, of course, the hermeneutical space of communicative praxis. In his attempt to refigure subjectivity, Schrag has, as it were, followed up on cues offered by Merleau-Ponty ("the greatest of French phenomenologists," according to Paul Ricoeur) who also did not believe—in opposition to Heidegger, in Merleau-Ponty's case—that the attempt to overcome the subjectivism, epistemologism, and anthropocentrism of modern philosophy necessitates an unqualified abandonment of philosophical humanism and the modern notion of subjectivity.[30] Schrag has developed this crucial point in ways that, due to his untimely death, Merleau-Ponty was not able.

By stressing the embeddedness of the subject in the intersubjective world of communicative praxis, Schrag has sought not to *deconstruct* the subject but rather to *decenter* it: "The emerging subjectivity within this space [of communicative praxis] will be that of a subject transfigured and transformed, a *decentered* subjectivity, bearing the wisdom gleaned from the arduous venture of deconstruction as a task never completed but rather to be performed time and again."[31] Thus the "dismantling [of] subjectivity as a positional center and a zero-point consciousness" does not lead to its dissolution in a sea of meaningless signifiers but to its recovery in the field (the "hermeneutical space," as Schrag would say) of communicative praxis, "the praxial space of discursive transactions."[32] As

Schrag says, "The disassemblage of the classical substance-attribute categorial scheme and the modern empirico-transcendental doublet does not entail a displacement of the subject in every sense you please." Such a disassemblage provides, rather, "a clearing for a restoration of the subject" by opening the path to "a transvalued subjectivity within a new space, making it possible to speak of a new humanism at the end of philosophy."

In short, "the metaphysical subject of the ancients and the epistemological subject of the moderns"[33] is displaced, and the living subject is restored, not as a mere "effect" of language but as the existential *implicate* of both language and action, of communicative praxis. Schrag's "phenomenological subject" is no longer the atomistic, monological subjectivity of modern philosophy but a dialogical subjectivity which is, accordingly, "intersubjective" through and through. As in the case of Merleau-Ponty, the ultimate purpose of Schrag's attempt to reconfigure subjectivity is to enable philosophy to reclaim its humanist vocation, to open up the possibility of what Merleau-Ponty referred to as a "new humanism" at the dawn of a new, global age, the "humanism of decentered subjectivity."[34]

Truth, Rationality, and Rhetoric

One of the major issues that Schrag has wrestled with "at the end of philosophy" is the issue of rationality. This issue goes to the very heart of the matter, since tied up with it is the fate of philosophy itself, "*la possibilité de la philosophie,*" as Merleau-Ponty would say. The only way philosophy can survive the "end of philosophy," the "end of metaphysics," is by becoming *postmodern* and *postmetaphysical,* and for this to occur it is necessary to elaborate a postessentialist and postfoundationalist conception of rationality. This is exactly what Schrag has done, and it constitutes one of the most significant features of his work.

Just as with the issue of subjectivity, so also as regards rationality Schrag has not attempted simply to deconstruct the notion of rationality as hitherto conceived by mainline philosophy, leaving in its place nothing more than some kind of agonistic and dissensual conflict of interpretations à la Lyotard or some kind of merely edifying "writing" à la Rorty. What he provides us with instead is a thoroughly reconstructed and thoroughly postmetaphysical conceptualization of reason, reason as communicative praxis. As he indicated in an article appropriately entitled "Reconstructing Reason in the Aftermath of Deconstruction," Schrag shares Habermas's belief that the poststructuralist deconstruction of reason "invites a self-effacing relativism and a suffocation within the historically specific."[35] However, unlike Habermas and his disciples, Schrag does not attempt merely to rehabilitate the modern and, so to speak, Kantian conception of universal reason. Above all, he does not, unlike Habermas, allow himself to be duped by the claims to "objective validity" on the part of scientistic reason. Unlike Habermas, Schrag simply does not believe that in this postmetaphysical age one can still appeal to " 'context-transcending notions of truth' and 'unconditioned truth.' "

What Schrag has aimed at is a "*reconstructed* rationality that is able to accommodate the requirements of deconstructive critique without sacrificing the resources for knowledge and truth claims."[36] What Schrag has always worked for is a plurivocal reason, a reason which speaks in many voices. Like Gadamer, he has sought to preserve the unity of reason in the very plurality of languages. He labels this "transversal rationality." Like the Frankfurters, Schrag wants to uphold the possibility of a philosophical critique of what-is; the "possibility of philosophy" is indeed contingent upon just such a possibility. The trouble with the genealogical and deconstructive positions of the poststructuralists is that they really do not allow for the possibility of a general, philosophical critique of things, that is, a critique effected in the light of universal principles or values. Derrida's treatment of otherness, for example, Schrag says, "leaves us pretty much at sea. It provides neither a standpoint for critique nor an occasion for a redress of social ills through responsible communal action."[37] Schrag, however, does not believe that we can override the contingency of our situation in such a way as to achieve the kind of context-free universalism that Habermas advocated in his critique of Gadamer, whose hermeneutics, he claimed, is essentially tradition-bound and thus lacking in critical force.[38] Speaking as a hermeneuticist, Schrag insists that we cannot "step outside the interplay of contextualized and conditioned beliefs and practices." This does not render critique impossible, however; it simply means that "criticism achieves its efficacy within the panoply of discursive and institutional practices because it is itself a praxis."[39]

If he is opposed to the reified universalism of the Frankfurt School, Schrag is equally opposed to the sort of radical "contingency" advocated by Rorty. His reconstruction of rationality does not amount to reducing reason to nothing more than a host of local narratives devoid of any kind of universal claim to validity (a position which, as Schrag sees it, leads to a self-defeating "conventionalism and conservatism").[40] He writes:

> The recognition of rupture and dissension within the wider socio-historical fabric does not entail the dissolution of transversality into a mere horizontality of random pluralization in which each paradigm

and each social practice remains isolated and self-sufficient, cut off from any transversal play of challenge and response through critical reflection and corrective action. Such is the myth of radical pluralization of postmodernity, which simply refashions the isolated epistemological subject of modernity into a serialization of equally isolated local narratives and cultural enclaves.[41]

Schrag is thus no apologist for a "weak reason" (as Gianni Vattimo might say). What he calls transversality (a matter to which I shall return) "opens a passage between the Scylla of a priori, universal truth conditions and the Charybdis of a criteria-bereft conventionalism and relativism."[42] Schrag chooses to "opt neither for a celebration of the incommensurable and paralogy nor for a serene faith in the logic of commensurable unities."[43] A move such as this is perhaps the only viable option for those who believe that philosophical reason has a vital role to play in the wider realm of human culture after the "end of philosophy."

If, in his defense of a reconfigured, contextualized universalism, Schrag was able to avoid the allures of theory unrelated to praxis—what, with reference to Habermas, he characterizes as a "penchant for theory construction in the grand style"[44]—it is owing to his interest in *rhetoric*. From its beginnings in ancient Greece, rhetoric has always been a mode of theorizing about communicative praxis that, rather than being an imposition of theory on practice, is, rather, a reflection upon, and an outgrowth of, the actual practice of communicative rationality. It is not only deconstructive postmodernists like Derrida who have sought to expose the rhetorical element in philosophical discourse, in the "language of reason." Contesting the rigid Platonic opposition between philosophy and rhetoric, episteme and doxa, has been one of the main features of postmodern thought in general. One of the main items on the hermeneutical postmodern agenda has been, as Schrag puts it, "the place of rhetoric at the end of philosophy."[45] Gadamer, it will be recalled, has insisted that the universality and ubiquity of rhetoric parallel that of hermeneutics itself.[46] It was no part of Gadamer's intention to diminish thereby philosophy's legitimate claim to universal rationality (logos). So likewise with Schrag.[47]

How exactly does rhetoric enter into the postmetaphysical picture? The issue of rhetoric arises—and, indeed, becomes all important—when the bankruptcy of traditional epistemologism becomes manifest and when it is realized that there are, and can be, no foundational, culturally invariant means (no "method," as Gadamer would say) for establishing the validity of various knowledge and value claims. Nevertheless, as rhetorical theory has always insisted, although we can never conclusively demonstrate the "validity" of our interpretations of what-is and our views of what ought to be, we can always seek to argue for them in a rational and persuasive manner. As Gadamer has observed:

> Rhetoric from oldest tradition has been the only advocate of a claim to truth that defends the probable, the *eikós* (verisimile), and that which is convincing to the ordinary reason, against the claim of science to accept as true only what can be demonstrated and tested! Convincing and persuading, without being able to prove—these are obviously as much the aim and measure of understanding and interpretation as they are the aim and measure of the art of oration and persuasion.[48]

Rhetorical theory, properly understood, furnishes an *alternative* to both scientistic rationalism and irrational "decisionism," to both Habermasian foundationalism and Rortyan conventionalism. To maintain that "truth" is a matter of rhetoric is not to maintain, as the Platonists would have us believe, that our claims to knowledge are, because of this, "groundless" and without criteria. Rhetoric is precisely that discipline which seeks to discover the criteria ("grounds") that, in actual practice, effectively allow us to discern good from bad arguments. As is the general rule in the case of a phenomenological hermeneutics inspired by classical rhetoric, Schrag's reflections on communicative rationality fall under the heading not of *philosophia speculativa* but of *philosophia practica*. His is not a free-floating, prescriptivist theory which, as in Habermas's case ("cataloguing the newest contributions by systems theory"), is meant to be "applied" to practice; it is a theory that is based upon and grows out of practice itself.[49] As the theoretical study of communicative practices, rhetoric, as Schrag might say, has for its object those criteria that "are called into being through the dynamics of an ongoing struggle for communication and understanding."[50] As the study of the practice of communicative rationality, rhetoric is nothing other than the study of what enables humans to become properly human, that is, humane.

Following up (as it were) on the groundbreaking work of the Belgian scholar, Chaïm Perelman, in the field of the "New Rhetoric," Schrag has shown how rhetorical rationality avoids the snares of both an antirationalist relativism and a rationalistic universalism.[51] As he remarks in this regard: "Contra the antilogos tendencies of postmodernism, which court an abandonment of the claims of reason and an invitation to a rampant relativism, I submit that there are criteria for our judgments about the better and worse argument and the more desirable and the less desirable course of action." However, as he also points out, these criteria "issue from a transversal, not a universal logos."[52] Schrag's interest in rhetoric reflects his uncompromising antilogocentrism, his belief, that is, that truth is basically a practical ("praxis-oriented") matter, not a "logical" one. The central issue raised by the hermeneutical-rhetorical challenge to the traditional, metaphysical conception of reason (as a "faculty" allowing for privileged, and monological, insight into the "nature of things") concerns the traditional theory/practice bifurcation. As Schrag sees it, a proper understanding of rhetoric enables us to overcome this bifurcation, the most basic, and perhaps most pernicious, of metaphysical oppositions. The task facing us at the end of metaphysics is that of "thinking beyond pure theory—theory of reality, theory of knowledge, theory of this and theory of that—so as to reclaim the space of praxis in which the manifold expressions of thought and action are situated."[53] What rhetoric teaches us is that "being rational" does not mean acting in accordance with the dictates of "reason," conceived of as a metaphysical "faculty" of the "mind"; it means behaving in a *reasonable* manner. To be rational is above all to be reasonable.[54]

To emphasize the rhetorical dimension of our communicative practices in general and of philosophical discourse or argumentation in particular is not to *reduce* philosophy to rhetoric, viewed as "mere" rhetoric, and it does not entail doing away with the notion of "truth." In line with his general approach to issues, Schrag seeks to steer a *via media* between unacceptable extremes, between, as he would say, the Scylla of metaphysical-epistemological foundationalism and the Charybdis of antiphilosophical relativism. He seeks not simply to substitute rhetoric for philosophy but to emphasize the rhetorical nature of philosophy and the philosophical status of rhetoric.[55] The relation between philosophy and rhetoric is one of "convergence without coincidence."[56] What is at issue in all this is the notion of *truth* itself.

Truth must no longer be conceived of metaphysically or epistemologically, as the correspondence of (subjective) ideas with so-called objective reality (an "entitative" reality which is supposedly just exactly *what* it is apart from our having anything to do with it). Truth must rather be seen to be a practical notion, an "implicate" of our being and acting. Truth is not something merely to be discovered; it is something we have the responsibility for making. As Schrag states: "The truth at issue in a rhetoric of truth is not that of an epistemic correspondence of a reified proposition with an equally reified state of affairs, but rather truth as the disclosure of possibilities for agreed upon perspectives on seeing the world and acting within it."[57] This is what Schrag calls "a hermeneutically informed notion of truth, liberated from its traditional epistemological paradigm." And thus, as he goes on to say: "This move beyond epistemology to hermeneutics within the field of formal rhetoric is itself part of the wider story of the 'end' of epistemology and the emergence of a new notion of philosophical truth."[58] Since, as Schrag remarks, "rhetoric as the directedness of discourse to the other, soliciting a response, is destined to slide into ethics," this new, praxial understanding of truth and rationality is no longer metaphysical or epistemological—it is ethical.[59] The term "praxis" has no metaphysical-epistemological significance; it designates a concept that is irreducibly ethico-political.

Philosophical Universalism

The defense of the philosophical enterprise "at the end of philosophy" necessitates a defense, not only of reason or rationality, but of *universal* reason, for reason is nothing if it is not universal (or, perhaps better said, universalizable). As Perelman has clearly shown, the principle of universalizability (the "reciprocity principle") is at the heart of communicative rationality as rhetoric understands it. The crucial question is whether philosophy's claim to universality can be divested of its traditional metaphysical trappings and be refigured in a suitably postmetaphysical way. Again like Merleau-Ponty before him, Schrag believes that it can. In opposition to the formalistic universalism defended by Kant, Merleau-Ponty argued for what he called a "presumptive" universality. In other words, Merleau-Ponty sought to disengage philosophy's claim to universality from its traditional "grounding" in universal essences which are supposed to be the selfsame always and everywhere. He rejected the metaphysical belief that an idea can claim to be rational only if it can be generalized in such a way as to possess a uniform (univocal) value in all situations, thereby making contact with some kind of objective absolute (the idea of universal commensuration, as Rorty would say). Although he was not able to develop the idea in any great detail, Merleau-Ponty said that the claim to universality is in reality an (existential) appeal or call "which a situated thought addresses to other thoughts, equally situated, and [to which] each one responds with its own resources."[60] When Merleau-Ponty said that "the germ of universality" is not to be located in, and is not guaranteed by, some metaphysical stronghold of absolute consciousness but "is to be found ahead of us, . . . in the dialogue into which our experience of other people throws us by means of a movement not all of whose sources are known to us," he was anticipating the position that Schrag was to work out in much greater detail.[61] The only viable way of conceiving of universality in a postmetaphysical age is by reconfiguring it in terms of communicative praxis as elucidated by rhetorical theory.

As was mentioned above, Schrag speaks in this regard of transversal rationality; universality needs to be reconfigured as transversality.[62] Transversality designates "a convergence without coincidence, an interplay without synthesis, an appropriation without totalization, and a universalization that allows for difference." Schrag believes, as Merleau-Ponty has said, that "we do not arrive at the universal by abandoning our particularity."[63] Schrag's "transversality" recalls the interesting expression Merleau-Ponty came up with when in the course of a discussion of alien cultures he sought to defend "a sort of oblique universality" and said: "The unity of the human spirit exists in each culture's lateral relationships to the others, in the echoes one awakes in the other."[64] Cultural relativists such as Rorty notwithstanding, there is indeed something like transcultural (and transhistorical) truth—not, to be sure, in any overarching, contextless sense, but in the hermeneutical, praxial sense that, given the requisite good will, people can always communicate *across* ("trans") cultural boundaries in such a way as to come to common understandings (compare Jaspers' notion of "boundless communication"). As Gadamer would say, the universal (the "same") exists always only in its "application" (difference); while always universal ("one") in its aspirations, reason is also always contextual ("many") in its actual existence.[65] Universality must be conceived of not in substantialist or essentialist (static) terms—as "identity" (in the metaphysical sense)—but in terms of process and performativity; not in terms of univocity, but of analogy and commonality. It is, as Schrag would say, a matter of convergence without coincidence.[66] The important thing to note in this regard is that the very notion of humanity—a philosophical notion par excellence, a creation of Greek philosophy—would be devoid of meaning if the notion of universality were not itself meaningful. This is something that, in their own perverse way, the antihumanist "philosophers of '68," who were all-too-eager to proclaim the death of "man" (and who, accordingly, had nothing of any real [theoretical] significance to contribute to the human rights movement that was then getting under way), understood all too well.[67] In contrast to the self-eviscerating thought of these writers, Schrag's thought, inspired by the great tradition of classical rhetoric, remained staunchly committed to the project of a philosophical humanism at a time when a Heidegger-inspired antihumanism dominated a large part of the philosophical scene.

In this context Schrag makes an important and much-needed distinction, one which is invariably overlooked by apologists for "localism" and "incommensurability." This is the distinction between " 'context-conditioned' (or 'context-informed') and 'context-determined.' "[68] While ideas or values are (it goes without saying) always culture-emergent, they are nevertheless not, necessarily, culture-dependent. Thus, while a given idea or value (such as, e.g., the idea of universal human rights) may be said to have originated "within" a particular culture, it cannot be maintained that its validity is necessarily *limited* to that culture. Just as an idea which first finds expression in a particular language can subsequently be creatively (interpretively) taken up in another language and become in this way part of its own repertory of ideas (this is a universal, hermeneutical, or phenomenological fact about human reality), so likewise a value first articulated in one culture can, in principle, be adopted as its own by any other culture.[69] The structuralist model when applied to human reality is false and grossly misleading. As in the case of natural languages (which, unlike formal or logistic languages, have no outer limits), human cultures are not closed-in, self-contained entities. Like consciousness itself (the intentional or "transcending" nature of which it was one of the chief tasks of classical phenomenology to demonstrate), every culture and every language is open to what is "outside" it, to the "other." It is precisely through the particularity of our being (as Gadamer suggests) that we are open to the universal, to the truth that we are.

Communicative rationality is, by its very nature, transcultural, that is, universal, "boundless." As Schrag sums it up: "The struggle for rationality is the struggle of transversal communication for understanding self and other in spite of the play of difference within our personal and social existence."[70] What this means is that, precisely because they are beset by the play of difference and are without metaphysical foundations, communication and the search for understanding (agreement) always involve a struggle, a struggle for openness to what is "other." Transcultural understanding is therefore never a fait accompli but always only a wager. Since it calls for effort on the part of intercoursing subjects, for resolve, the option for reason is, at bottom, an *ethical* matter. Reason is— or can be—a universal power of emancipation contributing to the unity of the human spirit (as Merleau-Ponty suggests) only if we conscientiously commit ourselves to making it be such.

Philosophical Universalism in a Global Age

With the advent of the twenty-first century, we are witnessing the emergence of a global civilization. Thanks to twentieth-century technological developments, the age-old philosophical idea of "humanity" is, for the first time in history, no longer *just* an idea, a philosophical abstraction, a referentless concept. It is an idea that is in the process of becoming an actual, lived reality. Communication in all the main arenas of human endeavor—cultural, economic, political—has become unbounded. Something like a global community is taking shape over and beyond the modern (Westphalian) system of nation-states, bypassing and ignoring it, and rendering it increasingly obsolete.

There are those who feel threatened by these developments, driven as they are by the forces of global capitalism. Cultural autarkists, for instance, would have us believe that globalization spells the end of cultural differences and the onslaught of global homogenization (by which they usually mean Americanization). As is now beginning to become hermeneutically manifest, however, this does not appear to be the direction in which the world is headed. As the Indian anthropological scholar, Arjun Appadurai, has stated, "globalization is not the story of cultural homogenization."[71] What culturalist arguments about "Americanization" and "commoditization" fail to consider, Appadurai observes, is "that at least as rapidly as forces from various metropolises are brought into new societies they tend to become indigenized in one or another way. The new global economy has to be seen as a complex, overlapping, disjunctive order that cannot any longer be understood in terms of existing center-periphery models."[72] In other words, the universalization of the human condition that globalization is bringing about is not of a "metaphysical" sort (which no doubt accounts for why criticisms of the new global economy on the part of both right- and left-wing critics are so often misdirected).

Whatever may be some of its more unsettling effects (and there will surely be no lack of these), globalization does signal the advent of some welcome changes in the human condition and in intersocietal relationships.[73] In regard to the human condition, it signals the end of cultural isolationism (the prime source of intercultural opposition and hostility) and the advent of a kind of cultural *métissage* or hybridity, a kind of "dialogized heteroglossia" (as Bakhtin suggests) on a worldwide scale.[74] In regard to intersocietal relationships, it signals the end of the Age of Empire which began in earnest in the sixteenth century (and which inaugurated the first phase of world history) and the advent of a new age which might appropriately be labeled the Age of Interdependence or the Age of Mutualism.[75] It is an age that is grounded on the rational principle of universal human rights and informed by an ethics of mutual recognition and responsibility—of identity within difference, solidarity— which follows from this philosophical principle.[76]

What is possible, what is even likely, is not always what is inevitable, however. The task of philosophy in the twenty-first century must be that of helping to translate the ideal into the real, of ensuring that the ideal does indeed become a living reality. This is to say that the supreme task of philosophy in the new millennium can no longer be metaphysical or epistemological (a "disinterested" attempt to discover the Truth as rationalists conceive of it, philosophy as the "mirror of nature") but must be ethical (a politically informed attempt to transform the world in which we live). The ultimate justification of philosophical theory (as, precisely, the theory of practice) is, and can only be, its significance for practice. If philosophy is to remain faithful to its age-old humanist vocation which dates back to the earliest of Greek rhetors, it has the moral obligation of seeing to it that the new humanity that is coming into being embodies, in all the realms of human agency, the philosophical virtue of humanness (what the Confucian humanist tradition refers to as *jen/ren*). Constructing humanness, assisting people to "be human" (*zuoren*), is philosophy's supreme responsibility.[77] A renewed philosophical humanism necessarily entails an ethic of responsibility, a responsibility for, as Gadamer would say, the "consciousness of a humanity that slowly begins to know itself as humanity."[78]

The prime theoretical means by which philosophy can contribute to this practical, civilizational end is by resolutely defending the notions of the individual subject and universal reason. For these two philosophical notions—individualism and universalism—are the twin cornerstones of the notion of universal human rights, which in turn is the only possible basis on which a humane global civilization, and a global community, can be built. These two notions can, however, be of relevance to the new global reality only if they are reconfigured in a suitably postmetaphysical (and, thus, nonhegemonic) fashion, in terms of unrestricted transversal communicative praxis.[79] And this is something to which Calvin Schrag's thoroughgoing reconfiguration of the guiding notions of phenomenological philosophy has greatly contributed.

Notes

1. Dating the inception of phenomenology from 1900, the year of publication of Husserl's *Logische Untersuchungen*, J. N. Findlay's English translation of the *Logical Investigations* appeared only many decades later, in 1970, by which time phenomenology had achieved a solid foothold in North America, thanks to the exertions of scholars like Calvin Schrag. For an account of the origins of American phenomenology, see E. F. Kaelin and C. O. Schrag, eds., *American Phenomenology: Origins and Developments* (Dordrecht: Kluwer Academic, 1989).

2. A symbolic testimony to this resurgent interest in the phenomenological tradition was the international symposium organized by Renaud Barbaras and

held at the Université de Paris-Sorbonne in 1995, "Merleau-Ponty: Les Figures du sensible." For an analysis of how the work of a "classical" phenomenologist such as Merleau-Ponty is actually more relevant to the contemporary, post-1989 world than the poststructuralism that displaced it for a time, see my "Merleau-Ponty Alive," *Man and World* 26 (1993): 19–44.

3. See Charles E. Scott, "Continental Philosophy at the Turn of the Twenty-First Century," in *The Columbia History of Western Philosophy*, ed. Richard H. Popkin (New York: Columbia University Press, 1999), pp. 745–53.

4. See in this regard my "Hermeneutics, the Lifeworld, and the Universality of Reason," *Dialogue and Humanism* (Polish Academy of Sciences) 7 (1995): 79–106.

5. The philosophical notion of universal human rights, which has now proven its practical effectiveness in the worldwide freedom and democracy movement, was, it may be noted, one that the "philosophers of '68"—as Luc Ferry and Alain Renaut have referred to them (*French Philosophy of the Sixties: An Essay on Antihumanism* [Amherst: University of Massachusetts Press, 1990])—chose to ignore in their haste to deconstruct philosophical reason. Richard Rorty also rejected the philosophical notion of human rights as being hopelessly "metaphysical."

6. See in this regard my *The Political Economy of Civil Society and Human Rights* (London: Routledge, 1998).

7. Maurice Merleau-Ponty, *Themes from the Lectures at the Collège de France: 1952–1960*, trans. John O'Neill (Evanston, Ill.: Northwestern University Press, 1970), p. 102.

8. This is true of all the outstanding heirs to Husserl: Heidegger, Gadamer, and Merleau-Ponty. A very significant and illustrative text in this regard (as regards his own phenomenological trajectory) is Paul Ricoeur's "On Interpretation," in *Philosophy in France Today*, ed. Alan Montefiore (Cambridge: Cambridge University Press, 1983).

9. Scott, "Continental Philosophy," pp. 745–46.

10. See in this regard the usage Schrag makes of Kierkegaard in his most recent book, *The Self after Postmodernity* (New Haven, Conn.: Yale University Press, 1997) (hereafter cited as *SP*).

11. Kaelin and Schrag, eds., *American Phenomenology*, p. 278.

12. Hans-Georg Gadamer, *Truth and Method* (New York: Continuum, 1975), p. xxv.

13. See Kaelin and Schrag, eds., *American Phenomenology: Origins and Developments*, p. 279. It should be noted that the "epistemological paradigm" of which Schrag speaks is *the* paradigm of modernist philosophy, and thus something that postmodern philosophy, in both its hermeneutical and deconstructive varieties, has sought strenuously to overcome. On the similarities—and differences—between hermeneutical postmodernism, on the one hand, and "poststructural" postmodernism (as represented by Rorty and Derrida), on the other, see my "Coping with Nietzsche's Legacy: Rorty, Derrida, Gadamer," *Philosophy Today* 36 (spring 1992): 3–19.

14. For a representative sampling of Schrag's work over the past several

decades, see his *Philosophical Papers: Betwixt and Between* (Albany: State University of New York Press, 1994).

15. See Roland Barthes, "The Death of the Author," in *Image, Music, Text* (New York: Hill and Wang, 1984), p. 145.

16. Indeed, Schrag's chief philosophical criticism of postmodern attempts at a dissolution of the subject is that they are altogether too "facile." See, e.g., his criticism of Jean-François Lyotard, "the most postmodern of the postmodernists": "The slide from diversity, plurality, and multiplicity to heterogeneity, paralogy, and incommensurability is too hurried, too facile, inviting a skewing of the phenomenon of discourse as it is lived through and more proximately experienced in our more quotidian existence" (Schrag, *SP,* pp. 29, 30).

17. Schrag's rejection of essentialist metaphysics goes all the way back to his student days at Harvard in the 1950s when he looked to Whitehead's process philosophy as an alternative to classical substance metaphysics; see Kaelin and Schrag, eds., *American Phenomenology,* pp. 277–78. Of Derrida, Schrag has said: "Personne n'a certainement apporté une plus grande contribution au travail de souligner les bizarreries des théories classique et moderne du sujet que ne l'a fait Derrida" (Calvin O. Schrag, "La Récupération du sujet phénoménologique," *Analecta Husserliana* 50 [1997]: 183–92). See also M. C. Dillon, *Semiological Reductionism: A Critique of the Deconstructionist Movement in Postmodern Thought* (Albany: State University of New York Press, 1995). For a critique of "semioticism" and a defense of a "postsemiological" theory of knowledge, see Gary B. Madison, "Being and Speaking," in *Beyond the Symbol Model: Reflections on the Representational Nature of Language,* ed. J. Stewart (Albany: State University of New York Press, 1996).

18. Calvin O. Schrag, *Communicative Praxis and the Space of Subjectivity* (Bloomington: Indiana University Press, 1986), p. 11 (hereafter cited as *CPSS*).

19. Ibid., p. 12.

20. Ibid., pp. 29, 170.

21. See my "Ricoeur and the Hermeneutics of the Subject," in *The Philosophy of Paul Ricoeur,* Library of Living Philosophers, ed. L. E. Hahn, vol. 22 (Chicago: Open Court, 1995), pp. 75–92, appearing also in Gary B. Madison, *The Hermeneutics of Postmodernity: Figures and Themes* (Bloomington: Indiana University Press, 1988), pp. 90–105.

22. Schrag, *CPSS,* pp. 170–71.

23. Calvin O. Schrag, "Traces of Meaning and Reference: Phenomenological and Hermeneutical Explorations," *Current Issues in Linguistic Theory* 73 (1992): 22.

24. Ibid., p. 23.

25. Calvin O. Schrag, *The Resources of Rationality: A Response to the Postmodern Challenge* (Bloomington: Indiana University Press, 1992), p. 89.

26. Schrag, "Traces of Meaning and Reference," p. 26.

27. Michel Foucault, *The Order of Things: An Archaeology of the Human Sciences* (New York: Random House, 1970), p. 387.

28. Calvin O. Schrag, "Subjectivity and Praxis at the End of Philosophy," in

Hermeneutics and Deconstruction, ed. Hugh J. Silverman and Don Ihde (Albany: State University of New York Press, 1985), p. 32. The mode of subjectivity that Schrag quite rightly rejects is described by him in this way: "Modernity turns on the principle of subjectivity, which grounds the human subject as at once rational and free, liberated from the fetters of tradition. The rationality of modernity resides in a centered subject, an immanent logos, functioning as an epistemological foundation from which all justification of knowledge claims proceeds" (Calvin O. Schrag, "Rationality between Modernity and Postmodernity," in *Life-World and Politics,* ed. S. K. White [Notre Dame, Ind.: University of Notre Dame Press, 1989], p. 83).

29. To allude to the title of a book by J. Van Den Hengel, *The Home of Meaning: The Hermeneutics of the Subject of Paul Ricoeur* (Washington, D.C.: University Press of America, 1982). Despite Schrag's criticism of Ricoeur (see above), the similarities between his work and that of Ricoeur are, in terms of their general thrust, quite remarkable. Both Schrag and Ricoeur have consistently, and resolutely, sought to divest phenomenology of the last vestiges of the "philosophy of consciousness."

30. For an analysis of Merleau-Ponty's endeavors in this regard, see my "Merleau-Ponty and Postmodernity," in *Hermeneutics of Postmodernity,* as well as my "Merleau-Ponty Alive."

31. Schrag, *CPSS,* p. 11.

32. Schrag, "Subjectivity and Praxis," pp. 26, 29.

33. See Schrag, "La Récupération," p. 183.

34. Schrag, *CPPS,* p. 198.

35. Calvin O. Schrag, "Reconstructing Reason in the Aftermath of Deconstruction," *Critical Review* 5, no. 2 (spring 1991): 248.

36. Ibid.

37. Ibid., p. 253.

38. See Jürgen Habermas, "The Hermeneutic Claim to Universality," in G. L. Ormiston and A. D. Schrift, eds., *The Hermeneutic Tradition: From Ast to Ricoeur* (Albany: State University of New York Press, 1990). For a defense of Gadamer against the misguided criticisms of Habermas, see my "Hermeneutics' Claim to Universality," in L. E. Hahn, ed., *The Philosophy of Hans-Georg Gadamer* (Library of Living Philosophers, vol. xxiv) (Chicago: Open Court, 1997), pp. 349–65.

39. Schrag, "Reconstructing Reason," p. 257.

40. Ibid.

41. Schrag, "Rationality between Modernity and Postmodernity," p. 99.

42. Schrag, "Reconstructing Reason," p. 259.

43. Schrag, "Interpretation, Narration, and Rationality," *Research in Phenomenology* 21 (1991): 111.

44. Schrag, *SP,* p. 80.

45. Calvin O. Schrag, "Rhetoric Resituated at the End of Philosophy," *Quarterly Journal of Speech* 71 (1985): 166.

46. For a detailed exposition of the intimate relation between hermeneutics and rhetoric, see my "The New Philosophy of Rhetoric," *Texte: Revue de critique et de théorie littéraire* (Toronto) 8/9 (1989): 247–77. As Schrag remarks: "The

rhetorician and the hermeneut alike are trained to recognize misunderstanding as it issues both from the infelicities of grammar and from deviations in the body politic" (Schrag, *Resources of Rationality*, p. 122).

47. "Indeed, our general continuing argument has been that a reclamation of the concrete intentionality of our doxastic lifeworld engagements does not entail a scuttling of the claims of a praxis-oriented logos" (Schrag, *Resources of Rationality*, p. 176).

48. Gadamer, *Philosophical Hermeneutics*, p. 24.

49. Schrag, *SP*, p. 81.

50. Schrag, "Reconstructing Reason," p. 258.

51. See Chaïm Perelman and Lucie Olbrechts-Tyteca, *The New Rhetoric: A Treatise on Argumentation*, trans. John Wilkinson and Purcell Weaver (Notre Dame, Ind.: Notre Dame University Press, 1969); originally published as *Traité de l'argumentation: La Nouvelle Rhétorique* (Paris: Presses universitaires de France, 1958). See also Chaïm Perelman, *The Realm of Rhetoric* (Notre Dame, Ind.: University of Notre Dame Press, 1982).

52. Schrag, "Reconstructing Reason," p. 259.

53. Schrag, "Rhetoric Resituated," p. 166.

54. See Schrag, *CPPS*, p. 194; see also Chaïm Perelman, "The Rational and the Reasonable," in *Rationality To-Day/La Rationalité aujourd'hui*, ed. Th. F. Geraets (Ottawa: Editions de l'Université d'Ottawa, 1979), pp. 213–19; as well as Gary B. Madison, "Pour une dérationalisation de la raison," in Geraets, ed., *Rationality To-Day/ La Rationalité aujourd'hui*, pp. 368–72.

55. See Schrag, *Resources of Rationality*, p. 147.

56. Calvin O. Schrag, "Communication Studies and Philosophy: Convergence without Coincidence," with David D. Miller, in *The Critical Turn: Rhetoric and Philosophy in Postmodern Discourse*, ed. Ian Angus and Lenore Langsdorf (Carbondale: Southern Illinois University Press, 1992).

57. Schrag, *CPPS*, p. 187.

58. Ibid., p. 188. Schrag writes (p. 194): "The inmixing of truth and communication in expressive rhetoric as hermeneutic . . . forges a new and expanded notion of rationality."

59. Ibid., p. 199.

60. Maurice Merleau-Ponty, *The Primacy of Perception*, ed. James M. Edie (Evanston, Ill.: Northwestern University Press, 1964), p. 8.

61. Maurice Merleau-Ponty, *Sense and Non-Sense*, trans. H. L. Dreyfus and P. A. Dreyfus (Evanston, Ill.: Northwestern University Press, 1964), p. 93.

62. See, in particular, Schrag, *Resources of Rationality*, chap. 6.

63. See Merleau-Ponty, *Sense and Non-Sense*, p. 92.

64. Maurice Merleau-Ponty, *Signs*, trans. R. C. McCleary (Evanston, Ill.: Northwestern University Press, 1964), p. 39.

65. For a discussion of the hermeneutical notion of "application," see my "Hermeneutics: Gadamer and Ricoeur," in *Continental Philosophy in the 20th Century*, Routledge History of Philosophy, ed. R. Kearney, vol. 8 (London: Routledge, 1994), pp. 317–18.

66. See Schrag, *SP*, p. 133: Schrag describes the unity as one that "functions as a coefficient of transversality in very much an open-textured process of unification, moving beyond the constraints of the metaphysical opposites of universality versus particularity and identity versus difference."

67. It should not be forgotten that during these antihumanist times one of the few responsible thinkers in France, Claude Lefort, a student of Merleau-Ponty, never faltered in his denunciation of totalitarian practices and in his commitment to the philosophical notion of human rights.

68. Schrag, "Reconstructing Reason in the Aftermath of Deconstruction," p. 257. See also Schrag, *SP*, pp. 107–9.

69. For a discussion of these matters, see my "Philosophy without Foundations," *Reason Papers*, vol. 16 (fall 1991).

70. Schrag, "Reconstructing Reason," p. 260 (emphasis added).

71. Arjun Appadurai, *Modernity at Large: Cultural Dimensions of Globalization* (Minneapolis: University of Minnesota Press, 1996), p. 11.

72. Ibid., p. 32.

73. For a discussion of both the challenges and the opportunities created by globalization, see my "Globalization: Challenges and Opportunities," working paper 98/1, Institute on Globalization and the Human Condition, McMaster University (electronic version available at http://www.humanities.mcmaster.ca/~global/workpapers/wp.ht m>).

74. See Fred Evans, "Voices, Oracles, and the Politics of Multiculturalism," *Symposium* (Journal of the Canadian Society for Hermeneutics and Postmodern Thought) 2, no. 2 (fall 1998): 179–89. See likewise Schrag's remarks on Bakhtin in *The Resources of Rationality*. He says, e.g., that "Bakhtin's vocabulary of the chronotope, heteroglossia, the centrifugal versus the centripetal, and dialogue is particularly helpful in addressing the issues at hand" (p. 83).

75. Although the Chinese were in advance of the Europeans in the staging of far-flung sea voyages (see in this regard Louise Levathes, *When China Ruled the Seas: The Treasure Fleet of the Dragon Throne, 1405–1433* [New York: Oxford University Press, 1994]), the world first became a "globe," in a real sense of the term, with the completion of the first known circumnavigational voyage of the world by Magellan's fleet in 1521—an appropriate date perhaps with which to mark the beginning of the Age of Empire. See my "Visages de la postmodernité," *Etudes littéraires* 27, no. 1 (summer 1994): 113–35.

76. For a discussion of some of the basic elements of a phenomenological hermeneutics of mutual recognition, conceived of as a universalist ethics of global solidarity, see my "The Ethics and Politics of the Flesh," in *The Ethics of Postmodernity: Current Trends in Continental Thought*, ed. G. M. Madison and M. Fairbairn (Evanston, Ill.: Northwestern University Press, 1999), pp. 174–90 and (notes) pp. 256–59.

77. "Being human" or "becoming human" (*zuoren*) is the central concept of Confucian ethical humanism. Current hermeneutical attempts in the wake of globalization to reconfigure traditional Confucianism with an eye to the "Western," liberal idea of universal human rights testify to the "transversal" relevance

of the latter in the new age of a globalized humanity. See in this regard Wm. T. De Barry and Tu Weiming, *Confucianism and Human Rights* (New York: Columbia University Press, 1998).

78. See Hans-Georg Gadamer, *Reason in the Age of Science*, trans. F. G. Lawrence (Cambridge, Mass.: MIT Press, 1981), p. 86.

79. Nonhegemonic, because no longer under the sway of the metaphysical notions of "unity, totality, identity, sameness, and consensus" (Schrag, *SP*, p. 7).

PART 2

TRANSVERSAL
RATIONALITY

"Where Are You Standing . . . ?": Descartes and the Question of Historicity

Robert C. Scharff

One topic that figures prominently in Calvin Schrag's philosophical work is the phenomenon of human historicity. Taking on this topic can prove to be a tricky thing, as one can see by comparing Schrag's surefooted treatment of it with, for example, its halting treatment by those analytic thinkers who now seek to distance themselves from the "Cartesian" idea that philosophy can be practiced as if from Nowhere. For as these thinkers show, often in spite of themselves, it is possible to speak *about* human historicity, both in general and in the thought of others, without recognizing its presence in one's own thinking. Our existence, says Nietzsche, is basically an imperfect tense that can never become a perfect one.[1] He intends this, of course, to be self-referential, but too many thinkers now repeat the statement without getting the message. What Putnam says of Rorty applies to many others: We hear that there is no God's Eye viewpoint from a God's Eye viewpoint.[2]

In this regard I can trace one of the lasting effects of Schrag's philosophical work by recalling his challenge to me in a seminar more than thirty-five years ago. After I had made some especially sweeping and decontextualized claim, Schrag turned to me and asked: "Where are you standing when you say that?" As I now see, this is in fact always a timely question—not because Schrag says so, but because it is always appropriate to reflect upon the way that we inevitably already *are*. All thinking, it seems, is hermeneutical—either candidly or in spite of one's best efforts to deny it. Here, I think, lies the real origin of Heidegger's early distinction between inauthenticity and authenticity. It is not a question of choosing between uninspired ordinariness and a specially elected option. Rather, it is a matter of recognizing, or failing to recognize, the determinate, located (or "sited"), concretely dwelling be-ing that we live through.

In what follows I try to say something about the importance of Schrag's question by showing its relevance in a place where it seems wrong to ask it, namely, in the famous *Meditations* of that very paradigm of the allegedly unsituated thinker, Descartes. For if it is true that one is always "standing" somewhere, however much one may try to cultivate a self-conception that denies this, then it must be possible to see this in any thinker. So I will argue that there is in the *Meditations* a Descartes who never achieves a God's Eye viewpoint, a Descartes who fails—and repeatedly acknowledges that he fails—to live up to the Cartesian ideal that Bernard Williams calls "the project of pure inquiry."[3] Descartes, I claim, always remains an "impure" thinker—a meditator who realizes that not even the most "resolute" use of his method can make him a Cartesian.

In the English-speaking world of Schrag's graduate student days as well as mine, of course, "Descartes himself" would not have been a proper philosophical topic. For in the heyday of logical empiricism, traditional figures were either treated with philosophical condescension (as somewhat backward contemporaries) or taken to have "merely" historical interest.[4] Today, however, even among English-speaking commentators, tradition is better treated. "Anachronism" is a serious charge; and it is even respectable to argue that contemporary philosophizing has not really gotten as free from its past as positivists wanted everyone to believe.[5] Descartes has, to some extent, benefited from this change. He is no longer routinely identified as just the first modern, that is, as the founder of rationalism, or the reason there had to be a Locke, or the purveyor of a method and a metaphysics that are now simply to be criticized or avoided. Nevertheless, in the Anglo-American tradition of Cartesian scholarship, Descartes still tends to be construed so much in terms of twentieth-century epistemic controversies that his own account of meditation is obscured.[6] I want to disrupt this interpretive tendency. I want to ask, *How is it to think "meditatively"?* Wilson once complained that Descartes "had little understanding of, or respect for, the concept of formalization."[7] I want to urge some admiration for this disrespect.

Reversing Williams's phrase, I want to praise Descartes for realizing that his project of inquiry will always remain unformalizable—and for recognizing that this is only understandable to those readers who are willing to "meditate with" him, but not to those who become preoccupied with purifying and "reconstructing" his "arguments." For only comeditators are able to see what is philosophically most striking about meditation—namely, that the inescapably determinate conditions of any inquiry place us forever "between" perfect truth and sheer blankness. It may be true, as I will mention at the end, that Descartes cannot pursue this realization because his inquiry is, by explicit methodological intention, pointed away from what his own procedure could have told him. Today, however, circumstances are otherwise. We find ourselves differently situated, and it may be worth pondering the idea that Cartesianism, far from "improving" meditation, may in fact have been a tradition of ill-conceived attempts to remove its essential limitations. First, though, I shall attend to something more modest. I simply want to show that an interpretation of Descartes which opposes the comfortable and familiar imagery of "pure" inquiry has considerable textual justification.

Meditation as "Impure" Inquiry

What, then, is the "meditation" that Descartes actually practices? It is not, of course, the introspective reporting of tickles, itches, pains, and mental acts—a kind of privately preoccupied psychological act that focuses on the present empirical state of how it is with me. Perhaps this should be self-evident, but in fact there remains some tendency among English-speaking commentators to run meditative reflectiveness and introspection together, especially among philosophers of mind. Typically, something called "(Cartesian) self-knowledge"—that is, a knowledge of our own thoughts, feelings, and volitions presumably obtained by a kind of "inward inspection" and accounted for in "folk psychological" terms—is interpreted as preceding or supplementing, or perhaps even competing with, everything from brain physiology to psychoanalysis and sociology.[8]

Descartes, however, is interested in something that is both narrower and more universal than this familiar empirical condition. Meditation is narrower because (as I will discuss later) the only features of one's current mental condition that concern Descartes are the ones that facilitate or retard the acquisition of the knowledge of figure, number, and nature. Meditation is also more universal because the knowledge to be attained has no special relation to Descartes himself but is supposed to be, like the mathematical knowledge he grew to admire at La Flèche, unconditioned by anything but the absolute test of clarity and distinctness. Analytic philosophers may find it disconcerting to hear meditation described in this way. For my description of the narrowing feature of its interest might suggest that there actually is something "empirical" or "psychological" about meditation, whereas reference to its intended universal reach seems nevertheless to expect the formalizing transcendence of all empirical/psychological contingencies. Both features are present, I think, in Descartes's meditation; but I will argue in a moment that this should be seen as its virtue, not its failure, and that neither "empirical" nor "psychological" is a good label for either the character or the goal of meditative practice.

How then should meditation be understood? We know at least that it is supposed to be a self-critically reflective affair—a monitoring of one's thinking under the "resolute" guidance of a model of truth extrapolated from mathematics. The fact that meditation always has "one's own" course of thinking as its concern seems as important to Descartes as the idea that it seeks certainty. Descartes tells us that in the *Principles of Philosophy*, he reasons "synthetically"—that is, *from* given principles *to* deduced conclusions. In his *Meditations,* however, his procedure is "analytical." When the synthetic method is employed, he explains, "people generally tend to think they have learned more than is in fact the case." The analytical method, however, "shows the true way by means of which the thing was discovered," and this allows the attentive reader to "make the thing his own and understand it just as perfectly as if he discovered it for himself."[9]

Yet to twentieth-century Anglo-American ears, Descartes's "personalized" accounts of his quest for certainty can sound formally sloppy and psychologically indulgent—insensitive to the need for keeping epistemic essentials separate from matters of contingent psychic detail. This insensitivity seems present both within and outside the *Meditations.* In the *Rules,* for example, Descartes says that "the greatest pleasure I have taken in my studies has always come not from accepting the arguments of others but from *discovering* arguments by *my own* efforts."[10] But what has objective epistemic analysis got to do with such pleasures, or with reforming a particular person's thoughts, or with learning to accept "the" criteria of thinking as "my own"?

We should be cautious, however, about taking this sort of objection at face value. Indeed, from the standpoint of the *Meditations* itself, a false dichotomy is at work in it. For Descartes, to "meditate" is precisely not to privilege an objective structure of Thought As Such over the contingencies of one's own actual thinking. He speaks throughout of "reforming his thought." Consider, for example, the famous assertion of methodological resolve in the First Meditation. Realizing that he must withhold assent not only from beliefs that are obviously false but also from all beliefs that are in any degree uncertain, Descartes concludes:

> It is not enough merely to have noticed this; I must make an effort to remember it. My habitual opinions keep returning . . . [to re-]capture my belief, which is as it were bound over to them as a result of long occupation and the law of custom. I shall never get out of the habit of confidently assenting to these opinions, so long as I suppose them to be what in fact they are, namely highly probable opinions . . . . In view of this, I think it will be a good plan to turn my will in completely the opposite direction, . . . pretending for a time that these former opinions are utterly false and imaginary.[11]

Here we can see that Descartes's famous hyperbolic doubt is primarily motivated, not by any interest in doing battle with skepticism, not by any recognition of inner logical necessities of his first rule, but by the desire to *retrain his mind*—that is, to discard the orientation of an ordinary believer for that of a disciplined knower.

In everyday life one simply tries to avoid obvious falsity and settles for probability. Our orientation toward the world is mostly sensuous and basically trusting. We seem to know when we are in the presence of real things; and we appear to be in possession of sufficiently reliable and "customary" criteria for knowledge about them. The important thing to notice here is that Descartes's main difficulty with this ordinary state of affairs has little to do with any of our usual beliefs in particular. Rather, he is concerned about the general and pervasive effect on our thinking of our basically sensuous orientation toward our surroundings. It is in relation to this concern that he finds he must work out his rejection of sense experience as a reliable guide for knowledge in two steps rather than one.

In the first step, Descartes finds it relatively easy to move from discrediting this or that sense-based belief to the *logical* conclusion that sense experience cannot guarantee certainty about the world. He finds, however, that it is much harder to actually accept this conclusion and to think against a sense-experiential orientation than it is to simply deduce its rejection. "Occasionally" my senses do deceive me, he admits. But in the case of so many other sense-based beliefs, it really seems "impossible" to doubt them. Descartes discovers that his orientation toward the sensually available is anchored, not just in an excessive trust of the senses, but in the additional assumption that I always know when I am awake and paying attention. This is why the logical conclusion in the first step that sense-based beliefs *should be* rejected failed to bring with it an *acceptance* of that rejection. For if I assume I can tell *when* sense experience is reliable, then I will continue to embrace those sense-based beliefs that seem "impossible" to doubt, and I will simply let go of the rest. It is the fact that there are times when it seems difficult to know if I am really awake and paying attention that finally brings Descartes to take a second step and employ for the first time his radical, hypothetical *reversal* of our normal, sensual/wakeful orientation. This, he reasons, is the only way to neutralize the pull of "highly probable" opinions. It is not enough to merely *notice* that we mostly settle for probability. I must take steps to "keep it carefully in mind." Indeed, he says, I see that "I cannot possibly go too far in my distrustful attitude" toward my normal orientation if certain knowledge is ever to be acquired.

In Descartes's eyes, then, to actually make this special effort, to admit that my own thinking tends to be repeatedly undermined by old mental habits, and to resolutely formulate a strategy of "pretense" for its self-correction—none of this is a mere matter of personal and psychological detail, something out of place in a truly rigorous epistemology. Later readers criticize Descartes for failing to make "a proper distinction" between psychology and logic.[12] But there are good reasons why meditators do not make this distinction.

Consider, for example, the *Meditations'* treatment of method. Descartes does not begin his inquiry with a discussion of his procedure, but it is commonly assumed that we must do so for him.[13] Ours is, after all, a technique-happy age, and it can seem natural to us to appeal to Descartes's *Rules* and *Discourse* to satisfy our sense of priority that cognitive success comes from following a method.[14] A careful reading, however, will show that for Descartes the *Rules* and *Discourse* are not preestablished guides for the *Meditations;* they only offer something more like "synthetically" useful abstractions from the meditative process. In this process itself even such infrequent passing remarks about method as Descartes does make are continually fleshed out by accompanying reports of *what it takes to set aside* common opinion, to *really adopt* a procedure, to *actually search* for certainty, and so forth. In this respect, Descartes still seems more ancient and dialogical than modern and formally logical.[15] On his map of the philosophical terrain, *knowing* and *knowing that I know* have not yet been split off into an anonymous system of rules on the one hand and the mere social-psychological fact of my using them on the other.

The *Meditations* display, then, a genuinely philosophical, not merely psychological, "my-ownness"—a feature of the meditative process occluded in "reconstructions" of its "Project" or epistemological "Gambit."[16] Descartes's self-monitoring way of thinking includes, as we might say, phenomenological remarks about what it is like to think and to be a knower. This feature of meditation is in evidence not only in the First Meditation's preparatory struggle against the influence of sense experience but also later, when doubts begin to be dispelled.

Consider, for instance, Descartes on certainty. Critics complain that Descartes alters his conception of it to suit the occasion—making it relatively narrow and demanding for the First Meditation's hyperbolically "skeptical" purposes, but then turning it into something looser and more forgiving when he later desires justifications for his metaphysical claims about mental, divine, and material substance. This, however, is a spectator's complaint—the criticism of a nonmeditating mind, demanding anachronistically from Descartes the sort of initial rehearsal of "criteria" that one might expect from a contemporary analytic colleague. To "think with" Descartes is not to discover a *shift* from one, initial, rigorous rule of certainty to another, later, more generous idea; rather it is to witness the *transformation* of an obvious minimum test for "indubitability" into an instrument of superior probative power that one comes to understand precisely by first employing the preliminary minimum test. Initially, as the *Discourse* reports and the opening lines of the First Meditation affirm, it seems obvious that whatever else it is, being certain must at least involve the rejection of any belief that can be doubted. In the Second Meditation, however, at least one thought emerges that is immune even to the hyperbolic doubt with which the First Meditation closes. Thus, Descartes refrains from generalizing positively about certainty until the beginning of the Third Meditation, because only then is he in a position to extrapolate from the Second Meditation's discovery of what it is like to have a certainty. First, he sees how even hyperbolic doubt cannot dislodge the insight that he must *be* a thinker while in the *act* of thinking. This, in turn, opens up the possibility of discovering something of the mind's essential nature. Only then, in light of clear and distinct perceptions thus gained— and not by prior analysis of what Rule 1 essentially "means"—is he finally prepared to speak of certainty "in general."[17] Hence, Descartes's understanding of the rules of method is just as cumulative as his understanding of the nature of the three substances he considers by means of them.

How misleading it is, then, to begin an exposition of the *Meditations'* order of reasons with a preliminary rehearsal of methodological generalizations Descartes makes in other places. For he is not being epistemically sloppy or devious when he does not begin the *Meditations* with an account of what techniques or criteria of rationality will guide him. In his "analytical" chain of reflection, such an account would be inappropriate, for at the outset the four rules are in just as "preliminary" a condition as is Descartes's sense of what will be discovered. Understanding what the rules involve is continually enriched as he employs them and benefits from this. One must think through this process from the inside, because *seeing precisely when and how the enrichment of the rules happens is an essential part of the meditative process.* It is, as we say, a matter of "coming to understand," of "making my own," what is there to be had.

In short, instead of trying, in twentieth-century Anglo-American style, to reconstruct Descartes's "pure theory of inquiry"—which only has the effect of making him look incautious and old-fashioned and of reinforcing contemporary vanities about our having superior epistemic habits—I would draw attention to Descartes's account of *becoming knowledgeable.* Small wonder that he finds "synthetic," or syllogistic, reasoning unsuitable for this task. The trouble with such reasoning is that it perverts the learning process and hypnotizes the mind by making it appear that there are

> certain forms of reasoning in which the conclusions follow with such irresistible necessity that if our reason relies on them, even though it takes, as it were, a rest from considering a particular inference clearly and attentively, it can still draw a conclusion which is certain simply in virtue of the form.[18]

For Descartes, then, one must "guard against our reason's taking [such] a holiday while we are investigating the truth"—because letting the mind "rest" on the form of an argument is the very opposite of actually learning something. Descartes does not mean, of course, that no truths are demonstrable. It is, rather, that he is concerned with "investigating" the truth, not just "explain[ing] to others arguments already known." His point is that even the most skilled thinkers cannot formulate a valid syllogism with a true conclusion unless they have already *gained an understanding* of the very truth, together with its grounds and their conditions, whose deduction can then be formally "displayed."

Of course, for those still living under the shadow of positivism's Maginot Line, according to which epistemic concern for reconstruction and justification is one thing and extraphilosophical interests in psycho-socio-historical contexts of discovery is another, Descartes's orientation will undoubtedly seem strange. For he concludes flatly that since increased understanding of truth never comes from studying the formal rules of demonstration, this latter study would best be "transferred from philosophy to rhetoric."[19]

Meditation versus Psychological Self-Discovery

In general, then, the *Meditations'* impure and first-person format should emphatically not be read as a sign that it is still to some unfortunate extent "psychological."[20] Descartes is concerned with discoveries that are not just personally possible for him but that are ontologically possible for others. He is concerned, that is, with learning *what it is like* to demand and obtain certainty in thinking, and to do so against the background of a widely shared set of received opinions and practices. What he expects from his readers is thus nothing more than what he requires of himself. As he explains:

> I wrote "Meditations" rather than "Disputations," as the [scholastic] philosophers have done, or "Theorems and Problems," as the geometers would have done . . . [because] I wanted to make it clear that I would have nothing to do with anyone who was not willing to join me in meditating.[21]

Even today, however, analytic commentators persist in fending off this first-person register, in order that analysis of Descartes's arguments can proceed in a presumably less contaminated way. Williams, for example, makes the *Meditations'* first-person mode of presentation a function of Descartes's being a pioneer and then explains the matter away with the observation that "the question of how many, other than himself, might be capable of fundamental scientific and philosophical discoveries [is] not very important if none remain to be made." This conclusion leaves Williams free to devote the rest of his book to explaining, in complacent mainstream retrospect, what remains "importantly true" about Descartes's project and arguments.[22] Wilson, too, separates Descartes's expository "style" from his "system." She grants that the system does "in some sense presuppose the availability of the concept of subject or self" and ventures to suggest that maybe the style was "intended to promote *identification* on the part of the reader." She then insists, however, that her focus must necessarily be on the *Meditations* "as the presentation of a philosophical *position* having some claim to general relevance, and not as history or autobiography."[23]

When the presentation of such depersonalized interpretations of Descartes is held against them, Williams and Wilson, like many other English-language commentators, think of themselves as unfairly accused of manhandling classical sources—of being given a "bum rap," as Wilson puts it. What they fail to see, however, is that their updating of Descartes's own allegedly impure presentation of his "arguments" silently reinstates precisely the positivists' forced option between doing real philosophy by focusing on philosophical systems and arguments and merely doing history or biography. Descartes asks for a response that is neither of these. He does not assume that the only alternative to history and biography is pure, third-person reconstruction of systems and arguments. We might call his alternative "comeditation," that is, the "resolute" decision by us to experience the intuitive force of each of his discoveries until we, too, apprehend it—or (it should be remembered) insist that we cannot. Adoption of this sort of resolve is essential to understanding how meditation works. Without it, we can only confront from the outside a Cartesian "system" of rules and arguments, and we are tempted to criticize that system by using whatever techniques of evaluation "one" uses today to evaluate someone's "statements." Dicker, for example, in puzzling over what Descartes means in the First Meditation when he says that he intends to "withhold belief from things that are not entirely certain," concludes that this must mean to "suspend judgment." After all, since this constitutes one of three *logically possible* "belief-postures," or (in Keith Lehrer's phrase) "doxastic attitudes" toward "statements" (the other two being either acceptance or rejection), he reasons that Descartes *must* mean by "withholding a belief" that he will neither accept nor reject it.[24] In this way, Dicker steps back from the meditative process, assumes the third-person perspective that brings the familiar machinery of twentieth-century epistemology into his commentary—and thus precisely misses Descartes's point.

Suspension of judgment may be the only *logical* alternative to the acceptance and rejection of *statements,* but it is not the only other attitude I can take toward my own thinking. As Descartes quickly sees in the First Meditation, the problem is not that he has this or that doubtful sense-based belief but that he is *disposed to think* that "whatever I have up till now accepted as most true I have acquired either from or through the senses."[25] It is this general *orientation* in his thinking, this tendency to settle for high probability no matter what the particular statement, that Rule 1 challenges; hence, the question is one of establishing the proper approach toward that orientation itself. Dicker and Lehrer's three "doxastic attitudes" may be suitable for evaluating particular statements while taking the orientation of a logical analyst of statements and arguments for granted. Descartes, however, is interested precisely in learning what it is actually like to privilege this orientation, when he can already see that it is neither natural to us nor capable of complete realization. And for that concern one needs to do something more than employ the comfortable concepts of true, false, and still-to-be-determined. He realizes that he must "turn my will in completely the opposite direction and pretend for a time" that the opinions I find myself accepting are false. The fact that such "pretense"—such epistemic resolve—is not a "belief-posture" will of course elude the mere observers of Descartes's reasoning; but as he famously says in his "Readers' Preface," those unwilling to meditate with me had best not read the work at all.[26]

To put Descartes's general point quickly, then, this meditator who seeks comeditators never expects to *be* the ideal Objective Thinker who haunts our inheritance of him. There is for him no moment of supreme insight when the rules achieve their final (re)construction, and no one ever actually becomes their flawlessly competent instrument. Hence, what the struggle is like for those aspiring to this ideal remains an essential phenomenon in Descartes's inquiry, continually prompting reminders of why and how we do not instantiate Reason Itself. Today, such personalization of epistemic inquiry can seem at once insufficiently logical and hopelessly subjective. If every cogito must follow the same rules to obtain truth and to avoid falsity (so goes the argument), then it is the analysis of these rules that matters, not psycho-biographical and historical accounts of their acquisition and use. Doesn't Descartes simply fail to properly distinguish questions of evidence and justification from questions of personal and historical discovery?[27]

Descartes: Not (Yet) a Cartesian

To be fair, however, we cannot deny that Descartes's own writings are full of "Cartesian" imagery that actually discourages a phenomenological reading of him. After all, a "thinking thing" has no personality, no body, gender, or emotional life; and ultimately also, no history. Studying tradition, Descartes says in the *Discourse,* is like traveling. It broadens mental horizons and combats provincialism. Yet eventually, "one who spends too much time traveling becomes a stranger in one's own country" and "remains ignorant" of its practices.[28] So, for the genuine thinker who returns home and employs the four rules, history (like biography, psychology, and social studies) is ultimately a distraction. One who really cares about the principles of sound judgment has little use for what other people, at other times or places, may happen to have thought.

In retrospect, Descartes's travel simile seems prescient indeed. For in later empiricist-positivist epistemologies, not just the personal and psychological history of individuals, but tradition generally came increasingly to be regarded as irrelevant to epistemic inquiry. Actual minds (so goes the reasoning) may continue to be shaped and bewitched by received opinion; but the criteria that constitute the test of opinion are themselves quite independent of such contingencies. And it follows that if the *topic* of epistemic analysis is ahistorical, then so, surely, is the *standpoint* from which that topic is to be analyzed. Besides, why label us anachronistic for refusing Descartes's call for comeditation, when the "discoveries" he asks us to experience are all so "old-fashioned"? Who today can seriously hope to achieve Descartes's "insights" concerning Mind, God, and Nature?[29] And now that his method, too, seems a merely surpassable legacy, what possible motivation is left for taking "comeditation" seriously? Isn't it obvious that biography and history are one thing and Real Philosophy another?

The trouble with writing Descartes's epitaph this way is not just, as I have been arguing, that it ignores what Descartes reports himself as actually doing. It also begins from the imperial assumption that our judgments about him originate from an unproblematic philosophical standpoint. It is not, of course, that contemporary critics actually tell themselves, "I'm starting from a viewpoint that is unproblematic." It is, rather, that many contemporaries who would never *say* such a thing nevertheless *act* as if they were so fully in control of their orientation that even dealing with predecessors at all is entirely a matter of choice. Rorty, for example, may be a bit more outspoken on this point than most, but he probably speaks for the mainstream majority when he insists that today's thinkers should be free "to seek out their own intellectual ancestors . . . or [even] claim to have no ancestors at all."[30] It therefore follows, he argues, that we must be tolerant about whether historical scholarship figures in someone's chosen "approach." Wilson agrees, noting that although some philosophers do develop positions "in conscious relation" to their predecessors, others "evince little or no direct concern with defining their positions in relation to . . . [tradition]; and the depth of their implicit historical knowledge is at best controversial."[31] To the Anglo-American mainstream, these democratic-sounding gestures seem self-evident. Indeed, doesn't the spirit of pluralism dictate precisely Wilson and Rorty's approach? Shouldn't we simply acknowledge that some of us do, and that others don't, "choose" to bring ourselves into a "conscious relation" with, say, Descartes?

Wilson and Rorty, like so many others in the analytic tradition, think that because they have spoken in opposition to positivism, they have earned the right to treat these questions rhetorically. But they are mistaken. One cannot escape the residual influence of positivism's hostility toward tradition by calling for tolerance about whether someone makes *conscious use* of intellectual ancestors and historical writing. In fact, such calls for tolerance only reinforce the positivist presumption that we *can* leave the past behind—that our relationship to tradition *is* a matter of choice. In this, moreover, there is more than just a recapitulation of positivism. There is the manifestation of something older and deeply Cartesian—namely, the Fourth Meditation's advice concerning the issue of how to avoid error. One avoids error, says Descartes, by first simply "entertaining" an idea to see if it is clear or clarifiable. Only then should one "affirm" it.

Here, without question, is the Cartesian ideal for a perfectly self-possessed mind—that is, a mind stripped of its premeditative past and wholly guided by the four rules. Error is then avoidable, if only the judging will allows itself to be restrained by the rules until reason determines that it is in the presence of clear and distinct thoughts. This ideal is inscribed in the very imagery of these rules and this mind as they are characterized in the *Meditations*.[32] It is the ideal toward which every move in the *Meditations* and every article in the *Principles* seem to be directed. And it is obviously also the ideal that dominates our modern legacy. It does not, however, accurately depict Descartes's own philosophical practice—that is, what he actually did, as opposed to what he says a perfectly self-controlled cogito would necessarily do.

What I want to say here is that I rejoice in the fact that the *Meditations* do not give a consistent description of what meditation can accomplish. For this offers us an opening to see how contingent and context-bound the very idea of philosophizing from Nowhere really is. It is true that Descartes's general, programmatic statements tend to speak of meditation in idealized form—that is, in terms of what happens when error is avoided, truths are clearly and distinctly seen, and a mathematicized and decontextualized rationality rules over sense. Yet it is equally true that when Descartes describes how matters are going for him in practice—that is, when he speaks from what we might call his immediately operative understanding of his own meditative process—he speaks as one who is never a pure inquirer. He fills his account with little reminders of just how far short of this ideal his actual thinking falls—repeated confessions, for example, that old habits are never entirely extinguished; that clarity fades when attention weakens; that one can have "some understanding" but never full "comprehension" of God; that nature in its full concreteness is too rich with possibilities for reason alone ever to know it; and that adventitious ideas may be "generally" reliable but no more.[33]

It is not only in the *Meditations,* moreover, that such humbling disclaimers appear. Recall, for example, the limits Descartes places on the application of his rules in the *Discourse.* Far from claiming that his method will cover all reasoning for all occasions, he specifically exempts politics, theology, and ethics from meditative scrutiny. In order to "live as happily as I could" while pursuing my meditative task, he says, I gave myself four provisional moral maxims and, having "set them aside together with the truths of faith . . . I judged I could freely undertake to rid myself of *all the rest* of my opinions."[34] "All the rest" of my opinions, he says—*not* including his opinions on politics, faith, or morals. Descartes's readers mostly ignored this qualification, of course, turning instead to his programmatic remarks about the need for uniformity among all the "sciences" and then widening this idea out in the direction of a universal, topic-neutral, "monological" logic that tests not only our knowledge of number, figure, and nature but also everything thinkable. Especially in the empiricist-positivist tradition, not only "the rest" of our opinions but also our thoughts on politics, faith, and morals came to be evaluated by this logic—albeit often just long enough to be declared deficient or even "noncognitive." Thus does Descartes's meditative practice disappear into a "system" that the *Meditations* now seem only partially and imperfectly to have anticipated.

Descartes himself, however, could never have accepted this totalizing extension of his method. Far from living up to this Cartesian ideal, the course of his own meditation traces a very different image of thinking as he actually tries to follow the four rules. What we find are descriptions of thinking that depict it not only as finite, forever beset by problems of intellectual inheritance and habit and incapable of transcending its roots even when it considers matters of number, figure, or nature, but also as mindful of extrascientific concerns that the *Meditations* leave behind—concerns that require, among other things, faith and "maxims" of a more worldly and sensible character. Descartes the meditator never entirely forgets the abstractive and derivative character of mathematicized thinking. He never imagines that *all* thinking, on *whatever* topic, might proceed as if from Nowhere, with concern for historical, social, and cultural inheritance suppressed or made "optional."

In short, Cartesian construals of the *Meditations* decontextualize meditation in two ways. First, by constructing a *logic of pure inquiry* that ignores Descartes's narrative of the *actual process of inquiring*, they produce a falsely idealized and ahistorical model of scientific understanding. Second, by ignoring Descartes's explanation about leaving extrascientific affairs behind, they totalize their idealized model. The first move glorifies the View From Nowhere; the second, scientism. The Descartes who actually thinks in the *Meditations* remains too modest and too worldly to do either one.

Conclusion: Descartes as Already Too Cartesian

In the end, however, we must face the fact that Descartes never consciously embraced the ideas of finite human consciousness and historically determinate rationality. Had he been able to do so, then meditation might not have been so easily occluded by the subsequent purifications and formalizations. Thanks to the excesses of the intervening Cartesian era, however, we should now be ready to recover and reconsider Descartes's operative and at least minimally phenomenological understanding.

But how might such a recovery proceed? At a minimum, it would require that we learn how to interrogate the meditative process according to Schrag's question, "Where is Descartes standing?" when he speaks as a finite thinker who makes idealizing epistemic pronouncements. This is the question I have considered above. As Schrag put it in the first article of his I ever read, philosophizing—self-consciously or not—always arises from and carries forward "the interdependent experiences and reflections of a [historical] community of selves."[35] "Philosophizing, self-consciously, from within a community of selves": This phrase might serve to identify a—if not indeed, the—guiding concern in all his work. My claim has been that this concern is also present in the *Meditations*—even if Descartes could only acknowledge its presence indirectly. My larger and undiscussed assumption, however, is that this sort of phenomenological construal of the *Meditations*[36] might help to explain—especially to the many English-speaking philosophers who are still more Cartesian in their practice than they think—the truly radical implications of Heidegger's calling knowledge a "*founded* mode of being-in-the-world."

Notes

1. Friedrich Nietzsche, "On the Uses and Disadvantages of History for Life," in *Untimely Meditations,* trans. R. J. Hollingdale (Cambridge: Cambridge University Press, 1983), p. 61. Some of the places where this topic figures especially prominently in Schrag's works are *Philosophical Papers: Betwixt and Between* (Albany: State University of New York Press, 1994), chaps. 3, 5, 9, and 12; *The Resources of Rationality: A Response to the Postmodern Challenge* (Bloomington: Indiana University Press, 1992), pp. 3–49; *Communicative Praxis and the Space of Subjectivity* (Bloomington: Indiana University Press, 1986), pp. 1–6, 158–76; *Experience and Being: Prolegomena to a Future Ontology* (Evanston, Ill.: Northwestern University Press, 1969), pp. 206–15, 253–69; *Existence and Freedom: Towards an Ontology of Human Finitude* (Evanston, Ill.: Northwestern University Press, 1961), pp. 3–25, 142–53.

2. Hilary Putnam, *Realism with a Human Face,* ed. James Conant (Cambridge, Mass.: Harvard University Press, 1990), p. 25.

3. *Descartes: The Project of Pure Inquiry* (Atlantic Heights, N.J.: Humanities, 1978). Hereafter cited as *PPI*.

4. I draw here on the two opposed genres of "historian of philosophy" and "intellectual historian" identified as the idealized forced options in the period of positivist ascendancy by editors Richard Rorty, J. B. Schneewind, and Quentin Skinner in their introduction to *Philosophy in History: Essays on the Historiography of Philosophy* (Cambridge: Cambridge University Press, 1984), pp. 8–13. My favorite examples of this period's philosophical attitude toward the tradition are A. J. Ayer's assurance, after fifty pages of unrelieved antitraditional critique, that matters are really not so bad because "the majority of those who are commonly supposed to have been great philosophers were primarily not metaphysicians but analysts" (*Language, Truth, and Logic,* 2d ed. [New York: Dover, 1952], p. 52); and Hans Reichenbach's proud announcement that logical empiricism's rational reconstruction of scientific knowledge finally gives "adequate . . . expression" to Socratic maieutics (*Experience and Prediction: An Analysis of the Foundations and Structure of Knowledge* [Chicago: University of Chicago Press, 1938], p. 6).

5. See, e.g., Charles Taylor's essay "Philosophy and Its History," in Rorty, Schneewind, and Skinner, eds., *Philosophy in History,* pp. 17–30. Among the earliest signs of the general thaw are the collection of essays by John Passmore, Maurice Mandelbaum, W. H. Walsh, and Eugene Kamenka, edited by Passmore in 1965 for *History and Theory, Beiheft 5: The Historiography of the History of Philosophy*; and *Philosophy and the History of Philosophy,* special issue of *The Monist* 53/4 (1969). See also Peter H. Hare, ed., *Doing Philosophy Historically* (Buffalo, N.Y.: Prometheus Books, 1988); *The Role of History in and for Philosophy,* special issue of *Synthese* 67/1 (1986); A. J. Holland, ed., *Philosophy: Its History and Historiography* (Dordrecht: D. Reidel, 1985); and Jonathan Rée, Michael Ayers, and Adam Westoby, *Philosophy and Its Past* (Brighton: Harvester Press, 1978).

6. Nevertheless, there is growing Anglo-American opposition to the practice of treating Descartes as if his *Meditations* were a somewhat less successful version of twentieth-century philosophy's epistemic inquiries. One should name first the pioneering study by L. J. Beck, *The Metaphysics of Descartes: A Study of the "Meditations"* (Oxford: Clarendon Press, 1965). See also, e.g., Amélie Oksenberg Rorty, "The Structure of Descartes's *Meditations,*" L. Aryeh Kosman, "The Naive Narrator: Meditation in Descartes's *Meditations,*" and Gary Hatfield, "The Senses and the Fleshless Eye: The *Meditations* as Cognitive Exercises," in *Essays on Descartes' "Meditations,"* ed. A. O. Rorty (Berkeley and Los Angeles: University of California Press, 1986), pp. 1–20, 21–43, and 45–79, respectively (hereafter cited as *EDM*); Marjorie Grene, "Idea and Judgment in the Third Meditation: An Approach to the Reading of Cartesian Texts," in her *Descartes* (Minneapolis: University of Minnesota Press, 1985), pp. 3–22; and Emmet T. Flood, "Descartes's Comedy of Error," *Modern Language Notes* 102/4 (1987): 847–66.

7. Margaret Wilson, *Descartes* (London: Routledge and Kegan Paul, 1978), p. vii.

8. See, e.g., Quassim Cassam, introduction to *Self-Knowledge,* edited by Quassim Cassam (Oxford: Oxford University Press, 1994), pp. 1–18; Owen J. Flanagan, Jr., *The Science of the Mind,* 2d ed. (Cambridge, Mass.: MIT Press, 1991), pp. 66–67, 193–200; and William Lyons, *The Disappearance of Introspection* (Cambridge, Mass.:

MIT Press, 1986), pp. 1–22. That Descartes's own method is "introspective" traces to the standard readings of Locke (namely, his analysis of the "ideas of reflexion" in *An Inquiry concerning Human Understanding*, ed. P. H. Nidditch [Oxford: Oxford University Press, 1975], II, i, pp. 2–5, 24–25). But see contra, J. Douglas Rabb, *John Locke on Reflection: A Phenomenology Lost* (Lanham, Md.: University Press of America, 1985).

9. Ch[arles] Adam and P[aul] Tannery, eds., *Oeuvres de Descartes*, new rev. ed., 11 vols. (Paris: J. Vrin, 1964–76), vol. 7 (Second Set of Replies), pp. 159, 155; also, pp. 9–10, vol. 9/1, p. 121. Translations are from John Cottingham et al., *The Philosophical Works of Descartes*, 3 vols. (Cambridge: Cambridge University Press, 1984–91), which includes AT pagination. For discussion of Descartes's analytic method, see E. M. Curley, "Analysis in the *Meditations:* The Quest for Clear and Distinct Ideas," *EDM*, pp. 153–76.

10. Descartes, *Rules for the Direction of the Mind*, AT 10.403, 10.367 (emphasis added). Elsewhere, he considers what sort of person will have difficulty with his approach, humbly contrasts himself with better minds, and says, "My plan is to reform my own thoughts and construct them upon a foundation that is all my own" (*Discourse on the Method of Rightly Conducting the Reason and Seeking the Truth in the Sciences*, AT 6.15).

11. Descartes, *Meditations on the First Philosophy*, in *The Philosophical Works of Descartes*, ed. John Cottingham et al. (Cambridge: Cambridge University Press, 1984–91), AT 7.22, cf. AT 7.47–48.

12. Frankfurt praises Descartes's *Meditations* because, like Plato's dialogues, "they do not emasculate the philosophical enterprise by severing the connection with the lives of men"; yet Frankfurt thinks the important respect in which Descartes's solution is superior is that he has managed to do this "without betraying the anonymity of reason" (Harry G. Frankfurt, *Dreamers, Demons, and Madmen: The Defense of Reason in Descartes' "Meditations"* [Indianapolis: Bobbs-Merrill, 1970], p. 3). Especially after Kant, increased epistemic efforts to avoid such a "betrayal" show markedly little corresponding worry over "emasculation."

The question of Descartes's "first-person viewpoint" has been reconsidered more recently by Gareth B. Matthews, who claims to avoid the forced option of merely personal thoughts versus thoughts that generalize by noticing that "reflexive" I-questions (e.g., "How can I be certain I exist?") translate/generalize into reflexive "he," "she," or "one" questions that preserve the first-person viewpoint (Gareth B. Matthews, *Thought's Ego in Augustine and Descartes* [Ithaca, N.Y.: Cornell University Press, 1992], pp. 3–6). Matthews, however, is primarily interested in Descartes's *answers* to such questions and in *their* generalization; hence, the issue of what Descartes wants us to learn, as philosophers, about the *experience* of (impure) thinking is not addressed. In chapter 9, e.g., Matthews offers lengthy treatment of the fact that Descartes never raises the problem of other minds; but Matthews is so intent on raising the problem himself, and on using what Descartes says to inform it, that he never asks why Descartes fails to raise it. The answer lies in a different direction of concern—not what I can *justifiably assert* about this or that, but *what it is like to say anything under mathematically inspired rules.*

Like mathematicians, whose relations, as mathematicians, are mediated by those rules, meditators "are" for each other only "as" other rule-users, not as minds, or minds within bodies, or unperceivable entities, etc.

13. Michael Williams even argues that we contemporaries must be wary of this methodological silence; for it is precisely "Descartes's artful method of exposition—which involves developing his doubts in a way that is initially rather vague"—that prevents us from realizing how unnatural and metaphysically loaded these doubts really are (Michael Williams, "Descartes and the Metaphysics of Doubt," *EDM*, pp. 117–39, quotation on p. 135).

14. In addition to the problem I stress here, there is also the widespread misperception that the *Rules* and the *Discourse* present the same picture of Descartes's "method." Among other differences, the *Rules* contains no discussion of the method of doubt. See, e.g., E. M. Curley, *Descartes Against the Skeptics* (Cambridge, Mass.: Harvard University Press, 1978), pp. 21–45.

15. Descartes's seemingly substantial, if mostly implicit, "emulation" of a Socratic model of inquiry, at least for the self-overcoming of ignorance (in the first half of the *Discourse*, in his introductory letter to the French translation as well as pt. 1 of the *Principles*), is argued for at length by Laurence Lampert in *Nietzsche and Modern Times: A Study of Bacon, Descartes, and Nietzsche* (New Haven, Conn.: Yale University Press, 1993), pp. 171–80. Lampert, however, is inspired by Nietzsche and is critically tracing the rise and development of modernism; hence he stresses all the evidence in Descartes's writings that show him "turning away" from Socrates. In the end, Lampert asserts, "flaunting wisdom rather than ignorance, [Descartes] broke with Socrates in order to begin his public life with a successful apology rather than a futile one" (p. 180).

16. The latter term comes from Peter J. Markie, *Descartes' Gambit* (Ithaca, N.Y.: Cornell University Press, 1986), in which Markie complains that "Descartes never makes a clear, detailed attempt to implement his strategy . . . say[ing] just enough to leave us holding a bag of interpretive and evaluative questions" (p. 23). It will surprise no one to learn that Markie comes at the text with a whole array of "premises, conclusions, definitions, and epistemic principles"—all laid out for handy reference in twentieth-century propositional style in an appendix— for the purpose of reconstructing the "complex argument for mind-body dualism" that constitutes the "position" Descartes wrote the *Meditations* to "defend" (pp. 30–31).

17. On the basis of my discoveries in the Second Meditation, he says, "I will cast around more carefully to see whether there may be other things within me which I have not yet noticed. I am certain that I am a thinking thing. Do I not therefore also know what is required for my being certain about anything? . . . So I *now* seem to be able to lay it down as a *general rule* that whatever I perceive very clearly and distinctly is true" (*Meditations*, AT 7.35 [emphasis added]).

18. *Rules*, AT 10.405–6; see also Descartes, *Meditations: Second Replies*, in *The Philosophical Works of Descartes*, ed. John Cottingham et al. (Cambridge: Cambridge University Press, 1984–91), AT 7.155–56. The best summary of this point is still L. J. Beck, *The Method of Descartes: A Study of the "Regulae"* (Oxford: Clarendon

Press, 1952), pp. 102–10; see also Curley, *Descartes Against the Skeptics*, pp. 26–32. The proximate enemy here is, of course, the medieval "dialecticians," but such criticism of syllogistic reasoning goes back to Sextus Empiricus.

19. Descartes, *Rules*, AT 10.406. Descartes, in fact, makes a number of different objections to syllogistic reasoning. John A. Passmore identifies four of these objections but then discusses primarily the one I mention here, in "Descartes, the British Empiricists, and Formal Logic," *Philosophical Review* 62 (1953): 546–50.

20. I ignore here the important and much debated questions of whether Descartes's thought implies intellectual elitism and for whom he can rightly speak. My point is simply that as first-person-like as his account clearly is, it is simultaneously and just as clearly intersubjective in its intent. Hence, I agree with Jonathan Rée that, in contrast to the *Discourse*, Descartes's "voice" in the *Meditations* is first-person more in the sense of a diarist than an autobiographer, for "if autobiographies such as the *Discourse* temptingly invite readers to take part in the story by making their own appraisals of the narrator's retrospective self-appraisals, diaries are a positive and almost irresistible provocation to do so" (Jonathan Rée, *Philosophical Tales* [London: Methuen, 1987], p. 23). Insofar, then, as Descartes has picked a form of writing that is virtually an "incitement to philosophical thought in its readers," he could not have made a more appropriate selection.

21. Descartes, *Second Replies*, AT 7.157. The strategy of "bracing oneself to attack the truth makes one less suited to perceive it" (ibid.). As Aristotle notes, lovers of wisdom and clever sophists, judged strictly from the outside in terms of the "pure form" of their reasoning, look just the same (*Metaphysics* 1004b, 22b).

22. *PPI*, pp. 30–31. Williams ends up rejecting "the project of pure and solitary inquiry," the "transparently rational mind," and the criterion of certainty, but he retains "Descartes' aspiration for an absolute conception [of reality] which abstracts from local and distorted representations of the world," and he argues that this is precisely what natural science gives us (302–3). For embracing this conclusion, Hilary Putnam singles Williams out as a good example of why analytic philosophy needs a radical revitalization that would finally overcome its inherited tendencies to be "either scientistic or irresponsibly metaphysical" (Hilary Putnam, *Renewing Philosophy* [Cambridge, Mass: Harvard University Press, 1992], pp. xi, 80–107).

23. *Descartes*, pp. 4–5 (emphasis added). This should be read together with her later identification of Descartes as one of those philosophers who in general "evince little or no concern with defining their positions in relation to the long history of philosophical thought" (Margaret Wilson, "History of Philosophy in Philosophy Today; and the Case of Sensible Qualities," *Philosophical Review* 101/1 [1992]: 191–243, quotation on p. 208). That Descartes does not "define" his "position" in such terms is not the same issue as whether "positions" ever leave their origins so "resolutely" behind that they can entirely *be* what a good "definition" makes of them.

24. Georges Dicker, *Descartes: An Analytical and Historical Introduction* (Oxford: Oxford University Press, 1993), pp. 13–14. Dicker goes on to explain that

Descartes's taking such an attitude toward propositions ensures that what he says is not just "idiosyncratic," but that he "means to speak for all of us" (p. 16).

25. Descartes, *Meditations*, AT 7.18. This, of course, turns out to be incorrect, according to the findings of the latter part of the First Meditation. But all this shows is that coming to clarity about how we think scientifically is a transformational process in which earlier "obvious" points, upon further consideration, need later modification. At work in this process is a kind of temporality that runs contrary to the official Cartesian doctrine of episodic time, that causes Descartes to balk, in the Second Meditation, at extending his recently confirmed "thinking self" from "one moment to the next."

26. Descartes, *Meditations*, AT 7.9.

27. The success of this sort of objection can already be seen historically in the move toward increasingly formalized interpretations of reasoning generally and of Descartes's meditation in particular—e.g., in the fact that earlier moderns still tend to follow Descartes in making epistemic inquiry focus on an idealized knower, with its faculties, powers, and connections with the outer world, whereas later inquiries increasingly tend instead to consider the ideal (logical and linguistic) conditions for knowledge. This shift of focus is already clearly defended in Mill's profoundly influential *System of Logic* (see John Stuart Mill, *System of Logic*, vol. 7 of *Collected Works of John Stuart Mill*, ed. R. F. McRae [Toronto: University of Toronto Press, 1973], e.g., p. 87, and McRae's introduction, pp. xxxix–xliv]).

28. Descartes, *Meditations*, AT 6.6.

29. One must be mindful of this historical shift in the primary meaning of "Cartesianism," or one may be tempted to settle too easily upon the idea that Descartes has been finally surmounted because one no longer adheres to his positive teachings. For reactions before the mid-eighteenth century, see, e.g., Nicholas Jolley, "The Reception of Descartes's Philosophy," in *The Cambridge Companion to Descartes,* ed. John Cottingham (Cambridge: Cambridge University Press, 1992), pp. 393–423. Jolley notes a "dramatic" and positive change in Descartes's fortunes at this time, but he suggests primarily increases in the appeal of his doctrines among nonscholastic theologians and antimaterialist philosophers as the main reason (p. 419). A more plausible explanation, I think, is offered by Peter A. Schouls, who argues (starting from a well-known passage from Condillac's *Essay*) that with the rise of the Enlightenment, what seemed most important in Descartes was not his "vain and ambitious" doctrines but his promotion of a philosophical method that, while "eager to know whatever is within reach," nevertheless "proportions [its] researches to the weakness of the human understanding" (Peter A. Schouls, *Descartes and the Enlightenment* [Edinburgh: Edinburgh University Press, 1989], p. 9).

30. R. Rorty, "The Historiography of Philosophy: Four Genres," in *Philosophy in History*, p. 67 (reprinted in R. Rorty, *Truth and Progress, Philosophical Papers*, vol. 3 [Cambridge: Cambridge University Press, 1998], p. 266).

31. Wilson, "History of Philosophy," pp. 208–9.

32. For an argument that Descartes's appeal to the "collaboration" of the will and the understanding in explaining correct judgments is integral to the formal

project of the *Meditations* and not a mere holdover from medieval psychology, see David M. Rosenthal, "Will and the Theory of Judgment," *EDM,* pp. 411–16.

33. See Descartes, *Meditations,* AT 7.22, 47, 52; *Discourse,* AT 6.64; and *Meditations,* AT 7.81–82, respectively.

34. Descartes, *Meditations,* AT 6.28. Hence, John P. Carriero may well be right in arguing that the *Meditations* were not directed against what twentieth-century epistemologists call skepticism but were concerned instead to "win the meditator over to nativism from scholastic abstractionism" (John P. Carriero, "The First Meditation," in *Descartes' Meditations: Critical Essays,* ed. Vere Chappell [Lanham, Md.: Rowman and Littlefield, 1997], p. 24). This, however, contextualizes the *Meditations* only in terms of its own project, not in terms of what this project explicitly leaves behind as inappropriate for the application of its rules.

35. Calvin O. Schrag, "Phenomenology, Ontology, and History in the Philosophy of Heidegger" (1958), in *Philosophical Papers,* pp. 33–47.

36. Maurice Merleau-Ponty locates the starting point of this sort of phenomenological interpretation in the task of "endow[ing] finitude with a positive significance and tak[ing] seriously the strange phrase in the Fourth Meditation that makes me 'a middle term [*medium quid*]' between God and nothingness." Merleau-Ponty argues that this task would involve at least two fundamental points which Descartes could not take seriously. One is that a meditator would have to come to "accept as a guarantee of itself human thought in its factual reality"—a move that would require a different understanding of lived temporality from the traditional, episodic conception of time that informs the *Meditations* and structures its descriptions of the thinking process. The other, which is, so to speak, a negative image of the first point, is that a meditator would have to come to realize that "the connection between essence and existence is not found in experience, but in the idea of the infinite"—which means that "in the last resort . . . analytical reflection rests entirely on a dogmatic idea of being, and . . . in this sense it is not a consummate act of self-discovery" (*Phenomenology of Perception,* trans. Colin Smith [New York: Humanities Press; London: Routledge, 1962], p. 44).

3

"Catch Me If You Can": Foucault on the Repressive Hypothesis

Sandra Bartky

The Repressive Hypothesis

Foucault's assault in *History of Sexuality, Volume 1* on what he calls the "repressive hypothesis" is widely regarded as a major theoretical advance in our understanding of sexuality and as one of the chief ornaments of Foucault's thought. I want to challenge this judgment; I shall argue that some of Foucault's reasons for urging us to jettison the repressive hypothesis fail to persuade. I want to argue too against Foucault's "dumbing down," that is, his rather egregious misrepresentation of the views of those influential twentieth-century theorists who put forward some version of the repressive hypothesis, namely, Freud, Reich, and Marcuse.

First of all, what exactly does Foucault take the repressive hypothesis to be? Foucault argues as follows:

> For a long time, the story goes, we supported a Victorian regime and we continue to be dominated by it even today. . . . At the beginning of the seventeenth century a certain frankness was still common, it would seem. Sexual practices had little need of secrecy, words were said without undue reticence and things were done without too much concealment. . . . But twilight soon fell upon this bright day, followed by the monotonous nights of the Victorian bourgeoisie. Sexuality was carefully confined; it moved into the home. The conjugal family took custody of it and absorbed it into the serious function of reproduction. On the subject of sex, silence became the rule. . . . These are the characteristic features attributed to

repression which serve to distinguish it from the penal law: Repression operated as a sentence to disappear, but also as an injunction to silence, an affirmation of nonexistence and, by implication, an admission that there was nothing to say about such things, nothing to see and nothing to know.[1]

Having said this, Foucault at once qualifies it: The Victorians knew that "infernal mischief" could not be made to disappear entirely; hence the mental hospital and the brothel, the prostitute and the pimp, the neurologist and his hysteric. According to the repressive hypothesis, the general regime of repression is adjusted to coincide with "the development of capitalism; it becomes an integral part of the bourgeois order."[2]

The repressive hypothesis has also a powerful utopian moment: the idea of liberation from repression. The project of liberation calls for an overthrow of the sexual status quo in which a new set of discourses and practices will link "sex, the revelation of truth, the overturning of global laws, the proclamation of a new day to come and the promise of a certain felicity."[3]

Foucault poses three questions ("serious doubts") to the repressive hypothesis: (1) "Is sexual repression truly an established historical fact?" In the course of answering this first question, it will become apparent that there are two questions at stake here. First, is there really such a thing as sexual repression, at least as (according to Foucault) it has been traditionally understood? Second, is the chronology associated with defenders of the repressive hypothesis correct? As we shall see, Foucault will answer both questions in the negative. (2) Are the workings of power, in a society such as ours, generally repressive, repression being characterized as "prohibition, censorship and denial," elsewhere as "refusal, blockage and invalidation"? This question is ambiguous. Given the multifarious forms that power can take, it might be the case that power operates differently in the sexual domain than it does in other orders of experience. So a more precise formulation of the question would be this: Does the regulation of sexuality per se take the form of "prohibition, censorship and denial"? Foucault answers this question in the negative as well. (3) Does the critical discourse that is addressed to repression by the repressive hypothesis represent a genuine challenge to it, or "is it not in fact part of the same historical network as the thing it denounces (and doubtless misrepresents)"? The very wording of this question suggests the way in which Foucault will answer it.[4] (For further discussion of this point later in the chapter, see the section entitled I Know a Secret).

Aware that the position he is developing runs counter to received opinion, Foucault tries to set the perplexed reader straight: "I do not claim that sex has not been prohibited or barred or masked or misapprehended since the classical age, nor do I even assert that it has suffered these things any less from that period on than before." The points that Foucault would like to score against the repressive hypothesis "are aimed less at showing it to be mistaken than at putting it back within a general economy of discourses on sex in modern societies."[5] So Foucault's predecessors were on to something, but they got it wrong. But did they, in fact, get it wrong?

"Catch Me If You Can"

If censorship and silence are part and parcel of repression, says Foucault, then how to explain the "veritable discursive explosion" around issues of sexuality of the past three centuries? Foucault concedes that "a whole restrictive economy" was introduced into the "politics of language" throughout society at large. But this seems far less important to him than the claim that "the multiplication of discourses" both issued from and was taken up by the "agencies of power."[6]

The Reformation encouraged everyone to be on the lookout perpetually for impurities in thought, word, or deed. Many Protestants (as we know from their diaries) were tormented by sexual thoughts and sinful desires they could not seem to expunge from consciousness. When Calvinists acceded to state power in places like Geneva, or Puritans in the Massachusetts Bay Colony, they established highly sexually repressive theocracies. But these are not histories that Foucault mentions, much less relates. Staying closer to home, that is, France, he tells us that the Counter-Reformation attributed ever more importance to "insinuations of the flesh."[7] Foucault cites a pastoral letter of the period:

> Examine diligently, therefore, all the faculties of your soul: memory, understanding, and will. Examine with precision all your senses as well. . . . Examine moreover all your thoughts, every word you speak, and all your actions. Examine even unto your dreams, to know if, once awakened, you did not give them your consent.[8]

Now we learned in *Discipline and Punish* that surveillance, especially unrelenting surveillance and of course self-surveillance, is profoundly disempowering. It is part of the production of "docile bodies"; it is, in a word, "repressive."[9] The Puritan theocracies, as well as the clergy of both the Reformation and Counter-Reformation, tried to put entire populations under a stricter surveillance than they had known before. We would expect too the same strongly implied condemnation of sexual repression here as Foucault offers of the disciplines in *Discipline and Punish.* Has Foucault changed his mind about the inextricability of surveillance and domination?

An "explosion of discourse" (albeit in language Foucault grants is extremely circumspect) occurs in such fields as biology, pedagogy, medicine, later criminology, sociology, anthropology, psychology, psychiatry— the "human sciences." Insofar as censorship and silence are crucial to repression, an explosion of discourses having to do with sex, it seems to Foucault, is surely at odds with the repressive hypothesis. But how can we ignore the fact that there was a discursive explosion—due to the rapid dissemination of print media in virtually every field? Foucault offers no evidence whatsoever to support the claim that in proportion to the total volume of publication, sexual matters get more attention than they had gotten—again, in proportion to total volume—in the Middle Ages. One can argue, of course, that late in this period, psychology and especially psychoanalysis, in which there does appear to be an "explosion" of discourse, are very much discourses about sexuality. But psychoanalysis, especially in its initial phases, is a renegade discourse, what Foucault sometimes calls "a subjugated knowledge," whose aim, in part, is to discredit other, more established discourses.

Seen in historical context, are the sexual discourses that appeared in the eighteenth and nineteenth centuries in any way unique? There was a passion during this period for the close observation and classification of all sorts of natural phenomena. Foucault recognizes that modern states come increasingly to require information as to the constitution, health, and augmentation of their populations; the authorities require knowledge in order to exercise "bio-power." But once again, are we dealing here with a unique phenomenon? During this period, instrumental rationality was brought to bear on every aspect of endeavor, from the improvement of productive techniques, to the control of populations and the radical reform of institutions. Foucault does not provide us with statistics or even a bibliography in support of his claim that there was a unique and disproportionate "explosion of discourse" concerning sexuality or a project of bio-control that differs in any important way from the "disciplinary practices" so meticulously described in *Discipline and Punish.*

It should be noted too that the texts of pedagogy, medicine, and so forth circulated within an extremely small circle of specialists—mainly white, privileged, European or Euro-American men. This information was not conveyed to the general public, many of whom, in the earlier phases of the modern period, were illiterate. When, in college, I tried to

56

SANDRA BARTKY

inform myself about sexual "perversions," I discovered that the sexually explicit passages in Krafft-Ebbing were all in Latin. My high-school trek through Caesar's Gallic Wars was insufficient. "Sex was driven out of hiding and made to lead a discursive existence."[10] One is tempted to add "a discursive existence, for those who knew medical Latin." I take it that most of the discourses to which Foucault appeals have scientific pretensions as well as the overt or covert aim of controlling sexuality. The application of science (or pseudoscience) to the project of controlling sexual behavior sounds more like ammunition for the repressive hypothesis than evidence against it.

Even if we grant, for the sake of argument, that there was, in the eighteenth and nineteenth centuries and down to our own time, an inordinate amount of talk and text dealing with sexuality, this fact, if fact it is, is not incompatible with the claim that sexual repression was, on balance, the order of the day. First, not everyone was authorized to speak or write about sex. Texts produced by scientists for other scientists were allowed; after all, they typically justified, directly or indirectly, the regulation of sexuality. Novelists had no such freedom. As late as 1890, the British censor banned Tolstoy's *Resurrection* from the mails as it portrayed a prostitute sympathetically. Journalists and feminists had to struggle for the right openly to discuss important social issues such as prostitution. William T. Stead, British journalist and author of *The Maiden Tribute of Babylon*, a high-minded exposé of "white slavery," containing neither sexually explicit language nor explicit description of sex acts, was nevertheless prosecuted by the Crown. Similar charges but a worse fate—terms of imprisonment—awaited those, like Margaret Sanger, who distributed birth control information. Second, it may be the case that sexual repression scars the soul so badly that when one finally wins the right to free expression, there springs the hope that speech or writing can be healing. It mostly cannot; hence the need for more speech and more writing. The obsessional preoccupation with sexuality that Foucault believes to be characteristic of modernity in the West may well be the discursive equivalent of the tongue's irresistible attraction to an aching tooth, or to the equally irresistible need to scratch at one's scabs. What he calls the "garrulousness" concerning sexuality in modern times is not incompatible with sexual repression.

But what was happening in the larger society while Foucault's "authorities" on sexuality were busily producing and consuming texts? What, in particular, was going on with children? Any evaluation of Foucault's critique of the repressive hypothesis must take into account the sexual socialization of children, for the patterns laid down in childhood are implicated in the formation of character, hence they are notoriously difficult to alter in adulthood. The lack of censorship that allowed a few "experts" (normally in the name of science) to publish on sexual matters is quite different than the society-wide sexual censorship that was imposed on children and, in the milieu in which I was raised, most adults.

As childhood sexual socialization varies greatly historically and also by race, class, ethnicity, and nationality, no comprehensive account has yet appeared or is likely to appear.[11] I therefore offer some typical features of my own childhood sexual socialization, this for three reasons: first, much of what I relate will be familiar to Foucault's readers, especially his older readers; second, while I was raised in Chicago in the 1940s and 1950s, I might just as well have been brought up in Freud's Vienna of the 1890s; finally, my sexual upbringing was what, before Foucault, virtually anyone would have called "repressive." Of course, much has now changed. How much has changed, where and for whom, is a matter for contestation. The larger question is this: What was happening to ordinary children in the familiar sites of social life during Foucault's "discursive explosion"?

Sex, for middle-class girls of my generation, was not driven out of hiding; whenever it threatened to appear, it was driven massively *into* hiding. We were forbidden to explore our bodies, indeed, we were not taught the proper names of our private parts; we were forbidden to engage in sex-play with other children, to masturbate, or to utter words relating to sexual matters. These things were not only forbidden, they were punished. Sex was never mentioned in my home, nor was there sex education in our schools. Sex was—not just a secret, but The Secret.

My first menstruation occurred when I was quite young; as I had no idea what was happening to me, I was terrified, believing that I was bleeding to death. The day this happened, my mother told me only that now I must not let a man touch me for I could get pregnant. I was quietly skeptical of this, knowing how often men brushed against women on the bus, especially during rush hour. I knew that all those women did not go home and get pregnant, though I had no idea then, or for years afterward, how women did get pregnant. My father mumbled something to me that evening in acknowledgment of the event, but we were both too embarrassed to discuss it then, and it was never mentioned again. While I knew next to nothing about human sexuality, I knew enough to be ashamed: I was covered in shame at the prospect that my father or brother might see traces of this monthly ordeal; I wrapped and removed used sanitary napkins surreptitiously from the bathroom so that they could be buried in the anonymity of the kitchen garbage. Four lonely years passed before I heard two schoolmates whispering about "it." I felt inexpressible relief in finding friends who got "the curse" every month, too. Keeping secrets can be a lonely business. As menstruation is a female affair, my very femaleness was implicated in my shame and in my need for secrecy.

The association of sex with what was dirty or filthy was then and is now a cultural given. There were "dirty jokes," "filthy pictures," and "dirty old men." The British, I learned later, speak of "dirty (i.e., adulterous) weekends." One would expect that a historian of sexuality would clarify— or at least notice—this association; why the absence of any discussion in Foucault's genealogy of modern sexuality of the pervasive identification of sex with dirt and filth?

Now a Foucaultian would be entirely unimpressed by my sad little childhood tale. Have I not become still another "confessing animal," typical of one who complains of sexual repression (censorship, denial, etc.) and then offers an intimate and uncensored narration? ("Western Man has become a confessing animal").[12] My reply to this is to set my story of the workings of sexual prohibition against a story of Foucault's. The passage is worth quoting at length:

> The medical examination, the psychiatric investigation, the pedagogical report, and family controls may have the over-all and apparent objective of saying no to all wayward or unproductive sexualities, but the fact is that they function as mechanisms with a double impetus: pleasure and power. The pleasure that comes of exercising a power that questions, monitors, watches, spies, searches out, palpates, brings to light, and on the other hand, the pleasure that kindles at having to evade this power, flee from it, fool it, or travesty it. The power that lets itself be invaded by the pleasure it is pursuing and opposite it, power asserting itself in the pleasure of showing off, scandalizing, or resisting. Capture and seduction, confrontation and mutual reinforcement . . . all have played this game continually since the nineteenth century. These attractions, these evasions, these circular incitements have traced around bodies and sexes, not boundaries not to be crossed, but *perpetual spirals of power and pleasure*. . . . The power which thus took charge of sexuality set about contacting bodies, caressing them with its eyes, intensifying areas, electrifying surfaces, dramatizing troubled moments. It wrapped the sexual body in its embrace. There was undoubtedly an increase in effectiveness and an extension of the domain controlled; but also a sensualization of power and a gain of pleasure.[13]

Foucault has now answered two of his original questions. The kind of power that is brought into play against bodies is not primarily repressive: It "intensifies areas, electrifies surfaces . . . wraps the sexual body in its embrace." Foucault is here claiming that increased surveillance in the modern period had the effect of heightening pleasure, though he does not clarify the mechanisms at work. However, he makes clear in the same passage that the analysis holds good for all sexual regulation, not just for the rooting out of sexual irregularities. The game of "capture and seduction" is played by "parents and children, adults and adolescents, educator and students, doctor and patients."[14] The point that Foucault will drive home over and over again is the productivity of the power that prohibits. In addition to erotic incitement, this power produces new knowledges and new social types.

If prohibition is regularly eroticized, as Foucault claims in this passage, then repression flies out the window. Repression is supposed to shut down sexuality, cancel it, annul it; a prohibition that incites, that excites both the one who surveys and the one who is put under surveillance is no kind of repression at all. " 'Sexuality' is far more a product of power than power was ever repression of sexuality."[15] I myself find it difficult to accept the claim that domination (and the power of which Foucault speaks is a project of domination) is, for most people, regularly eroticized, except for those with sadomasochist sensibilities.[16] At any rate, Foucault's conclusion is clear enough: "We must therefore abandon the hypothesis that modern industrial societies ushered in an age of increased sexual repression," and later in the same text, "It appears unlikely that there was an age of sexual restriction."[17] Foucault underscores this claim elsewhere:

> The notion of repression is quite inadequate for capturing what is precisely the productive aspect of power. In defining the effects of power as repression, one adopts a purely juridical conception of such power, one identifies power with a law which says no, power is taken above all as carrying the force of prohibition. Now I believe that this is a wholly negative, narrow skeletal conception of power, one which has been curiously widespread.[18]

Foucault's story is considerably less depressing than mine. Indeed, he describes a perpetual game of "catch me if you can." The constant preoccupation with watching is eroticized for the regulator, while for the one regulated, there is the "pleasure of showing off, scandalizing, or resisting."[19] For me there was no pleasure in showing off; the sense of taboo that attached to all things sexual both at home and at school hung over me so heavily that the punishments I anticipated from its violation were terrible, even though they were never articulated clearly. No pleasure was kindled in me at having to evade this power. What I have described—bits and pieces only of a much longer and even sadder tale—is not a story of "perpetual spirals of power and pleasure." My surfaces were not electrified, nor, as far as I knew, was my body wrapped by power in a sexual embrace. On the contrary, the point was to hide and keep hidden from authority all things pertaining to sex. There was no "sensualization of power," and certainly no "gain of pleasure"; indeed, I believe that the effect upon me of sexual taboo was, overall, an erotic loss of considerable dimensions.

The *kind* of regime toward which my story points is far more typical (esp. for women) than Foucault's exciting game of catch me if you can. He writes of titillation but not of pain. The profound absence at the heart of *History of Sexuality, Volume 1* is the shame and guilt that is associated with sexuality in the minds of countless individuals whose sexuality was silenced, annulled, circumscribed, even proscribed, tabooed, punished, made shameful and guilt-ridden. Where is the recognition of shame in this text, where the theorization of guilt? There is no acknowledgment that the sexual repression of children is responsible for much sexual suffering in adults. Prohibition and injunctions to hide are not, of course, limited to childhood. There are, for example, large numbers of homosexual adolescents who are even more at risk of suicide than at-risk heterosexual adolescents. There are homosexual adults who are forced to live the lie that they are heterosexual, in constant fear of exposure, hence of shame and the rejection by their families, the possible loss of livelihood and, in some states, criminal prosecution. Theoreticians of the repressive hypothesis had much to say about sexual shame and sexual guilt. I shall argue in the next section that Foucault presents a radically impoverished account of the more influential versions of the repressive hypothesis. This stacks the deck against Foucault's theoretical rivals; also, in my opinion, it obfuscates the entire issue of sexual regulation.

I Know a Secret

Foucault ascribes to theorists of the repressive hypothesis the view that repression is nothing but the "affirmation of (the) non-existence" of sex. This affirmation is buttressed by silence, prohibition, censorship, nullification, denial, or taboo. The repressive hypothesis puts forward only an "emaciated form of prohibition." . . . "It never establishes any connection between power and sex that is not negative: rejection, exclusion, refusal, blockage, concealment or mask."[20] His view, on the contrary, is that the power that came to be exercised over sexuality is productive—

of "perpetual spirals of power and pleasure," of new knowledges (e.g., psychiatry), of new identities (the pervert, the homosexual, the nymphomaniac). The idea that Freud, Reich, and Marcuse believed that the effects of repression were merely negative and unproductive is flatly false. Knowledge and pleasure are, for Foucault, results of sexual prohibition that defenders of the repressive hypothesis are said to ignore. But how can anyone at all familiar with Freud overlook the fact that for him, the phenomenon of sexual repression, in all its complexity, is indeed a source of new knowledge about the human psyche? New pleasures emerge from Freudian discourse as well, for example, anal eroticism.

Moreover, Freud, as every schoolchild knows, believed that sexual repression is productive of (pause here for emphasis) *civilization!* How much more productive can anything get?

It is impossible to overlook the extent to which civilization is built up upon a renunciation of instinct, how much it presupposes precisely the non-satisfaction . . . of powerful instincts. This 'cultural frustration' dominates the large field of social relationships between human beings.[21]

And elsewhere, in the same passage from *Civilization and its Discontents,*

Sublimation of instinct is an especially conspicuous feature of cultural development, it is what makes it possible for higher psychical activities, scientific, artistic or ideological, to play such an important part in civilized life.[22]

Furthermore, for Freud, Reich, and Marcuse, shutting down, nullifying, prohibiting, and so forth, sexual feeling is *impossible* because all believe that sexual energy is a crucial dimension of the human organism: Dammed up in one place, it will find new channels in which to flow; denied satisfaction of its original object of desire, it will substitute (sublimate) another. Now none of this should be interpreted as in any way a defense of Freud's instinct theory, or of his ideas concerning "the vicissitudes of the instincts" or of his claim that civilization is based on sexual repression. My aim here is solely to expose Foucault's gross misreading of Freud.

Moreover, quite apart from the merits or demerits of instinct theory, it seems to me that Freud has a concept of repression that is more complex and intellectually sophisticated than Foucault's truncated version. For Foucault, repression is interpersonal. Other people, acting in accord with prevailing discourses and social practices, exercise upon me a series of "deployments" whereby my sexuality is "constructed" in ways that are specifically modern.

For Freud, on the contrary, repression is both interpersonal and intrapersonal. The prohibitions that originate with external authorities are internalized: Repression becomes something that I do to myself. Tabooed desires as well as an elaborate internalized repressive apparatus—the Censor or Superego—keep these desires at bay even while allowing them some disguised expression. Many of my desires as well as my Censor or Superego are largely unconscious, in spite of the fact that they determine critical aspects of my behavior and personality. Foucault's rejection of psychoanalysis is so total that nowhere in *The History of Sexuality, Volume 1* is there any suspicion that important dimensions of our sexual ideas or sexual desires might be unconscious. This results in impoverished portraits of those whose "deployment" of sexuality socially constructs the sexual self as well as those selves targeted by the same "deployment."

Let us return to Foucault's example of one site in the genesis of "spirals of power and pleasure," the secondary schools of the eighteenth century. Let us imagine a monitor who patrols the halls and peeps through small glass windows in the boys' rooms to see if they are masturbating. It is Foucault's contention that there are two pleasures at work here: the pleasure the boys must take in outwitting the monitors and the pleasure of the monitor himself, "a pleasure that comes of exercising a power that questions, monitors, watches, spies, searches out."[23] Ostensibly, the pleasure of the monitor consists in his contribution to the extirpation of a prohibited sexual act; it is, by his own lights, the kind of pleasure that one takes in performing moral actions. But neither we nor Foucault are so naive as to believe that this is the whole story. The monitor is excited by his proximity to acts that are, in his own eyes, sinful; he is able to indulge a forbidden, but fascinated, voyeurism that secretly, indeed unconsciously, is excited by the very thing that it condemns. He is titillated by prohibited behavior in the very act of prohibiting it. He may very well have sought out such a position in order to persist in his own bad faith; he lacks what most philosophers think is essential to the moral life, that is, even a rudimentary understanding of his own motives. Indeed, if his unconscious enjoyment of "sin" were somehow to burst into consciousness, the monitor's psychic economy might be shattered. His is a pleasure that dare not know its name.

Foucault speaks simply of "pleasure" in his discussion of "spirals of pleasure and power." But there are all kinds of pleasures. There are pleasures so threatening to the individual that they can be enjoyed only in the act of rooting them out of others. There are guilty pleasures, pleasures that remain in the darkness of the unconscious because they are power-fully suffused with feelings of guilt, shame, and fear. The masturbating schoolboy must endure, we may assume, a large portion of guilt, shame, and sense of sin as price of his pleasure. Once again, one is struck by the absence in Foucault of any recognition of how troubled sexual pleasure can be precisely because of its attempted repression.

Wilhelm Reich, like Freud, believes in the productivity of sexual repression. Reich, Freud, and Marcuse believe that the working of re-pression in modern societies creates certain character types, a view that Foucault himself endorses. According to Reich, the character structures that have come into being in our sexually repressive regime help to repro-duce the class structure of capitalism, hence the exploitation of human labor that produces wealth in class societies. Reich, in his earlier years, believed that sexual repression, in particular the prohibition of sexual play and exploration among children and the denial of the compelling sexual needs of adolescents, are ways to break the spirit:

> Capital defends the maintenance of sexual repression with all at its disposal. . . . 1. It is a powerful prop of the church, which, with the assistance of sexual anxiety and guilt feelings, is deeply anchored in the exploited masses. 2. It is a prop of the institutions of family and marriage which require a stunting of sexuality for their existence. 3. It requires children to obey their parents, and prepares for the later obedience of the adults to the authority of the state and capital by producing fear of authority in all individuals in society. 4. It lames the critical intellectual powers of the oppressed masses. Sexual repression consumes a great deal of psychic energy that otherwise would be utilized in intellectual activity. 5. It damages the psychic ability of an immense number of people. It creates inhibition and cripples the power to rebel in materially oppressed individuals.[24]

Now there is a great deal here that no one today would want to defend. But it seems absurd to say that for Reich, sexual repression is nothing but a denial, a shutting down, a censoring, a taboo. While Reich may well be mistaken, it is a fact that he believed repression to be an important factor in the maintenance of an entire system of social relations, a powerful and resilient economic structure with powerful institutions that still dominate most people's lives.

Foucault takes Reich to task for errors in Reich's periodization of his account of repression. One would expect, on Reich's analysis, that first and foremost, in the early modern period, "the young adult man, possessing nothing more than his life force, had to be the primary target

SANDRA   BARTKY

of a subjugation destined to shift the energy available for useless pleasure toward compulsory labor." But this is not what happened. Indeed, it took several centuries to bring the working classes into line. (Foucault's admission that whatever the chronology, sexuality was eventually "deployed" against the workers, appears to be a significant concession to Reich.) "The most rigorous techniques were formed and, more particularly, applied first, with the greatest intensity, in the economically privileged and politically dominant classes." The sexual economy of the rising bourgeoisie was concerned with its own "vigor, longevity, progeniture, and descent."[25] The significance of the body of the bourgeoisie differed markedly from that of the landed aristocracy. The latter justified its rule in part on the basis of "blood," that is, on the purity of its lineage. The former, as befits a militant rising class, was anxious to keep its youth from squandering its energies and vital bodily fluids in debaucheries that come increasingly, in the public mind, to expose the decadence of the aristocracy, hence its unfitness to rule. The close monitoring of its sexual substance, a saving that requires self-mastery and self-control, worked, at least in its own eyes, as a moral justification of the bourgeoisie's accession to power. Finally, however, Foucault and Reich are not so far apart after all. Foucault did not believe that capitalism produces the discourses and practices it needs; rather, local practices and policies arise for a variety of reasons. The ones that serve the needs of the bourgeoisie survive; the rest do not. The eventual success of the sexual repression of the working class, though it differs from place to place in character and quality, is sufficiently widespread to conclude that it must indeed serve the interests of the bourgeoisie. Foucault takes a view that can as easily be regarded as a contribution to Reich's analysis as a critique of it, namely, that sexual repression can play itself out differently in different classes:

> If it is true that sexuality is the set of effects produced in bodies, behaviors and social relations by a certain deployment deriving from a complex political technology, one has to admit that this deployment does not operate in symmetrical fashion with respect to the social classes, and consequently, that it does not produce the same effects in them.[26]

It should be noted that what I continue to call "sexual repression," not convinced that this term can or should be abandoned, Foucault begins to call "sexuality" or "the deployment of sexuality" in the last half of *History of Sexuality, Volume 1.* I diagnose Foucault's eccentric language use as follows. Having diagnosed (or narrowed and misdiagnosed, as I have been arguing) the concept of "repression" as erroneous and misleading, Foucault is forced to invent a terminology that will do, more or less, the same work. The choice of the term "deployment," with its military echoes, suggests that more is going on there than mere sexual regulation.

Finally, Marcuse.[27] Like Freud, Marcuse accepts an instinct theory. Like Foucault, Marcuse believes that individuals resist the imposition of sexually repressive regulation. (Foucault believes that individuals tend to resist the imposition of disciplines tout court.) Whatever the status of the instinct theory, Marcuse can at least offer an explanation for this resistance—its instinctual basis; Foucault cannot. Both thinkers are hostile to normalization in the sphere of sexuality. Marcuse rejects Freud's (and Reich's) claim that only heterosexual genitality is psychosexually normal: He is drawn to another model of sexuality, "polymorphous perversity," that is, the reeroticization of those parts of the body whose sexual sensitivities, according to the Freudians, have to be repressed to allow the "normal" adult to focus on genitality. This is echoed by Foucault's plaintive call for a return to "bodies and pleasures":

> It is the agency of sex that we must break away from, if we aim—through a tactical reversal of the various mechanisms of sexuality—to counter the grips of power with the claims of bodies, pleasures and knowledges, in their multiplicity and their possibility of resistance. The rallying point for the counterattack against the deployment of sexuality ought not to be sex-desire but bodies and pleasures.[28]

LaDelle McWhorter interprets this rather obscure passage in the following way: "Sex-desire" refers to sexual identity, a concept that carries too heavy a weight of normalization, that is, too many norms that are thought to cling necessarily to particular identities. In the antihumanist tradition of postmodernism, Foucault imagines a state of affairs whereby individuals, no longer modern subjects constructed along disciplinary lines, are free to explore the multiplicity of bodies and pleasures. "Sex is the linchpin of sexuality; desire is sex-desire. The desiring subject, thoroughly normalized, is the sexual subject. Affirmation of desire, even in the plural, will do nothing to undermine the *dispositif de sexualité*."[29] While Marcuse believes in the existence of a core sexual self, this self may be deeply buried, never, for want of opportunity, to see the light of day. The core self may be nothing but a potentiality; what shows itself is socially constructed according to what Marcuse calls "the established order of domination." The parallels between Foucault's utopia of "bodies and pleasures" and Marcuse's "polymorphous perversity" are evident, as is the idea that the subjectivities we are have been constructed in conformity to an exploitative regime.

Reich's conception of sexual repression has been historically super-seded by a far more permissive sexual regime that now allows (in some of its incarnations) sexual behavior that was disallowed in Reich's day—premarital intercourse, abortion, homosexuality, pornography, and so forth. Foucault recognizes this phenomenon and the ways it too can be "repressive," but he does not pursue this issue theoretically.

The lifting of taboos has not ushered in a period of sexual satisfac-tion. The commodification that is so prominent a feature of capitalism invades consciousness, especially the consciousness of embodiment, and both men and women try to package themselves for success in the "meat market." Billions of dollars are spent each year for toning and exercising the body, on diets, makeup, clothes, plastic surgery, and so forth. Since women are still the primary targets of sexual objectification, it is women who are the major consumers of products and services that will pre-sumably make them deserving of male attention. This regime, as I have argued elsewhere, creates in contemporary women low self-esteem and a very specific set of anxieties about embodiment (that can turn pathologi-cal, as in bulimia or anorexia nervosa).[30] Now insofar as older taboos have been lifted, there has occurred a "de-sublimation," but this desublima-tion is still repressive, only in new ways. So contemporary sexuality is im-portantly, for Marcuse, as it is for feminists, a "repressive de-sublimation." Foucault is widely admired for having brought to sexual theory the idea that sexuality, as well as subjectivity, is "socially constructed." But, as I have suggested, this idea was developed earlier, both by Marcuse and by feminist theorists; indeed, one can trace the rather detailed development of this notion, at least in reference to subjectivity, to Simone de Beauvoir. And John Stuart Mill had argued in *On the Subjection of Women* that it would be impossible to know what woman's true nature in fact is, until the current "social construction" of the female character is abolished. Until recently, however, feminists stopped short of the Foucaultian claim that the deep or core self, our roles and representations, as well as our biologies, are socially and historically constructed.[31]

While Reich believed that sexual repression was necessary only for the perpetuation of capitalism, Marcuse takes the more conservative view that there is a certain "necessary" repression required by an organized and productive social life; he believed that the requirements of capital-ism (and, as he later admitted, patriarchy) require "surplus repression." Hence, repression is not just nugatory; like Reich, Marcuse believed that it produced and reproduced the central features of contemporary social life in the "developed" societies. Since Marcuse believed in the possibility of an overthrow of macrosystems of domination (with varying conviction at different stages in his career), he is often optimistic about the possibility of a life free of "surplus repression," that is, a much freer and happier sexuality. There is thus a utopian moment in Marcuse that is developed theoretically out of his analysis of repression and its relationship to advanced capitalism. This utopian moment is ridiculed by Foucault, even though he has his own utopian moment ("bodies and pleasures")—a moment that gets nothing more than a mere mention and whose normative status (given Foucault's resistance in this text to a ranking of discourses) is unclear.

While, as I have shown, Foucault is quite clear about the relationship between the bourgeois order and "the deployment of sexuality," this does not suggest to him (as it did to Marcuse) a strategy of liberation. While Foucault appears to have abandoned his agnosticism in regard to values in his discussions of Greco-Roman sexuality in volumes 2 and 3 of *The History of Sexuality,* in volume 1 he has been widely taken to be a relativist, seeing in history only a march of discourses and practices ("regimes of power/knowledge"), none of which will produce either an overarching truth or a liberated sexuality. Calvin Schrag's analysis of the consequences of Foucault's moral and epistemological relativism in the texts on which his reputation is based seems particularly apt here:

> Numerous challenges addressed to more traditional views of reason surface in Foucault's politics of power. If the logos is itself an effect of power, then any appeal to theory for a comprehension and management of the constraints of power would become useless. If the rational subject is a product rather than an agent of power, then the grammar of autonomy and emancipation is deprived of any significant function. If everything, from our specialized disciplines of knowledge to our pre-reflective everyday practices, is imbued with power, there is neither resource nor standpoint to combat the specter of ideology that always hovers over the power relations in a given society.[32]

An instance of the relationship between power and truth, for Foucault, is the confession. The West for many centuries has believed that truth could be obtained through confession. This ancient belief, religious in origin, has been taken over by the manifold schools of psychology, as well as by contemporary movements of sexual liberation:

> The obligation to confess is now relayed through so many different points, is so deeply ingrained in us, that we no longer perceive it as the effect of a power that constrains us; on the contrary, it seems to us that truth, lodged in our most secret nature, "demands" only to surface; that if it fails to do

so, this is because a constraint holds it in place, the violence of a power weighs it down.

Sex, "lodged in our most secret nature," constitutes the core, the veritable essence of the self, and if this core can be articulated, truth will be revealed. For Foucault, however, the idea that there is a sexual core that constitutes the essence of our being is not only a myth, it is part of the technology of subjugation developed within the deployment of sexuality. Foucault has now answered his third original question: Does the critical discourse that is addressed to repression represent a genuine challenge to it, or "is it not in fact part of the same historical network as the thing it denounces?"[33]

Here, as in other postmodern texts, liberation discourse stands accused of essentialism. It is said to be equally bad to have a sexual essence ascribed to oneself (a core self) by others as to ascribe an essence to oneself. Ascriptions of this sort are always embedded in relations of power; "normalization" is here a principal weapon in the deployment of sexuality. Hence to be labeled a "queer," a "pervert," or a "slut" is to be exiled beyond the borders of normalcy; it is to be eternally defective in one's essence. Liberation movements remain, Foucault thinks, within the knowledge/power regimes that they are trying to combat. Of Reich's vision, for example, he says "it always unfolded within the deployment of sexuality and not outside of it or against it."[34] Foucault is quite right about this. Reich agitated for a sexual revolution but regarded homosexuality as infantile and regressive.

But what of the modern Gay Rights movement itself? How vulnerable is it to Foucault's criticism? Movements for gay liberation accept the distinction between heterosexuality and homosexuality; they try only to valorize the persecuted partner in this duality. Hence, they have not gotten beyond a fundamentally oppressive way of carving up human sexuality; they have not broken through the "deployment of sexuality" to the freedom of "bodies and pleasures."[35] Furthermore, in its struggle to gain respectability for the movement, many of its participants stigmatize the flamboyance of swishers, cross-dressers, drag queens. In this way, a liberation movement may create new norms that push to the margins some of those it ought to be liberating.

The history of Second-Wave feminism tells a similar story (though it is hardly the main plot). It too has a history (in some, but not all of its manifestations) of exclusion and marginalization. Working-class women, women of color, and lesbians have complained that Second Wave feminism has either ignored them, or else failed to grasp the complex forms of oppression that are peculiar to their situation. Some lesbian separatists, in response, have declared sexual love between women, or else celibacy, to be the only legitimate choices for true feminists, hence marginalizing heterosexual feminists in a new discourse of normalization.

Since lesbian love was thought to be not only politically correct but more gentle, nurturant, and productive of true intimacy than heterosexual relations, the confessions of members of Samois, an organization of lesbian sadomasochists, that burst upon the scene in San Francisco in the late 1970s, were profoundly shocking to many lesbian—and heterosexual—feminists; lesbian sadomasochists were roundly condemned and entirely excluded by many (not all) from the community of "true" and "normal" feminism.[36] Examples of this sort could be multiplied at great length for both liberation movements, but I think that the general point is clear.

But Foucault's theoretical ambivalence in regard to these movements is somewhat shortsighted.[37] While political movements tend often to rehearse the very oppressive practices against which they are agitating, there is no comparison between the marginalization visited upon individuals by social movements and the marginalization and exclusion that is typically visited upon these same persons by the "established order of domination."

In spite of the flaws and deficiencies in social movements for sexual liberation, there is something about them that Foucault may have noticed but about which he has failed to remark. I refer to the life-altering and life-enhancing effect they have had on myriads of people. This "failure to remark" is an absence less striking than Foucault's failure to understand sexual misery, but it bears resemblance to it: Here that about which he fails to remark is joy. There is inexpressible relief in "coming out" or, as in women's consciousness-raising groups, "speaking bitterness." Joy and relief are proportional, perhaps, to the corrosive effects of having to live a lie at best, at worst, having to live under highly repressive circumstances, that is, in fear of exposure, persecution, and disgrace. There is an extraordinary joy too in breaking out of the isolation that is imposed by rampant sexism and homophobia; why else would solitary confinement be the most dreaded punishment? The joy we feel in being thus released is a measure of our fragmentation and of the alienation from others we experience in everyday life; the joy of temporary escape is a measure of the unhappiness many feel for life in "normal" bourgeois society. Other girls bleed every month, not just me. Others have suffered what I have suffered. The "confessions" heard in these movements build solidarities among the participants, and since every political movement needs solidarity, such confessions are empowering, not disempowering, as Foucault suspects are all confessions. In consciousness-raising and in "coming out," a renegade discourse takes shape. There is, for many, an inexpressible joy in so speaking and in standing in solidarity with others, especially if one has felt, all her life, weak, defective, and despised. This joy is transformative: It releases the individual from the prison house of personality—in which the disciplines (and their internalizations) have no doubt been inscribed—into a wider human arena. Foucault felt an extraordinary rush of solidarity during the early stages of the Iranian revolution. There is little indication in his published work that he knew the joys of solidarity closer to home.

It is inevitable that movements that challenge the established order will bear its stamp. While we need to hold tightly to our vision, insofar as we are persecuted, our persecutors determine in large measure our political agenda. Radically new regimes of power/knowledge cannot be invented out of whole cloth at the moment that antagonists of the established order recognize its bankruptcy. Typically, movements of contestation combine genuine innovation with elements that are older and more familiar. The polarities which structure current regimes of "truth" and power and in which contemporary social movements are imbricated— male / female; masculine / feminine; gay / straight; black / white; self / other—can, it is true, be deconstructed. Poststructuralist theory, critical race theory, queer theory—all have demonstrated the possibility of such an overcoming.[38] If all that Foucault is telling us, in his talk of the "deployment" of sexuality, is that we must reexamine the terms and concepts with which we theorize our oppression and liberation, then he is certainly correct. But what Marx said of Hegel, namely, that he had overcome alienation in thought, but only in thought, is true here as well. Race, gender, and "sex-desire" may indeed be fictions, but they have been overcome, if at all, only in thought; they structure the psychic and material reality of everyday life; we cannot cease to struggle against them, like it or not.

Notes

I would like to thank Isaac Balbus and William McBride for helpful comments on an earlier draft of this chapter. I would particularly like to thank Jana Sawicki, LaDelle McWhorter, and Elaine Miller for very detailed and careful critiques of the chapter. Their efforts are all the more appreciated in view of the fact that all three reject the central claims I put forward here about Foucault and the repressive hypothesis.

1. Michel Foucault, *The History of Sexuality: Volume 1, An Introduction* (New York: Vintage Books, 1990), pp. 3–4.

2. Ibid., p. 5.

3. Ibid., p. 7.

4. Ibid., pp. 10–11.

5. Ibid., pp. 12, 11.

6. Ibid., pp. 11, 18.

7. Ibid., pp. 19 ff.

8. Foucault's reference here is to Segneri, *L'Instruction du pénitent* (n.p., n.d.), pp. 301–2.

9. See Michel Foucault, *Discipline and Punish: The Birth of the Prison* (New York: Pantheon, 1977), pp. 135–69.

10. Foucault, *History of Sexuality*, p. 33.

11. However, for a fascinating attempt to periodize epochs of child-rearing in the West, see Isaac Balbus, *Marxism and Domination: A Neo-Hegelian, Feminist, Psychoanalytic Theory of Sexual, Political and Technological Liberation* (Princeton, N.J: Princeton University Press, 1983).

12. Foucault, *History of Sexuality*, p. 59.

13. Ibid., pp. 44–45. On the sexualization of domination, see also Michel Foucault, *Politics, Philosophy, Culture* (New York: Routledge, 1990). According to Foucault, "There is about sexuality a lot of defective regulations in which the negative effects of inhibitions are counterbalanced by the positive effects of stimulation" (p. 9)

14. Foucault, *History of Sexuality*, p. 45.

15. Michel Foucault, *Power/Knowledge: Selected Interviews and Other Writings, 1972–1977* (New York: Pantheon Press, 1980), p. 120.

16. For a provocative account of the way in which severe childhood sexual repression may give rise to a fully masochistic sexuality, see Robert Stoller, *Perversion: The Erotic Form of Hatred* (London: Karmac Books, 1994), and *Pain and Passion: A Psychoanalyst Explores the World of S and M* (New York: Plenum Press, 1991).

17. Foucault, *History of Sexuality*, pp. 49, 122.

18. Foucault, *Politics, Philosophy, Culture*, p. 119. In spite of the apodeictism of these statements, Foucault never articulates a fully coherent position on sexual repression. We must remember, in regard to the unconditionality of the first two statements above, that Foucault said earlier in the text that he did not so much want to deny the existence of repression as to recontextualize it. In the passages quoted, however, he does deny it. Nevertheless, he excoriates as "detestable" the press and popularizers for condensing his work into a slogan: "Sexuality has never been repressed" (p. 45). He finds the notion of repression "insidious" and admits that he can hardly free himself of it (p. 119). "Why," he asks elsewhere, "do we speak with so much passion and so much resentment against our most recent past, against our present?" (Foucault, *History of Sexuality*, p. 8). Foucault answers this question, but the answer seems obvious: The passion and resentment spring from the experience of repression and the pain that it causes. Foucault seems to

waver between two positions: first, that there is no such thing as repression, at least as he claims repression has been understood, and second, that repression is real enough but it needs to be recontextualized. We think of repression in juridical terms, on the model of law and not, more appropriately, as thoroughly modern power—diffuse, bureaucratized, and disguised. The concept rests on a series of "psychological reference points borrowed from the human sciences" (Foucault, *Power/Knowledge*, p. 108). Here, Foucault admits that he finds it difficult to avoid Freud, as elsewhere Marx. The principal objection to the "human sciences" as they emerged in the nineteenth century is that they are, as postmodernists like to say, "imbricated" in new forms of the exercise of power. For Foucault, however, this is the case with all discourses that claim to be "true." The first claim predominates in *History of Sexuality, Volume 1,* which is the text on which the present chapter focuses.

19. Foucault, *History of Sexuality,* p. 45.

20. Ibid., p. 83.

21. Sigmund Freud, *The Freud Reader,* ed. Peter Gay (New York: W. W. Norton, 1989), p. 742.

22. Ibid.

23. Foucault, *History of Sexuality,* pp. 27–29, 45.

24. Wilhelm Reich, *Sex-Pol, Essays 1929–1934,* ed. Lee Baxandall (New York: Random House, 1972), pp. 245–46.

25. Foucault, *History of Sexuality,* pp. 120, 121.

26. Ibid., p. 127. Foucault's position in many ways echoes that of the Freudo-Marxists: Capitalism "would not have been possible without the controlled insertion of bodies into the machinery of production and the adjustment of the phenomena of population to economic processes" (Foucault, *History of Sexuality: Volume 1,* p. 141). While Foucault did not believe that the economic base produces superstructural effects as its epiphenomena (a position that Reich appears to have held), he believed that mechanisms of control with varied histories and contingent causes get taken up and "colonized" by the bourgeoisie if these mechanisms further its interests (p. 94). For all three—Reich, Marcuse, and Foucault— mechanisms of sexual control in the modern era are closely tied to the capitalist economic order.

27. See Gad Horowitz's extremely acute comparison of Marcuse and Foucault and his compelling defense of Marcuse against Foucaultian claims (Gad Horowitz, "The Foucaultian Impasse: No Sex, No Self, No Revolution," *Political Theory* 15, no. 1 [February 1987]: 61–80). For another trenchant critique of Foucault on sexuality, see Anthony Giddens, *The Transformation of Intimacy: Sexuality, Love, and Eroticism in Modern Societies* (Stanford University Press, 1992). Giddens questions whether it is possible, as Foucault does, to write meaningfully about sexuality in the modern period without reference to love.

28. Foucault, *History of Sexuality,* p. 157.

29. LaDelle McWhorter, "Foucault's Attack on Sex-Desire," *Philosophy Today* 41, nos. 1–4 (spring 1997): 160–65.

30. See Sandra Bartky, *Femininity and Domination: Studies in the Phenomenology*

of Oppression (New York: Routledge), chaps. 3 and 5. See also Susan Bordo, *Unbearable Weight* (Berkeley and Los Angeles: University of California Press, 1993).

31. John Stuart Mill, *On the Subjection of Women,* in *Essays on Sex Equality,* ed. Alice S. Rossi (Chicago: University of Chicago Press, 1970), p. 148.

32. Calvin O. Schrag, *The Resources of Rationality, A Response to the Postmodern Challenge* (Bloomington: Indiana University Press, 1992), p. 37.

33. Foucault, *History of Sexuality,* pp. 60, 10.

34. Ibid., p. 131.

35. This is Foucault's fundamental critique of the Gay Rights movement. But he recognizes the impossibility of escaping from sexual specification, especially when a specific range of practices are condemned, outlawed, etc. See Foucault, *Power/Knowledge,* pp. 220–21.

36. See Samois, *What Color Is Your Handkerchief?* (Berkeley: Samois, 1979), and Samois, *Coming to Power* (Berkeley: Samois, 1981). See also Robin Linden et al., eds., *Against Sadomasochism: A Radical Feminist Analysis* (Palo Alto, Calif: Frog-in-the-Well Press, 1982).

37. Foucault's theoretical stance vis-à-vis the women's movement is far more positive than his response to the Gay Rights movement. Women, unlike gays, have made a "veritable movement of de-sexualisation, a displacement effected in relation to the sexual centering of the problem, formulating the demand for forms of culture, discourse, language, and so on, which are no longer part of that rigid assignation and pinning-down to their sex which they had initially in some sense been politically obliged to accept" (Foucault, *Power/Knowledge,* p. 220). This has not been true of most feminist activists, and true only of poststructuralist feminist theorists who have "deconstructed" sexual difference. Ladelle McWhorter has told me that Foucault was active in gay rights movements and took part in gay politics; further, he was interviewed by virtually every major gay periodical in the United States and in France. She asserts too that he espoused a gay identity. This seems to contradict his denial that there is a core sexual self but to recognize, as I shall shortly claim, that we have little choice but to accept, albeit provisionally, the identities foisted upon us by a misogynist and homophobic culture. "Queer theory," which began to blossom only after Foucault's death, is far closer to the poststructuralist feminism he praises than the self-understanding of the gay liberation movements that were active during his lifetime.

38. See, e.g., Judith Butler, *Gender Trouble: Feminism and the Subversion of Identity* (New York: Routledge, 1990).

4

Transversality and Geophilosophy in the Age of Globalization

Hwa Yol Jung

To think is to confine yourself to a single thought that one day stands still like a star in the world's sky.

—*Martin Heidegger*

Only connect!

—*E. M. Forster*

Prologue

In their joint work *What Is Philosophy?* Gilles Deleuze and Félix Guattari define philosophy as that discipline which is engaged in creating and advancing concepts.[1] Transversality and geophilosophy are taken to be two transformative and paradigmatic concepts. By reterritorializing the traditional boundaries of conceptualization both cultural and disciplinary, they have momentous imports and consequences for the future of philosophy and the world which is said to have become a global village or cosmopolis.

The idea of interfacing transversality and geophilosophy dawned on me as a direct result of Calvin O. Schrag's response to my review, in *Philosophy and Social Criticism,* of his most recent work *The Self after Postmodernity.*[2] In concluding my review of Schrag, I intimated that the concept of the "ecological self" would be thought of as an extension of, or addendum to, his definition of the "self after postmodernity," or, if you will, the "post-postmodern self," which is meant to transverse rather than to sublate modernity and postmodernity. The importance of the "ecological self" can no longer be ignored or underestimated because today the very fate of the earth hangs in precarious balance. The earth (*oikos*) is the dwelling place of all beings and things both human and nonhuman. It is no mere accident that we are fondly called earthlings. No doubt the well-being of the earth as a whole should continue to be our ultimate concern and the defining moment of humanity on earth in the new millennium.

Transversality and the Overcoming of Eurocentrism

The discovery of transversality is Schrag's seminal and paradigmatic contribution to philosophy in general and to phenomenological hermeneutics in particular.[3] Inspired directly and indirectly by the philosophical insights of Merleau-Ponty, Sartre, Deleuze and Guattari, Lyotard, and Foucault, Schrag develops transversality as dialogical engagement and enrichment across differences and embraces the conception of truth as the way of communicability. He contends that transversality moves "beyond the constraints of the metaphysical oppositions of universality versus particularity and identity versus difference. Transversal unity is an achievement of communication as it visits a multiplicity of viewpoints, perspectives, belief systems, and regions of concern."[4] As a "refiguration" of rationality, transversality is for Schrag a passageway *between* modernity and postmodernity, that is to say, *between* the modernist overdetermination and the postmodernist underdetermination of reason and its claims. His transversal shifter is meant to scale the continental divide between modernity and postmodernity. It intends to dissolve, as it were, their difference(s). By way of transversality, he means to subvert and to transgress the dichotomy between modernism and postmodernism, by splitting *diagonally* the difference between the pure verticality of modernist "transcendentalism" and the pure horizontality of postmodernist "historicism." By administering a double-edged *pharmakon* to both, transversality is best described as the future-oriented Maitreyan middle way between the two extreme tendencies of modernity and postmodernity: between, in Schrag's own words, "the Scylla of a hegemonic unification" on the one hand and "the Charybdis of a chaotic pluralism" on the other. It, in other words, unlocks the deadlock between the two. In the very words of Schrag himself:

> Thus truth as communicability [i.e, transversality] . . . is at once a
> disclosure of similarity and difference, unity and multiplicity, the

commensurable and the incommensurable. Historicism forgets similarity, unity, and commensurability; transcendentalism forgets difference, multiplicity, and incommensurability. And each forgets the other because both decontextualize the intentionality of communicative praxis.[5]

Within the phenomenological movement, Schrag's formulations of transversality or "transversal universals" are, as he himself acknowledges, "somewhat reminiscent" of the "lateral universals" of Merleau-Ponty, for whom history is an open notebook full of ambiguous pluralities (*Vielseitigkeit*) and culture has a multiplicity of ethos. Transversality advances the cause of cross-cultural fertilization or hybridization as well as cross-disciplinary engagement in which truth as communicability privileges, and is monopolized by, neither the West nor philosophy alone. Here we cannot resist comparing Schrag's construction of truth as communicative praxis with the dialogism of Mikhail Bakhtin, the Russian literary theorist and philosopher.[6] Listen to the deep and prodigious voice of Bakhtin. Speaking of Dostoevsky, who is his philosophical protagonist, he writes without equivocation:

> At the center of Dostoevsky's artistic worlds must lie dialogue, and dialogue *not as a means but as an end itself. Dialogue here is not the threshold to action, it is the action itself.* It is not a means for revealing, for bringing to the surface the already ready-made character of a person; no, in dialogue a person not only shows himself outwardly, but he becomes for the first time that which he is—and, we repeat, not only for others but for himself as well. *To be means to communicate dialogically. When dialogue ends, everything ends.* Thus dialogue, by its very essence, cannot and must not come to an end. At the level of his religious-utopian world-view Dostoevsky carries dialogue into eternity, conceiving of it as eternal co-rejoicing, co-admiration, con-cord. At the level of the novel, it is presented as the *unfinalizability of dialogue,* although originally as dialogue's vicious circle.[7]

There is indeed the difference between the dialectical and the dialogical of Bakhtin (cum Dostoevsky). The dialectic from Plato to Hegel, Marx, Kojéve, and now Francis Fukuyama privileges a transcendental and teleological ending or closure, whereas the dialogical of Bakhtin is without "finalizability." Thus, Bakhtin's dialogism is very much like the Sinitic logic of yin and yang as mutually complementary, which produces a familial circle of sixty-four hexagrams.[8] In other words, the dialectic ends in the identity of identity and difference, whereas the dialogical refuses to identify difference with identity, that is, homogenize the two. In the tradition of Western metaphysics, there exists the underlying assumption, though never warranted or proven, that truth is universal in that it is immutable, timeless, and objective for all humanity. The idea manifests itself in the guise of "human nature." The logic of sublated identity has been the regulative idea of modernity and modernization which is decisively Eurocentric or Orientalist in its formulation of both knowledge and power. Not only does modernity place Europe at the center of what has happened and will happen, but modern Europe also has legislated for itself the zoning laws of universality: What is particular in Western modernity is universalized, while what is particular in the non-West forever remains particular. European ethnophilosophy lays monopolistic claim on universality. For good reason, this Eurocentric orientation is often called a "white mythology." Since the West is the central focus of truth as universal, the non-West in its knowledge and power has been marginalized or ignored. The logic of transversality challenges Eurocentrism or Orientalism—as well as, for that matter, Occidentalism such as Sinocentrism or Afrocentrism—and attempts to go beyond it.[9] It opens up a brand-new space for comparative philosophy and comparative culture which is neither Orientalist nor Occidentalist.

Merleau-Ponty contends that the arrogant and dialectical path of Hegel excludes Oriental thought from absolute and universal knowledge and draws "a geographical frontier between philosophy and nonphilosophy." Philosophy is destined to examine its own idea of truth again and again because truth is "a treasure scattered about in human life prior to all philosophy and not divided among doctrines." If so, Western philosophy is destined to reexamine not only its own idea of truth but also related matters and institutions such as science, economy, politics, and technology. Merleau-Ponty writes with telling poignancy and profundity:

> From this angle, civilizations lacking our philosophical or economic equipment take on an instructive value. It is not a matter of going in search of truth or salvation in what falls short of science or philosophical awareness, or of dragging chunks of mythology as such into our philosophy, but acquiring—in the presence of these variants of humanity that we are so far from—a sense of the theoretical and practical problems our institutions are faced with, and of rediscovering the existential field that they were born in and that their long success has led us to forget. The Orient's "childishness" has something to teach us, if it were nothing more than the narrowness of our adult ideas. The relationship between Orient and Occident, like that between child and adult, is not that of ignorance to knowledge or nonphilosophy to philosophy; it is much more subtle, making room on the part of the Orient for all anticipations and "prematurations." Simply rallying and surbordinating "non-philosophy"

to true philosophy will not create the unity of the human spirit. It always
exists in each culture's lateral relationships to the others, in the echoes
one awakes in the other.[10]

In his lateral pursuit of truth, transversal truth, Merleau-Ponty
means to take nothing for granted. It is just here that he makes a decisive
break with the "conceit" of Hegelian Eurocentrism or vertical and universal transcendentalism. As childhood and adulthood are one inseparable
ontological order of the human, so Oriental and Occidental cultures and
societies are made up of one continuum of the life-and-death cycle of
humanity everywhere, thereby pointing the way to philosophical truth.
We expect to learn as much from "primitive" societies as from "civilized"
ones regarding the conditions of common humanity unless we believe
in cultural evolutionism which is "the old accomplice" of European eth-
nocentrism. Merleau-Ponty thus contends that "there is not *a* philosophy which contains all philosophies; philosophy as a whole is at certain
moments in each philosophy. To take up the celebrated phrase again,
philosophy's center is everywhere and its circumference nowhere."[11] In
the final analysis, truth is a diffused and decentered happening. The
value of transversality is squarely placed in seeing what is ours as alien
and what was alien as our own.

To be sure, ethnography—especially phenomenological ethnography—is invaluable for philosophy's transversal search for truth. Transversal truth must be sought and proven by understanding all sociocultural life-worlds. Thus, Merleau-Ponty is forthright in suggesting that
transversal truth is acquired "through ethnological experience and its
incessant testing of the self through the other person and the other person through the self," which is, by the way, no easy task to accomplish.[12]
It is in this context that he pays his fitting tribute to French ethnography,
the ethnography particularly of Marcel Mauss and Claude Lévi-Strauss.
In turn, in his inaugural lecture in 1960 at the Collège de France, Lévi-
Strauss echoed the transversal voice of Merleau-Ponty in paying moving
homage to the "savage mind" of "primitives", whose "pupil" and "witness"
he was, to the end of preserving the *lateral continuity* of all humanity, not
the vertical hierarchy of the "civilized" (Western) on top and the alleged
"primitive" at bottom.[13]

Interfacing Transversality and Geophilosophy

Transversality and geophilosophy are imbricated concepts. They overlap
and complement each other. Transversality is a geometric concept. Were

etymology any marker of truth, then it should be relevant to geophilosophy as the disciplined study of the earth (*geo*). Geophilosophy is not just
a recent Western invention; indeed, it is global, stretching from the East
to the West and from the North to the South. Transversality as communicative praxis, too, cultivates neither the narcissistic conversation of the
West with itself nor the conversation between modernity and postmodernity within the Western Hemisphere alone. Rather, it creates, as Schrag
himself—who has also an interest in comparative philosophy—puts it,
"a new space"—the brand-new space of intercultural discourses between
the West and the non-West—in order to attend to the urgent matters of
the earth.

What is geophilosophy? It is the philosophy of the whole earth as
elemental of all elements, of the affairs of all earthly inhabitants both
human and nonhuman. To draw a cue from Deleuze and Guattari, "the
earth is not one element among others but rather brings together all
the elements within a single embrace."[14] It is a grave mistake to identify
geophilosophy simply with environmental philosophy for the reason that
the earth is also quintessential to the interhuman condition.[15] The purpose of geophilosophy is comprehensive and inclusive in investigating
the interdependent zone between the interhuman and the interspecific
realm. In alliance with transversality, geophilosophy claims to be a topology of Interbeing.

The most basic principle of the ecological is placed in the notion
that everything is connected to everything else, that is, not one thing
exists in isolation from others in the universe. In a nutshell, reality is
nothing but consummately social process. Indeed, Interbeing—to borrow the deep and felicitous concept of the Vietnamese Zen Buddhist
Thich Nhat Hanh who now lives in southern France—is the geophilosophical paradigm. M. C. Escher's *Verbum* (1942) is the genealogical and
geometric rendition of the ecological as a Great Chain of Interbeing.

The Great Chain of Interbeing is always already embodied or en-
fleshed, that is to say, it is first and foremost intercorporeal. Only by way
of the body or flesh are the self and the world said to be intertwined or
chiasmic. The body is the material precondition for our (inter-)being-
in-the-world. As Merleau-Ponty puts it, the world and the body, which is
the locus of the sensible and sensuous, are made of the same material.[16]
Thus corporeality or embodiment as intercorporeality may be said to be
"archisociality"—to borrow the expressive term of Dany-Robert Dufour.[17]
But for the body or flesh, sociality itself is unimaginable. For that reason
alone, we are compelled to somatize sociality. In this respect, it is wrong
or only half-right to say that the body is the medium of communication;
rather, it *is* communication, or in itself a primordial "interbeing."

Interbeing is a transversal of time and space, that is, "chronotopical"—to use Bakhtin's idiosyncratic but pithy language. The body, which intersects or transverses the boundaries of time and place, is preeminently a geophilosophical idea. The aim of body politics (in the plural), in turn, reterritorializes philosophy itself. According to Merleau-Ponty:

> [The body as] flesh is not matter, is not mind, is not substance. To designate it, we should need the old term "element," in the sense it was used to speak of water, air, earth, and fire, that is, in the sense of a *general thing*, midway between the spatio-temporal individual and the idea, a sort of incarnate principle that brings a style of being wherever there is a fragment of being [interbeing]. The flesh is in this sense an "element" of Being [Interbeing]. Not a fact or a sum of facts, and yet adherent to location and to the now.[18]

The contribution of contemporary feminism to the body as a geophilosophical idea is unsurpassed. It overturns the history, and radicalizes the geopolitical culture, of the body and thus philosophy itself. On the temporal plane, the "calendar of the flesh" is synchronized with the calendar, solar or lunar, of nature's passage.[19] Adrienne Rich's new "politics of location" begins with the body. By returning to the body, which is for her a place-name, she means to rebel against "the idolatry of pure ideas" and to break loose from the "universal shadow of patriarchy."[20]

The ecological destruction of the earth constitutes the ultimate limits of Western modernity which has disenchanted the world in the name of humanity's infinite progress based on the cultivation of "enlightened" reason that demystifies "soft" magic by "hard" science and technology or what Heidegger calls "calculative thinking" (*Gestell*) as opposed to "meditative thinking" (*Gelassenheit*).[21] Let us take Descartes and Bacon as the paragons of the calculative thinking of Western modernity.

Descartes regarded men as the "masters and possessors" of dumb nature. His cogito hypnotized and dazzled Western modernity in which epistemology has become *prima philosophia*. "The French," Deleuze and Guattari declare, "are like landowners whose source of income is the cogito."[22] The epistemological subject or the "I" of the "I think," which is for Descartes disembodied, is by necessity egocentric or monological. The cogito exemplifies a thinker's desire to seal himself/herself off from the world and to keep his/her thinking pure or uncontaminated by the presence of the Other. The true philosopher is, for Descartes, one who takes infinite delight in the permanent state of solitude, social isolation, and hibernation. As the "I" of the "I think" is a cloistered self, in the final analysis, the Cartesian mind as *res cogitans* is in the perpetual state of social paralysis and is incapable of socializing with others both human and nonhuman. The cogito, in other words, is a fatal abstraction for sociality. The "I" of the "I think" is the epitome of an "invisible man" in total isolation from others, both other minds and other bodies. As a thinking substance, the mind needs nothing more than itself to think: It signifies *cogito ergo non-sum*. For this reason, Schrag is well aware of the importance of the primacy of the "agentive self" over the "cognitive self."[23]

Bacon initiates the technological élan that establishes and justifies the total domination by men of nature or, as he himself calls it, "the inquisition of nature." Bacon's experimentalism allegedly improves on, and supersedes, Scholastic book learning whose "cobwebs" produced neither substance nor profits. For the fruits of science do not grow in books. For Bacon, instead, the "dignity" of human knowledge is maintained by "works of utility and power." The framework of modern technological rationality, or *Gestell,* was laid down by Bacon when he insisted on the unity of knowledge and power in one (i.e., *scientia et potentia in idem coincidunt*) and discovered "in the womb of nature many secrets of excellent use" in overcoming the necessities and miseries of humanity (i.e., *philanthropia*). The earth or nature is for Bacon, in short, nothing more than a dead pile of use-objects for humans.

What is to be done in order to overcome the "death of nature" or the "ecological crisis"? In Chinese the expression "crisis" is composed of the two logograms of "danger" and "opportunity." Crisis means to turn danger into opportunity. Geophilosophy, whose epicenter is Interbeing, is meant to seize an opportunity to overcome the ecological danger which humanity is confronting today in two interrelated ways. In the first place, it is predisposed to the abiding sense of community among all beings and things, not just among humans alone.[24] In the second place, in opposition to anthropocentrism, geophilosophy favors the ecocentric approach in which the earth becomes first and primary and humans are caretakers/givers and agents of responsibility for the well-being of the whole earth. The earth does not belong to, or is not possessed by, humanity, but rather humanity itself belongs to the earth. It is a matter of shifting or transforming our "mentality" and perspective. The ecocentric question is "Why do humans build the road where animals cross?" whereas the anthropocentric question is "Why do animals cross the road we build?"

The eleventh-century Chinese neo-Confucianist Chan Tsai wrote a most celebratory passage which exudes with a touch of humility the cosmic and ecological sense of Interbeing and elevates the abiding sense of piety as unyielding reciprocity: "Heaven is my father, and Earth is my mother, and even such a small creature as I find[s] an intimate place in their midst. Therefore that which fills the universe I regard as my body and that which directs the universe my nature. All people are my brothers and sisters, and all things are my companions."[25] The "land ethic" of the imcomparable American conservationist Aldo Leopold, whose weighty and poetic deliberation of "thinking like a mountain" is legendary and exemplifies Heideggerian *Gelassenheit* (serenity), is also predicated upon the notion of "a biotic community" in which the land designates a composite term for an extended sense of community. For Leopold's topophilic idea of community, which preceded James Lovelock's hypothesis of Gaia as a living organism by exactly three decades, includes soil, water, plants, worms, microorganisms, and of course animals. He is right to advance the idea that all ethics rest on the "single premise" that "the individual is a member of a community of interdependent parts."[26] Echoing the Kantian sentiment about ethics, however, he bemoaned the fact that "there is as yet no ethic dealing with man's relation to land and to the animals and plants which grow upon it. Land, like Odysseus' slave girls, is still property. The land-relation is still strictly economic, entailing privileges but not obligations."[27] I find no fundamental lacuna or contradiction between Leopold's "biotic community" and Schrag's "self in community," which may be stretched to include nonhuman beings and things. The "ecological self" is indeed an extended, added, or modified—if you will—dimension of Schrag's communal self. Schrag sums up what he means by "the self in community," which combines, I think, the received wisdom of Alfred Schutz, Edmund Burke, John Donne, and Merleau-Ponty, as follows:

> The self in community is a self situated in this space of communicative praxis, historically embedded, existing with others, inclusive of predecessors, contemporaries, and successors. Never an island entire of itself, the self remains rooted in history but is not suffocated by the influx of historical forms and forces. The communalized self is *in* history but not *of* history. It has the resources of transcending the historically specific without arrogating to itself an unconditioned and decontextualized vision of the world.[28]

But for difference, there would be no meaningful diversity. But for diversity, there would equally be neither reciprocity nor community, that is, no "communal self." Indeed, without difference the notion of Interbeing based on the primacy of the Relation (*primum relationis*) is ultimately unthinkable. The connective *inter* in Interbeing designates asymmetrical reciprocity. The necessity of (ecological) communication exists because, on the one hand, human community consists of distinct individuals who are, as Schrag puts it, "agentive" and, on the other hand, (external) nature is made up of myriads of distinct beings and things or "ten thousand things"—to use the poetic expression of Sinism. The communal self is neither unitarian nor communitarian. Both unitarians and communitarians are not fully aware of the fact that difference is a marker of communication, community, and all relationships. Heidegger's *Differenz* as *Unterschied* is an "adventure of difference" which plays and feeds on the combined meaning of the words which double or couple difference with the between (*Unter/schied*) that at once connects, preserves, and promotes *both* difference *and* the relational. Difference (*Unter/schied*) is capable of conserving the principle of complementarity in our relationships with other humans and nonhumans alike. Heidegger's fourfold crossing (*das Geviert*) *transverses* sky, earth, gods, and mortals (humans who are most mortal of all mortals and nonhumans).[29] Because the biotic community is an interconnecting gathering of many distinct beings and things which are together capable of orchestrating, it produces *harmony*, the harmonics of invisible sounds, in other words, the communal self whose regulative idea is harmony is quintessentially ecological.

The most fundamental thrust of geophilosophy based on the "earth first" or ecocentrism is first and foremost ethical. There is no ethics involving egocentrism or a mere plurality of monadic subjects for whom, as Merleau-Ponty puts it elegantly, "the world and history are no longer a system with [multiple] points of entry but a sheaf of irreconcilable perspectives which never coexist and which are held together only by the hopeless heroism of the I."[30] The ethical can never be sanitized by the heroism of the I whoever he/she may be. Separately, we are condemned to perish.

I would contend, moreover, that only heteronomy or the primary of the Other over the self is the ethical site of responsibility if not the site of the ethical itself. For the making of heteronomy in which ethics becomes first philosophy and responsibility becomes first ethics, we need the guidance of Lévinas. Schrag is well aware of the importance of Lévinas's "ethics of alterity." While Lévinas refuses to interface the ontological with the ethical, that is, the ethical is for him fundamentally "meonotological" (nonontological) mainly because of Heidegger's impasse, Schrag attempts to promote—correctly, I think—his phenomenology of communicative praxis, by interfacing the "ontological" order of "descriptive responsivity" with the "ethical" issue of "normative responsibility" based on the Greek concept of *kathakonta* ("the fitting"). The responsible self is the "agentive" self who *answers* the world by first *authoring* it—to use the formulation of Bakhtin's dialogism.

The discovery of heteronomy, of a "Thou" as alterity, is truly the Copernican revolution of social and ethical thought. Heteronomy was first discovered in modern European philosophy by Ludwig Feuerbach in the mid-nineteenth century. It may judiciously be called "Copernican" simply because of the fact that what egocentrism/ethnocentrism is to geocentrism, heteronomy/interculturalism is to heliocentrism. Lévinas continues and preserves Feuerbach's Copernican revolution of heteromony in which the face of the Other as ethical transcendence is elevated to the altar of both interhuman and interspecific relationships (i.e., "altarity," as if it were).[31]

Now the heteronomic ethic of responsibility confronts and runs counter to the Anglo-American institution of "rights talk" or the talk of "the I's have it" which places the self as the dead center of the moral and political universe and lends a deaf ear to the issue of responsibility. Indeed, rights talk is deeply implanted and entrenched in American soil and unshakably embedded in the American soul. It is no accident that Americans are called "born Lockeans" who honor, guard, and defend jealously entitlements, the inviolable sovereignty of the individual, and possessive individualism. Locke is the possessive individualist par excellence since for him the concept of the human as laborer or exploiter of nature is necessary for the acquisition of private property as absolute rights. The utilitarianism of labor and industry in exploiting and dominating nature or the land, which when uncultivated by human labor (i.e., wilderness) is called by Locke "waste," builds the society of acquisitive individuals (or *homo oeconomicus*). For Locke, things of nature are useless unless they acquire "value" on account of labor and industry. In the end, Lockean possessive individualism incorporates the antisocial principles between humans on the one hand and between the human and nature on the other hand.[32] Mary Ann Glendon speaks most critically of the scotoma of Anglo-American "rights talk." "The American rights dialect," she writes, "is distinguished not only by what we say and how we say it, but also by what we leave unsaid."[33] As every "want" is being translated into a "right" whose language is extended now to trees and animals, we tend to trivialize the magnitude of the dire plight of the wounded, weakened, and fragile earth whose well-being is indispensable for the sustainability of all earthbound creatures including humans.

There is indeed a paradox and incongruity when "rights talk" is anthropomorphically extended, albeit in a well-intended way, in all quarters of environmental ethics, to stones, trees, and animals, that is, "rights" of stones and trees and "animal rights." For example, in his recent work entitled *The Natural Contract*, Michel Serres expresses the innovative and imaginative sentiment of a holistic and global approach to environmental philosophy with the intent of making peace with the ruined world of nature, in the same way that his compatriot Rousseau intended to make peace with the interhuman world by way of social contract.[34] It was also the visionary Rousseau who warned that "you are lost, if you forget that the fruits of the earth belong to all and that the earth belongs to no one."[35] So far, so good. Nevertheless, there is a conceptual flaw, something unnatural and incongruous, about Serres's use of the language of "contract," Rousseau notwithstanding, in order to overcome the wretched and unbearable condition of inhumanity in the warlike "state of nature" but not to overcome inhumanity to the nonhuman world (i.e., the domain of nature).

Epilogue

I hope that transversality and geophilosophy based on a Great Chain of Ecological Interbeing will govern the future of philosophy, which is becoming global in approach and content: cross-disciplinary and cross-cultural. Transversality is no doubt a hermeneutical principle which demands the disciplined listening to the Other and is predisposed to the (Gadamerian) idea that the Other might very well be right. Geophilosophy measures the earth as the all-encompassing element which brings all the elements into its range. In its holistic method and content, environmental philosophy is the geophilosophy par excellence for the reason that it is concerned with the very question of how to dwell properly on earth. In his attempt to construct a geophilosophical paradigm, Félix Guattari raises a weighty and timely question:

> The ecological crisis can be traced to a more general crisis of the social, political and existential. The problem involves a type of revolution of mentalities whereby they cease investing in a certain kind of development, based on a productivism that has lost all human finality. Thus the issue returns with insistence: how do we change mentalities, how do we reinvent social practices that would give back to humanity—if it ever had it—a sense of responsibility, not only for animal and vegetable species, likewise for incorporeal species such as music, the arts, cinema, the relation with time, love and compassion for others, the feeling of fusion at the heat of cosmos?[36]

Indeed, responsibility as first ethics becomes an ethics of the future world which is hurrying into a global village. To apostrophize my conclusion: The new millennium belongs to heterocracy, which, as the moral habitus of humanity's conduct, is neither egocentric nor anthropocentric. It cannot be otherwise: By ceasing our investment in the long misguided theories of egocentrism and anthropocentrism, heterocracy is destined to reenchant the world—the earth and humanity in one and the same embrace. It is destined to embrace the earth as an intimate and felicitous home for all beings and things.

Notes

1. Gilles Deleuze and Félix Guattari, *What Is Philosophy?* trans. Hugh Tomlinson and Graham Burchell (New York: Columbia University Press, 1994), p. 5.

2. See my "Review Essay," of Calvin O. Schrag's *The Self after Postmodernity* (New Haven, Conn.: Yale University Press, 1997), also published in *Philosophy and Social Criticism* 22 (1998): 133–40 (hereafter cited as *SP*).

3. Schrag began to explore the issue of transversality in earnest in 1989. See "Rationality between Modernity and Postmodernity," in *Philosophical Papers: Betwixt and Between* (Albany: State University of New York Press, 1994), pp. 255–306. See also Calvin O. Schrag, *The Resources of Rationality: A Response to the Postmodern Challenge* (Bloomington: Indiana University Press, 1992), and *SP*. For an extended discussion of Schrag's quest for transversality, see my "The *Tao* of Transversality as a Global Approach to Truth: A Metacommentary on Calvin O. Schrag," *Man and World* 28 (1995): 11–31.

4. Schrag, *SP*, p. 133.

5. Schrag, *Philosophical Papers*, p. 274.

6. See Mikhail M. Bakhtin, *The Dialogical Imagination,* ed. Michael Holquist, trans. Caryl Emerson and Michael Holquist (Austin: University of Texas Press, 1981), and *Problems of Dostoevsky's Poetics*, ed. and trans. Caryl Emerson (Minneapolis: University of Minnesota Press, 1984). See also my "Bakhtin's Dialogical Body Politics," in *Bakhtin and the Human Sciences,* ed. Michael Mayerfeld Bell and Michael Gardiner (London : Sage Publications, 1998), pp. 95–111.

7. Bakhtin, *Problems of Dostoevsky's Poetics,* p. 252 (emphasis added).

8. In François Jullien, *The Propensity of Things,* trans. Janet Lloyd (New York: Zone Books, 1995), p. 124, Jullien observes that Chinese reason does not function in the same way as Western reasoning. "Chinese reasoning," he writes, "seems to weave along horizontally, from one case to the next, via bridges and bifurcations, each case eventually leading to the next and merging into it. In contrast to Western logic, which is *panoramic,* Chinese logic is like that of a possible journey in stages that are linked together." In other words, Chinese reasoning is pragmatic, concrete, existential, and inductive, whereas Western reasoning is theoretic, abstract, essentialist, and deductive.

9. See Fred Dallmayr, *Beyond Orientalism: Essays on Cross-Cultural Encounter* (Albany: State University of New York Press, 1998). See also my *The Question of Rationality and the Basic Grammar of Intercultural Texts* (Niigata: International University of Japan, 1989). Edward W. Said's *Orientalism* (New York: Pantheon

Books, 1978) is an influential critique of the ideology which places the West at
the center of world culture and power and marginalizes the non-West.

10. Maurice Merleau-Ponty, *Signs,* trans. Richard C. McCleary (Evanston, Ill.:
Northwestern University Press, 1964), p. 139. See particularly "Everywhere and
Nowhere," pp. 126–58.

11. Ibid., p. 128.

12. Ibid., p. 120.

13. See Claude Lévi-Strauss, "The Scope of Anthropology," in his *Structural
Anthropology,* vol. 2, trans. Monique Layton (New York: Basic Books, 1976), pp.
3–43.

14. Deleuze and Guattari, *What Is Philosophy?* p. 85. The most classic work
on phenomenological geophilosophy is Gaston Bachelard's *The Poetics of Space*
(Boston: Beacon Press, 1969). Bachelard's poetics reverberates with the "sonority
of Interbeing," as it were. For a recent comprehensive and systematic contribution of phenomenology to geophilosophy in Bachelard's tradition, see Edward S.
Casey, *Getting Back into Place* (Bloomington: Indiana University Press, 1993), and
The Fate of Place (Berkeley and Los Angeles: University of California Press, 1997).

15. When Homi K. Bhabha entitles his major work *The Location of Culture*
(New York: Routledge, 1994), he means to treat culture as a geophilosophical
idea.

16. See my "Phenomenology and Body Politics," *Body and Society* 2 (1996): 1–
22. For Merleau-Ponty, psychoanalysis needs the concept of the flesh, whereas the
body is an anthropological idea. According to him, "a philosophy of the flesh is
the condition without which psychoanalysis remains anthropology." See Maurice
Merleau-Ponty, *The Visible and the Invisible,* ed. Claude Lefort, trans. Alphonso
Lingis (Evanston, Ill.: Northwestern University Press, 1968), p. 267.

17. See François Dosse, *Empire of Meaning,* trans. Hassan Melehy (Minneapolis: University of Minnesota Press, 1999), p. 130.

18. Merleau-Ponty, *The Visible and the Invisible,* pp. 139–40. We would be re-
miss if we failed to recognize the difference between Merleau-Ponty and Deleuze
and Guattari concerning their respective conceptions of the earth. For Merleau-
Ponty, the earth is one element among others, whereas for Deleuze and Guattari
it is the all-encompassing element of all elements.

19. See Luce Irigaray, "Love between Us," trans. Jeffrey Lomonaco, in *What
Comes after the Subject?* ed. Eduardo Cadava, Peter Connor, and Jean-Luc Nancy
(New York: Routledge, 1991), p. 170.

20. See Adrienne Rich, "Notes toward a Politics of Location (1984)," in her
Blood, Bread, and Poetry (New York: Norton, 1986), pp. 210–31.

21. For extended discussions of the Weberian theme of "the disenchantment
of the world" (*die Entzauberung der Welt*), including the desacralization of nature,
see particularly Mircea Eliade, *The Myth of the Eternal Return,* trans. Willard R.
Trask (New York: Pantheon Books, 1954); Morris Berman, *The Reenchantment
of the World* (Ithaca, N.Y.: Cornell University Press, 1981); and Marcel Gauchet,
The Disenchantment of the World, trans. Oscar Burge (Princeton, N.J.: Princeton
University Press, 1997).

22. Deleuze and Guattari, *What Is Philosophy?* p. 104. An unusually perspicacious non-Cartesian contribution to the discourse of nature is Robert Pogue Harrison, *Forests: The Shadow of Civilization* (Chicago: University of Chicago Press, 1992). "An identical 'humanism' [anthropocentrism]," he writes, "underlies both Cartesian rationalism and the [French Enlightenment] encyclopedia's empiricism, a humanism that finds fulfillment in what Descartes called the mastery and possession of nature" (p. 118). For another sober and stimulating anti-Cartesian inquiry into the moral sense of nature, see Erazim Kohak, *The Embers and the Stars* (Chicago: University of Chicago Press, 1984).

23. Cartesian epistemocracy based on the cogito is necessarily ocularcentric as well as disembodied and egocentric/monologic. In pursuit of "clear and distinct ideas," which happen to be all visual terms, there is in the cogito the transparent identity between the mind's *I* and the mind's *eye*. The cogito is unmistakably *video ergo sum*. It is interesting to note that there are two ways of translating the notion of 'subjectivity' into Chinese: *zhu/guan/xing* and *zhu/ti/xing*—both in three ideograms. The middle ideogram (*guan*) in the first stands for visualized "ideas," whereas the middle ideogram (*ti*) in the second is "body" signifying subjectivity as already embodied. Li Zehou, who is China's foremost aesthetician today, coined "subjectality" for *zhutixing* in order to distinguish it from "subjectivity" for *zhuguanxing*. Subjectality is for him the material and embodied foundation of subjectivity: the former informs the latter. See Li Zehou, "Subjectivity and 'Subjectality': A Response," *Philosophy East and West* 49 (1999): 174–83. In the long-established and venerable tradition of Confucianism, the good (ethical) and the beautiful (aesthetic) are inseparably linked by way of harmony: What is good is beautiful, and what is beautiful is also good. Moreover, "humaneness" or "benevolence" (*ren*), which is the highest Confucian moral virtue, is closely affiliated with music. For the youthful Nietzsche, too, music stands for a consummately aesthetic phenomenon. In *The Ideology of the Aesthetic* (Oxford: Basil Blackwell, 1990), Terry Eagleton is most suggestive when he sums up the Nietzschean legacy of the aesthetic (*aisthesis*) in two related ways: (1) the aesthetic is preeminently a carnal and performative affair; and (2) born of the discourse of the body and cultivated by the senses, it is the revolt of the body's praxis against the tyranny of the theoretical (*theoria*), which is purely spectatorial.

24. For my intimation to apply the idea of sociality to interspecific as well as interhuman relationships, see "Toward a New Humanism: The Politics of Civility in a 'No-Growth' Society," *Man and World* 9 (1976): 283–306. The first original work in English on Heidegger's philosophy of the earth is Vincent Vycinas, *Earth and Gods* (The Hague: Martinus Nijhoff, 1961). See also Michel Haar's recent study, *The Song of the Earth*, trans. Reginald Lilly (Bloomington: Indiana University Press, 1993).

25. Wing-tsit Chan, ed., *A Source Book in Chinese Philosophy* (Princeton, N.J.: Princeton University Press, 1963), p. 497. For my discussion of Sinism (Confucianism, Taoism, and Ch'an/Zen Buddhism) and geophilosophy, see "The Way of Ecopiety: An Essay in Deep Ecology from a Sinitic Perspective," *Asian Philosophy* 1 (1991): 127–40.

26. *A Sand County Almanac,* special commemorative ed. (New York: Oxford University Press, 1987), p. 203.

27. Ibid.

28. Schrag, *SP,* p. 109. If we were to define narrowly the notion of community as bonding or cementing of so-called rational beings alone, there would be no "biotic community" and we would be forever condemned to confine ourselves to interhuman relationships. In order to speak of interspecific relationships, we should bring the idea of communication down to primordial, prelinguistic, sensuous, and bodily contact. Listen to what Toni Morrison has to say: "No, it was not language; it was what there was before language. Before things were written down. Language in the time when men and animals did talk to one another, when a man could sit down with an ape and the two converse; when a tiger and a man could share the same tree, and each understood the other; when men ran with wolves, not from or after them" (Toni Morrison, *Song of Solomon* [New York: Penguin Books, 1977], p. 278). In other words, interspecific relationships are possible at the level of the sensible and sensuous, which is the locus of the bodily. See David Abram, *The Spell of the Sensuous* (New York: Pantheon Books, 1996); and Morris Berman, *Coming to Our Senses* (New York: Simon and Schuster, 1989).

29. See my "To Save the Earth," *Philosophy Today* 19 (1975): 108–17, and "Heidegger's Way with Sinitic Thinking," in *Heidegger and Asian Thought,* ed. Graham Parkes (Honolulu: University of Hawaii Press, 1987), pp. 217–44.

30. Maurice Merleau-Ponty. *Adventures of the Dialectic,* trans. Joseph Bien (Evanston, Ill.: Northwestern University Press, 1973), p. 205.

31. See my "Difference and Responsibility," *Phänomenologischeol et Forschungen,* special issue (1999): *Phänomenologie der Natur,* ed. Kah Kyung Cho and Young-Ho Lee, pp. 129–66. See also two classical works on the postmetaphysical or antifoundational subject of responsibility: Hans Jonas, *The Imperative of Responsibility* (Chicago: University of Chicago Press, 1984); and Werner Marx, *Towards a Phenomenological Ethics,* trans. Stefaan Heyvaert (Albany: State University of New York Press, 1992). "Difference and Responsibility" also explores the invaluable contribution of feminism to geophilosophy on the basis of "feminine difference." The heteronomic ethics of care or "earthcare," as Carolyn Merchant calls it in her *Earthcare* (New York: Routledge, 1996), marks "gynesis," which is coined by Alice A. Jardine in her *Gynesis* (Ithaca, N.Y.: Cornell University Press, 1985), both to valorize the feminine and to trace the genesis of things and ideas in the feminine. It is neither trite nor commonplace to emphasize the fact that feminism itself is a multiple phenomenon. For example, see Barbara Johnson, *The Feminist Difference* (Cambridge, Mass.: Harvard University Press, 1998). She writes that "conflicts *among* feminists require women to pay attention to each other, to take each other's reality seriously, to face each other. This requirement . . . places difference *among* women rather than exclusively between the sexes. Of course, patriarchy has always played women off against each other and manipulated differences among women for its own purposes. Nevertheless, feminists have to take the risk of confronting and negotiating differences among women if we are

ever to transform such differences into positive rather than negative forces in women's lives" (p. 194).

32. Because of its "enlightened" faith and optimism in the infinite progress of humanity even at the expense of nature, e.g., its economism and productivism, Marxism fares no better than its counterpart, possessive individualism. Both ideologies intend to milk nature to death, and the only difference between the two is the question of distributing the wealth that both intend to accumulate. Both capitalism and Marxism equally failed miserably in ecology. So far, Marxian socialism has failed to compete and to outpace capitalism, a situation which is called by Francis Fukuyama "the end of history." See my "Marxism and Deep Ecology in Postmodernity: From *Homo Oeconomicus* to *Homo Ecologicus,*" *Thesis Eleven,* no. 28 (1991): 86–99.

33. Mary Ann Glendon, *Rights Talk* (New York: Free Press, 1991), p. 76.

34. Michel Serres, *The Natural Contract,* trans. Elizabeth MacArthur and William Paulson (Ann Arbor: University of Michigan Press, 1995).

35. Jean-Jacques Rousseau, *Rousseau's Political Writings,* ed. Alan Ritter and Julia Conaway Bondanella, trans. Julia Conaway Bondanella (New York: Norton, 1988), p. 24.

36. Félix Guttari, *Chaosmosis: An Ethico-Aesthetic Paradigm,* trans. Paul Bains and Julian Pefanis (Bloomington: Indiana University Press, 1955), pp. 119–20.

5

The Ethics of the Glance

Edward S. Casey

M y topic in this chapter is "The Ethics of the Glance." This title is doubly unlikely. First of all, I am not an ethicist—not by a long shot. I am a phenomenologist with special interests in aesthetics who has been much influenced by psychoanalysis and poststructuralism. Even worse, what can the glance have to do with ethics? How can anything so momentary and light-headed as a mere glance have anything important to do with something so momentous and serious as ethics? Does not the glance epitomize the superficial in human experience by concerning itself with the sheer surface of things, their gleam and glitter, and not at all with their depths? Is not the glance directed at the merely phenomenal—if not the sheerly epiphenomenal—rather than with the noumenal, wherein the ethical is supposed to find its foundation on a Kantian model? What can the glance have to do with the idea of the good or the intuition of the right? Given its fragile and fickle waywardness, how can it relate to what is a matter of principle, of imperatives and rules, normativities and values? What does the utterly impractical glance—so easily lured into any trivial pursuit—have to do with pure practical reason, which writes its own rationally sanctioned laws and speaks with the spirit of gravity?

Despite these plausible initial objections—some of them common-sensical, some coming from the philosophical tradition—I shall persist in pursuing my unlikely topic. I take special encouragement from two inspiring sources. Wittgenstein said memorably that "the depths are on the surface." William Earle, my mentor in philosophy, advocated the investigation of what he called "peri-phenomena": supposedly marginal phenomena that turn out to be far more significant than we might have imagined. Earle's own last book, *Evanescence,* is an eloquent case in point.

So that you will not think that I am off on the wildest of tangents, let me mention just to start with a fairly frequent experience that gives to the glance an initial place in the ethical domain. I refer to our sudden perception of someone as ethically exemplary. When I witness on the evening news a person who dives without hesitation into icy waters to save people whose plane crashed in a Washington, D.C., river, I see arrayed before me an exemplary instance of human heroism. I can tell from a glance at Frank Hurley's haunting photographs of the ill-starred Shackleton expedition to Antarctica that extraordinary moral strength was at play in this drama of impacted polar ice. The same goes for many other less dramatic actions of which a mere glimpse suffices to tell me that they are ethically exemplary in some particular way: such as a gesture of sheer generosity (at Bennington's in Chicago one night a waiter told me he was not charging me for dinner: He just "felt good that day").

The striking thing about exemplary actions—and this is true of those that are aesthetically or politically as well as ethically exemplary—is that a mere glance suffices to persuade us of their indisputable value. In part, this is because they are not mere tokens of a type that would invite comparisons with other such actions; they bristle with the type itself. They are the very essence of being or doing good, creating beauty, acting in a politically efficacious way. Think of films of Picasso or Matisse painting; or photographs of Gandhi practicing satyagraha. Because the type is present in the token, fully present there, I can grasp it by the bare perception of the token. This stands in contrast with all those cases in which I must *infer* what is right to do, or beautiful to create, or politically efficacious to enact: either by putting an individual instance under a preexisting rule, or by collecting many such instances to argue for a general law of the good or the right or the beautiful. Precisely because of the immediacy of its perception, I am all the more likely to want to undertake the same kind of action myself: The exemplary, grasped in a glance, is always exemplary *for me,* carrying with it the implication that I, too, this mere glancing witness, can do these things. The ethical force is not just that of observation but of internalization and change within myself.

Martin Buber writes that "in the deadly crush of an air-raid shelter the glances of two strangers suddenly meet for a second in astonishing and unrelated mutuality; when the All Clear sounds it is forgotten; and yet it did happen, in a realm which existed only for that moment."[1] Here Buber captures the gist of the matter, adding that "even in the tiniest and most transient events which scarcely enter consciousness," something important between human beings transpires—important both for ethical enactment and for a phenomenology of the ethical itself.[2]

Some Instances

My strategy is to present you with various peri-phenomenological instances of the glance as it figures formatively into ethical situations. Several of these situations come from life on city streets; others from the natural environment. These are very different contexts, yet they share one thing in common: the unsuspected power of the glance in ethically charged circumstances.

As it so happened, I began writing on the glance on Martin Luther King Day this past January. All that King did—all the changes he instituted—came from his concrete perceptions (and those of others inspired by him) that injustice was being done in very specific ways: ways so specific that they could be gleaned in a glance. Just walking onto a bus in the Deep South in the 1950s showed in an instant the reality of Jim Crow seating policies; the same was true of segregated classrooms, segregated restaurants and theaters and businesses—and of the bathrooms and water fountains found in each of these institutions. As we say revealingly, "a moment's notice sufficed" to see the pervasiveness and tenacity of such segregationist practices. A glance was quite enough. Enough to ignite outrage for all who had eyes to see. Not that it had not been seen before. But given the right overall situation—given a certain readiness in the social and political environment—the particularly powerful look of a moral leader such as Martin Luther King, Jr., could detect instantly what was wrong and how to go about remedying it. As he proceeded to do—over years and years of concerted and engaged exemplary action. In order to enlist others in this action, he had to get them to take in the awryness of segregation: He had to get them to glance, too. Change came from the massive concatenation of all these onlookers—all those who took the time, the intense moment, to look evil in the face and to take certain decisive actions—until the very laws of the land were changed in response to this vast canvas of interwoven glances.

Of course, gaining civil rights for blacks was a massive historical event with many determinants, among which the immediate confrontation with evil was only one ingredient. Granted. Yet have we ever fully pondered how crucial this confrontational moment can be? Sartre singled out the brief moment early in the French Revolution when tiny groups of three or more citizens gathered on street corners to form the critical "groups in fusion" that, linking up with other such groups, made the revolution as a whole happen. But this moment—which is the moment of the glance, with the concerned citizens exchanging glances even as they exchanged heated words—is itself swept up and lost in the larger movement of *The Critique of Dialectical Reason,* the book in which the very idea of such groups in fusion was first set forth in 1960, premonitoring the social movements of the decade to come.

A minor and personal but no less revealing episode in the same vein from later in the same decade comes to mind. It was 1967 and in Chicago (where I was then a graduate student at Northwestern): I was walking back from the El to get to my apartment on Hudson Street when I suddenly noticed a man beating up a woman across the street, striking her head repeatedly against a car. I saw this at a glance, I felt it was wrong, I walked right over to the scene—and my merely heading toward the couple in such a concerted way distracted the man sufficiently so that the woman could flee. He was trying with his glances back at me to figure out what kind of a threat I posed. Rash behavior on my part? Probably. I might have made things *worse* for the woman, and endangered myself to boot. But my point is not about appropriate or effective behavior. It is about the glance that precipitates conduct, wise or not. Not just *at* a glance but still more important *in* the glance, I saw injustice occurring; I saw immediately that things were not right in that street scene; what I did about it was something else, but it certainly followed from the initiatory moment of the glance.

Emmanuel Lévinas would probably hold that this Chicago street scene is an instance of his notion of justice as requiring a "third" (*le tiers:* curiously, the same term used by Sartre in his description of a group in fusion, in which each member is a third in relation to the other two). As he says in a 1981 conversation with Philippe Nemo, "How is justice possible? I answer that it is the fact of the multiplicity of human beings, the presence of the third beside the Other, which is the condition for laws and institutes justice."[3] Justice implies judgment, and judgment (as we know from Kant) is a synthesis of concepts, that is, another kind of thirdness. On that Chicago street I was the third who judged the couple to be engaged in a damaging circumstance that was manifestly unjust (given that the greater strength of the man was being employed to hurt the woman in a truly dangerous way; she may well have provoked his anger, but the particular expression of that anger was injurious as well as unjust).

Lévinas distinguishes stringently between such a situation of justice—in which equality of treatment is always at stake—and ethics proper.

In ethics proper there is no third person who judges; indeed, there is no judgment yet, nor even any concepts at play. Instead, there is "the ethical relation," which is not mediated by any concept or judgment. The concrete form taken by this ethical relation is that of the face-to-face, in which my face confronts another's, each in an essential "nudity" that implies not just lack of clothing but the absence of any justifying apparatus whereby the Other can arrogate worldly power over me. On the contrary, the Other appeals to me in his or her destitution, need, poverty—commanding me in effect to help him or her. This means that I am not "for myself" (as Sartre had insisted in *Being and Nothingness*) but "for the other" (in Lévinas's phrase) and thus ready to substitute myself for that other—as I was doing in effect on Hudson Street: putting myself in the place of the woman as the potential target of her male friend's wrath. (Fortunately, he decided that I was not worth the trouble to mess with; but by that time, the woman had disappeared.)

In the ethical relation of being face to face with the Other—the other with a capital "O", the Other as both transcendent and infinite in regard to myself—I am in "proximity" with him or her: not in spatial nearness (that is a matter of literal "interval") but in genuine intimacy. Here I should like to ask Lévinas: Is not the glance, mine to the Other, the Other's to me, part of this intimacy, thus integral to the ethical relation?

Contributions of the Glance

Perhaps you are willing to grant that the glance may at least play an important role in the very first moment of ethical encounter. In this role, it sets the stage for considered ethical thought and reflection. Not that these things happen in some simple sequence. Often, they happen together, all at once. No sooner did I see that woman in distress than I began to act; here there was no separate moment of reflection. Had I not glanced at what was going on, I would not have acted; but once I had glanced, action ensued. In such a case as this, ethical action is not precipitated by sheer thought but by concrete perception. More generally, there needs to be a compelling call for action before action itself is undertaken; and this call is often first grasped in the moment of the glance. (It may also be *heard*, as in a cry of distress; but then we have to do with the auditory equivalent of the glance—for which there is, significantly, no exact word in European languages: The power, even the linguistic power, is accorded to the glance. This is not, I think, a simple case of oculocentrism.)

Beyond its special virtue as the opening moment of ethical action, what are the specific contributions of the glance in ethical life? Here I shall single out only a few aspects of what is in fact a very complex situation:

1. The glance provides direct *access* to the Other: to his or her mood, thought, interest, attitude at the moment: what the Other *feels* right now. This is crucial for ethics, since, as Scheler has argued, ethical values are conveyed by emotions as their "bearers" (*Träger*): To get a glimpse of a particular emotion is to get a sense of what ethical issue is at stake.

2. The glance also captures a sense of *less manifest* aspects of the Other, say, the darker thoughts (beyond the physical fear) of that woman who was being pummeled; here something is "intimated," as we say. In this case, the glance exercises its penetrating power, its ability to go *under* the manifest phenomenon—yet still staying on the perceived surface and without any interpretive activity on my part. Here, indeed, the depths are on the surface.

3. This is not to mention certain telltale *signs* which the glance picks up instantly and which may be pertinent to ethical activity: class, gender, race, way of dressing (betokening niche within class), even educational level; these are external indicators of the Other's identity, history, and present milieu; they are often (I do not say always) evident in a glance, and they have everything to do with my ethically tempered behavior.

4. Not to mention, either, the *exchange of glances* that may be extremely relevant to ethical matters; in this dense dialectic, the Other shows himself only insofar as he engages my glance with his; and it is the engagement itself, its duration and quality and direction, that becomes significant for ethical thought and action. (Strangely, for all his emphasis on the importance of the face-to-face relation, Lévinas does not attend to the *interchange* of glances—a curious lacuna that can only be explained by his focus on the first-person experience of the ethical actor: I in relation to You in your destitution.)

In these four ways—of which I here give only cursory indications— the glance can be said to *give witness* to the Other: to testify to that Other's compelling and demanding presence in the ethical field. The witness given by the glance is to the *place of the Other.* By "place" I do not mean merely location but something far more complex, namely, the situation of the Other vis-à-vis myself—a situation which Lévinas designates expressly as "ultimate."[4] It is ultimate because there is no further court of appeal in the ethical relation (again in contrast with justice, which is a matter of lawyers and courts, judges and concepts). Rather than comment on the situation, much less pass judgment on it, in the ethical relation I am there primarily to witness to the suffering of the Other: I say "witness *to*" and not just "witness," for here it is not a matter of sheer observation (which would unduly objectify the situation) but of being there *for the Other*, assuming responsibility for his or her suffering and need. To be there for the Other in this testimonial sense is accomplished in the blink of the eye, the *Augenblick* effected by the glance. To glance at the Other is to give witness to that Other—immediately and unconditionally, without any compensatory action, any reward or even acknowledgment, expected or required on the Other's part.

At the same time, and by the same bare glance, I *welcome* the Other: the Other, who, no matter how fortunate in other regards, is nevertheless always in need of feeling welcome—indeed, *being* welcome. For all his stress on welcoming (in many ways it is the inaugural ethical move), Lévinas does not tell us anything about how this is concretely accomplished, except to say that it occurs in intimacy and especially in feminine gentleness.[5] But this intimacy and gentleness, and their many successors in every subsequent act of welcoming, surely include the glance as a constituent part of their operation: In welcoming the Other into one's domestic domain, the glance is the minimal but powerful opening moment. (Such welcoming is the converse of the threatening that is also a resident power of the glance, as we know from the animal kingdom as well as from dangerous street scenes.)

In spite of his explicit recognition of the centrality of witnessing to, and welcoming of, the Other in the ethical relation—they are in effect its double pillars—Lévinas does not spell out the exact ways by which these are accomplished. I submit that they are realized in the fourfold way I have just outlined—the way of the glance. The glance fills the void left by Lévinas's refusal to consider the precise means by which witnessing and welcoming occur. In this regard, it is the missing member of any complete description of the ethical relation.

The Relevance of Perception

The primary reason for Lévinas's conspicuous neglect of the glance is not far to seek. It arises from his critique of perception as a form of knowledge. Ethics, however, is not a matter of knowledge; no amount of knowledge of the Other will help one to become ethical in relation to that Other. Instead, the ethical is a matter of desire, and desire bears on what transcends the known or knowable.[6] If this is the case, then any approach to the Other as an object of knowledge, as something thematically or synoptically grasped, is bound to miss the (ethical) mark.

EDWARD S. CASEY

I do not know if one can speak of a "phenomenology" of the face, since phenomenology describes what appears. By the same token, I wonder if one can speak of a look (*un regard*) turned toward the face, for the look is knowledge, perception. I think, rather, that the access to the face is ethical straight off.[7]

Lévinas adds that "the best way to encounter the Other is not even to notice the color of his eyes"—or, for that matter, his nose, forehead, or chin.[8] Any such perceived feature of the face takes us down the primrose path of the knowable and the representable, and thus away from the true path of ethics, for "the Infinite does not show itself."[9]

This is a moment of double crisis. On the one hand, Lévinas here departs from phenomenology—his discipline of origin—while, on the other hand, he denies any relevance of perception to the ethical relation as this is embodied in the face-to-face encounter. In short, he rejects a phenomenology of perception as playing any significant role in ethics. I wish to show, on the contrary, that such a phenomenology (and thus in effect *all* phenomenology—as Derrida argues in *Speech and Phenomena*, "phenomenology . . . is always phenomenology of perception") remains not just relevant to ethics but essential to it, both in its delimited human format and in a more extended sense as is found in the ethics of the environment.[10]

Despite his outright denial of any place for perception (and thus for the glance as the vanguard act of perception), Lévinas ends by conceding a place for a certain delimited form of perception. In a conversation with Philippe Nemo, published in English under the title *Ethics and Infinity*, Lévinas speaks of the face as "a signification without a context," as "uncontainable" within the bounds of perception, as a "rupture" with perception, and so forth.[11] Indeed, "one can say that the face is not 'seen' (*vu*)."[12] Yet later in the same interview, Lévinas says suddenly that "there is in the *appearance* of the face a commandment, as if a master spoke to me"![13] Now I ask you: How can there be an "appearance" (*apparition*) without a perception of that appearance? A nonperceived appearance makes no sense at all; and if this is so, then surely perception is, after all, ingredient in the relation to the face.

That Lévinas himself is not entirely averse to this conclusion is indicated by a further remark he makes that bears specifically on perception:

The relation with the face can certainly be dominated by perception [indeed, he is conceding that it *is* so dominated], but that which is specifically face is that which cannot be reduced to it.[14]

Lévinas also remarks:

Access to the face is not of the order of perception pure and simple, of
intentionality that aims at adequation.[15]

In the first statement, Lévinas admits the very great difficulty of
separating out perception from the ethical relation to the face; by saying
that the relation cannot be *reduced* to perception, he is backhandedly
admitting that perception remains the natural conduit for this relation—
that in which it comes clothed even if in the end the relation must doff
the clothing itself. And by speaking of "perception pure and simple" in
the second statement, he implies that there is some mode of perception
that is *not* so pure and simple and that might therefore be at stake in the
ethical relation with the Other's face.

What, then, would this impure and nonsimple perception be? Pre-
sumably, it would be the very thing designated as "apparition" elsewhere
by Lévinas. Let us call it (after Leibniz) *apperception,* a form of "petite
perception" that precedes and in any case undoes the otherwise invet-
erate tendency of full-blown perception to objectify—to be a matter of
knowledge, of comprehension and thematization, and so forth. In our
relations with the Other, apperception is always already at work. I would
like to suggest that the primary form it takes is the *glance,* which in its
mobile entrainment on the surfaces of things does not consolidate into
robust perception. Indeed, the glance deconsolidates obdurate perceptual objects with their determinate edges and sides, definite volumes and
weights, and so forth, thereby making possible the nuanced interplay of
apperceptions of which it is the continual outpost.[16]

Glancing at the Environment

I shall move to the environmental case first of all, before returning to
the street. James J. Gibson says suggestively that "the perception of the
[surface] properties of the persisting substances of the habitat is necessary if we are to know what they afford, what they are good for."[17] To
be "good *for*" is a species of *being* good. Gibson is intimating that an
ethics of the environment, one which concerns itself with what is good
for that environment as well as its intrinsic goodness, must attend to the
presenting surfaces of that environment. Ethical action must direct itself
at these surfaces if it is to be efficacious at all. For it is on these surfaces
that environmental problems will be made visible, and it is these same

surfaces that furnish the place where we must try to begin to cure them of their distress.

If vision indeed plays a central and not merely peripheral role in ethics, then the perception of surfaces will be crucial, whether these surfaces belong to human beings (especially their faces) or to the environing world. In either case, we pick up distress—the signal of difficulties of an ethical order—*directly from the surface.*

Now, surfaces are precisely where glances alight: in particular, we are drawn to glance at the distress etched on surfaces. This distress conveys itself to us as an imperative to change the material conditions of the environment so that its surfaces may no longer appear as diseased or damaged but fall back into their rightful healthy place. Surfaces have the requisite expressivity to be telltale signs of environmental malaise; they transmit this malaise to the watchful look of the person who cares about their destiny. They also have the requisite simplicity to reflect this same malaise in what Gibson calls an "ecological optics": The simpler the surface, the more it is able to convey complex contents, including those that bear on environmental disorder and depredation. We are reminded here of Lévinas's statement that "ethics is an optics."[18] Of course it is, if it is indeed the case that the primary instigator of ethical action is the glance, which *sees* distress expressed on the surfaces of human beings, animals, and other natural entities.

When I glimpse clear-cutting on a mountain slope or the dumping of waste in a swamp, I am witnessing disorder in the environment. The natural order itself is not just complicated but has been disrupted. I am witness to a *corpus contra naturam,* nature in manifest disarray. The distress I take in by my glance is that caused by environmental turpitude as this is reflected—expressively—in the surfaces shared by a given group of natural entities.[19] The signs of such distress are telling something to us; they are expressing a wound to the ecosystem, a tear in its fabric, an illness in the landscape.

To those who had eyes to see, the early effects of nineteenth-century industrialism in England and America were manifest in the country as well as in the city—as acute observers from Blake to Dickens, Thomas Cole to Thoreau, all saw so poignantly. These ecologists of perception, before there was any science of the subject, grasped in one fell glance the destruction that was billowing in the air and poisoning the ground. So we, too, at the beginning of this century can apperceive at once the ill effects of clear-cutting as well as the imperative to restore at least a semblance of the natural order of forest growth.

For a glance apperceives not just distress and disorder. It also picks up the imperative to do something about that disarray. Here we take the crucial step from being *noticeable* to being *compelling*. Certain surfaces of the environment are noticeably in trouble, and we see this at a glance; but we also grasp with equal celerity the ethical demand that we find a way out of this trouble. Analogues to this double-edged aspect of the glance abound: The practiced medical doctor knows by a mere glance what her patient is suffering from *and* that it must be treated in a certain way, the painter knows by the briefest of looks what is missing from his work and thus what has to be added to it to make it persuasive. The same goes for the poet and her text, the cook and the dish under preparation. In each of these cases, a bare apperception, a mere moment of attention, is enough to detect the problem and to know that a certain remedy must be pursued.[20]

To expressivity and simplicity of surface we must add one final factor that figures into the glanceful perception of environmental difficulties and the imperative to rectify them: the *intensity* of the conflict that engendered these difficulties. This factor is present as well in other ethically compelling circumstances. In that Chicago street scene, it was not just the noticing of the fight between the man and woman that drew me across the street but the intensity of the struggle—an intensity that betokened a dangerous and violent edge. Not dissimilarly, I once beheld the devastation wrought upon the slopes of the Crazy Mountains in Montana. My backpacking companion, David Strong, confirmed my apperception: There had indeed been a great deal of destruction here. In fact, he had already taken action against it, filing a suit on behalf of a local environmental action group that indicted the logging company for environmental infringements. From my own brief glance at this scene, I could not doubt the rightness of this action: The decisive and compelling evidence lay before me, set forth in the intense contrast between the healthy verdancy of growing trees and the mud-clogged patches of tree stubs. The apperception of disruption and the imperative for ecological action stemmed from the intensity of the scene itself, its devastated surfaces speaking dramatically to my dismayed glances. This intensity was such as not only to appall and anger any sensitive witness but to call out for action of the sort that my friend, more forthright and knowledgeable than I, had engaged in: Where I took in the interpellation, he acted on it overtly. But both of us started with the same dispiriting experience of a disrupted landscape whose imperative to undertake action was located *in the environment,* not in "the moral law within." The disruption was out there in the scarred surfaces of the land, and it drew my anxious glances *there*—there where something cried out to be done.

City Glances: Letting the Other Be

But back to the streets from whence we came. Back to Chicago—which is virtually nothing but streets—from the mountains of Montana, which is strictly streetless. Despite the diremptive difference in these two settings, the glance shows its acute ethical force in both.

On city streets human beings do a great deal of glancing about. To be on these streets is to be in a virtual Glance-orama, with everyone glancing every which way. Check this out for yourself: Notice how people glance up and glance down, they glance around and across, they glance all over the place. They glance at buildings and cars and the sky. They glance distractedly into thin air. But they glance above all at each other—and even here in very diverse ways, indirectly as well as directly, lewdly and reassuringly, furtively and straightforwardly.

It is the interpersonal street glance on which I shall concentrate here, leaving aside the larger thematics of urban looking. In this ordin-ary—and yet quite extraordinary—glancing, I see an unsuspected ethical significance. Ethical significance?! I have probably already strained your credulity to the breaking point. But is it not outright preposterous to claim that the bare, and often barren, glancing we do on the street is *ethi-cally* charged? It is one thing for the glance to discern intensely displayed environmental damage along with an imperative to do something about it. That is a tall enough order, but I hope to have convinced you of the rightness of my reading. It is another thing, however, to claim any ethical significance in the mere fact that people glance at each other as they pass each other by in the busy course of everyday life. *Absurdum per absurdum.* How can this possibly be?

But consider what these passing glancers ("slipping glimpsters," as DeKooning calls them) are really doing. They are not just noting the existence of others, or satisfying some idle curiosity in the manner of the classical nineteenth-century flaneur, or getting some good aerobic exer-cise as might happen more recently. They may be doing these things too, but they are also *acknowledging each other.* This is not merely to recognize others' sheer existence, but their being *as persons*—their personhood no less. It is to see the person in the face of the other: in that peculiarly po-tent surface in which the person expresses himself or herself and comes to gestural and visual and vocal articulation. A long shot, you will say. But consider further.

The key here is the *passing glance,* in which there is eye contact with the other on the street, even if this lasts only a few seconds. The effect is that of catching the other out of the corner of our eye. In casting such a glance, our interest is not in becoming better acquainted or in learning anything in particular about the other. Having no utilitarian purpose, the primary point of the passing glance is to acknowledge the other's being and, if the other returns the glance, to have one's own existence acknowledged as well. This involves a dialectic of the singular and the universal. In a passing glance, I affirm the other's being as a singular fact: I am looking *just at you* and *at no one else*. At the same time, I also affirm something much more expansive in scope: I also affirm you as a member of the human race, as (fully and truly) *another human being*. The singular you I recognize by my glance is not the autobiographically unique you— *that* I may know nothing about, since you are very likely to be a stranger to me on the modern street—but a singularity that manifests the universal of human being in just *this* place and at *this* time and with *this* flesh. My glance in effect salutes Everyone in You, and conversely You as Everyone.[21] This remarkable, yet frequently encountered, circumstance exemplifies the strange logic of the glance: Something quite exiguous, seemingly trivial, shows itself to be immensely significant in its scope and effect. A narrow defile opens onto a vast vista.[22] This is the very opposite of the law of diminishing returns, or any comparable entropic phenomenon of ineluctable exhaustion. It is, rather, a law of diminutive support, by which a quite undramatic and ordinary act leads to an extraordinary augmentation of being.[23] Such augmentation holds for many phenomena of the glance, whose brevity belies its enormous effectuality in the visual world.

In the case before us, a meager look assures us of our being human: We are upheld in the look of the other. Remember Buber: "In the deadly crush of an air-raid shelter the glances of two strangers suddenly meet for a second in astonishing and unrelated mutuality . . . in a realm which existed only for that moment." The importance of this moment exceeds what we might first imagine. We can grasp this importance from the counterfactual circumstance: a world in which others never offered any such confirmation of my human being—there would be a disturbing place indeed. Others' passing looks at me do not prove my existence— this is not necessary, being supplied by consciousness (as Descartes would argue) or by my body (as Merleau-Ponty would insist)—but they do act to *acknowledge* it. Without the confirming glances of others cast at me *en passant*, I would be less than myself: I would be adrift in a Sargasso Sea of generality in which my very identity, as well as my singularity, would be dissolved in a morass of indifference.

To be adrift in a sea of strangers who do not pay attention to me even in this minimal form is to experience anomie of an especially acute sort. I begin to wonder: Is there something wrong with me? Or worse, do I really exist? I certainly do not exist in the eyes of others—I seem to have lost my social being. It is one thing for these others not to speak to me: This is too much to expect if I have recently come to town or am in a district where I am not known. But for them not even to glance at me! This seemingly trivial loss of visual support is in fact a dead serious matter. The others, on whom I count for at least momentary confirmation, might as well have killed me off.[24] But I can be restored to life by the merest passing glance, which acknowledges me to be the singular universal which I am for the other—and the other is for me when I glance back at that same other.

Not that this mutual confirmation always happens. Sometimes the glance, even the passing glance, is lacking. I set out for a stroll near my apartment on North Winchester, and I cannot help but notice the rarity of any significant glance received in the street. Not only are looks averted; I do not even encounter the "blank stare." Indeed, I am confronted with *no look at all,* no noticeable glance either given or received. The street on which I am living seems swept clean of the glance: The Glance-orama is empty.

I begin to suspect that I am not even worth a glance! For I am here experiencing not just a lack of glances exchanged but a situation of *no glance at all:* a no-looker in short! It feels almost as if I were being given a lesson in HOW NOT TO GLANCE! Or shall we call it "the art of glancing away"—so radically far away that I cannot even catch the first glimmering of a glance, much less any effective follow-through.

Admittedly, this situation is an extreme case and reflects a quite specific historical moment in a quite specific place. On other streets, in other cities and at other times, I find a great deal more glancing going on. All is not lost in the glance-world. Nevertheless, there is today in almost any city a sizable reduction of the glance's public presence, compared not just to the great boulevards of a century ago but also to the small town sidewalks that were a central feature of life in the Middle West during my youth. In the latter case, people not only looked at each other with open eyes but often stopped to talk as well: Indeed, they *lingered* to talk.

I do not wish to wax nostalgic. Times have certainly changed; but, short of the desperation of my experience in north Chicago, one will usually find in cities a modicum of glancing going on: Enough, at least, to say that walkers are acknowledging each other's presence by their looks *en passant.* Standard ways of glancing in public may be less conspicuously and less openly pursued than they once were, but the role of glances exchanged on city streets has not fallen altogether fallow.

This bare remnant is more important than it may seem at first. A failure to look at the other person, albeit just in passing, is a failure to affirm that other as a fellow member of the species. I would go so far as to say that there is an *obligation* to acknowledge the other by one's mere look: quite apart from, and well before, any obligation to say or do other things. We owe it to our fellow beings—before we owe them anything else—to affirm their presence before us and with us. A glance at another person in the street (or anywhere, for that matter) is the *first* sign of respect for that person. This is why the withholding of the glance can be so puzzling and so painful. The reclusion of the look amounts to an exclusion of the unacknowledged person from the sphere of the human: it is acting as if the unacknowledged other did not belong to the Kingdom of Ends, as if You were not an integral part of Everyone. There is much more at stake in the glance than meets the eye of the beholder.

A brief example illustrates this. A woman of my acquaintance lives in a "dangerous" neighborhood in south Chicago. When she is out walking on the street, she sometimes passes by gangs of young men gathered at a street corner. Instead of looking the other way, she makes sure that she looks at each member of the gang: not defiantly but just to acknowledge their being there. At one level, she takes this to be an ethical obligation; at another level, it is quite effective in a much more practical way: Those at whom she looks realize that she is not cringing before them or trying desperately to bargain for her safety (both of which ploys might invite the very violence they are explicitly trying to avert). Her assuring look encourages others to regard her as a person who shares a common humanity rather than as someone who is an object of prey.[25]

Acknowledging the other person by means of the glance means taking in this other *as a person*—not only as a (singular) member of a (universal) species but as someone who is on the way to becoming something other than she has been so far. Just by recognizing the other as other in the glance, I free that other to be herself: *I let that other be by my glance.* By looking alone, I in effect release this other to be the person she wants to be, tacitly encouraging her to *become* the very person she is capable of bringing into being. This is a version of what W. B. Yeats calls the "brightening glance" that transfigures what it sees.[26] My mere glance sanctions the other to become still more other—still more singular than singular, still more his or her own person (though not more universal: there are no degrees in this latter case). The converse of this is the fixated and fixating stare that confines the other to how the other appears on just this occasion, as if it were definitive for all future occasions.

The stare—a species of the gaze—reduces the other to the realm of *appearing*. It embodies the spirit of gravity, which delimits and pins down. The glance that acknowledges affirms the other as other, a matter of *being*. At the same time, it alleviates the other with its light touch, allowing the other to realize an otherness previously unknown to himself or herself: and this is an issue of *becoming*. Contributing to the being and be-coming of the person and not merely to its appearing, the glance—even (and especially) the passing glance—shows itself to be a major player in the ethical arena.

The Glance in Relation to Character

An appreciative but skeptical reader of an earlier version of this chapter had this to say: "No conscious reflection [is needed in] the glance . . . [because] a lifetime of character formation, of the development of con-science, previous experiences of manifest injustice, parental or other examples, the moral imperatives of religion—all these and more must have operated in the choice before you [on Hudson Street]. To be sure, the glance was enough to move you, but only because it exposed a moral nerve, so to speak. Another man [i.e., with another kind of moral nerve, or with little such nerve at all] would have [stayed] on the other side of the street, like the Pharisee in Jesus's parable of the Good Samaritan."[27] My friend adds: "A glance at a virgin forest may rejoice a man's heart for different reasons, one of which might be the chance of making a fortune in cutting it down. Think of the first viewers of the great redwoods! Maybe a glance of awe and thanksgiving, but as likely a calculation of board-feet. No, without 'the moral law within,' there is no [respect for the] landscape. The glance is the trigger, not the powder or the gunsight." My good friend makes a powerful point, and it is best to confront it squarely before drawing any smug conclusions as to the ethicality of the glance. He is certainly right to insist that the glance which is sensitive to ethically charged situations cannot be naive—a matter of a chance encounter or some arbitrary whim. It must be a glance that knows what it is doing: not consciously, much less reflectively, but nevertheless effec-tively. It must *know its way about* in the ethically challenging circumstance. It must have discernment of an ethical sort if it is to be a glance that instigates effective action instead of merely noting the circumstance. But how does this happen? What enables the glance to be so adroit in the ethical realm—or so maladroit in the case of the entrepreneur with board-feet eyes?

It is undeniably true that without an extensive, or at least intensive, moral education no glance (or any other ethically relevant action) could be consistently effective. It is a matter of a "knowing look," not of a literal "first look" that has no idea what it is looking at or what the stakes are. One is not born with a knowing look; it arises from the very experiences mentioned by my friend: the exemplary actions of others, religious injunctions, the cultivation of conscience, and so forth. All of this makes up our ethical *Bildung*—the history of the formation of our character. The difficult question becomes how such *Bildung*, which arises from the long haul of one's whole life, finds its way into something so merely "passing" as a glance: how it seeps into the extremities of one's active body, one's eye or hand or foot, informing them with its practical wisdom.

What Aristotle terms *hexis* is the crucial formative factor. By means of the slow acquisition of the right habitual actions—learned from example as well as precept—one's "customary body" literally incorporates the ethical, which insinuates itself into the appropriate sinews of one's "momentary body."[28] One comes to act as one is formed. One does not have to reflect on what one has already become. Instead of thinking on it, one acts on it. *Ça suffit.* If it is true that (as Heidegger affirms) thinking is in the hands, it is equally true that ethics is in the eyes.[29] Far from inhibiting the glance, it inhabits it.

Rather than a model in which ethically informed character is self-contained—confined to pure practical reason (as in Kant) or to the superego (as in Freud)—we ought to think of character as suffusing the entire person, especially the entire body of the entire person. Suffusing it right down to the toes of the feet (which propel one to cross the street or to stay on the same side), the fingertips (which tell us just where to direct our body vis-à-vis other tangible bodies), and the outer edges of our eyes (with which we glance about). Nor is it a matter of a complemental series in which we could say simply "the more of X, the less of Y, and vice versa." It is not as if the more (or better) our *Bildung*, the less the body needs to be involved. On the contrary: The more the one is acquired, the more the other will benefit and the more effective it will be. The glance may not be a reflective action—far from it!—but it *reflects* one's moral background, brings it to bear on any given occasion just as a mirror might refract a ray of light onto an object toward which it is tilted. The whole ray finds its way onto the surface of the whole object, just as the whole of one's ethical habitus comes to be concentrated in a single glance that falls on an ethically charged situation.[30]

Hence we cannot separate the trigger from the gunpower or the gunsight—in my friend's bellicose analogy. The trigger is an integral part of the circumstance of firing a gun. It is mechanical in nature, but it is not blind in its operation. For the finger that releases the trigger is an educated organ; it is as much a thinking finger as the glance is the activity of a knowing eye. The gunsight through which the marksman looks is not limited to the scope on the barrel of the gun but extends to his index finger, which has its own form of sight, and is completely continuous with the action of this finger. And the gunpowder that will explode when that action is taken is remarkably analogous to the habitual mass of inculcated responses: These, too, will be instantly released when the appropriate bodily action is undertaken—when the hand touches what needs to be felt, the foot steps forward forthrightly, and the eye glances with discernment.

The glance is indeed an instigator of ethical action, but it is a far more complex precipitating event than it usually presents itself as being. It instigates by being the delegated agent of a lifetime of ethical learning and practice. For nothing, not even the bare glance, is a mere mindless trigger in matters of morals. It is not that everything ethical is predetermined—hardly so!—but there is a decided proclivity to act in certain ways rather than others; the glance often leads the way, scouting out new circumstances in which to enact new versions of that deep penchant.

The ever-lengthening shadow of one's ethical *Bildung*, far from precluding a diversity of response on the part of different individuals, allows for it. The Pharisee and the redwood leveler are not simply unethical; they do not fail to see, much less to glance; but they see and glance differently from the Good Samaritan and the environmentalist, respectively. They look in accordance with their own habitus. We can criticize the intention and effect of this habitus—that is part of the task of ethical reflection—but we should not be dismayed, or even surprised, by such disparate responses. In fact, we should expect them in a world that does not enforce exactly the same stringent moral education on all its human inhabitants.

One result is certain. The celerity of the glance is not undermined by the formative influence of *Bildung;* rather, it is reinforced. It is just because one has so fully incorporated the pertinent principles and exemplary instances that one can glance so tellingly in such a brief span of time. In this case, we do observe a complemental relationship: the more deeply embodied the ethical upbringing, the less time one needs for reflecting on a new problematic situation—or even for deciding what to do in that situation.

In the same way, we can now understand better why the glance has been so neglected in ethical theory. The contrast between the *longue durée* of one's ethical formation and the alacrity of the glance has led philosophers to assume that the glance cannot be of any real significance for ethical action: How can something so literally momentary be of genuine moment for morally challenging circumstances? The glance is something of a Trojan Horse (or should we say a Trojan filly?): In its apparent innocence, it is admitted into the fortified walls of serious ethical life, only to show itself to be capable of decisive if not disruptive action within those walls.

The glance is not a creature of "the moral law within," but is itself an active agent of that law, its deputy in the visual world. The glance not only acts "in the eyes of the law"; *it is the very eye of the law,* its silent sentinel. It bears the moral law in incarnate form into the seen world—not just recognizing it there (as when an ethical imperative is grasped) but also carrying it out and realizing it in ever more effective ways.

Concluding Comments

Permit me to make six brief comments in conclusion:

1. If the glance is to play an important role in ethics—as I have been proposing—then it is at once more nuanced and more powerful than we are apt to admit if we are doing ethics in a traditional manner. It must be more *nuanced* if it is to be able to detect what is good or right to do in certain circumstances; not only must it sort out alternatives, but it must also bring to bear on these circumstances a history of previous looking. This history is culturally informed and socially instructed. A large portion of the nuance of the glance has to do with its being a discerning and knowing action, thanks to the continuing influence of the *Bildung* on which I have just put so much stress. It should be clear by now that I am not advocating a return to a guileless eye but, rather, recommending a renewed appreciation of the educated look. (Which includes the very real possibility of a *mis*educated look that sees only with bigoted eyes—that, instead of acknowledging the other as an intrinsically valuable being immediately, and in the glance itself, reduces that other to a shrunken and stereotypical image of that being: Black, Jew, Muslim, Southern Baptist, thereby losing all nuance.) But another portion of the subtlety of the glance stems from its status as an apperception which does not require whole stable objects as its specific content; as a mode of "petite perception," it penetrates into the interstices of robust perceptual objects—and things and persons and places—so as to comprehend their subtly wrought infrastructures.

The glance must also be more *powerful* than we are likely to suppose. If it is to make a difference in ethical life, it cannot be a mere registration of difference, much less the bare registration of fact. It has to be suffi-ciently forceful to do the active witnessing and welcoming I first ascribed to it, as well as to respond to environmental imperatives in the wild and to acknowledge other persons on the street. The basis of this power of the glance lies in its ability to seize its object instantaneously and to size it up—to see it for what it is and to sense its significance without hesitation or reflection. In large measure, this is a function of its culturally encoded state (again: the better grounded at a habitual level, the more swift and certain it can be); but it is also a matter of the glance's impatience, its refusal to linger, its saccadic swings from one item to another, its zigzag motions.

2. The combination of these two aspects of the glance—its nuance and its power—is sufficient to support another ethically relevant dimension of glancing, its *subversiveness*. Despite the embedding of the "acquired treasure" of character and culture in its very manner of looking, the glance does not always enact the commonly affirmed norms and values. It is under no compunction to submit to ethical conventionalities, but may question them and even act to undermine them. By a mere flicker of the eye, a modulation of its gleam, a redirection of its look, the glance may make clear its disdain for accepted normativities and its desire for something quite different. We say that "he has a certain devilish look in his eye," and we speak tellingly of the glance as "arch," "skeptical," "sardonic," "withering"—all of which are forms of visual subversion. The glance as lance: cutting down to size, cutting through social pretentiousness, hypocrisy and presumption. But also the glance as pointing to new directions of ethical conduct, adumbrating them if not explicitly articulating them. "Knowing where to glance" is not just knowing *how* to glance (which is a matter of skill and tact and personal history) but a reflection of where one wishes value to be placed and actions to be done. One thinks of the way in which young monks are trained in Zen monasteries in Japan. There, the leanest look of the master monk tells all: what should be done; in what style to do it; in what spirit; and with what state of mind.

3. Pondering these larger reaches of the glance, it becomes clear that we cannot regard it as something merely preliminary that precedes ethical action. Indeed, it is *part of the action itself.* It goes right to the imperative that calls out to it by its intensity. Not only does it detect this imperative; as a form of vigilance, it belongs to the action the imperative calls for. The matter is even more dramatically evident in glancing at others: In so doing, we actively recognize them as other. Here the acknowledgment is the action itself, not just part of it; which is to say that it is performative in character. In neither case, however, does the glance merely precede the ethically pertinent action: It inaugurates it and may even accomplish it. In my experience on Hudson Street, my glance uncovered a compelling circumstance, but it was itself noticed by those at whom it was aimed; their glances back at me (with their inherent effort to

figure out my intentions) were already forms of acting—acting differently than they would have had they gone undetected by my look. The point is not just that the glance makes a difference in such a circumstance; it is itself part of the difference it makes.

4. One aim of this essay is to recommend an expanded descriptivism in ethics. This is the imprint of my phenomenological heritage, first learned from William Earle, a master of close description. I have pursued the glance as a leading instance of a "peri-phenomenon" into some rather unaccustomed corners—as unaccustomed for ethics as for the glance itself. If we put ethics entirely under the heading of the prescriptive, then the unaccustomed will become the merely bizarre: For then there is no meaningful connection between what ought to be the case in ethics and what is in fact the case when ethics is enacted. There is no room for the glance in the abyss that separates the "ought" from the "is." But if we stay descriptive—which is not the same as staying merely factual, much less statistical—there will be room for the glance. Room enough not just to bear on the ethical but to bear out the ethical itself: to bring it into being with nuanced power.

5. Ironically, Lévinas is right after all, despite my own earlier-expressed reservations. Regarded as an integral part of ethical action, the glance is not just another perceptual act. Its ethical efficacity does not consist in its being a mode of perception per se; if anything, it is an apperception, and in any case, it has shown itself to be actional and not merely observational. But this does not mean (as Lévinas would doubtless insist) that the glance is not a form of knowledge (I have insisted on the knowingness of the glance) or that it is not synoptic (a single sweeping glance can be quite comprehensive). It can be both of these things and yet still remain inactive in essence—just as the fact that it takes only a moment to enact does not undermine its effectiveness in the actual world. The truth of the matter is that the glance cuts to the quick of the ethical matter; it belongs to what Lévinas calls pointedly the "ethical relation" and is not something standing apart from it.

6. This is not to say that the glance is *all* of this relation or that it makes up 100 percent of the action—nor even that it is the only factor of the quick at work in ethics (the hand, not to mention memory, can be equally dextrous and discerning). Of course not! But the quicksilver action of the glance, its mercuriality, allows it to get at the heart of the matter. It comes to this heart in a single moment of disclosure. This is not the moment of *kairos*—the time of the decision that turns time itself around—but the moment of such poignant apperception as to make a decisive difference in how we live out the ethical dimension of our lives.

Strange indeed, how such a puny action can make such a momen-tous difference. "Even in the tiniest and most transient events which scarcely enter consciousness" (in Buber's words once again) something ethically quite significant can happen. It can happen in a glance. This is the case whether we merely glance at a clear-cut forest or glance at others whom we pass rapidly in the street. Both ways, the law of diminutive support remains in effect. Little as the glance may look to be—it presents itself as the slenderest form of looking—it proves to matter a lot when we are being or becoming ethical. It matters a lot more than we might have thought . . . at first glance. . . .

Notes

1. Martin Buber, *Between Man and Man,* trans. R. G. Smith (London: Kegan Paul, 1947), p. 204. Buber also cites an example from the cultural realm. Two people are at an opera listening to Mozart. Between them is "a relation which is scarcely perceptible and yet is one of elemental dialogue, and which has long vanished when the lights blaze up again."

2. Ibid.

3. Emmanuel Lévinas, *Ethique et infini: Dialogues avec Philippe Nemo* (Paris: Fayard, 1982), p. 94 (hereafter cited as *EI*). Translations from this work are my own unless otherwise indicated.

4. "The face to face remains an ultimate situation" (Emmanuel Lévinas, *Totality and Infinity,* trans. Alphonso Lingis (Pittsburgh, Pa.: Duquesne University Press, 1969), p. 81 [hereafter cited as *TI*]).

5. See Lévinas, *TI,* pp. 155–58, 154–55. Strictly speaking, welcoming is part of dwelling and habitation, and is thus not yet ethical; yet the Other does here figure in the form of the "thou": "The Other who welcomes intimacy is not the *you* [*vous*] of the face that reveals itself in a dimension of height, but precisely the *thou* [*tu*] of familiarity: a language without teaching, a silent language, an understanding without words, an expression in secret" (Lévinas, *TI,* p. 155).

6. "Ethical witnessing is a revelation that is not [a matter of] knowledge" (Lévinas, *EI,* p. 114). He adds that "the relation to the Infinite is not [a form of] knowledge, but of Desire" (Lévinas, *EI,* p. 97).

7. Lévinas, *EI,* p. 89. Compare this statement: The Infinite "does not appear, since it is not thematized, at least not originally" (Lévinas, *EI,* p. 112).

8. See ibid., p. 89. I am grateful to Peter Atterton of San Diego State University for drawing my attention to this, and related passages, on the problematic perception of the face.

9. Lévinas, *EI,* p. 113. He adds: "It is by this witnessing, whose truth is not that of representation or of perception, that the revelation of the Infinite is produced."

10. Jacques Derrida, *Speech and Phenomena,* trans. D. Allison (Evanston, Ill.: Northwestern University Press, 1967), p. 104.

11. Lévinas, *EI,* pp. 90, 91. Elsewhere, Lévinas ties perception to the tendency to be comprehensive and synoptic: "The experience of morality does not proceed from [eschatological] vision—it *consummates* this vision; ethics is an optics. But it is a 'vision' without image, bereft of the synoptic and totalizing capability, a relation or an intentionality of a wholly different type" (Lévinas, *TI,* p. 23).

12. Lévinas, *EI,* p. 91.

13. Ibid., p. 93 (emphasis added).

14. Ibid., p. 91.

15. Ibid., p. 102.

16. Like sensibility—as the vanguard of sensibility itself—the glance "establishes a relation with a pure quality without support" (see Lévinas, *TI,* pp. 136, 137: "I enjoy this world of things as pure elements, as qualities without support, without substance"). The glance is also prerepresentational—again like sensibility and enjoyment: "Sensibility is therefore to be described not as a moment of representation, but as the instance of enjoyment" (Lévinas, *TI,* p. 136). The same is true of the glance, which does not represent but only grasps. It grasps not things but part-objects; thus the fact that the glance is prerepresentational goes hand in hand with its evasion of things (and thus sides of things). If "things have a name and an identity" (Lévinas, *TI,* p. 139), then they also have the status of something represented (cf. Lévinas, *TI,* pp. 138–40 for this linkage).

17. Lévinas, *EI,* p. 110.

18. See note 11 above. See also Lévinas, *TI,* pp. 29, 78 (where he speaks of a "spiritual optics"); on p. 174 he says:. "The 'vision' of the face is inseparable from [the] offering of language. To see the face is to speak of the world. *Transcendence is not an optics but the first ethical gesture.*" Peter Atterton suggests that "possibly, by 'optics,' he means something like the 'law' governing ontological vision, which would again suggest the primacy of ethics as the ground of ontology" (Peter Atterton, letter to author, November 12, 1998).

19. This is not to deny that appearances on this surface may be misleading—especially when their full virulence is still masked—but it is to emphasize that there is a great deal we can trust in our perception of environmental disorder: We can by and large rely on our "perceptual faith," as Merleau-Ponty calls it, or our "animal faith," in Santayana's term. (On perceptual faith, see Maurice Merleau-Ponty, *The Visible and the Invisible,* ed. Claude Lefort and trans. Alphonso Lingis [Evanston, Ill.: Northwestern University Press, 1968], pp. 50 ff.; on animal faith, see George Santayana, *Skepticism and Animal Faith* [New York: Scribners, 1923].)

20. Here the glance is strangely the counterpart of the earth, which, as Lévinas says, also suffices in its own way: "The earth upon which I find myself and from which I welcome sensible objects or make my way to them suffices for me. The earth which upholds me does so without my troubling myself about knowing what upholds the earth" (Lévinas, *TI,* p. 137). This last sentence could well be a statement about surfaces, about whose support we also do not concern ourselves; even the ground to which they ultimately relate is itself, as J. J. Gibson avers, a surface of its own.

21. On the strong but tacit collusion between the singular and the universal, see Gilles Deleuze, *Difference and Repetition,* trans. P. Patton (New York: Columbia University Press, 1994), esp. pp. 1–5, 189–213, 276–84.

22. The "narrow defile" refers to Freud's metaphor in the opening passage of chapter three of *The Interpretation of Dreams:* "When, after passing through a narrow defile, we suddenly emerge upon a place of high ground, where the path divides and the finest prospects open up on every side, we may pause for a moment and consider in which direction we shall first turn our steps" (Sigmund Freud, *The Interpretation of Dreams,* trans. J. Strachey [New York: Avon, 1998], p. 122).

23. I borrow the phrase "augmentation of being" (*Seinszuwachs*) from Hans-Georg Gadamer, *Truth and Method,* translation revised by J. Weinsheimer and D. G. Marshall (New York: Crossroad, 1991), p. 155.

24. To be confirmed by others in this way is the intersubjective equivalent of glancing at oneself in the mirror. Here, too, I am supported by a mere look back—in this case, the literal reflection of my own looking at myself. This look, stemming from me in the most spontaneous way, is captured in the mirror, held there in such a way as to acquire a momentary existence of its own. It is as if it had become, for a brief second, the look of another—hence our sense sometimes that it is the look of someone we do not know: Can this be me, we ask ourselves? This is an alienated look that seems to look back at me from its place in the mirror, a displaced place that is no longer my own. Developmentally, this is the moment of Lacan's celebrated "mirror stage," in which the emerging ego is built from its false identification with its own image, a merely fictitious and alienated version of a self that until then had been wholly fragmented and uncoordinated. Such identification is based on a fundamental *méconnaissance,* a failure of self-acknowledgment. For I am identifying with a petrified image of myself, a self who is in fact another: In Rimbaud's famous phrase (very much on Lacan's mind) "je suis un autre." I am an other because I do not recognize that I am in fact identifying with my own awkward, uncoordinated bodily self. For adequate acknowledgment to occur, I would have to realize that this mirror image is in fact *me,* albeit a me that is slightly distorted (e.g., in terms of right/left reversal) and more steadily presented than I experience myself by myself without a mirror. Short of this acknowledgment, my ego has gotten off to a false start; it is formed in a "fictionalized direction." But the importance of this bare recognition, however fraught with egological danger it may be, is again indicated by the shock I would experience if I glanced into a mirror only to see *no image of myself* at all there. I would be quite literally—visually—*wiped out* by this experience, self-blinded as it were.

25. My informant is Ginger, who does what I here report not just from the standpoint of the most effective strategy but because of an obligation she feels to acknowledge everyone she meets, including dangerous figures in the environment. My point in citing this example is not that this tactic always works or that it is always appropriate. Of course not. In other circumstances, it might well be ill-advised and even disastrous. But for the glance to play such an affirmative role as it does in Ginger's situation is nevertheless revealing of its persuasive power, its ethical force, even in a rather risky setting.

26. See W. B. Yeats, "Among School Children," in *The Poems: A New Edition,* ed. Richard J. Finneran (New York: Macmillan, 1983), p. 217. I am grateful to Richard Kearney for this reference and for suggesting the line of thought that is developed in this section of my chapter.

27. Comment in correspondence with Stanley A. Leavy, M.D., June 25, 1999. I am indebted to Leavy for his incisive remarks.

28. The terms "customary body" and "momentary body" are those of Merleau-Ponty. See Maurice Merleau-Ponty, *Phenomenology of Perception,* trans. C. Smith (New York: Humanities, 1962), pp. 142–47.

29. Martin Heidegger, *What Is Called Thinking?* trans. J. Glenn Gray (New York: Harper, 1968), p. 16: "Every motion of the hand in every one of its works carries itself through the element of thinking. . . . All the work of the hand is rooted in thinking." The original inspiration for Heidegger's statement is found in Aristotle, especially in his statement that "there is an analogy between the soul and the hand; for, as the hand is the instrument of instruments, so the intellect is the form of forms" (Aristotle, *De Anima,* trans. R. D. Hicks [New York: Arno Press, 1976], 432a, p. 145).

30. I am using "habitus" in Bourdieu's sense, which locates it between nature and culture as their essential intermediary. See Pierre Bourdieu, *Outline of a Theory of Practice,* trans. R. Nice (Cambridge: Cambridge University Press, 1977), pp. 72–85.

6

Decentered Subjectivity, Transversal Rationality, and Genocide

Bruce Wilshire

Schrag's Decentered Self

From Calvin Schrag's first book, *Existence and Freedom* (1961), until what I take to be his most recent, *The Self after Post-Modernity* (1997), his work exemplifies the basic insight that phenomenological description must precede scientific explanation. When this principle is ignored, we get premature and misleading explanation. The diversion typically takes this form: The coherence of the directly lived world is missed. The world is parceled out, partialed out, into reified abstractions. The most obvious divide isolates self, mind, ego, subjectivity, on the one hand, over against the material or "external" world on the other. Phony problems are generated: How can "nonextended" mind possibly influence "extended body," mine or any other's? How can minding self know there is anything beyond whatever is given in subjectivity—one's own privacy? Is there a world out there at all? How can value judgments possibly be true of ourselves and the rest of the world rather than being mere expressions of each of our subjective and idiosyncratic feelings and opinions? Et cetera.

Schrag's phenomenology restores the integrity of the world-immediately experienced and undercuts and collapses artificial polar oppositions and dichotomies. It explodes as well attendant reifications. The history of substantialism in all its forms is overhauled, particularly the notion of the autonomous self as the seat of pure reason, or as that which looks on while the phenomenal world is constituted out of eternal Ideas or by an Absolute Mind. The corollary is that the physical or extended world is regarded as the mere instantiation of eternal Ideas. The phenomenal presence of the physical world in all its amplitude, contingency, resistance, intimacy, and fluency—perhaps radiance—is cut into fragments and frozen, including one's own body as essential for one's self.

Thus premodern substantialist notions are discarded by Schrag, particularly the view of self (or Self or Mind) as center and ground of all reality and all knowledge. But also postmodern critiques of modernism are severely criticized by Schrag. He believes that the postmodernists have not husbanded the integrity of the world-phenomenon, but have themselves fallen into mindless dichotomies that, ironically, are left over from modernism: reason/irreason, universal/particular, self/nonself. As if the previously hidden member of Siamese twins were to be shockingly turned to the fore by the postmodernists. From supposedly all-unifying pure reason, they flip to the utter fragmentation of reason. From self they flip to the fear—or is it bravado?—that there is no self, no powers of unification or direction, at all.

Schrag gladly grants that the premodern idea of the substantial self must be discarded. But the postmodern notion of no-self does not follow. He plots a third way, his idea of a decentered self—all the while realizing that the notion of centeredness, and its companion decenteredness, is a crude spatial idea applicable only to an "external world" and its polarized companion, the "internal" domain.[1] He quotes William James in *Essays in Radical Empiricism,* "The world experienced . . . comes at all times with our body as its centre, centre of vision, centre of action, centre of interest." But on James's own idea of prereflective consciousness ("-sciousness"), body is not given at the center of the field of the world experienced, but as the ever warm and abiding presence on the margins of the field. Though marginal, it can usually be made central when occasion calls for this (when the body is injured, say). And even when marginal, it is the anchor of acts of abstraction, reasoning, and goal directedness when that is appropriate.

Connected most intimately with the concept of decentered self is that of transversal rationality.[2] Gone is the "autonomous rational subject" issuing dicta to the contingent world beneath it. Present is the idea of an earthbound and earth-navigating reasoning that cuts across petrified dichotomies, reifications, hierarchies. Schrag develops Sartre's appropriation of Husserl's early *The Phenomenology of Internal Time Consciousness,* the concept of intentionalities transversing the stream of consciousness; that is, the past immediately retained and the future immediately protended tie together to a considerable extent the recollected and anticipated time of one's whole life. Schrag also develops Charles Peirce's and William James's notion of reason as navigational "seat of the pants" reasoning that has evolved over millions of years because it has gotten us where we need to get often enough to satisfy basic needs and interests (see, e.g., James's "The Sentiment of Rationality"—rationality as the flowing of feelingful, working, discovering awareness). Given our survival needs, experience is self-organizing if it perdures at all. Also found throughout Schrag's work are key references to A. N. Whitehead and his ideas of prehension and creativity.

Transversal rationality is chastened rationality. It aims for convergence of viewpoints and interests, personal and cultural, instead of strict identity or isomorphism of them. It sorts the world into kinds, universals, but without assumptions concerning the ontological status of universals. It is an achievement of needy and interested body-selves intimately involved, more than likely mimetically engulfed, in the rest of the world. Rationality is an achievement of selves that are over their heads in the world.

As a great achievement it is also subject to great failure at any time. For example, Schrag quotes Félix Guattari on transversal rationality in groups.[3] How do the various staff members of a hospital, say, in their different roles and immediate interests, coordinate their activities to promote the welfare of the whole? A difficult task easily collapsing in failure. Moreover, since selves are not born autonomous, they can only hope for, and work for, moral autonomy. And since the individual's identity is all tied up with the identity of the group, any threat to the identity of the group body may translate into frenzied purging of anything perceived to be alien—genocide. Schrag's work opens this gruesome topic for further inquiry.

This philosopher's thought over his lifetime so far exhibits a marvelous consummatory sweep and balance. He recognizes that reason must be chastened, but to throw it away is mad. Likewise we must confront our finitude, vulnerability, contingency as bodily and social selves, but to simply discard belief in self—or to try to—is mad. We must recognize that our world has in fact fragmented into different spheres, the technological, the political-economic, the private, the institutional-religious. But to simply throw up our hands and despair over this malcoordination is senseless. We must find our way through the whole world. Without this, individuals, ineluctably social and communicative on so many levels, come unhinged.

The ultimate challenge to transversal rationality is to achieve transversal transcendence—not an idling on the top of an imagined pyramid, not an attempted domination of the spheres of human activity, but a connecting and chastened ordering of them insofar as they are knowable and changeable by us, a rationality that navigates and orients itself through them as best it can. Not to be swallowed up in one or other of

DECENTERED SUBJECTIVITY, TRANSVERSAL
RATIONALITY, AND GENOCIDE

these spheres requires the recognition that none of them is our ultimate concern, only preliminary and contingent. Our ultimate concern is with the ground of Being, that within which we emerge stage by stage, which sustains us every minute, and to which we will wholly return at death. Our ultimate concern is to be overfull, to pour ourselves out in unconditional respect and love, and to be prepared to receive it. If we cannot transcend contractual relationships—even subtle ones in which friendship is between equals who can expect to get, more or less, as good as they give—we will live stunted. We learn with little surprise that as a graduate student at Harvard years ago, Schrag was Paul Tillich's assistant—Tillich, the author of *The Courage to Be*. Tillich, also the author of *Systematic Theology*, in which the "God beyond the God of Theism" seems to be some complex notion of time.

One of Calvin Schrag's keenest insights into postmodernist thinkers is that some in this brightly bannered camp (e.g., J.-F. Lyotard) have muddled together the ahistorical and the transhistorical. In throwing out the former, they tend to throw out the latter. But to do that is to miss the abidingly human, our primal needs developed in the course of evolution. Our primal need for symbolical meaning distinguishes us from the other creatures, but does not separate us—not if we are wise.

"The Rational Animal" and Genocide

Calvin Schrag's development of the ideas of decentered subjectivity and transversal rationality gives us powerful clues in trying to grasp genocide. We need all the help we can get. Genocide seems so irrational. But there must be reasons. What are they?

By "genocide" I mean the systematic persecution of a group of persons simply because they are members of that group—men, women, children, infants, the unborn, it makes no difference. The ultimate in genocide is famously exemplified by Hitler's persecution of the Jews. After exterminating them from Europe, he apparently planned to rule the world and exterminate every last Jew from the planet. Would he have pursued them into outer space if he had thought some might be there?

Now why? In ordinary warfare the main job is to kill as many combatants as possible. In genocide, the "others" are killed indiscriminately. Now, sticking with the Jews example—unfortunately there are many other cases of genocide—it might be said that Jewish babies could grow up to be nefarious people of the Jewish sort, exploitative bankers, for instance. So kill them.

But all more or less "rational" explanations prove inadequate in the face of the palpable ferocity and fanatical frenzy of genocidal persecution. Thus, for example, Nazi-types, tools of the ruling junta in Argentina (1976–83), would at times press electric cattle prods into the engorged breasts of pregnant women charged with being "subversives." As one torturer is quoted, "The swollen nipple invites the prod." What is "rational" about that? But there must be reasons.[4] So what are they?

Radovan Karadžić, Bosnian Serb leader, said of the Muslims, on a television documentary, "They will vanish"—as his generals poured artillery shells into the Sarajevo hospital, including of course the maternity ward. They also targeted the great Oriental Museum and its irreplaceable manuscripts depicting the history of the Ottoman Empire, and the more recent history of multicultural coexistence in Bosnia. Every trace of Muslims, past, present, and future, was to be expunged—as Hitler had razed Jewish cemeteries, for example. All memory must be obliterated, all occasion for thought of them, and of their thinking.

I will not multiply examples beyond necessity. The point is not to spew them out and deceive ourselves that since the examples are horrifying, and we are suffering a little in recounting them, we must be understanding what is happening. The point is to grasp the peculiar horror of genocide, the sweep of it, the mad intensity and endurance of it. Three more examples may be sufficient.

Pol Pot ordered his communist militia into the capital of Cambodia, Pnom Penh, rounded up all the "corrupted, westernized intellectuals and merchants and their families" they could find, and led them into the surrounding rural areas where they killed them, about a million and a half of them, largely through clubbing (not wanting to waste ammunition on such trash). And by all accounts Pol Pot was an unassuming, quietly charming man living modestly, who until the day of his death assured himself and others that he did it all "for his country."[5]

The "lower caste" in Rwanda, the Hutus, finally gained the upper hand over the tall, "European-type Blacks," the Tutsis, after the colonializing Europeans left Africa. In just a few months over a million Tutsis were massacred, mainly by machetes.[6] But one incident is particularly memorable. Many of the bodies were dumped into a river leading north into Ethiopia, from where the Tutsis were believed to have originally come. One person reported seeing a woman's body washed up on shore. Tied to her arms and legs were four young children and infants. No other marks of violence showed on their bodies.

Finally, the indigenous peoples of what is now California were systematically exterminated by various Europeans. They had bounties placed on their heads, as if they were predatory animals. Festivals were held honoring their deaths.[7] Finally only one "wild Indian" was left, Ishi, protected by the anthropologist, A. L. Kroeber. He lived for a few years, and the job was done: They had all vanished.

When we postpone the search for explanation in terms of causes, and just describe in rudimentary ways what we see, salient features of genocide begin to appear. First, genocides can appear universally, or so it seems—they are not the province of any particular nationality or ethnic group (the genocide of the Armenians was perpetrated by people of Muslim belief, that of millions of Chinese landowners by Mao Tse-tung, etc.). This suggests that there is something about human identity itself which prompts genocidal frenzy under certain conditions. Second, the presence of others in the corporate body of the group—the presence of aliens—is intolerable to that group's identity and for many of its members. The others are extruded, exterminated, just because they are other. (Thus, Jews were considered germs infecting the corporate body of the German nation, *Volkskorper,* and ought to be exterminated.)[8] All of them must be persecuted, tortured, corralled for slaughter. (Animals kill, but not in order to kill all their prey.) Third—and with this we face the "under certain conditions" clause—in every case of genocide in this century of which I am acquainted, the corporate body of the group is in some way threatened—beleaguered, unstable, apprehensive, nascent—and responds genocidally to rid itself of aliens, others, "intruders," "germs."

I believe this latter epithet, "germs," supplies an important clue. As even one germ may infect the whole body, so all "germs"—no matter how small or apparently innocuous—must be extruded from the "corporate body." Now that we have some idea of what is to explained— and perhaps a clue for beginning to explain it—let us look for a full-fledged explanatory hypothesis. Schrag's ideas of decentered subjectivity and transversal rationality come into play, in some form. Let us look first at decentered subjectivity. Selves are no longer centered primally and ineluctably in themselves, autonomous rational subjects comfortably insulated from the world, looking down and around to calmly assess an encircling panorama of alternatives. But we are bodily beings caught up in the world, trying to find our way, and we are immensely porous, vulnerable, fragile.

We are inherently relational beings, becoming human because mimetically engulfed bodily in beings already humanly formed, and who recognize us to be human along with them. Moral autonomy must be achieved, and we can easily fail to achieve it.[9] One fearfully misguided way to try to achieve it is to engulf one's threatened individual identity in the identity of the group, and then to protect the group from infectious, infiltrating, polluting "others," those who for some reason don't fit into the corporate body.

Schrag's idea of transversal rationality helps explain how reason can go so desperately wrong. For Schrag, there is no showcase of finished, eternal Forms or Ideas in terms of which we perceive the world's events as instances. We sort the world into kinds as a result of what furthers our needs and interests—or so we think—in this world into which we have been thrown: thrown corporately over multitudes of millennia, and individually from the moment we were born. There is always more to be known than we can ever presently know, and we are fairly often shocked and disrupted when we come up against the unexpected. Amidst the precarious we have only the relatively stable.

This tells us something about our identity. Each of us is an individual, subject to all the hazards and contingencies of occupying always a particular place and time. What may rub against us, infect us, hit us? And we are also who we are because recognized as playing a certain set of roles within the corporate body of the group. The group has habitually sorted the world, and absorbing this mode of categorizing things and events is essential in forming the experienced world for each of us. And since each of us is a being in and of the world, the group's categorizing is essential for each of us to become who we are.

Really tuning in and describing closely our immediate involvements with others shows how vulnerable and entangled we bodily selves are. This is what I seem to hear when I hear the other: the sound from within a body-processing-the-world heard from within this body-processing-the-world, and all within the matrix of how my community has and is processing the world.

The experienced world and our place in it is constituted by our sorting. A group that sorts differently—that finds things supremely important and holy, say, different from what we find—threatens to infect our very being. Especially when our group is exhausted, nascent, or unstable and threatened by any number of causes. The *others* are too much, they traumatize us and must be exterminated.

As William James knew, belief is the very sense and feeling of reality. Dualistic views that divide us into minds and bodies and place beliefs in the mind cannot begin to grasp the gravity of beliefs. They are our ways of responding as whole beings to various circumpressures, openings, threats, or blockages in the world. Sorts of belief are sorts of response. Or, they are sorts of initiative, from routine actions initiated in routine situations, to the upsurge of deep affirmation by the whole self in the face of unusual challenges. Without our beliefs about the world we would not be who we are.

Alien modes of believing rip across our transversal patterns of responding and initiating, and, particularly if we are also threatened by other factors, prompt rage and condemnation. The others threaten our very existence and must be exterminated—genocide.

At this point what Schrag says can complement what Mary Douglas writes in her monumental *Purity and Danger*.[10] Her analysis of what pollutes the corporate body is profound. She is not distracted by "rational" explanations—of Jewish dietary laws say, such as that the Jews discovered that certain creatures carry deleterious substances and should not be ingested. She studies Hebrew purification practices integral to their origin myth. These embody the belief that clean things live and move properly in their environments, while dirty things do not. Eels, for instance, have no fins and move improperly in the water and hence are unclean according to Hebrew law. It is particularly the eating of these creatures that is polluting, for a disordered thing that enters the body tends to disorder the self. What is disordered must be kept outside the body.

Schrag and Douglas complement each other. Transversal rationality is an achievement easily disrupted. If we cannot achieve through categorizing, responding, initiating what is workable and fitting for us, we will die. What cannot be categorized and accommodated will pollute or infect us. Whatever lives and moves improperly in the world threatens us, as eels threaten Jews. The gravity of this cannot be overemphasized: Since the world experienced is constituted through the expectations and leadings of our believings or beliefs—the means we employ to make meaning—what contradicts our beliefs contradicts our lives. We suffer earthquake terror. Normally we order and are ordered in regenerative cycles of Nature and culture. To be disordered is to be dead. When others' modes of categorizing, responding, initiating rip across ours in situations of stress from these or other sources, they must be exterminated.

And they must be so because of what *they are*. Who they are in particular is irrelevant. *They* are those who think and act in ways that disrupt our ways of being in the world. They threaten to dissolve our world and ourselves. Even the thought of them must cease because we may think their thinking and so imperil our being. So not only they themselves but every memory of them must be expunged. And every possibility of their procreating and recreating themselves must be eradicated.

Certain horrifying features of genocides finally become somewhat understandable, for example, the torture of pregnant women, the disembowelment of pregnant women.[11] The very possibility of new alien life must be nipped. Or, the violation by rape of women who are other. The man releases his seed into the woman who bears the consequences: Her lineage is compromised, violated, or diluted. The alleged violators are violated, the alleged polluters polluted. The violating rapist goes scot-free, so it is thought, for his sperm which violates the woman's egg may itself be compromised, but it no longer resides in his body, so cannot infect him.

And, again, why must *all* the others be pursued? Because one "germ" can infect the whole corporate body and each of its members. Because any one of the others instantiates Otherness, the freakish, haunting universal that has spun off crazily from the precarious transversal rationality Schrag describes. The urge for transcendence does not find unconditional love, but only terror seeking to smother one's own terror. Perpetrators of genocide do not transcend into unconditional love, to be given or received, as Schrag argues that we should. They fail utterly to transcend, for they sort the world so fearfully and rigidly that the other among them becomes intolerable.

We are selves who are also bodies in the most intimate communion with others, hence our vulnerability is immense. Genocide is a kind of demonic possession: We cannot center ourselves morally, and we are possessed by fear of the other. But that is too abstract. In our desperation our bodies take on a life of their own, a frenzied urge to survive, as if we were cornered animals—cornered, but not really understanding by what, which adds to the panic. And as we reduce the aliens to mere meat, the killing gets easier. Philip Gourevitch wonders why Hutus killing Tutsis with machetes did not weary of their work. But mere exhaustion means nothing when one is demonically possessed—a frenzy of desperate life affirmation that means death for others.

In genocide "the rational animal" goes crazy. Our glorious powers of symbolizing and classifying go berserk. Genocide seems to be rage against Nature herself, against having vulnerable animal bodies, nerve and flesh, possessed of precariously balanced powers of classification and symbolization. It is not clear that we philosophers have anything but a tenuous hold on an explanatory hypothesis for genocide. I think, however, that it is better than nothing.

But Heidegger may have been right at the end of his life when he reportedly said, "Only a god can save us."

Notes

1. See Calvin O. Schrag, *Communicative Praxis and the Space of Subjectivity* (Bloomington, Ind., 1986), pp. 139 ff.
2. See first and foremost Calvin O, Schrag, *The Resources of Rationality: A Response to the Postmodern Challenge* (Bloomington, Ind., 1992), pp. 148 ff.

3. Calvin O. Schrag, *The Self after Postmodernity* (New Haven, Conn., 1997), pp. 131–33.

4. Marguerite Feitlowitz, *A Lexicon of Terror: Argentina and the Legacies of Torture* (New York, 1998), p. 67.

5. David P. Chandler, *Brother Number One: A Political Biography of Pol Pot,* rev. ed. (Boulder, Colo., 1999).

6. Philip Gourevitch, *We Wish to Inform You That Tomorrow We Will Be Killed with Our Families: Stories from Rwanda* (New York, 1998).

7. William Doty, "We Are All Relatives," *Soundings: An Interdisciplinary Journal 81, nos. 3–4* (fall/winter 1998): 516. "Communities offered bounties for Indian Scalps—to the point where whites ended up killing one another and dying the hair black, since there were no more Indians left—and public holidays in California featured Indian hunts as the principal form of celebration. Some carried banners that their wives had embroidered with the slogan EXTERMINATION!, and between 1849–56, 50,000 of an initial population of 120,000 were murdered." I can find no reference in A. L. Kroeber's 1,000-page *Handbook of the Indians of California* (New York, 1976 [1925]) to these massacres. He seems to have followed the best "scientific" or positivist practice of confining his data to indigenous cultures. Their annihilation did not count.

8. Robert Jay Lifton, *The Nazi Doctors: Medical Killing and the Psychology of Genocide* (New York, 1986).

9. For mimetic engulfment, its role in identity, and the capacity of theater to reveal it, see my *Role Playing and Identity: The Limits of Theatre as Metaphor* (Bloomington, Ind., 1991 [1982]).

10. Mary Douglas, *Purity and Danger: An Analysis of the Concepts of Pollution and Taboo* (London, 1966), pp. 55–56. I use her book prominently in my *Wild Hunger: The Primal Roots of Modern Addiction* (Lanham, Md., and New York, 1998), p. 127.

11. See Gourevitch, *We Wish to Inform You,* p. 98. Similar atrocities committed by Serbs against Bosnians and Kosovars have been reported. Perhaps similar atrocities have been committed against Serbs by Croats. Not to mention the hundreds of years of unmentionable crimes committed against Serbs by Ottoman Turks.

PART   3

THE SELF AFTER
POSTMODERNITY

7

Transversal Liaisons: Calvin Schrag on Selfhood

Fred Dallmayr

In our age of consumerism and proliferating technical gadgetry, basic existential questions are prone to be sidelined or repressed—though perhaps never completely erased. Despite the pervasive amnesia or absentmindedness cultivated by the media, a certain mindfulness stubbornly persists, giving rise to such anxious questions as: What are these gadgets all about, and how are we to live our lives properly in their midst? As can readily be seen, such worries harken back mindfully to older, nearly perennial themes of human self-search and discovery, epitomized in such classical mottoes as "know thyself" and "the unexamined life is not worth living." In a long string of publications, the philosopher Calvin Schrag has persistently endeavored to "examine" human life—the very point or meaning of being human—in the midst of our turbulent and fast-paced century. More recently, Schrag has offered his readers a relatively slender treatise which elegantly and concisely summarizes the fruit of his lifelong examination: *The Self after Postmodernity* (which is a revised version of his Gilbert Ryle Lectures of 1995). The title of the book refers to a certain debunking or dismissal of selfhood often associated with postmodernity, evident in such popular phrases as the "death of man," the "death of the author," or the "deconstruction of the subject." As Schrag comments wryly and acerbically, "the postmodern announcement of the death of the subject, like the news release of the death of Mark Twain, was a bit of an exaggeration."[1]

In a way, *The Self after Postmodernity* seeks to clear a path through contemporary philosophical thickets: above all, beyond or between the conundrums of modernity versus postmodernity, foundationalism versus antifoundationalism, reason (logos) versus storytelling (mythos). In large measure, the path favored by Schrag endeavors to recapture or reenergize individual agency or the role of the human subject—though now a subject concretely situated in finite social, cultural, and religious contexts. To be sure, it might be possible to find a different sense in the cited postmodern announcements, by reading them not as parallels to the news release about Mark Twain but as code words signaling a profound decentering or problematization of the modern subject, triggered not by consumerist amnesia but precisely by a deepening of self-reflection. Questions like these may be seen as a kind of background noise to Schrag's text—though they can initially be held in abeyance to permit an attentive scrutiny of his perspective. The following presentation proceeds in three steps. The first section offers a condensed synopsis of the book's main lines of argument, while the second part raises a number of afterthoughts or reservations having to do mainly with the issue of a revitalized subject. By way of conclusion, an effort will be made to indicate the relevance of Schrag's approach to contemporary social and political developments, especially to the emergence of a global civil society or community.

The Self after Postmodernity

In modern Western philosophy, selfhood, in the sense of individual subjectivity, has traditionally functioned as a crucial cornerstone or linchpin; but this cornerstone has come under increasing pressure in the course of our century. Appropriately for the occasion, Schrag's text pays tribute to Gilbert Ryle as a pioneer who early on punctured the Cartesian conception of the "thinking substance" (*ego cogitans*) by caricaturing the latter as a "ghost in the machine." The lasting contribution of Ryle's work, Schrag notes, was "a dismantling of the Cartesian portrait of the human subject as an interiorized mental substance"; to this extent, his work may "indeed find a place in the history of twentieth-century philosophy as one of the early illustrations of deconstructionist thought."[2] Partly in response to Ryle (as well as to Wittgenstein), the puncturing of the subject was carried forward under the auspices of the "linguistic turn," which became a prominent leitmotif in Anglo-American analytical philosophy. Concurrently and largely independently of Ryle, a similar movement arose in Continental European philosophy, prominently triggered by Heidegger's pathbreaking *Being and Time* and subsequently

deepened and expanded by a host of existentialist and structuralist writers from Marcel to Merleau-Ponty and beyond. In the wake of structuralism, the puncturing or deconstructive project was pursued with single-
minded vigor by a group of thinkers variously labeled "poststructuralists"
or "postmodernists" whose agenda culminated in the postmodern announcements mentioned before. In this postmodern ambience, Schrag
observes, "questions about the self, and particularly questions about the
self as *subject*, are deemed anathema." To the extent that the older vocabulary is retained, the self is associated with "multiplicity, heterogeneity,
difference, and ceaseless becoming, bereft of origin and purpose. Such
is the manifesto of postmodernity on matters of the human subject as self
and mind."[3]

It is chiefly the single-mindedness of this manifesto which triggers
Schrag's objections. Although concurring with Ryle and his successors in
their assault on the Cartesian thinking subject and the entire traditional
"substance-theory" of self, he insists that a debunking of this foundationalist model does not and should not entail "a jettisoning of every sense
of self." In Schrag's view the valuable lesson to be learned from the anti-
Cartesian moves in our century is that modernity's portrayal of the mind
as a "transparent mental mirror" and epistemological bedrock has little
to contribute to a proper understanding of the human self "in its manifest
concretion as speaking and narrating subject." The basic deficiency of
the modern portrayal resided indeed in the construal of "an abstracted,
insular knowing subject" severed or shielded from "the context and contingencies out of which knowledge of self and knowledge of the world
arise." Once this abstract model is put aside, however, we are by no means
left empty-handed or at the mercy of chaotic multiplicity. According to
Schrag's text, precisely the debunking of the erroneous traditional view
clears the way to a more genuine grasp of selfhood. In the aftermath
of deconstruction, he notes, what happens surprisingly is that "a new self
emerges, like the phoenix arising from its ashes"; this self is no longer abstract but concrete, a "praxis-oriented self, defined by its communicative
practices." Seen against this background, the postmodern manifesto—
despite some of its merits—can be seen as an "overreaction" which ex-
cessively denudes human selfhood, leaving behind only "a subject too
thin to bear the responsibilities" of concrete engagement. Correcting
this excess prompts an inquiry into a new vision of the self "as subject
after postmodernity."[4]

In focusing on a concretely situated subject, defined by its "communicative practices," Schrag also seeks to make a contribution to the
modernity/postmodernity conundrum in another sense; namely, by situating himself vis-à-vis the so-called "differentiation of culture-spheres."

In the wake of Kant's three *Critiques*, modern social and sociological theorists—led prominently by Max Weber—had argued that the gist of modernity and modernization consists in the progressive separation and indeed "stubborn differentiation" of the value-spheres of science, morality, and art. Reacting to this proliferation of spheres, modern dialectical thinkers—from Hegel to Marx and beyond—sought to overcome the divisiveness of the modernizing process by emphasizing either the unifying role of universal reason or the unifying potential of a political movement. In a modified vein, Jürgen Habermas in recent times has sought to reconnect the value-spheres under the rubric of a "communicative rationality," a conception which—by stressing the respective integrity of science, morality, and art—also aims to salvage the "project of modernity," seen as a commitment to reason and rationalization. On the other side of the spectrum, postmodern thinkers have shown pronounced disinterest in the problem of value-spheres and their interconnections, delighting instead in the prospect of infinite dispersal, dissemination, and multiplication. Here again, Schrag takes exception to postmodernism's excess. As indicated before, his text relies on the integrative role of "communicative practices"—practices which, in contrast to Habermas's approach, are anchored not in abstractly rational claims but rather in modes of concrete engagement in the life-world. In Schrag's account situated selfhood inserts itself into the unfolding trajectories of science, morality, and art—amplified by the sphere of religion—while simultaneously articulating itself in the modalities of discourse, action, social community, and transcendence. While the latter modalities, we read, constitute the "ingredients of a synchronics of self-understanding," the four culture-spheres represent "the moving figures within a diachronics of historical constitution."[5]

The successive chapters of the *Self after Modernity* move step by step through the different "synchronics" of self-understanding, always paying due attention to the historical context of value- or culture-spheres. Paying tribute to the linguistic turn, the opening chapter on "Self in Discourse" seeks to uncover the self or "who" involved in discursive practices—where the question of "who" is sharply distinguished from the "what" question of Cartesian metaphysics and the substance-theory of self. As Schrag notes, inquiry into the "who" is not of an "abstract universal nature" but rather aims at a "concrete and historically specific questioner." Seen from this angle, the notion of discourse or discursive practice challenges or disrupts prevalent dichotomies in contemporary linguistic philosophy: especially the dualisms of speech and language, of parole and langue, and also of linguistic behavior and the semantics of meaning. For Schrag, speaking and meaning are "closely intertextured"; hence, discourse involves the "symbiotic event of an intercalation of speaking with a language *from* which one speaks." Functioning in a discourse or discursively, selfhood is not fixed or static but rather dynamically "emergent" or becoming; its unfolding and recognition signal an "adventure of hermeneutical self-implicature." As he acknowledges, this notion of discursive selfhood is to some extent indebted to the teachings of Wittgenstein, Ryle, and Austin, but also—and perhaps in a major way—to Gadamer's discussion of the "linguisticality of being." What matters most to Schrag at this point is that discourse should not be seen as an isolated or fragmentary occurrence but as constituent of an overarching cultural framework which integrates discourse into a broader narrative. Such narrative is said to provide the "ongoing context in which the figures of discourse are embedded." Viewed against this background, discourse emerges as a critical midpoint: a point located "between the constitutive elements of speech and language and the wider contextual and holistic intertexture of narratives." This midpoint, the zone of the discursive event, is the place where "the who is called into being."[6]

By emphasizing narrative and its role in discourse, the text finds it important to demarcate itself from a narrowly scientific narratology, which, obeying the canons of modern epistemology, distances narrative into an empirical object. In making this move, narratology ruptures the linkage of narrative and discourse; in such a scheme of things "the who has no voice." Countering this reifying project, the text celebrates the figure of a narrating self, a *homo narrans,* or a "story-teller who both finds herself in stories already told and strives for a self-constitution by emplotting herself in stories in the making." In Schrag's account, this narrative perspective provides a sheet anchor, both against the Cartesian cogito and also—still more important—against the disassembling and disaggregating tendencies fostered by postmodernism. Turning to a leading postmodern author, Schrag objects to Lyotard's conception of a radical "heterogeneity of language games" and his segregation of speech genres into isolated, mutually unrelated enclaves. Associating this outlook with the rhetorical devices of ancient Sophists, he cautions against the equation of difference and plurality with radical separation and/or antimony; the slide, he notes, "from diversity, plurality, and multiplicity to heterogeneity, paralogy, and incommensurability is too hurried." Returning to the notion of *homo narrans,* Schrag insists that narrative allows for a certain unification of selfhood amid diversity—although the latter should not be misconstrued in terms of a rigid "sameness." Borrowing a leaf from Paul Ricoeur, one might distinguish here between "idem-identity" and "ipse-identity"—where the former involves an appeal to fixed criteria of identification, while the latter refers to a flexible process

of self-formation, to the "occasioning of personal identity" linked prominently with the forging of character. Under the rubric of ipse-identity, we
read, selfhood has "much to do with ethos, and particularly with ethos as
the formation of character."[7]

Narrative, in Schrag's presentation, involves not only storytelling
in the sense of reciting a tale but also story-enactment through concrete
engagement in an unfolding life-praxis. Taken in the latter, "stronger"
sense, narrative points to the "dynamics of the self as life-experiencing
subject," to the "emplotment of a personal history"—which not merely
is mental exercise but a concretely embodied enterprise. Drawing on
the lessons on phenomenology, the chapter on "Self in Action" underscores the importance of "embodiment" for a proper understanding of
the active life—where embodiment serves again as an antidote to Cartesian metaphysics and especially to the "mind-body" conundrum (where a
"ghostly interior" resides in a causal mechanism). Due attention is given
at this point to Merleau-Ponty's notion of the "lived body" (*le corps vécu*),
to Gabriel Marcel's celebration of "incarnate" existence, and to Sartre's
definition of the body as a "synthetic totality of *life* and *action*." As Schrag
elaborates, formulations of this kind do not at all coincide with a merely
accidental conjunction according to which the self would just happen to
"have" or be located in a body seen as a disposable garment (or, in Plato's
terms, as "prison house" of the soul). In fact, the notions of incarnate
existence or embodied being require a radical rethinking or reconfiguration of modern conceptions of space or spatiality which present "space"
simply as an outer container or as a serialized juxtaposition of spatial
points. The focus on bodily praxis or enactment, by contrast, brings into
view a different mode of in-dwelling, a mode where the body does not
occupy space, but rather "*inhabits* space," moving freely in a realm of
"embodied spatiality." For Schrag, the self in action designates an "embodied who," in the sense that the body as lived is "veritably *who I am*."
Thus, he continues, "we can say with Marcel 'I am my body,' and by this
we mean that the self-identity that one articulates in one's storytelling is
always entwined with a self-identity of bodily intentionality and motility."[8]

Having portrayed narrative from the (embodied) actor's perspective, the text quickly adds some caveats designed to shield selfhood from
a simple relapse into traditional subjectivity. Faithful to his contextual
starting point, Schrag reminds readers of the complex interlacing of
action and reaction in every concrete "interactive" situation. Seen from
the angle of interaction, narrative involves a "dialectic of acting and suffering" which discloses the who of action as "at once agent and patient,"
as *both* "an active or originating force and a reactive or responding force."
In more strictly philosophical terms, human selfhood coincides neither

with "a sovereign and autonomous self" completely impervious to forces of "alterity," nor with a self caught in "the constraints of heteronomy" and fully governed or determined from outside. Rather, the self in action lives "*between* autonomy and heteronomy, active and reactive force, pure activity and pure passivity"; it articulates itself grammatically in the "middle voice." Support for his mediating or midpoint position, in Schrag's view, can be found in Deleuze's portrait of the "rhizomatic self" energized in its self-formation by the play of active and reactive forces and also in some of Foucault's comments on the role of "bio-power" in human life. As he insists, however, none of these interactive models can, or should, detract from the importance of active self-initiative and above all from the vital function of choice or decision seen as the catalyst constituting human selfhood. It is at this point that Kierkegaard enters prominently into the discussion, especially with his accent on the "either/or" quality of self-formation. In Schrag's words: "It is this accentuation of choice that provides the peculiar hallmark of Kierkegaard's existential reflections on the experience of self"—a hallmark which enables him to transform the Cartesian motto into "I choose, therefore I am." Choice presides over the transition from the "aesthetic" to the "ethical" stage of life whereby self-identity is achieved "through a baptism of the will"; it functions even more crucially in the epiphany of the "religious" through an existential "leap" of faith. With regard to the latter domain, Schrag speaks of an important "Kierkegaard-effect" evident in the reshaping of modernity through the addition of religion to the trilogy of science, morality, and art.[9]

Returning to the aspect of interaction—and bracketing Kierkegaard for the time being—the next chapter shifts the focus to political praxis and specifically to the "Self in Community." The notion of "communicative praxis" or "communicative practices," mentioned before, surfaces here again by disclosing human selfhood as "discovering and constituting itself in relation to other selves." Compounding its other flaws, postmodernity is found to be particularly deficient in this domain. Seconding Richard Rorty, Schrag considers it difficult "to situate any positive role for community within the parameters of postmodern discourse." To be sure, the point for him is not to privilege community or the "we-experience" over individual selfhood or "I-experience," since both can be shown to be intricately "entwined"; to this extent, both "sociologism" and "egologism" are equally unacceptable alternatives. As Schrag acknowledges, community seems to be particularly elusive in our century, where it has been (and continues to be) so often overshadowed by domination, alienation, and oppression. Moreover, profound philosophical problems beset the task of conceiving community properly as the relation of selfhood to another self as "other." In his famous *Cartesian*

Meditations, Edmund Husserl boldly shouldered this task—but without being able in the end to escape Cartesian premises (reducing the other to an alter ego). In Schrag's view, egology must more resolutely be left behind, meaning that "the otherness of the other needs to be granted its intrinsic integrity, so that in seeing the face of the other and hearing the voice of the other I am *responding* to an exterior gaze and an exterior voice rather than carrying on a conversation with my alter ego." Not unexpectedly, the testimony of Emmanuel Lévinas is invoked at this point, and especially his notion of the "face" of the other as the inaugural event of moral awareness. In Lévinas's "ethics of alterity," we read, "the who is able to assume the voice and visage of the teacher issuing the commandment 'Thou shalt not kill.' "[10]

Although endorsing the accent on alterity, Schrag finds it important to caution against a narrow reading of that term. As he notes, self in community should not be restricted to "face-to-face" encounters or close interpersonal relationships, since being-with others acquires its full meaning only "against the backdrop of wider historico-cultural forces." Above all, self-formation implies also an understanding of oneself in larger contexts: "as a citizen of a polis, a player in an ongoing tradition of beliefs and commitments, a participant in an expanding range of institutions and traditions." To be sure, community cannot, or should not, be reduced to the rule of customs and conventions, heralding a lapse into mere conventionalism; rather, as lived practice we-experience is always suffused with "ethico-moral" concerns in an unfolding social context. Hence, it is important to define community as "principally a creative and self-affirming modality of being-with-others in society," as contrasted with conformism as a mode of self-effacement. Recognizing this creative modality as silhouetted against a sociohistorical background yields again a dialectical interplay of forces, paying heed both to contextual or situational features and to the "ethico-moral fabric of self-actualization." The operative notions governing this interplay are "responsivity" and "responsibility" (the former more descriptive, the latter more ethical in character). The basic task of the self in community is to be both responsive and responsible in social interactions, that is, to cultivate the virtue of responding "in a fitting manner" (according to the "ethic of the fitting response"). In pursuing this task, crucial guidance is provided by the voice of "conscience," defined by Heidegger as a liberating call to "authentic" self-being. Amplifying Heidegger's account (and correcting its shortcomings), Schrag turns to the eighteenth-century philosopher Joseph Butler whose theory of the "moral sense" presented conscience as a "superior principle of reflection" able to guide individual and social life with practical discernment. What is important in this insight, for purposes of communicative praxis, is that conscience emerges as "a mode of moral understanding, a manner of knowing one's way about in moral predicaments, a practical wisdom of what the situation requires." Imbued with reflective discernment, conscience also provides criteria for evaluation and critical judgment, that is, for "praxial critique."[11]

The notion of praxial critique implies a distantiation of the self from prevailing conventions—which opens the path to a consideration of the "Self in Transcendence," the theme of the final chapter. As Schrag notes right away, there are different modes of transcendence which need to be carefully distinguished. In a sense, language transcends speech performance, just as action—in Sartre's sense—implies a self-projection transcending present conditions. In these and similar instances, transcendence is still narrowly circumscribed, lacking (so to speak) a vertical dimension. In Schrag's words, usage of the term here remains "quite mundane and domesticated," disclosing only its "weaker sense": something like "transcendence-in-immanence." There is, however, also a stronger sense pointing to an alterity exceeding "the economy of intramundane forms." Steps in this direction can be found in Plato's Ideas, in the Kantian "noumenal" realm, and in the metaphysical notion of God as an infinite and supremely perfect being. More recent and still more poignant examples are provided by Rudolph Otto's notion of the "holy" (*das Heilige*) and by Karl Jaspers's doctrine of the "Encompassing" functioning as the ultimate limit of rational comprehension. Particularly in these latter instances, the term "transcendence" signals an encounter with what Emmanuel Lévinas has named a "radical exteriority," a phrase motioning toward a transcendent realm "residing on the other side of the economics of human experience." At this point, the voice of Kierkegaard reenters the discussion and, in fact, begins to modulate or structure the book's remaining argument. Returning to the "Kierkegaard-effect," Schrag locates the Danish thinker's significance both in his religiosity and in his transformation of modernity, in the sense that the "inclusion of religion" should be seen as "one of the more urgent requirements" for updating the doctrine of modern culture-spheres. In terms of the issue of transcendence, Kierkegaard's importance resides in his distinction between "religiousness A" and "religiousness B"—where the former designates a mundane "religion of immanence" while the latter points to a radical leap beyond or rupture of immanence, a leap "fracturing all efforts by the self to find the God-relationship within itself" and thus clearing the way to the encounter with "a radically transcendent Other." Any relation of that "Other" with the self is paradoxical, and "incarnation" the emblem of an "Absolute Paradox."[12]

With regard to the culture-spheres of modernity, Kierkegaard's religiosity (religiousness B) provides, in Schrag's view, several important lessons. First of all, as a mode of distantiation, radical transcendence or alterity furnishes a "critical principle," permitting the critical assessment of conditions in the "intramundane" spheres of science, morality, art, and (organized) religion. By relativizing all situational contexts, religiousness B supplies "the requisite safeguards against ideological hegemony, irrespective of whether such hegemony has staked its claims in the spheres of science, morality, art, or institutionalized religion." Kierkegaard's biting attack on "Christendom" (meaning mainly the established church of Denmark) was in many ways a continuation and intensification of Kant's critique of clericalism defined as a combination of "fetish-worship" and "fetish-faith." The second major lesson of Kierkegaard's work resides in its contribution to the "unification" of modern culture-spheres, an issue which, in Schrag's view, constitutes the "storm center" of the modernity-postmodernity dispute. While many modern philosophers saw reason as the gateway to synthesis, most postmodernists revel in the unleashing of difference and incommensurability. Here, Kierkegaard comes to the rescue by offering a unity grounded not in reason but in radical alterity and faith, while simultaneously banishing the specter of chaotic dispersal. Schrag invokes at this juncture the metaphor of "transversality," suggesting a process which achieves "convergence without coincidence," "conjuncture without concordance," or "union without absorption." By allowing for a coordination without assimilation, he writes, transversality can be helpful "in elucidating the unifying function of [Kierkegaardian] transcendence." The third major lesson operates on the level of the culture-spheres themselves, where religiousness B shows its transformative quality by contributing to the "transfiguration and transvaluation of the life of self and society." In our time, this Kierkegaard-effect is amplified by Lévinas's accent on transformative ethics (the latter seen as response to "the Other as absolute exteriority"). In Schrag's view a prime example of alterity's incursion is the paradox of gift giving in the sense that such giving bars any expectation of a return or a "counter-gift"; in fact, gift giving escapes the "economy of production and consumption," transcending radically the "requirements of reciprocity." In this respect, giving is closely related to caritas or the Kierkegaardian "works of love" where love—even if unrequited—is freely offered and thereby exceeds the bounds of Aristotelian friendship. An outgrowth or corollary of grace, the benefits of alterity in fact leave behind all forms (ancient and modern) of moral theorizing and even the "edicts of institutionalized religion," making room instead for the recognition of "Absolute Paradox."[13]

Critical Afterthoughts

Although condensed, the preceding review should convey both the broad sweep and the intellectual subtlety of Schrag's text. Having moved through the different modalities of selfhood, the reader is prone to come away with a sense of exhilaration, a sense of having participated in a rich adventure journeying through the multiple dimensions of the human condition. A small chef d'oeuvre, the text elicits praise both in terms of its style and its content. Like few professional academics today, Schrag is able to express his thoughts in lucid language free of jargon, manifesting his desire to engage his readers reflectively rather than impress them with obscure or murky rhetoric. In terms of content, praise is due especially to the impressive scope of his intellectual horizons, ranging from Plato and Aristotle to Kant and Hegel and to the leading figures of twentieth-century philosophy (including figures unjustly sidelined today, like Marcel and Merleau-Ponty). Although cognizant of the latest intellectual developments, his writings—and this text in particular—always exude the aura of mature seasoning, of a perspective wedded to the *longue durée* disinclined to fragmentation and neat compartmentalization.

It is precisely on the latter score, however, that qualms may arise regarding the very title of the text: the suggestion that postmodernity somehow denotes a distinct historical phase which we have now left behind as survivors "after postmodernity." This suggestion is awkward and disorienting in several ways. First of all, the title may give aid and comfort to all those "survivors"—quite large in numbers—who have habitually bemoaned postmodern initiatives as a stark assault on, and an insult to, the finer qualities of Western civilizations. To critics of this kind, the announcement of postmodernity's demise may be welcome news— but a news which, as in Mark Twain's case again, may be premature. In Schrag's presentation, the term "postmodernity" designates an array of diverse (and not very admirable) features—a profusion which is disorienting in its own way. On the one hand, and perhaps predominantly, postmodernity is associated with dispersal and dissensus, with the "celebration of difference and diversity." On the other hand—perhaps but not necessarily as a corollary—postmodernity is said to be marked by an overvaluation of aesthetics (in the theoretical sense of that term). Pointing to developments from Nietzsche to Foucault, Schrag finds in this overvaluation a "problem endemic to postmodern thought" as such: "In valorizing the economy of the aesthetical, placing a premium on matters of style, postmodernists have responded to the separation of culture-spheres in modernity by according a ubiquity to the aesthetical." This ubiquity exerts a constraining effect on science and morality, and especially on the latter, where the "postmodern ethos" shows tendencies toward "a global aestheticism." More constraining still, in Schrag's view, is the effect on everyday social praxis—a domain liable to disappear in a "postmodern pantextualism" that sees the world only through the lenses of textuality and discourse."[14]

To readers familiar with "postmodern" writings, these judgments will appear summary and neglectful of important nuances. Most important, they seem to shortchange the innovative contributions of these writings in the fields of metaphysics, ethics, aesthetics, and even politics— contributions which are unlikely to have run their course or to have reached their full fruition. As it happens, Schrag himself does not fully subscribe to postmodernity's demise. Repeatedly (as stated before) he pays tribute to postmodern initiatives in debunking the Cartesian cogito seen as a transparent mirror or fixed substance. In this respect, he even extols Ryle as a postmodern pioneer by presenting his *The Concept of Mind* as "one of the early illustrations of deconstructionist thought." Occasionally, he also enlists individual postmodernists (or thinkers labeled as such) as useful accomplices in his own project of redefining selfhood. This is particularly true of Deleuze and his portrait of the "rhizomatic self." Deleuze's portrait, he writes, is "particularly germane to my own project of devising a sketch of the human subject." Wedged between fixity and random indeterminancy, Deleuze's self develops "against the backdrop of his notion of the *chaosmos,* the world as a *becoming*-world" in which the subject emerges "not as a 'substantive *hypokeimenon*' but rather as a task and a performance in the 'theater of philosophy.' " To a lesser degree, some affinity is also claimed with the work of Foucault and especially with his conception of "self-scripting" (*l'écriture de soi*), a conception which proves helpful "for articulating what is at issue in our depiction of the self in discourse."[15]

Despite these and similar concessions, the overall tenor of the book is that of a postscript or epilogue which, in a literal construal of the title, attempts to uncover the self as "subject *after* postmodernity." This literalness may have something to do with a certain restorative tendency of the book, the tendency to bracket (indeed) the Cartesian cogito but only by replacing it with a more concretely situated and thus more robust subject. Despite the shift from the what-question to the who-question, the text— over long stretches—pays ample homage to the traditional "modernist" notions of self-constitution, self-enactment, and self-actualization. Thus, in discussing the "self in discourse," Schrag presents speaking as a mode of self-discovery, but also and emphatically as a "creative act," an act of "self-constitution"; by participating in speech and discourse, the self is said to emerge as an agent "constituting itself as it lives in and through a maze of speech acts and a plethora of language games." Even the self as storyteller or *homo narrans,* although finding herself in stories already told, basically strives for "a self-constitution by emplotting herself in stories in the making." Likewise, the portrayal of the self in action makes ample room for self-enactment and actualization. Turning against a certain postmodern valorization of "desire," Schrag finds it important to reaffirm "the role of rationality in the life of the self-constituting subject." Despite the need to recognize human finitude and its constraints, action theory—in his view—must pay heed to the "odyssey of self-constitution" and also to the "dynamics of decision-making" where "the who of action is called into being as an agentive subject"; for, as Kierkegaard has insistently demonstrated, it is "through the act of choice that the self constitutes itself." Even the chapter on community reveals a similar accent. In encountering and responding to others, the self is claimed to effect "a self-constitution, a constitution of myself, in the dynamic economy of being-with-others"; proceeding in this manner, the self can reach an "authentic mode of creative intersubjective self-actualization."[16]

In fairness to Schrag—and this must be added quickly—the retrieval of the subject is not simply a modernist agenda. As presented by Schrag, self-constitution is not simply a Husserlian enterprise where the self constitutes both itself and the other as alter ego; nor is self-enactment equivalent to a Sartrean mode of self-making. Two devices above all protect his approach from this equivalence. One is the emphasis on "embodiment," the notion that the body is not merely an external costume but rather part of the self's very being. As previously mentioned, following in the footsteps of Marcel and Merleau-Ponty, Schrag stresses that both in discourse and in action the self is "called into being as an *embodied who*"; to this extent, the self's identity is always entwined with "a self-identity of bodily intentionality and motility." The second protective device is the correlation between action and reaction, or challenge and response. In Schrag's account, the dynamic of human action occurs in the tension span between "an active or originating force and a reactive or responding force"; in this sense, the who of action is "at once agent and patient, an initiator of action and a receiver of action." This positioning of action "*between* autonomy and heteronomy, pure activity and pure passivity," is said to find grammatical expression in the notion of the "middle voice." Despite their importance in the general argument, however, the preceding devices at best modulate, but do not really undermine, the preeminence of self-constitution. In the case of embodiment this fact is evident in the focus on "bodily intentionality" (which merely amplifies Husserlian phenomenology). In the case of action-reaction, the correlation is instantly disrupted in the text by the turn to Kierkegaardian decision making where the self "constitutes itself" through the act of choice. The same conclusion results from another passage where Schrag positions himself *versus* Gadamer by insisting that responsiveness for him is "an active—and not a reactive—force."[17]

The real break with self-constitution occurs only in the last chapter devoted to self in transcendence. Here selfhood in all its embodied robustness is suddenly beleaguered and assaulted by nonself, by a combination of Kierkegaardian religiousness B and Lévinasian radical alterity. At an initial glance, this change of perspective seems to involve an inconsistency or contradiction (or perhaps just another Kierkegaardian "paradox"). At a closer look, however, the change amounts only to a reversal, a look at the other side of the (same) coin. Just because the self was never really dislodged or "decentered" from its traditional interiority, self-transcendence requires as its supplement recourse to a radical outside or exteriority; just because agency in earlier passages was persistently linked with self-constituting autonomy, its antidote must now be found in heteronomy; just because the self was said to be identical with, and thus equal to, itself, refuge has now to be sought in inequality and asymmetry. In the text the preceding terminology is largely borrowed from Lévinas—although it can perhaps plausibly be extended to Kierkegaard as well. Reacting critically to the Husserlian constitution of the other, Schrag sides solidly with Lévinas's approach "from the other." "No longer an alter ego, issuing from the depths of subjectivity," he writes (sensibly), "the other displays an integrity and existential resiliency, advential and supervenient." On this point, he adds, "it is prudent to side with Lévinas rather than with Hegel, avowing an original asymmetry within the self-other relation. The radical exteriority of the other as other needs to be acknowledged, attested, and assented to." This assent carries over to Lévinasian ethics, where the ethical is seen to be anchored in heteronomy and asymmetry rather than "reciprocity" and to derive from "an encounter with and response to the Other as absolute exteriority."[18]

Here one can wonder, first of all, how a radical or absolute exteriority—say a rock on the moon—can have ethical relevance for the self. More to the point, these assenting comments place considerable pressure on Schrag's own earlier presentation which continuously resisted any leap "outside." To recall again a quoted passage (exuding seasoned judgment): The human self is "neither a sovereign and autonomous self whose self-constitution remains impervious to any and all forces of alterity, nor a self caught within the constraints of heteronomy, determined by forces acting upon it." To the extent that a connection exists between heteronomy or exteriority and heterogeneity (as seems plausible), one is also reminded of Schrag's earlier rebuke of Lyotard. Criticizing the

latter's postmodernism, he writes that a recognition of diversity and multiplicity "does not warrant claims for heterogeneity"; the multiple does
not necessarily imply something that is "radically 'other,' as is suggested
in the use of *heterogeneous*." Most important, the accentuation of an exterior otherness and its claims upsets and disengages the intricate balance
between action and reaction, between acting and suffering, which served
as the hallmark of the action chapter. The same or similar problems
beset the endorsement of Kierkegaardian religiousness B. Kierkegaard's
radical distinction between a "religion of immanence" and a "religion of
transcendence" seems to go counter to the main thrust of Schrag's earlier
arguments, which precisely sought to dislodge and surmount metaphysical binaries (like those between mind and body, inside and outside,
immanence and transcendence). Moreover, the insistence on a "God-
relation" which ruptures immanence and consists in a wholly nonreciprocal exposure to a "radically transcendent Other" seems to disavow the
"covenantal" character of Judaism and of all genuine "religion" (to the
extent that the latter term denotes a mutual bonding or rebonding).[19]

The virtues of Kierkegaardian (and Lévinasian) nonreciprocity are
illustrated by Schrag with the help of two examples: gift giving and friendship. Echoing Kierkegaard, his text finds a deep paradox in the giving
of a gift, a paradox which is not properly grasped by anthropologists
who placed their emphasis on exchange. To be genuinely a gift, a gift
must be presented without any expectation of a "countergift" or a return.
To this extent, he writes, the gift remains necessarily "outside, external
to, the economy of production and consumption, distribution and exchange" and hence "radically transcendent to the requirements of reciprocity." The qualities of gift giving are said to extend to other domains,
like the rendering of services, the helping of a friend, the offering of
words of counsel, or the paying of a visit; in all these instances, giving
operates without mutuality through a "surplus of significations." Here
some critical discernment seems called for. Nonmutuality certainly deserves a hearing to the extent that gift giving is meant to be shielded or
segregated from commercial or market transactions, from the inroads
of "distribution and exchange." However, reciprocity is not necessarily
restricted to these mundane or instrumental forms of interaction but
may also operate on a more refined, "spiritual" and noninstrumental
plane. As it appears, this subtler type of reciprocity seems also to be at
work in gift giving. Although shunning the expectation of a countergift,
a gift must surely be received by the beneficiary "*as*" a gift, that is, to
be properly understood and assessed as such. The giving of a gift would
certainly misfire if the receiver (say a policeman or public official) took
it to be a bribe or if the recipient mistakenly assumed that it involved

an item the giver had previously borrowed. Thus, gift giving, to function as such, inevitably involves some mutuality of understanding and discernment. This conclusion cannot be "news" to Schrag himself who, in other contexts, consistently stresses the "as" character of all encounters—for instance, by stating that the "taking something as something flags the interpretive moment in our inquiry into facts" which do not exist "without interpretation."[20]

Perhaps the most prominent type of nonreciprocal giving, according to the text, is friendship. Close attention here is paid again to Kierkegaard, and especially to the latter's *Works of Love* which celebrates "a love that loves for the sake of loving," a "nonpossessive love" which "expects nothing in return." As Schrag recognizes (following Kierkegaard), this type of loving bears indeed a resemblance to the Aristotelian notion of friendship (philia) seen as a dedicated mutual engagement. However, in the wake of Christian teachings of caritas and agape, Kierkegaardian loving transcends or "leaps beyond" classical Greek insights. In Schrag's words: "It is the Augustinian view that brings into relief the limitations of Aristotle," whose idea of friendship remained "rooted in the requirements for reciprocity" and who saw *philia* as possible "only between equals." By contrast, Augustinian and Kierkegaardian agape escapes the vagaries of mutuality and reciprocity, opening itself up instead to "the paradoxical intervention of the gift of love in the leap of religiousness B."[21] Here, again, the critical reader may remonstrate on several grounds—first of all, by pointing to the "as" character even of loving. Even the most gracious and nonpossessive agape is liable to misfire if it is seen by the beneficiary as a mode of condescension or paternalism. More important, the contrast between agape and Aristotelian friendship seems overdrawn in several respects. Pace Kierkegaard, Aristotelian philia is not mundanely instrumental but nonpossessive in character—as is evident from his repeated statements that genuine friendship means loving the friend "for the friend's sake." The connection between philia and equality is, of course, undeniable; but its significance is misconstrued. The point is not that philia presupposes equality but rather that it is an agent effectively equalizing unequals, especially those unequal in rank, age, or gender. It is for this reason that Aristotle saw philia as the equalizing bond in political regimes, including democracy—whereas the accent on inequality and asymmetry has dubious (if any) democratic credentials.

Apart from its intrinsic quandaries, the turn to nonreciprocity and unilateralism has detrimental effects on two of Schrag's most fruitful and appealing insights: his plea for practical wisdom and his emphasis on "transversality." Critiquing a certain postmodern concern with desire, Schrag argues that the "self in action" displays a "praxis-oriented reason," bringing into view "a dynamics of discernment, an economy of practical wisdom" that carries its own weight without requiring the sanction of "pure cognition and pure theory." Elaborating on the "common sense" approach to morality, he comments that, in Butler's theory, conscience issues not just arbitrary fiats but manifests "a mode of moral understanding, a manner of knowing one's way about in moral predicaments, a practical wisdom of what the situation requires." It is this kind of practical moral discernment which allows the "self in community" to respond properly to other selves, thus providing the contours for an "ethic of the fitting response"—which in many ways is close to Aristotle's (and Gadamer's) notion of *phronesis* seen as preeminent practical virtue. The problem that arises here is the compatibility of these statements with unilateralism, that is, with a resort to "radical alterity" or to a Kierkegaardian "leap of faith." Clearly, practical discernment is not instantly acquired but, like piano playing, needs to be assiduously practiced; as Aristotle has taught (correctly), phronesis and all practical virtues need to be steadfastly cultivated—and no one can relieve the self of this burden of cultivation. By contrast, on a certain reading of Lévinas, ethics seems to be suddenly bestowed on the self by a radical exteriority— apparently without the need for self-care and the practice of virtues. Even more explicitly, Kierkegaard's radical fideism cancels or disavows practical discernment, relegating it to a "lower" ethical realm. Schrag quotes approvingly Kierkegaard's statement that "God does not think, he creates"—a phrase which seems to place God below the aptitude for practical wisdom accorded to humans.[22]

Nonmutuality is even more damaging to perhaps the most significant contribution of Schrag's text: the notion of transversality. As previously mentioned, the notion is invoked chiefly as a means of correlating or "unifying" the different culture-spheres of modernity and more generally the multiplicity of diverse life-forms. In Schrag's presentation, transversality is meant to replace the traditional notion of an abstract "universality," namely, by shifting the accent from a finished result to an ongoing dynamic process of unifying by correlating: "The unity at issue is a coefficient of thought and communication moving across differentiated belief systems, interpretive viewpoints, and regions of concern." In exploring this dynamic process, Schrag finds support in Deleuze's discussion of Proustian reminiscence (as a memory-work opposed to Platonic recollection) and in Félix Guattari's inquiry into group interactions in psychiatric hospitals where a certain kind of transversal ordering is achieved "through a diagonal movement across the groups, acknowledging the otherness and integrity of each." As Schrag comments, echoing these writers: "Transversal unity is an achievement of communication as it visits a multiplicity of viewpoints, perspectives, belief systems, and regions of concern." The problem here is the conflict between this aspect of processual correlation and the simultaneous emphasis on transcendence and alterity seen as an exodus from reciprocity. By definition, such alterity/exteriority is placed outside or beyond the concrete labor of transversal interactions. As Schrag comments with reference to Kierkegaard's religiousness B: "It is this radical alterity that supplies the standpoint for an external critique of the four culture-spheres." Seen from this angle, religiousness B has already achieved—through a radical leap—that superior or transcendental standpoint through which all "immanent" perspectives are transgressed and relativized, seemingly without the need of lateral engagement. Noticing the metaphysical bent of this proposition, Schrag cautions against a precipitous exit from the world, emphasizing the need to give "due regard to the integrity of particularity and the play of diversity." Yet, the book concludes by celebrating transcendence as standing "outside" the various culture-spheres and thus as a mode of "robust alterity."[23]

Social and Political Lessons

Having voiced these critical observations, it seems appropriate to return to the mode of friendly engagement and appreciation. After all, these observations were offered precisely in a transversal spirit and by no means as the fruit of a higher standpoint immune from critique. What seems desirable, by way of conclusion, is to highlight aspects of the broader social and political significance of Schrag's arguments, especially as they are applicable to our age of rampant consumerism and ethnic cleansing. Here one may, first of all, wish to applaud Schrag's own sense of public awareness and responsibility, his self-interpretation as an academic philosopher shouldering the task of a public intellectual. As he writes in the preface to his book, in our time of growing specialization the responsibility placed upon the intellectual is considerable; for he/she is called upon "to forge lines of communication across several academic disciplines" and to explore the relevance of arguments "for citizens of a public world." Schrag at this point evokes the long and complicated history of the involvement of philosophy and public life in the development of Western civilization since its beginning. "We need but to recall the Athenian Socrates," he notes, "who at the dawn of Western philosophy exemplified the life of philosophical inquiry in dramatic manner by mingling with the citizens of Athens in the local marketplace, engaging them in conversations about the achievement of self-knowledge." The steady rise of scientific and technological expertise in our time lends a new sense of urgency to the Socratic example. Without demeaning or eliding their possible academic functions, public intellectuals today need also to reconstrue their philosophical task: namely, "along the lines of a rhetoric of inquiry directed *to* the public and crafted *for* the public."[24]

Lucidly written and eminently accessible to nonacademic readers, *The Self after Postmodernity* clearly fulfills Schrag's self-imposed task. The publicity of the text, however, is manifest not only in its style but also in many of its substantive arguments; some of these arguments, in effect, have a crucial import for contemporary social and political life. An example is the recuperation of practical wisdom and of ethics seen not as an inventory of abstract principles but rather as an ongoing responsible life-praxis. "The ethical," Schrag notes (distantly echoing Heidegger), "has to do with *ethos* in its originative sense of a cultural dwelling, a mode or manner of historical existence, a way of being in the world that exhibits a responsibility both to oneself and to others." This kind of lived ethics is not only recuperative but also evaluative, giving rise to a "praxial critique"— though a critique that does not simply deny its cultural dwelling. Every culture, one needs to note here, is a tensional fabric, a tapestry of "difference" or multiple strands—where some strands may be marginalized at a given juncture but can be mobilized for purposes of resistance. In this context one may wish to take a leaf from the work of Julia Kristeva, a professional linguist and psychoanalyst who has also shouldered the role of public intellectual and political theorist. Particularly significant in the latter repect is Kristeva's conception of a "politics of marginality" which seeks to enlist the agency of sidelined or subaltern groups for purposes of political transformation. In her view given the postmodern (and post-Freudian) decentering of the subject, emancipatory politics can no longer rely on grand ideological schemes entrusted to a collective agent, but must instead operate in the interstices of prevailing constellations (i.e., on the level of Foucault's micropowers). As Schrag writes, crediting Kristeva: "The most effective resources for social change are found in the interventions of marginal groups, after one has become duly suspicious of the grandiose aims of collective political programs."[25]

Even more timely and significant on a global scale is the text's endorsement of transversality. Schrag is eloquent in castigating traditional conceptions of unity and universality for relying on centralized command structures and on homogenizing or totalizing metaphysical premises. "In the traditions of both the ancients and the moderns," he states persuasively, "unity has fraternized with identity, and in concert unity and identity have waged war against plurality and difference." Operating on both a metaphysical and a political plane, the quest for unity—in his view—was driven "by a nostalgia for a primordial and unblemished *arché,* an untrammeled beginning, and an appetition for a fixed and universal *telos.*" Against this background, postmodernity's merit resides precisely in its accent on difference and multiplicity—provided this accent is not transformed into an atomistic "foundationalism," into a doctrine of radically isolated substances. It is here that transversality comes into play with its emphasis, not on a fixed or pregiven unity or universality, but on the open-ended search for self-transgressing horizons and correlations; ranging freely across and between elements or domains of life, the transversal quest proceeds as "an open-textured gathering of expanding possibilities." Seen in this light, transversality bears a close resemblance to Jean-Luc Nancy's notion of an "un-managed or inoperative community" (*communauté désoeuvrée*), a phrase which means to defy both a prearranged synthesis and an antisocial heterogeneity. In Nancy's portrayal, community of this kind involves neither a totalizing metaphysics nor a compact empirical presence, but rather something like a calling, an advent or perhaps a promise. Eluding both fusion and segregation, the gathering of elements proceeds here through "communication"— but a communication which, exceeding information exchanges, operates on a deeper experiential level: that of the "sharing and co-appearance (*com-parution*) of human finitude." Reflecting an unplanned and unprogrammed mutuality, *communauté désoeuvreé* for Nancy signals the place of "the *between* as such": "You *and* I (between us)—a formula where the *end* does not imply mere juxtaposition but exposition or exposure."[26]

Amplified by Nancy's insights, transversality inserts itself—as a calling—into contemporary global politics: by challenging both hegemonic global power structures (often parading as "universal") and the traditional anarchy of states and societies. Wedged *between* universalist arrogance and forms of particularistic (ethnic, religious, or cultural) belligerence, transversal communication invites individuals and societies to participate in open-ended encounters geared toward neither appropriation nor exclusion. Seen in this light, transversality opens an arena for what Schrag describes as a lived practical ethics—now projected onto the global scale. As in the case of personal relations, global interactions urgently need the cultivation of an ethics of the "fitting response"— where responding responsibly involves both a mutual learning experience and an element of "praxial critique." In the final pages of his book, Schrag himself points to the global or cross-cultural significance of his argument by referring to Christian-Buddhist encounters, and especially to the affinities and divergences between Christian and Buddhist understandings of love and compassion (the latter illustrated by the writings of Keiji Nishitani). What transversality contributes to such encounters is the promise of a responsive engagement which resolutely stops short of a totalizing or coercive synthesis, thus "letting difference be." As Schrag concisely observes by way of conclusion: "This is what I have named *transversal communication,* striving for convergence without coincidence, conjuncture without concordance, seeking to understand within the context of difference."[27]

Notes

1. Calvin O. Schrag, *The Self after Postmodernity* (New Haven, Conn.: Yale University Press, 1997), p. 61 (hereafter cited as *SP*). For some of Schrag's earlier writings, see esp. *Communicative Praxis and the Space of Subjectivity* (Bloomington: Indiana University Press, 1986), and *The Resources of Rationality: A Response to the Postmodern Challenge* (Bloomington: Indiana University Press, 1992). For a detailed review of the latter book, see my "Splitting the Difference: Comments on Calvin Schrag," *Human Studies* 19 (1996): 229–38.

2. Schrag, *SP,* pp. xii, 4. The reference is to Gilbert Ryle, *The Concept of Mind* (New York: Barnes and Noble, 1949).

3. Schrag, *SP,* p. 8.

4. Ibid., pp. 8–9, 25, 28.

5. Ibid., pp. 5–7. As Schrag adds, against the backdrop of our explorations it would appear "that the culture-spheres of science, morality, and art cannot be that facilely divided. There is more of an inmixing of the constative or descriptive, the normative or prescriptive, and the expressive or aesthetic across the domains of science, morality, and art than the framers of the modernity problematic are wont to acknowledge" (p. 32). In his discussion of Habermas, Schrag seems to overestimate the integrative function of "communicative rationality," since Habermas repeatedly insists on the separate trajectories or "logics" of science, morality, and art.

6. Ibid., pp. 12–13, 16–17, 19–20. Regarding Gadamer's "linguisticality of being" (*Sprachlichkeit des Seins*), see his *Truth and Method,* 2nd rev. ed., trans. Joel Weinsheimer and Donald G. Marshall (New York: Crossroad, 1989), pp. 405–28.

7. Schrag, *SP,* pp. 22, 26, 29–30, 35, 38. The reference is to Paul Ricoeur, *Oneself as Another,* trans. Kathleen Blamey (Chicago: University of Chicago Press, 1992), pp. 147–48.

8. Schrag, *SP,* pp. 42–43, 46, 48–49, 54–55.

9. Ibid., pp. 56, 59, 62–63, 66–67, 70. Regarding the notion of the "middle voice," see Suzanne Kemmer, *The Middle Voice* (Philadelphia: John Benjamins, 1993); and John Llewelyn, *The Middle Voice of Ecological Conscience* (London: Macmillan, 1991).

10. Schrag, *SP,* pp. 77, 79–80, 83–84. The reference is to Emmanuel Lévinas,

Totality and Infinity, trans. Alphonso Lingis (Pittsburgh: Duquesne University Press, 1996), chap. 3.

11. Schrag, *SP*, pp. 86–88, 91–92, 96–99. The reference is to Joseph Butler, *The Works of Joseph Butler*, vol. 2, *Fifteen Sermons on Human Nature* (Oxford: Clarendon Press, 1986).

12. Schrag, *SP*, pp. 111–16, 118–21. The reference is chiefly to Søren Kierkegaard, *Philosophical Fragments; or, A Fragment of Philosophy*, trans. David Swenson (Princeton, N.J.: Princeton University Press, 1936), and *Concluding Unscientific Postscript*, trans. David Swenson (Princeton, N.J.: Princeton University Press, 1941).

13. Schrag, *SP*, pp. 124–29, 134, 137, 139–46.

14. Ibid., pp. 27, 67, 69, 75.

15. Ibid., pp. xii, 38, 56. At other points, however, Schrag is quite critical of Foucault and especially of his "read on the Stoic ethics," which "tends to blur the distinction between ethics and aesthetics" (p. 38). In a later context Schrag basically concurs with Richard Rorty's "swipe" at Foucault and other current French philosophers (p. 29).

16. Ibid., pp. 16, 19, 26, 56–57, 60–62, 84, 95.

17. Ibid., pp. 54, 59, 62, 100.

18. Ibid., pp. 100, 137.

19. Ibid., pp. 30, 59, 120. Why Kierkegaard's bifurcation of types of religiousness should have "nothing to do" (as Schrag writes, pp. 135–36) with "the distinction between the finite and the infinite, the temporal and the eternal," thus setting aside "traditional metaphysical binaries," remains obscure. The obscurity deepens in the face of Kierkegaard's statement, quoted in the same passage, that "God does not exist, he is eternal." See Kierkegaard's *Concluding Unscientific Postscript*, p. 296.

20. Schrag, *SP*, pp. 93, 139–40.

21. Ibid., pp. 141–42. Further accentuating Kierkegaard's distinction, a recent (Augustinian) scholar writes: "I want to suggest, hesitantly but firmly, that a Christian ethic ought to recognize the ideal of civic friendship as essentially pagan, an example of inordinate and idolatrous love." See Gilbert C. Meilaender, *Friendship: A Study in Theological Ethics* (Notre Dame, Ind.: University of Notre Dame Press, 1981), p. 75. Schrag himself cites approvingly A. N. Whitehead's statement that "religion is what the individual does with his own solitariness"— probably one of Whitehead's more dubious propositions. See A. N. Whitehead, *Religion in the Making* (New York: Meridian Books, 1960), p. 16; Schrag, *SP*, p. 89 n. 7.

22. Schrag, *SP*, pp. 57, 97–98, 135. The passage occurs in Kierkegaard's *Concluding Unscientific Postscript*, p. 296.

23. Schrag, *SP*, pp. 126, 129–33, 147–48. The references are to Gilles Deleuze, *Proust and Signs*, trans. Richard Howard (New York: George Braziller, 1972); and Félix Guattari, *Molecular Revolution: Psychiatry and Politics*, trans. Rosemary Sheed (New York: Penguin Books, 1984).

24. Schrag, *SP*, pp. ix–x.

25. Ibid., pp. 40–41, 99, 101. The reference is to Julia Kristeva, *Revolution in Poetic Language*, trans. Margaret Waller (New York: Columbia University Press, 1984), and "The System and the Speaking Subject," in *The Kristeva Reader*, ed. Toril Moi (New York: Columbia University Press, 1986), pp. 24–33. For Heidegger's notion of ethics as "ethos," see his "Letter on Humanism," in *Martin Heidegger: Basic Writings*, ed. David F. Krell (New York: Harper and Row, 1977), pp. 233–35.

26. Schrag, *SP*, p. 129. See also Jean-Luc Nancy, *The Inoperative Community*, ed. Peter Connor and trans. Peter Connor et al. (Minneapolis: University of Minnesota Press, 1991), pp. xxxviii–xxxix, 29–31. For a closer review of Nancy's work, see my "An 'Inoperative' Global Community? Reflections on Nancy," in *Alternative Visions: Paths in the Global Village* (Lanham, Md.: Rowman and Littlefield, 1998), pp. 277–79.

27. Schrag, *SP*, pp. 146–47. Regarding Keiji Nishitani, see his *Religion and Nothingness*, trans. Jan Van Bragt (Berkeley and Los Angeles: University of California Press, 1982); also my "Nothingness and *Sunyata*: A Comparison of Heidegger and Nishitani," *Philosophy East and West* 42 (1992): 37–48, and "*Sunyata* East and West: Emptiness and Global Democracy," in *Beyond Orientalism: Essays on Cross-Cultural Encounters* (Albany: State University of New York Press, 1996), pp. 175–99. To be sure, the encounter with Nishitani, and with Asian Buddhism in general, may involve a greater challenge to Schrag's argument than he realizes—given the Buddhist emphasis on emptiness and no-self. See in this regard Jean Stambaugh, *The Formless Self* (Albany: State University of New York Press, 1999).

8

Schrag and the Self

Bernard P. Dauenhauer

C alvin Schrag's *The Self after Postmodernity* is a slender volume that nicely exemplifies the saying that "good things come in small packages."[1] It presents a sophisticated case for a humanistic conception of the self, a conception that maintains a strong distinction between selves and other sorts of entities or events. While acknowledging the merits of postmodern critiques of modernist conceptions of the self, Schrag shows that it is still necessary to recognize that there are irreducible differences between selves and nonselves.

To make his case Schrag investigates the self by asking *who* the self is rather than *what* it is. In his words: "Framing the discussion in terms of 'who' questions instead of 'what' questions, I shall conduct explorations of the self in discourse, the self in action, the self in community, and the self in transcendence against the backdrop of such inquiries as 'Who is speaking?' 'Who is acting?' 'Who responds to other selves?' and 'Who stands within and before transcendence?' "[2] His aim is to focus on the "who experience" that shows up in the course of our communicative practices of speaking, narrating, working, and doing. Attention to this "who experience" reveals that the reason exercised by the self is "transversal."

This approach allows Schrag to engage irenically such postmodernist thinkers as Deleuze, Derrida, Gadamer, Guattari, and Lévinas. It also allows him to draw on crucial resources that Kierkegaard provides. It is these latter resources, above all, that enable Schrag to bring his investigations to fruition.

In this chapter I want first to point out what Schrag's "who" questions have brought into the open. Then, using Paul Ricoeur's recent work, I will propose a way to enrich Schrag's conclusions.[3] This proposal is an amplification rather than a criticism. Finally, however, I will make mention of a few problems that, in my view, indicate that Schrag's account of the self needs further refinement.

For present purposes, I will focus primarily on Schrag's discussions of (a) discourse, (b) action, and (c) community. What he says about transcendence is by no means of small moment.[4] Here, however, I will not give it the attention it deserves.

The first step in Schrag's inquiry deals with the self in discourse. Discourse has the character of an event that involves both speech acts, or what Saussure would have called parole, and language, Saussure's langue. The discursive event is not a simple atomic event. It is always made up of parts that together constitute a narrative. Furthermore, each identifiable narrative comes to the fore against an encompassing horizon of narratives. This narrative character is not merely a feature of certain segments of discourse. It displays itself in the discourse belonging to the learned culture-spheres (science, art, morality, and religion) as well as in the discourse of everyday life. Modernist doctrine notwithstanding, narrativity draws these spheres into an overlapping that cannot be fully disassembled.[5]

From another vantage point, one sees that discourse takes place in multiple ways. With Wittgenstein, one can distinguish a number of language games. Nonetheless, Schrag argues, there is a who of discourse, a self, that remains present to itself throughout the course of its engagement in these several games. That is, the who is not merely a function wholly constituted within a particular language game. The who of discourse maintains its self-identity across different language games. This identity is "concretely manifest in narration . . . emplotting the multiple and changing episodes of his or her communicative endeavors."[6]

Schrag finds support for his conception of the who of discourse in the works of Ricoeur, Michel Foucault, and Julia Kristeva. In *Oneself as Another* Ricoeur distinguishes two sorts of identity, namely, idem-identity and ipse-identity. Roughly, an entity's idem-identity is that by which the entity remains, in some important sense, continuously the same over some nontrivial span of time. This is the kind of identity that persons, in their bodiliness, share with other sorts of entities. There are objective criteria for determining the presence or absence of this kind of identity.

Ipse-identity, by contrast, does not consist of a stable persistence through a temporal span. Rather, it "develops with and in the temporal becoming of the self, occasioning a presence of the self to itself that is borne by a recollection of that which has been and an anticipation of that which is not yet."[7]

The temporality of the ipse-identity is, for Schrag, a "narrative identity," the kind of temporality involved in understanding oneself as a story-telling animal.[8] The self's story of itself is the story of creative advances, new perspectives on the past, and still open possibilities. In short, the self, in its ipse-identity, "exists as temporalized. Temporality enters into the very constitution of who the self is."[9]

Schrag also finds resources for his position in Foucault's work, particularly in the notion of *l'écriture de soi,* or "scripting of the self."[10] Drawing on the Stoics, Foucault develops the notion of a self that scripts for itself an ethos for forming an appropriate character to deal with the vicissitudes of life. The scripting of the self is constitutive of the distinctive sort of identity that the self has. And the scripting takes place in the narrative mode.

Kristeva's account of what she calls the "subject of enunciation" is also called upon to buttress Schrag's view of the who of discourse. She conceives of the subject as being in process, or in Schrag's words, "a dynamic speaking and acting subject in the throes of a creative becoming."[11] With Kristeva, Schrag holds that, because the speaking subject is always also an acting subject, the proper description of the process of character formation through which the self achieves its identity in the course of hearing and telling stories must not neglect the role of decision and action in the building of character. Furthermore, he agrees with her that "the subject constitutes itself at the same time as speaking and agentive subject against the backdrop of an ethos and a body politic of common goals and institutional involvements."[12] Thus Schrag finds in Kristeva support for adding to his account of the narrative self an account of the self involved in action.

When one shifts focus from discourse to action, one finds it impossible to disregard the self's embodiment. Of course, the who of discourse already shows its bodiliness. But the full force of embodiment becomes clearer when one examines action.

For Schrag, as for Merleau-Ponty, the acting body is something other than just another objectifiable physical entity. Rather, it is a "lived body." It is the site of projects to be undertaken and deeds to be performed. It is the point of origin, the spatiotemporal zero point whence doings and makings issue.

The lived body does not occupy space, as a physical thing or a mechanical contrivance does. Rather, it inhabits space. It lives its space as its opening for movement and engagement with its surrounding world. Because the who is bodily, it can perceive things, use tools, and interact with other persons by kissing, punching, smiling, scowling, and so forth. In all these sorts of involvements, the lived body is not some "ur-device" that a basically disembodied mind makes use of to satisfy its interests and implement its design. Rather, "the body as lived is veritably who I am. We can say with Marcel 'I am my body,' and by this we mean that the self-identity that one articulates in one's story-telling is always entwined with a self-identity of bodily intentionality and motility. . . . My body as lived is who I am."[13]

The bodily who of action is by no means a wholly independent, "sovereign" agent. To be sure, there is some moment when the agent, after deciding, on the one hand, to act rather than to refrain from acting and, on the other hand, to do x rather than some alternative y, inaugurates a new action. But this inauguration is not a creation ex nihilo. It is always the beginning of an action whose meaning depends on its being like some prior meaningful actions. Thus, for example, if I were to tackle you, the meaning of what I do depends on a context of other tacklings and what they have come to mean. Tackling in football is not the same action as tackling a fleeing robber. Furthermore, when one inaugurates an action, he or she is always responding to some previous action. Hence, in a way reminiscent of Hannah Arendt, Schrag can rightly say: "The who of action, implicated in the experience of making a decision, is thus at once agent and patient, an initiator of action and a receiver of action, doing the action while responding to prior action."[14]

The fact that an agent is always also a patient makes it clear that the self of action is not and cannot become literally autonomous, independent of all external influences. But neither is the self wholly heteronomous, fully constrained and determined by the forces that impinge upon it. The who of action inhabits a region between pure autonomy and pure heteronomy, between pure activity and pure passivity.[15]

To admit that the self cannot be purely autonomous is, however, by no means to downplay the significance of its capacity to act, to inaugurate real changes in the world. Nor does it diminish the importance of its initiatives in its own self-constitution. The self of action exercises a genuine freedom that can either empower or enfeeble itself or others. Though it is neither a fixed metaphysical substrate nor a sovereign, radical independent observer capable of judging sub specie aeternitatis, the self has "the power to become an effective agent of social change and cultural transformations."[16]

The self's capacity to be an efficacious agent brings with it a responsibility for how it exercises that capacity. In Schrag's view, Kierkegaard has given the best account of the self-constancy and existential continuity that characterizes the who of action. For Kierkegaard, a self achieves its identity and self-constancy in and through the act of choice. By virtue of its self-constancy, a self can bring its past and future to bear upon its present and thereby achieve integrity.

Furthermore, one achieves self-constancy only through linking one-self with others. That is, the "integrity that is won through self-constancy is sustained not only through a proper relation of the self to itself but also in and through the self's relation to others. . . . Kierkegaard makes it explicit that 'this self is not merely a personal self but a social, a civic, self.' "[17]

When one thinks together the characteristics of the self of discourse and the self of action, one finds that this kind of self is inextricably bound up not with its contemporary other selves. It is also tied to its predecessors and, in some real but not easily specified respects, to its successors. Hence this self is a thoroughly temporalized self. The self constitutes and makes sense of itself in terms of a narrative that is always enmeshed in the already told stories of others and that always points forward to stories not yet told. Similarly, the self that acts is always embedded in social practices that form a tradition and that recall persons and things of the past while at the same time its own actions prepare the way for its, and others', future deeds.[18] All of this is just to say that every self is always a self in community.

The phenomenon of being-with-others shows the need for a counterweight to the heavy emphasis that postmodernism places on the alterity of one person to another. Being in a community is constitutive of selfhood. The self is not just present to itself. It is simultaneously present to, for, and with others. Furthermore, this being-with-others is not confined to face-to-face encounters with just a few others. Face-to-face encounters themselves make sense only in the context of the pervasive historical and cultural forces that are at play in the formation both of the individual self and of society. As Schrag puts it: "Just as events of discourse and action require for their intelligibility an insertion into the history of discursive and institutional practices, so also the face-to-face encounters of the self with the other take on meaning only against the background of a tradition already delivered and the foreground of one yet to be enacted. Self-understanding entails an understanding of oneself as a citizen of a polis, a player in the ongoing tradition of beliefs and commitments, a participant in an expanding range of institutions and traditions."[19]

Precisely because the self is always a member of a community of selves, it cannot avoid involvement in ethico-moral considerations. It makes ethical judgments and its own actions stand open to ethical assessment. Thus the self in community has two dimensions. Self-constitution always has anterior sociohistorical sources. But it also involves ethico-moral considerations that the self ought to bring to bear to evaluate and criticize these sources.[20]

Schrag proposes to pull these two dimensions together by way of reflection on the notions of responsivity and responsibility. Whereas responsivity is a descriptive notion, responsibility refers to "an ethos, a way of dwelling in a social world that gives rise to human goals and purposes, obligations, duties and concerns for human rights."[21]

The self never begins itself. It always finds itself already under way by reason of its responsivity to what others do and say. When its response is fitting or appropriate, then it is responsible. The determination of what counts as a fitting response is the work that conscience does.

The fitting response is not one that simply accommodates itself to prevailing mores and practices. It is a critical response that at bottom acknowledges that others have binding claims on one and that discerns how, in concrete practice, one ought to respond to those claims. Ethically proper conduct, then, is "a fitting response to the alterity of the discourse and action of those with whom the self shares a concrete lifeworld. This [account] clearly places a premium on the contextuality of local and historically specific social practices."[22] Schrag emphatically denies that his conception of a fitting response is either relativistic or nihilistic. Truth claims concerning ethical conduct and effective criticism of these claims play themselves out in the "space of communicative praxis, transversally textured, enabling a transhistorical assessment and evaluation to guide a fitting response that is neither ahistorically absolutist nor historically relativistic. . . . The communalized self is in history but not of history. It has the resources for transcending the historically specific without arrogating to itself an unconditioned and decontextualized vision of the world."[23]

A crucial part of Schrag's reply to postmodernist dissolutions of the self is his contention that the sort of rationality that the self exercises is "transversal."[24] The self is born into a world that contains several distinct culture-spheres, each with its own sort of rationality. Specifically, these are the spheres of art, morality, science, and, on Schrag's account, religion. The life task of the self is to effect some sort of unification of these several sorts of rationality.[25]

Consider again Schrag's who of discourse. The who, he says, is an achievement, a performance. Its presence to itself is fragile to be sure. Nonetheless it does have a species of self-identity. Its self-identity is not underpinned by any permanent substratum. Rather, it is "acquired through a transversal extending over and lying across the multiple forms of speech and language games without coinciding with any one of them. This transversal dynamics, effecting a convergence without coincidence, defines the unity, presence, and identity of the self."[26]

In support of his conception of transversality, Schrag cites approvingly Sartre's view of consciousness as that "which unifies itself, concretely, by a play of 'transversal' intentionalities which are concrete and real retentions of past 'consciousness.'" Similarly, Schrag endorses the notion of transversality that Deleuze employs in his discussion of Proust.

Schrag says: "Placing the accent on what he calls the 'importance of a transversal dimension in Proust's work,' Deleuze is able to conclude that the unity at issue 'is always within this dimension of transversality, in which unity and totality are established for themselves, without unifying or totalizing objects or subjects.' Proust's search for lost time thus proceeds via a congruence of viewpoints without concordance, a convergence of remembered moments of time that does not congeal into a coincidence of identity." This unity, Schrag adds, is "a unity that is achieved rather than a unity somehow given beforehand."[27]

What holds for the self of discourse holds also for the self of action and the self in community. Transversal reason is operative in all domains of human activity. Unlike a Cartesianesque reason, which supposedly is the preexperiential source of a comprehensive unity in human life, transversal rationality achieves convergences and conjunctions without canonizing any particular method, belief system, or set of practices as universally obliging requirements of reason. Recognizing reason's transversality "allows us to acknowledge the contingency and contextuality of our historically specific scientific, moral, aesthetic, and religious claims, while nurturing an appetition to see how things might hang together, however loosely. In effect, to tap the resources of transversal rationality and transversal consciousness is to split the difference between the demands for the solidity of an impermeable unity by the moderns and the demands for the vacuity of a porous plurality by the postmoderns."[28]

I concur with David Carr's assessment that the case Schrag makes for his conception of the self is, in the main, persuasive.[29] And it can, I believe, be significantly buttressed by taking note of a distinctive sort of evidence that, in the simplest terms, shows both the irreducibility of selves to things and the complexity of the kind of identity that a self has. This is the kind of evidence that Ricoeur calls "attestation" and that he uses to defend his distinction between idem-identity and ipse-identity.[30]

His own investigations into the constitutive characteristics of selves yield results that Ricoeur says are attested to rather than empirically verified. The distinction between attestation and verification is epistemological, not psychological.[31] Attestation, according to Ricoeur, is "the sort of assurance or confidence . . . that each person has of existing in the mode of selfhood. In saying assurance, I do not say certitude. In saying confidence, I do not say verification. . . . Assurance is, if one wishes, a belief, but it is a non-doxic belief, if one means by doxic belief that which is expressed by the 'I believe that. . . .' I would prefer to speak of credence, as opposed to belief-opinion. The grammar of credence would be expressed in terms of 'believing something' or 'believing in something or someone.' The witness believes what he or she says and one believes in the witness's sincerity. One believes in his or her word. . . . Assurance is linked with confidence in the sense in which someone's word is believable or not."[32]

The importance of the distinction between attestation and verification appears when one considers the nature of the link between action and its agent. For Ricoeur, "the bond between the action and its agent is not a *fact* that one could *observe*. It is a *power* that an agent thinks itself, with complete confidence, capable of exercising."[33] Unless one accepts the validity of the agent's attestation to his or her own power, then Ricoeur's distinction between ipse-identity and idem-identity, and Schrag's invocation of it, remains without experiential support.

Put in other terms, one can say that the crucial evidence in favor of both Schrag's and Ricoeur's cases for insisting on the distinction between selves and other sorts of entities is evidence that finds expression in first-person discourse that is irreducible to third-person discourse. First-person discourse is the discourse that logically demands that we impute our sayings and doings to ourselves as our own. Third-person discourse, by contrast, simply gives an account of what was in fact said and done or happened. At bottom, it is because first-person discourse is irreducible to third-person discourse that Schrag's and Ricoeur's shift of focus from the what of discourse to the who of discourse makes such good sense.[34] To accept attestation as valid evidence is to accept the irreducibility of first-person discourse and vice versa. There is no "external" verification of attestation. Attestation is either self-authenticating or it is irrelevant.[35]

Though Ricoeur's conception of attestation in the main supports Schrag's overall case, it also leads one to notice certain tensions in Schrag's account of the self. Schrag's overall picture of the self is pretty clear. But there is at least one part of it that remains murky. This is the part that concerns how one is to understand the self as agent. There are two aspects of this matter that I want to draw attention to.

Consider first some of the passive-voice locutions that Schrag uses to talk about the self. He speaks of an economy of discourse that is both event and system, both an articulation of something new and a repetition of what is old. Within this economy of discourse "the self is called into being." In this same vein, he says that "the critical zone in which the who is called into being is the zone of the discursive event." Again, he speaks of "the self as emergent, a self emerging from the panoply of communicative practices in which it always already finds itself implicated." And "in the dynamics of decision making the who of action is called into being as an agentive subject."[36]

These locutions provoke one to ask: Who or what does the calling? In fairness, Schrag himself points out the "irony of discourse without speakers, texts without authors, and actions without actors." Furthermore, "the self as the who of action lives between autonomy and heteronomy, active and reactive force, pure activity and pure passivity. The grammatical voice of action is the middle voice, neither a sovereign active voice nor a subordinated passive voice."[37]

The objective of Schrag's "middle voice" talk is clear. It is meant to avoid falling into the trap of a substance metaphysics of any sort. Nonetheless, one can reasonably doubt whether this stratagem can ultimately succeed. Simply put, could a particular self—let us call her Mary— "emerge" from persons, things, forces, and so forth, that are in all respects antecedent to *and* separate from her such that she would be nothing but their product or effect? Would there not have to be some "Mary-potential" that comes to actualization through the influences it undergoes? Perhaps there is nothing that we can concretely predicate of this "Mary-potential" except retrospectively to say that it must have been an "I-know-not-what."[38] But without this "Mary-potential," could Mary ultimately be said to be radically different from other things, things that are exhaustively the effects of their respective causes?

Another way to approach the same issue is to reflect on the emphasis Schrag gives to choice in the self's constitution. Following Kierkegaard, Schrag claims that the act of choosing "centralizes the self and occasions its unity and continuity." By far the most important choice is the choice to be self-constant over time. That is: The self in action is a unified self to the extent that it displays a constancy in discourse and action, in the keeping of its word and in the coherence of its actions, in the delivering of its past promises and in its preenactment of commitments for the future."[39]

Again Schrag finds himself constrained to speak in a middle voice. The self that acts exists in a region "between" the poles of activity and passivity. It exercises there a genuine freedom as one who is "implicated as a seat and source of empowerment within the wider economy of prior and contemporary co-actors."[40]

I do not want to challenge what Schrag says about choice. But I believe that there is room for refinement. One can rightly distinguish the act of choosing from what is chosen. The medievals drew this distinction in terms of liberty of exercise, the liberty to engage in choosing, and the liberty of specification—the liberty to determine which of several possibilities one would actually select. Think again of Mary. Unquestionably, Mary's context predelineates the candidates among which she may choose. Without her context she would have no candidates. But her context can only prompt or provoke her into engaging in choosing. There is nothing like predelineation here. In other words, Mary *initiates* the choosing.

Ricoeur has shown the importance of focusing on initiative. Initiative displays "a *disjunctive* stage, at the end of which we recognize the necessarily antagonistic character of the original causality of the agent in relation to the other modes of causality; and a *conjunctive* stage, at the end of which we recognize the necessity to coordinate in a synergistic way the original causality of the agent with other forms of causality."[41] Without the conjunctive stage, without gearing into the world's causal sequences, initiatives would have no efficacy. But without the disjunctive stage, the break introduced into an antecedent sequence of events, there would be no genuine agency.

Here again I would ask: Must one not acknowledge a specific antecedent "Mary-potential" if there is to be a Mary who ever actually initiates a disjunction? Without this potential, how would Mary ever become a genuine initiator, a true person rather than simply the product of antecedent causal processes? So far as I can see, one has to accept something like a Lockean distinction between being born to freedom and being born in freedom. We are not born in freedom. But unlike other entities we are born to freedom.

Of course, as Schrag says, the self always finds itself already under way, responding to what others say and do and to its material surroundings. This fact is not only empirically verifiable but is also well attested to. But when the self reflects on its always-situated existence, it also finds strong attestation to its own extracontextual capacity to take unique initiatives. Mary's initiating capacity is uniquely her own. So is John's his. Each of them discovers that he or she has not been born initiating but has been born to initiate. Their capacities to initiate are not wholly explicable by the contexts they inhabit. Without trying to set forth a metaphysics for this capacity, I can say that the phenomenology is compelling.[42]

Another angle from which to approach the basic issue here, the issue of how to describe the individual initiating agent, is through a reflection on Schrag's conception of transversal reason and its exercise. Recall that Schrag holds that the self's identity is an *acquisition*. Its unity does not antedate the contingency and context of its historical experience and the articulation of that experience in a multiplicity of discourses and their respective culture-spheres. Though there is some ambiguity in Schrag's talk about reason's transversality, it does not appear that, on his view, there is any antecedent who or self to acquire an identity. We seem to have an acquisition made by no one. I would suggest that Ricoeur has provided a way to avoid this perplexity.

Consider Ricoeur's view that the fundamental mode of being a person is action. As he construes it, action encompasses doing, making, and receiving as well as enduring, the latter being a composite of receiving and doing. Indeed, acting encompasses "saying inasmuch as it is doing, ordinary action inasmuch as it is intervention into the course of things, narration inasmuch as it is the narrative reassembling of a life stretched out in time, and finally, the capacity to impute to oneself or to others the responsibility for acting."[43] Hence, the mode of being of action as Ricoeur conceives of it corresponds to Heidegger's conception of care as the fundamental way in which persons exist and inhabit the world.[44]

Ricoeur's expansive conception of action, or Heidegger's conception of care for that matter, is not incompatible with Schrag's view of reason functioning in, and across, multiple spheres. By its very nature, action stands opposed to completeness. There is no first action or last action, either in terms of time or in terms of status. As long as there is a self there is action. And no self is, in principle, first self or last self. Furthermore, action both unifies and breaks open. It is neither exclusively dispersive nor totalizing, but rather is always in some sense both. Hence Ricoeurian action is thoroughly "transversal." Its voice, one might say, is the middle voice. But this self is still a unique source of initiative and hence is not wholly "called into being" by its context. It is endowed with something of its own that is the ground of its unique capacity to be the unique person that it is.

To conclude, then, Schrag's study of the self after postmodernism serves as a pertinent and valuable rejoinder to some postmodernist efforts to "dissolve" the self. Amplifying his work through leads that Ricoeur supplies can substantially enhance its effectiveness.

Notes

1. Calvin O. Schrag, *The Self after Postmodernity* (New Haven, Conn.: Yale University Press, 1997) (hereafter cited as *SP*).

2. Schrag, *SP*, p. 4.

3. Ricoeur's work on the self is in overall harmony with Schrag's, as Schrag makes plain in his several references to it. See in particular Paul Ricoeur, *Oneself as Another*, trans. Kathleen Blamey (Chicago and London: University of Chicago Press, 1992) (hereafter cited as *OA*).

4. See David Carr's review of *SP* in *Continental Philosophy Review* 31, no. 4 (1998): esp. 449.

5. Schrag, *SP*, pp. 19–20, 32.

6. Ibid., p. 33.

7. Ibid., p. 36.

8. Ricoeur's account of the distinction between ipse-identity and idem-identity is richer and more complex than Schrag suggests in *SP*. But, for present purposes, it is not necessary to delve further into this matter. For a somewhat

fuller presentation of Ricoeur's distinction, see my *Paul Ricoeur: The Promise and Risk of Politics* (Lanham, Md.: Rowman and Littlefield, 1998), pp. 110–11, 120–22.

9. Schrag, *SP,* p. 37.

10. Foucault, "L' écriture de soi," *Corps écrit* 5 (1983), pp. 3–23; "Self Writing," in *The Essential Works of Foucault, 1954–1984,* vol. 1, *Ethics, Subjectivity, and Truth,* ed. Paul Rabinow (New York: The New Press, 1997): 207–22.

11. Schrag, *SP,* p. 40.

12. Ibid., p. 41.

13. Ibid., p. 54.

14. Ibid., p. 59.

15. Ibid.

16. Ibid., p. 61. To support his conception of the self of action Schrag cites, with varying degrees of approval, Deleuze and William James as well as Foucault, Kristeva, Ricoeur, and Ryle. And, as I will point out shortly, it is in his account of action that Schrag's strong affinity for Kierkegaard is particularly evident.

17. Ibid., p. 66.

18. Ibid., p. 71.

19. Ibid., p. 86.

20. Schrag makes it clear that his own position seeks to synthesize the strengths of Charles Taylor's *Sources of the Self: The Making of Modern Identity* (Cambridge: Harvard University Press, 1989); and Jürgen Habermas's *The Theory of Communicative Action,* trans. Thomas McCarthy (Boston: Beacon Press, 1984).

21. Schrag, *SP,* p. 91.

22. Ibid., p. 102.

23. Ibid., p. 109.

24. Schrag draws on Sartre and Deleuze, among others, to develop his conception of transversal rationality and consciousness.

25. Schrag proposes that the kind of rationality operative in Kierkegaard's religiousness B can provide a transversal unification of the culture-spheres (Schrag, *SP,* pp. 128 ff.). For present purposes I need not take up this proposal.

26. Ibid., p. 26.

27. Ibid., pp. 128, 131.

28. Ibid., p. 134. For a full account of Schrag's conception of transversal rationality, see his *The Resources of Rationality: A Response to the Postmodern Challenge* (Bloomington: Indiana University Press, 1992), esp. pp. 148–79.

29. Carr, review of *SP,* p. 450.

30. In a passage dealing with Lévinas, Schrag himself uses the word "attest." But he does not indicate that he takes it to refer to a distinctive form of evidence. See Schrag, *SP,* p. 100.

31. See Paul Ricoeur, "L'Attestation: entre phénoménologie et ontologie," in *Paul Ricoeur: Les Métamorphoses de la raison herméneutique,* ed. Jean Greisch and Richard Kearney (Paris: Cerf, 1991), esp. p. 382. For a fine discussion of Ricoeur's conception of attestation, see Jean Greisch, "Testimony and Attestation," *Philosophy and Social Criticism* 21, no. 5 (1995): 81–98.

32. Ricoeur, "L'Attestation," pp. 381–82. See also Ricoeur, *OA,* pp. 21–23, and Paul Ricoeur, "De l'esprit," *Revue philosophique de Louvain* 92, no. 2 (1994): 251, and "Autonomie et vulnérabilité," in his *Le Juste 2* (Paris: Editions Esprit, 2001), pp. 85–105.

33. Paul Ricoeur, "Morale, éthique et politique," in *Pouvoirs: Revue française d'études constitutionnelles et politiques* (1993), p. 7 (emphasis added).

34. It is not irrelevant to recall here Edmund Husserl's argument against naturalism; see his "Philosophy as Rigorous Science," in *Phenomenology and the Crisis of Philosophy,* trans. Quentin Lauer (New York: Harper and Row, 1965), esp. pp. 79–122.

35. It does not, of course, follow that all claims appealing to attestation are true. Rather, the only way to assess and, if necessary, to rectify such claims is to appeal again to attestation. This is not odd. We take it that the way to test visual perceptions is by way of other visual perceptions.

36. Schrag, *SP,* pp. 17, 20, 26–27, 61.

37. Ibid., pp. 61, 59. Ricoeur also situates the self between autonomy and heteronomy. See Ricoeur, *OA,* pp. 274–76.

38 Perhaps it would not be folly to borrow from Duns Scotus and speak of Mary's *haecceitas.*

39. Schrag, *SP,* pp. 62, 64.

40. Ibid., p. 60. Throughout his discussion of choice, Schrag makes it clear that he has learned much from Ricoeur. He refers explicitly in this context to Paul Ricoeur, *Freedom and Nature: The Voluntary and the Involuntary,* trans. Erazim Kohák (Evanston, Ill.: Northwestern University Press, 1966). And it also seems clear that he draws on Ricoeur's later work as well.

41. Ricoeur, *OA,* p. 102.

42. In informal discussion of my critique, Schrag objected that cause-effect talk about selves was metaphysically mistaken. He considered it to be an expression of a now deconstructively discredited metaphysical "doublet." For my part, I consider it impossible to make sense of the self as an agent without granting that it has some capacity for causally efficacious initiative.

43. Paul Ricoeur, "De l'esprit," p. 248. On Ricoeur's metaphysics of action, see François Dosse, *Paul Ricoeur: Les Sens d'une vie* (Paris: La Découverte, 1997), pp. 651–52.

44. Paul Ricoeur, *Critique and Conviction,* trans. Kathleen Blamey (New York: Columbia University Press, 1998), pp. 74–75.

9

Calvin Hears a Who: Calvin O. Schrag and Postmodern Selves

Linda Bell

W hen asked to participate in a Festschrift for Cal on the occasion of his impending retirement, I accepted eagerly, delighted by the opportunity and knowing how deserving Cal is of such a tribute.

Not to accept, in fact, would have been unconscionable. After all, it was he who introduced me to existentialism in general and to Sartre in particular, thus to what would become a central focus of my philosophical efforts. That was my first year as a graduate student at Northwestern University, and Cal was a visiting professor. Even more important were the tools he thereby gave me for fighting the sexism with which I was being assaulted. Existentialism's denial of essences fortified me in those early battles as I defended myself from challenges, by both fellow graduate students and professors, to my right to be in graduate school and to my dreams of becoming an academic philosopher.

As the male students harassed me with snarls that women had made no significant contribution to philosophy or, for that matter, to any other area, a claim they took not only to be true but also to constitute compelling evidence that *I* had no business trying, I became more and more committed to existentialism. I appealed to it over and over, sometimes explicitly, often implicitly, as I argued against those who would thrust me so violently out of academe and back into what they conceived to be my place. Against their misogyny and naive metaphysical essentialism, I drew on Sartre's challenges to essences, trying to unsettle my tormenters' strange combination of arrogance, mean-spiritedness, and complacency.

Quietly rehearsing to myself those objections also lessened (not much, but some) the sting in the professor's pronouncement—in my presence and to the admiring nods of male graduate students—that fellowships are "wasted" on women since they will only marry, get pregnant, and drop out of school. This was the same professor who had begun one of my first graduate classes by reading my name on the roll with such a sneer, especially the title of "Mrs." that he insisted on including—and stressing.

Not only did existentialism provide much-needed ammunition for my counterattacks, but also it buoyed me as I tenaciously pursued my studies in spite of the persistent opposition. Sartre's emphasis on freedom and responsibility suggested the importance of trying, even if I did not succeed, to change the world as I found it but also to alter the effects of society's expectations and conditioning that I carried in me (as Sartre would say, to make myself into something slightly different from what I had been made). This two-pronged sense of agency, directing efforts toward self as well as toward the world, encouraged me as I fought the habits and other effects of my upbringing, particularly the self-doubts that all too easily reverberated with the claims of female inferiority that I was encountering. I tried to feel what Sartre calls metaphysical uneasiness to my very bones. The assurance that I was free and responsible led to a greater stubbornness on my part, probably kept me in philosophy, and no doubt helped me to stay relatively sane.

Given the significance of a theory of agency in my own life, I was baffled and chagrined to see some of those connected with the recent movement of postmodernism proclaiming not only that subjects can no longer be said to exist but also that our society is now postfeminist. The latter claim astounded me and left me wondering if I had kept myself too busy fighting sexism to notice such a remarkable transition in the society. But then I decided that this was just hyperbole and not even a recently invented one, the claim that we are postfeminist having been affirmed as early as 1919 in response to the success of the women's suffrage movement.[1] Nor is such hyperbole surprising since movements, as well as reactionary forces, seem prone to exaggerate and to view even the tiniest of steps as revolutionary, global upheavals.

The death knells for subjects are, however, more troubling to me and to others. Many feminists have voiced legitimate suspicions concerning a movement in which practitioners seem to undermine notions of agency and self just as a critical mass of white women and of men and women of color are gaining voices and some ability to direct attention to the complex network of oppressions that affect them. This move within postmodernism appears just a bit too well timed and convenient, particularly given the way it serves to subvert forces of change and to uphold the status quo. It is difficult not to see it as part of the backlash against feminism.

Thus, it intrigues me to see Cal leap into the fray, attempting, in *The Self after Postmodernity*, to uphold what is legitimate and even salutary about postmodernism while disagreeing with practitioners who deny subjects and who plunge into relativism. As he tries to avoid relativism and to keep agency from being swept away along with the Cartesian subject, even while acknowledging and affirming the postmodern move generally, Cal adds an importantly nuanced and level-headed discussion to the debate.

In this chapter I examine these two aspects of his book. The first section, "*Homo Narrans* and Agency," presents Cal's rethinking of self: unfolding agency in the context of acting, embodiment, language use, community, and storytelling. While questioning Cal's emphasis on continuity and constancy in the creation of self-identity, I nonetheless support his depiction of what is basically an existential self and his general argument that this self is fundamental to action and need not be denied by those who reject the Cartesian subject. The second section, "Transcendence and Relativism," develops various types of transcendence, their connections to this narrating self, and the ways Cal uses them to challenge the postmodern move into relativism. Though I reject, as unnecessary, intimations of religion or God in any of these, I conclude that Cal's discussion offers important strategies for avoiding both relativism and absolutism.

Homo Narrans and Agency

Cal takes the discussion of subjects in a non-Cartesian direction suggested by his retelling of a possibly apocryphal story about Morris Cohen. When confronted by the question of a profoundly serious student, "Professor, *do I exist?*" Cohen supposedly answered, "Who wants to know?" Instead of disavowing Descartes by denying all subjects, Cal suggests "a refiguration of our mode of questioning, putting us in quest not of an abstract universal nature but rather of a concrete and historically specific questioner."[2]

Turning to Descartes himself, the archvillain of the postmoderns, Cal focuses attention on "the who of Descartes as actor in the world of public affairs," a rather different subject from that described in the *Discourse* and the *Meditations*. In particular, Cal finds in Descartes's letters a writer who is not a subject separate from a body, not an "accomplished master of scientifically oriented methodological doubt," but rather who is an individual concerned with "various bodily ailments and possible medical cures." The Descartes of these letters, for Cal, is a self "called into being as the who that is speaking and listening, writing and reading, discursing in a variety of situations and modalities of discourse."[3]

This "who," Cal observes, is not the infamous Cartesian "translucent cogito struggling to apprehend itself and the variegated furniture of the universe as unblemished *cogitata*, oriented toward a theoretical grounding of all knowledge in a foundationalist epistemology." Rather, the who of Descartes's letters is "a narrating self, a *homo narrans*": "a storyteller who both finds [him]self in stories already told and strives for a self-constitution by emplotting [him]self in stories in the making." Not "a self-identical monad, mute and self-enclosed, changeless and secured prior to the events of speaking, . . . not a 'thing,' a pregiven entity, a ghost in a machine, or whatever," it is instead "an achievement, an accomplishment, a performance, whose presence to itself is admittedly fragile, subject to forgetfulness and semantic ambiguities." In short, this is an existential self, acting, hence embodied, "at once agent and patient, . . . neither a sovereign and autonomous self, . . . nor a self caught within the constraints of heteronomy, determined by forces acting upon it."[4] This is a self always in the process of becoming.

For Cal, postmodernism can—and should—dismiss the "sovereign and autonomous subject, secure in an abiding and monadic self-identity" but without rejecting what he describes as "the concretely functioning intentionality that is imperative in embodied communicative practices." Thus, he affirms "a genuine agent of change," a "self-identity achieved through the emplotment of the who of discourse [that] blends with the bodily self-identity achieved through the enactments of the who of action." Such self-identity, Cal tells us, "in this wider context . . . appears in the guise of *self-constancy* and *existential continuity*."[5]

Cal relates this self-identity to Judge William in Søren Kierkegaard's *Either/Or:* "The self in action is a unified self to the extent that it displays a constancy in its discourse and actions, in the delivering of its past promises and in its preenactment of commitments for the future. It is thus that conjugal love becomes for Judge William a telling exemplar of self-constancy and existential continuity."[6] As one who has always found it difficult to see Judge William as an exemplar of anything very positive, much less of the ethical life, I resist the sort of constancy he exemplifies and particularly the suggestion that it is vital to self-identity. Moreover, and quite apart from my reaction to Judge William, I am far too convinced by Jean-Paul Sartre's analyses of bad faith and radical conversion to place such a high value on constancy. Besides, I read Cal's emphasis on narrative, particularly on the story a self tells itself and others about itself, its thoughts and especially its actions, as allowing for significant breaks with "past promises and . . . pre-enactment of commitments for the future."

In my own case, I can point to a past quite unlike my present. Thinking about self-identity and Cal's claims, I find myself remembering the abstinence cards I signed with such regularity as I was growing up in a southern Methodist church and how lacking in constancy I have been vis-à-vis all those promises to avoid alcoholic beverages. Remembering this aspect of my history, I am amazed at how easily I became unfaithful to my earlier promises, really to much of my early life. On the other hand, I remember with considerable pain how difficult it was—and frequently still is—to throw off some of my early enculturation into values. While much of that training did not actually elicit explicit promises from me, surely my responses can be seen as involving at least implicit commitments. The net effect of that southern upbringing was to develop me into a rather fearful young girl, quite tangled in the knots of convention and convinced that any questioning of the status quo was tantamount to blasphemy, a horrifying prospect to someone who was at that point religious, albeit probably much too conventionally so for Kierkegaard.

Still, though, I readily turned my back on those numerous and enormously sincere pledges never to touch a drop of alcohol. Since then, I have had no problem whatsoever telling people that I earnestly made such promises and then later broke them without a single pang of guilt. Never, though, did I feel that this change or lack of constancy left my self-identity hanging in the balance. When I try to tell the rest of my story, however, I do encounter difficulties, no matter how sympathetic the listener. I feel guilt, both about my ever having been the least accepting of many of the values I was taught *and* about my having tried to extricate myself from them. I feel tainted by my past, by my earlier easy acquiescence in my culture, as well as by my later acts of betrayal, the latter never seeming quite strong or sharp or ultimately pure enough.

One thing I cannot find in all of this, though, is a problem with self-identity. My lack of constancy seems to me just the opposite of a lack of self-identity. Rather, it is a significant part of the way I see myself. It is in fact part of my self-identity. Puzzles and problems, even inconsistencies, abound in this; but, no matter how serious, these too are vital aspects of who I am. I am far from translucent to myself, so the story I tell myself and others is not apt to be much clearer—unless I deliberately impose an artificial and somewhat extraneous constancy and singularity of purpose.

Over the years, I have made other commitments that I now recognize to be *mine*, rather than something others or society thinks *should be* mine; and I readily admit that inconstancy in the face of at least some of these would constitute quite a problem for me, given who I now am.

Whether it would constitute a problem of self-identity, I am not so sure. Such lack of constancy would seriously challenge part of the story I tell myself and others. It would demonstrate that I am not the person I now claim to be and that I do not really cherish the values to which I have told myself and others I am committed. Then I would have to recognize that I am not what I claim to be and that I am not thus committed, but is that a lack of self-identity? Why would it be so when I experienced no crisis of identity as the result of being untrue to those earlier promises and implicit commitments?

I suppose someone could argue that my youth prevented an identity crisis, that I had been simply and fairly thoughtlessly osmosing values, trying to be a "good girl" in the ways set out for me by the conventionalism of my culture and by the dictates of others who convinced me for a while that they knew best what I should do and what my society should be like. While I agree and even incorporate such a recognition into my story, I am not at all sure that my youth makes any important difference. Had I still been mired in the virulent racism of the Jim Crow South when I was in my thirties or forties or fifties, rather than in my teens, even had I been tied into it with the most convoluted of bad faith that Sartre or anyone else could imagine, would I more likely have been catapulted into self-doubt, self-questioning, and an identity crisis by a radical conversion in which I left behind my fierce allegiance to this racism? I think not and for the simple reason that, having left this allegiance behind, I would have a story to tell about that conversion that would make sense of it, given who I am rather than who I was. This seems to me exactly what Cal has recognized when he proposes that we see the human being as *homo narrans*.

Admittedly, my story after my conversion would involve a chasm if I tried to tell it from both perspectives at once, both the earlier bad faith and racist perspective and the later converted and trying-to-move-beyond-racism perspective. To do so would, in fact, be decidedly schizo-phrenic and *would* suggest a crisis in my identity. While I see this duality in perspectives as a problem that I *might* have faced, especially had I remained horribly divided between my racism and my rejection of it (or, for that matter, between my promises of abstinence and my later rejection thereof), it is not what I went through and is clearly not inevitable. After all, I was not and could not be required to adopt both perspectives at once. Surely, after a conversion, no matter how radical, I can tell my story, to myself and to others, from the converted perspective. Although I grant the merit of trying to understand and to help others understand my earlier perspective and how I could have lived for so long within it, still the who, as Cal would say, now attempting to understand her earlier self is the present self, not the previous one to whom the conversion would no doubt seem preposterous and completely unmotivated. For my converted self, however, many good reasons for the change would be apparent, and many compelling motivations could be teased out of my previous existence.

Cal's *homo narrans* seems quite adequate to my demand that it allow for the possibility of conversion, even a radical one. Moreover, it seems to me that wanting or demanding any greater degree of coherence or constancy from this self retrieved from postmodernism's rejection of modernism is itself a hangover from our long and enthusiastic imbibing of the all-too-heady drafts of Cartesian accounts of a unitary and enduring self.

Let me conclude this section with a final caution. As I read back over what I have said in response to Cal, it occurs to me that I may have far too readily and even carelessly shifted my discussion from agency to identity. The more I found myself discussing identity, the more I began hearing my own doubts as to whether my topic was still agency. Agency does seem to be what Cal is discussing with his *homo narrans* or narrating self. This is a self ahead of itself, in the sense that it is *constructing* the story that it tells itself and others about who it is. As soon as a story is constructed, that story is my identity—for now, until I revise my story and thus my identity by taking something else into account, perhaps something that I only then see as important or no longer see as having the significance I previously ascribed to it, perhaps something radically new like a conversion. Identity thus should be recognized as a construct; as such, it should be distinguished from agency in something like the way Sartre distinguishes the ego from the freedom that constructs the ego and projects it out in the world with other objects.

This caution does not affect the case Cal makes against postmodernists who would deny agency and self nor, I think, does it negate anything I have said about its importance. It simply complicates that response in a way that I think is vital and with which, I suspect, Cal would agree.

Transcendence and Relativism

Now, what can we say about Cal's sense that an affirmation of transcendence is necessary if we are to avoid plunging with this narrative self into relativism? I think his attempt to avoid relativism, like his rescue of agency and self, is important for postmodernism, though I have reservations about the intimations of God and religion to which he appeals in the former effort.

Cal begins his discussion of transcendence by continuing his critique of modernism, rejecting "the Cartesian prejudice of determining the rules of method prior to the actual investigation of events and processes." Challenging the framing of the dispute over relativism, historicism, and nihilism "in terms of a conceptual either/or—*either* the theory of relativism *or* the theory of absolutism, *either* the theory of historicism *or* the theory of universalism, *either* the theory of nihilism *or* the theory of a priori values," Cal asks: "Might it be, however, that what is troublesome, disconcerting, or even scandalous is not that no correct theory for resolving the problem has yet surfaced, but rather that the conceptual construction of the issue has somehow been sold as a *genuine problem* and that 'correct' theories continue to be sought?"[7]

Undercutting modernism's dichotomy of mind and body and proposing instead an embodied self begins to create a way between these theoretical either/or's. Another important step in this direction is Cal's affirmation of community. Each embodied, acting self is embedded in social practices: "The praxis in which particular actions are embedded encompasses not only a history of skills and techniques but also a background of habit formation, social customs, and institutional norms." This in turn means, Cal says, that "the we-experience and the I-experience are more intricately entwined than has been acknowledged by proponents of either the social doctrine of the self or the individualist doctrine." Thus, the self embedded in social practices is neither the self defined by the social doctrine ("as simply an ensemble and product of societal relations") nor the individualist "self-constituting individuality that proceeds independently of relations with other selves."[8]

The self "called into being through community and communication" is enmeshed in a complex network of social practices and relations with others. This means, as Cal recognizes, that the criteria for evaluation and justification, for truth and falsity as well as for right and wrong, are not laid out in advance, as Cartesians would have it. Rather they are "contemporaneous with the occurrence of events and processes to be evaluated, . . . *conditioned* by historically specific contexts, but . . . not *determined* by such contexts." It means, too, that "human thought is nonetheless able to transcend the particularities of its social and historical inherence, stand back, establish a distance from both traditional and occurrent practices, suspend beliefs about them, revise and revamp some, and completely overturn others."[9] Here, then, is Cal's middle course between relativism and absolutism with what he calls "a standpoint of critique." As he says,

It is this refusal to be determined by a particular tradition, a particular
conceptual system, or a particular form of behavior that enables
a standpoint of critique that delivers us from a relativism and a
hermeneutical anarchy in which all interpretations and perspectives are
granted an equal claim to thrive because they are simply determined
by their particular place in society and their particular time in history.
Herein resides the mistake of all relativisms, historicisms, and nihilisms,
equating *the context-conditioned* with *the context-determined.*

He finds "the obverse side of the same mistake," however, in "the appeals to universal, unconditioned, and context-independent norms and
principles by the antihistoricism absolutists." Such absolutists share with
relativists the mistaken belief that "no transcendence of the contextualized and contingent particular practices is possible . . . and yearn . . .
for a foundationalist universality and necessity wherewith to ground a
transcending critique that is wholly contextless."[10]

To cut a middle path between relativism and absolutism, Cal proposes a "communalized self," one that "is *in* history but not *of* history,"
one that "has the resources for transcending the historically specific without arrogating to itself an unconditioned and decontextualized vision
of the world." So what, then, is the need for any further discussion of
transcendence? In part, the answer to this is that we are being reminded
of previously argued aspects of the self. The self, as Cal has noted, is
immersed in language; and language involves transcendence since language "is transcendent to the act of speaking." The self in action is also
"a self in transcendence—moving beyond that which it has become and
going over to that which it is not yet." Finally, in the self in community, "transcendence is operant not only in the face-to-face encounter
with the other self as other, but also in the self's recognition that the
totality of received social practices exceeds its particular hold on the
world."[11]

Each of these forms of transcendence in which the self is engaged—
in language, in action, and in community—is different; but each in turn
differs from a final sense that Cal introduces, namely, that of an unconditioned and nondependent existence. Such metaphysical transcendence
is suggested by Emmanuel Lévinas's "radical exteriority," Rudolph Otto's
idea of the Holy, and Karl Jaspers's "Encompassing," the latter two, Cal
tells us, being less informed than the first by metaphysical categories and
emerging more from within experience. Otto's idea of the Holy points
to "an unfathomable depth within the dynamics of religious experience"
and Jaspers's "Encompassing" "mark[s] . . . out an encounter with an
indeterminate range of the possible beyond all world horizons."[12]

These introduce a new notion of transcendence, one that involves radical alterity and that adds important theoretical dimensions to the attempt to chart a postmodernism that avoids the pitfalls of relativism as well as of absolutism. First, Cal maintains, this transcendence serves as a "principle of restraint." As such, it

> curb[s] any absolutization of methodologies, conceptual frameworks, beliefs, creeds, and institutional practices within scientific, moral, artistic, and religious endeavors. It relativizes the culture-spheres and installs a vigilance over their claims and presuppositions, curtailing any temptations to achieve a God's-eye view of the panorama of human history.[13]

Such transcendence has a second function: "its role as a condition for unification." This role nevertheless allows us to agree with the postmodern rejection of a foundationalist epistemological and metaphysical unity and to join in the "celebration of diversity, plurality, heterogeneity, and incommensurability." Inspired by Sartre's claim that consciousness "unifies itself, concretely, by a play of 'transversal' intentionalities which are concrete and real retentions of past consciousness," Cal proposes "a notion of unification, operating transversally in an extending across given contents, converging without becoming coincident, that can be found helpful in elucidating the unifying function of transcendence." This concept "illustrates a dynamic and open-textured process of unifying that allows for plurality and difference and neither seeks the metaphysical comforts of stable beginnings and universal telic principles nor displays an epistemological enchantment with zero-point epistemic foundations."[14]

Finally, Cal claims, transcendence as radical alterity has a third function, "that of providing a space and a dynamics for a transfiguration and transvaluation of the life of self and society within the intramundane culture-spheres."[15] While the first two functions can be read as quite secular, this last function takes us into the explicitly theological realm even as Cal tries to avoid the metaphysical trappings thereof along with the endless quibbles to which they give rise.[16] Thus, with Kierkegaard, he refuses to talk of the existence of God and suggests, with Tillich, "the 'God beyond God,'" speaking approvingly of Tillich's "displacement of the recurring theism-versus-atheism conundrum." Cal goes on to discuss the paradox of giving a gift and the generosity of nonpossessive love, suggesting that in this third function transcendence acts as a lure.[17]

With this last function, Cal seems to have found, or to think he has found, a cross-cultural anchor of some sort, "a transcendence that is older than religion itself." This offers a point of "convergence without coincidence, conjuncture without concordance," toward which those with cultural, and especially religious, differences can strive to understand and to appreciate their similarities and differences.[18] But just why is such transcendence necessary? What exactly does it do that has not already been done by the other types of transcendence—of language, of action, and of community—in which the narrating, embodied, and communal self as previously described is thoroughly ensconced?

As I see it, the existential self that Cal wrenches from the devouring jaws of postmodernism is engaged in the world with others, using language or languages that transcend the users. Each self is itself multiple, telling stories to itself and to others that tie together not only the multiplicity within each self but that reinforce, reinterpret, and/or establish connections between it and other selves. Some of the multiplicity within and among selves reflects the diversity of languages and institutions and the ways these may affect each individual differently, even within the same society, and sometimes so that the individual is conflicted within herself or himself. Some of the multiplicity may result from individual choices and conversions, from betrayals and broken promises to oneself and to others, and even from fairly simple failures of communication.

This means that an individual self confronts a problem with its narrative construction of self-identity that is remarkably similar to that faced by selves who attempt to understand one another and to create a communal identity. The problems of constructing a self-identity that unifies in some way the gaps and multiplicities within an individual are, of course, compounded for those who try to create a communal identity. Even those who find themselves already in relation and in a more or less common language that calls them into existence as selves must communicatively bridge enormous differences in order to maintain their connections with one another. Do not their narratives collectively create a sense of common humanity and of common interests, as well as defining their sense of a shared world, just as individual narratives create for each a sense of self?

Transcendence certainly plays an important role in all of these narratives, both those of individuals and those of groups and communities; but the transcendences that first and foremost make these narratives possible are those of the world in which they find themselves, of their embodied connections with that world and with others who are a part of it, of the institutions and the language that call them into existence as selves, and of the ideals of consistency and cohesiveness that would seem to emerge from the very structure of narration.

In addition, though, Cal thinks transcendence as alterity is necessary, serving as it does the three functions of providing (1) a principle of restraint from absolutism and hegemonic tendencies, (2) a condition of unification consistent with both postmodernism's rejection of foundationalist epistemological and metaphysical unity and its affirmation of diversity, and finally (3) a lure for generosity, nonpossessive love, and crosscultural communication. Cal's hope seems to be that the transcendence of alterity, particularly its third function, will "relativize . . . the belief systems of the particular historical religions and restrain . . . overtures to ecclesiastical colonization." This third and last function does more than simply curb the hegemonic tendencies of various institutionalized religious views, a function already served by the previously delineated and more secular-sounding first function (that of operating "as a principle of restraint, curbing any absolutization of methodologies, conceptual frameworks, beliefs, creeds, and institutional practices within scientific, moral, artistic, and religious endeavors"). Cal's third function is more, as he says, a "beckoning."[19]

While all of these functions seem important, I resist the theological overtones. Of course, Cal will probably object to my characterization of them as theological, desirous as he is of undercutting the distinction between atheism and theism. However that may be, I am convinced that what Cal is attempting with the notion of transcendence as radical alterity and its three functions in fact can be accomplished without any hand waving in the direction of religion or God, by explicitly disavowing both.

What Sartre does with the idea of God offers an example. According to Sartre, human beings are "haunted" by the idea of God and in bad faith often pursue this idea as though it represents a unity that is possible. We may, however, authentically aim for the unity within ourselves and in relations with others that the idea of God can represent when understood and pursued as a regulative idea, as an ideal that can guide human behavior but that cannot be actualized. While such an ideal can offer both lure and critical edge, we need not—indeed must not, according to Sartre—postulate it as real in any sense, whether as existing or as "beyond" existence; this is what it means for an ideal to be taken as regulative.

I conclude, then, that, without appeals to transcendence that assume any more than ideals as regulative ideas, Cal's narrating self, immersed with others in language and more broadly in a world, together with his proposal of a critical standpoint, can be developed in a direction that includes restraint on hegemonic tendencies and that offers sufficient lures to generosity, nonpossessive love, and cross-cultural communication. What is the source of such ideals for those of us who can see no reason to entertain the idea of God as pointing to some sort of reality, either existing or beyond existence? Cal's notion of *homo narrans,* though it hints at an essentializing that may make postmodernists edgy, offers a better answer than Sartre's rather cryptic claims about the idea of God, particularly since these occur so often in connection with his analyses of bad faith. Existential selves, embodied and immersed in language and in a world with others, create identities and communities through their action and through their storytelling. Their actions and their narratives take place within constraints imposed by language, by embodiment, and by preexisting and ongoing relations with others. As they are experienced, those constraints may give rise to a more radical notion of transcendence—transcendence as alterity—suggesting restraint, unity, and generosity beyond the ideals of unity and adequacy required by the very structure of the narratives as narratives.

With Cal's critical standpoint, not only are reconfigured selves pulled from the wreckage after postmodernism's demolition of modernism but also a way around relativism has been opened. This is a discussion that I have found enormously helpful and that, I think, can steer postmodernism in more fruitful directions and away from disastrous affirmations of relativism and denials of agency.

Notes

With apologies to Dr. Seuss and with thanks to my writers group—Valerie Fennell, Elizabeth Knowlton, Libby Ware, and M. Charlene Ball (to the last especially for the subtitle)—and to David Weberman, for their helpful comments.

1. Valerie Bryson, *Feminist Political Theory: An Introduction* (New York: Paragon House, 1992), p. 102.

2. Calvin O. Schrag, *The Self after Postmodernity* (New Haven, Conn.: Yale University Press, 1997), pp. 12–15 (hereafter cited as *SP*).

3. Ibid., pp. 15–17.

4. Ibid., pp. 25–26, 33, 59.

5. Ibid., pp. 57, 61, 62.

6. Ibid., p. 64.

7. Ibid., pp. 106, 103.

8. Ibid., pp. 71–72, 79.

9. Ibid., pp. 87, 107–8.

10. Ibid., p. 108 (emphasis added).

11. Ibid., pp. 109, 111.

12. Ibid., pp. 111, 114–17.

13. Ibid., p. 124.

14. Ibid., pp. 127–30.

15. Ibid., p. 134.

16. Actually, all three can be read in a religious way. First, one might very well ask if the very fact that Cal proposes three functions is itself suggestive of

LINDA BELL

Trinitarian thought. Second, a less suggestive and more direct indication of the Christian Trinity itself squishing under the door is Cal's actual delineation of these functions—restraint, unification, and transfiguration/transvaluation/nonpossessive love. Not just the content but even the order of these fit the traditional order of Father, Son, and Holy Ghost.

17. Schrag, *SP,* pp. 136–37, 139–44.

18. Ibid., pp. 147–48.

19. Ibid., pp. 148, 124.

10

Romantic Love

Martin C. Dillon

> Transcendence in its threefold function as a principle of protest
> against cultural hegemony, as a condition for a transversal
> unification that effects a convergence without coincidence,
> and as a power of giving without expectation of return, stands
> outside the economies of science, morality, art, and religion as
> culture-spheres. This defines transcendence as a robust alterity.
>
> —*Calvin O. Schrag*, The Self after Postmodernity

This essay is a critique of romantic love. The critique turns on the
idea of transcendence. Calvin O. Schrag is a philosopher of transcendence: He transcends the borders that demarcate the cults of
contemporary philosophy, and he transcends himself in each new writing venture; he does these things by maintaining the wonder that sustains philosophy, the wonder that feeds on attunement to transcendence.
Schrag has provided a measure for my own thinking about transcendence: His writing provokes me, it goads me and guides me, it reassures
me in moments of convergence, and it challenges me in moments of
dissonance. Both of these moments will be apparent in the text below.

The themes of transcendence, self-transcendence, and love have
been intertwined as far back as our histories can take us, and the ways of
thinking about them and acting upon them are diverse and conflicting.
Schrag's musings on these themes in the concluding pages of *The Self
after Postmodernity* jolted me: The quest for the unconditional reflects the
finitude to which philia and eros are responses, but are such responses
fundamentally ill conceived?

If the quest for the unconditional is "older than religion itself," if
it transcends religion itself, if (now in my terms) it has led to noble lies,
mystifications, the self-deceit of "metaphysical comfortizing," and all the
other pernicious foibles that seem always to attend humankind's highest

venture, then maybe that quest has been misconceived.[1] Nietzsche certainly makes a strong case in favor of that suspicion, at least so far as philia is concerned. What, then, of eros?

The critique of romantic love offered here is my best attempt to "protest against [the] cultural hegemony"of the romantic model of love. I will try to show that we suffer under its insidious sway. And I shall argue in favor of another manner of loving that seeks "convergence without co-incidence" in exactly those terms. But I shall argue against the unconditional expressed as a "giving without expectation of return," a giving that stands outside the economy of reciprocity. It is my view that love is always conditional, subject to the limitations of human embodiment, and can deny expectation of response only in self-dissembling modes of wistful denial: Altruism and commitment must be conceived in different terms than those which appeal to the unconditional. My view of the love that is beyond romance draws upon Merleau-Ponty's notion of reversibility of flesh, hence it takes reciprocity in both its brighter and darker hues as intrinsic to love's peculiar response to alterity. On this point, Schrag and I obviously diverge.

Beyond the obvious, however, it may be that Schrag and I are trying to do the same thing, trying to do what philosophers have always tried to do: to articulate the primordial sense of transcendence that is the prime mover of thought. Perhaps it would be appropriate to think of this phase in our dialogue as a venture in *transversal communication:* "striving for convergence without coincidence, conjuncture without concordance, seeking to understand within the context of differences."[2]

Introit

The ancient Greeks tell two stories about the coming into being of Eros. In one account, love is the oldest of gods, the first to emerge from primal chaos, and the one responsible for the creation of world order. In the other, Eros is among the younger gods, a fair and delicate creature who needs a peaceful environment in order to exist, but disrupts it with random darts of love.[3] In my view, these two apparently competitive accounts are compatible and mutually reinforcing: Love must be seen as both primordial and a new arrival on the cosmic scene.

Past, present, and future are dimensions of time which flow uninterrupted from one mode to another, but each has its own characteristics which set it apart. We know the past in detail, but cannot change what has already happened. We know the future only generically—we know that certain kinds of things will happen, that there will be weather, politics, and fluctuations in the stock market—but we do not know concretely what determinate shapes these events will take, although we can try to anticipate them, even to influence how they play out. One dominant characteristic of the present is its capacity to engage and envelop us. The present is now, it is urgent, it is more real than past or future. It is the context of our moods, our sense of reality, and it governs our thinking in moments of decision and action. Lessons from the past and forebodings about the future certainly play a part, but only as they insinuate themselves into the decisive moment. This characteristic of the present generates temporal myopia, an unobtrusive arrogance that accords the horizon of the present in which we live a privilege it may not deserve. We differ in age, gender, cultural heritage, and so forth, and have some awareness that others look at the world through different perspectives. Indeed, it is a fact of life that others force us to this awareness; they demand respect and a measure of humility to accommodate our differences. This tempers our arrogance, our egocentricity. The constraints on our temporo-centricity, however, are not enforced in this way: We *all* live in the present.

The ideal of love that governs the present time is romantic love. In the essays I have written on the subject, I have adopted the consensual view of European scholars that romantic love had its inception among the noble classes in twelfth-century France and was shaped by the social and religious thinking of that time and place. I continue to think that this narrowly focused snapshot of romance is exquisitely revealing, perhaps more revealing of romantic love than any other picture that could be put in a tight frame. But as I probe the romantic ideal to uncover its latencies—the power that makes it so robust and pervasive despite its conspicuous flaws and the disasters it invites—I have learned to recognize its features in times and places far removed from the court of the countess of Champagne. The rape or abduction of Helen by Paris recounted by Homer in the *Iliad* has romantic tendrils that reach back into the murk of prehistory. The same could be said of the *Pillow-Book* of Sei Shōnagon.

Romance is the name of the god of love that reigns in the present, and it was christened for the congregation of our era just as the scholars say. In cosmic time, the godling of romantic love is a newborn, but this parvenu is also as old as Father Time, a glint on the scythe he carries, a response to human finitude and the passage of time that leads us all from darkness into darkness. Romantic love is a peculiar way in which we answer to the call of transcendence; it is one of the ways we respond to the awesome appeal of what lies beyond us, the way that now has us in its thrall. Romantic love is an unmindful invocation of catastrophe. Romance is vertigo, the swoon into an infantile dream. Romantic love is not our only erotic option, and it is certainly not the best one. We are so caught up in the present, however, that we take the form of love that now prevails, romantic love, as the only form, as love itself.

Romantic love is a swerve in cosmic time, a phase in the development of humanity comparable to adolescence. It is a passage that we may have had to make, given our global history and its interdependencies, but there are other ways we might have gone and other ways that we might now go. The love-hate continuum that has ever ruled over our relations with each other and ourselves can express itself over a wide spectrum of psychological structures and social forms, and these patterns can vary in degrees of intensity, gratification, tumult, and tranquillity. This variance in love style is apparent to cultural historians, but it is also discernible within our own culture as individuals mature and pass through different phases of life. The emotional and cognitive forms of human relations among grandparents are different from those apparent among parents, those involved in mate selection, children, and infants. The variance in love styles within each of these age-groups is also evident. There are choices that can be made, options that can be sought or avoided.

It is doubtless true that we do not live in a free space of infinite possibility. Sexlove is highly regulated by law, custom, cultural expectation, family circumstance, and the like. We internalize the values that circulate about us like the air we breathe, and we take them in with as little thought as we draw a breath. When the air turns noxious, however, as now it has in many places, we begin to pay attention. Such is the case with the values of sexlove which we have tacitly adopted and allowed to govern our lives. I will leave it to others to document the sexual malaise of our time; it is tedious work because the list of ills is long. AIDS, of course, but also chlamydia, herpes, and all the other sexually transmitted diseases. Unwanted lives being yanked into the world or aborted in huge numbers. Rape, molestation, commercialization, depersonalization, harassment, and public humiliation. Name your poison. The one that strikes me as particularly emblematic is the ambivalence of values that turns our leaders into hypocrites. The private lives of our statesmen cannot stand scrutiny, and neither can the lives of our spiritual leaders, including our athletes, military heroes, and other celebrities. Not to mention the clergy. If, as Aristotle argued, tragedy consists in the fall of persons of great magnitude from happiness to misery and makes them "worse . . . than the men of the present day," then we have more tragedies in a decade of evening news than Sophocles and Aeschylus could have depicted in their lifetimes.[4] Perhaps it has long been thus, perhaps the ridicule is in the eye of the TV camera. I leave the historical point moot; the collision between public values and private lives, however, is rampant on both sides of the TV screen and brings misery upon us all. Perhaps we are privileged to have our noses rubbed in it. Maybe we are now in a position to do something about it.

There are those who argue that it is impossible to achieve erotic fulfillment in a cultural climate rife with political and social injustice. First we must change the air, then we can breathe. The metaphor makes my point: It is impossible not to breathe. One does what one can under the circumstances. Hide in a closet or carry a banner in a parade, there is no way not to be engaged in love-hate; genuine indifference is not an option in the spectrum of human relations (or it is pathology in its starkest form).[5]

Is the romantic ideal of love responsible for the erotic malaise of our times? My answer to this question will emerge throughout the course of this essay, but it may be well to give a preliminary sketch here at the beginning. Hitherto I have argued that the deep source of our troubles lies in the demonization of sex that begins with Socrates, consolidates in medieval Christianity, and sustains itself through a kind of metaphysical inertia or perpetuation of values despite attenuation of belief in the underlying religious doctrine. Romantic love feeds on the sexual ambivalence of this tradition: It is aimed toward ecstatic unification and affirms sexuality as the means, but in its quest for a purely spiritual union it negates the flesh of sexual desire and posits the body as the matter that separates us from one another without acknowledging that our bodies also allow us to come together.[6] I continue to believe that this is the case, that romance is the unhappy form that love must take in a milieu governed by the demonization of sex, but here I want to temper my critique and seek a primordial truth of love that manifests itself through the distortions of romantic illusion.

A Genealogy of Romance

The past is murky, but origins are discernible. Not absolute origins: They require some sort of creator god who is cause of itself and all things that follow, and what is named in the term *causa sui* is a classical contradiction in terms that can be celebrated as a mystery of religious truth or rejected as a form of anthropomorphic projection and self-mystification. The origins of which I speak do not have to be retrieved from relics and runes, but are evident in the present. Organic beings are born; they grow, reproduce, decay, and die. Like all things, we come into being and pass away. We seem to be more acutely aware of this than other beings; we are reflective. Reflection on our transience is the source of philosophy, literature, religion, and their derivatives. It is also a main source of love: eros, philia, agape, and their derivatives. The source or origin named here is primarily psychological, although it manifests itself historically and can be traced in relics, runes, and ruins.

In classical terms, to know a thing is to know its causes and effects, why it came into being, and its contribution to cosmic destiny. The principle of sufficient reason is one expression of the desire to know things in this way: For a thing to be, there must be a reason which suffices to account for its being. Reflection is characteristically narcissistic; it is concerned with itself, wants to know itself, and gives rise to the questions of provenance and destiny. The first truth of reflection is the ignorance it betrays in its interrogation. The first truth of reflection is awareness of transcendence, that what we seek lies beyond us, else we would not be seeking it. The second truth, which bubbles to the surface of awareness long after the first, is that we must have some sense of what lies beyond us, else we could not begin to look for it or hope to recognize it if we found it. The third truth takes longer still to formulate itself: This is the truth that the transience, finitude, or temporality that is the source of the interrogation precludes arriving at an answer that is final and absolute, yet nonetheless affords a growing awareness of the thing we cannot but understand since we *are* it. Alpha and omega can never be known, but the progress in understanding the processes of birth and death is indisputable.

Socrates is generally acknowledged to be the thinker who brought the essentially narcissistic flavor of reflection to the forefront of philosophy. Know Thyself was his Delphic motto, and Socratic ignorance his wisdom: He knew that he did not know, and in that knowledge demonstrated his awareness of transcendence. He articulated the first two truths of reflection mentioned above.[7] Whether it is Socrates or Plato who is to be held accountable for obscuring the third for better than two millennia is a question I leave for scholars better equipped than I to answer, and I will content myself to argue that it did get obscured in the Platonic dialogues and that in that occultation lies the germ of romance.

In the *Symposium*, the classic work on love that is cited by nearly every important writer on love in the Western tradition, Plato sketches a theory of human development that mirrors the analogy of the divided line in the *Republic*. Life is a quest for permanent possession of the ideal in which truth, beauty, and goodness coincide. The motive force of this quest is Eros or love, the striving for transcendence driven by desire for what we do not possess but do glimpse in a sort of prescience as that which will answer our need and make us happy. In the *Symposium*, Plato emphasizes the beautiful aspect of the triadic ideal and says that we begin life fascinated by images of beauty, fleeting appearances. Some do not pass beyond this stage of thralldom to passing fantasies; perhaps these are the artists Plato criticizes in the *Republic* for dwelling in fascination with things that evanesce and that are thrice removed from reality. For Plato, permanence in time is the essential feature of genuine reality, and images are destined to fade. Others, however, respond to the call of Eros and grow out of this stage into the next, where the object of desire is a physical object, something that lasts longer than a fantasy, perhaps a human being whose physical being radiates beauty. Those whose lives are structured around the quest to possess beautiful persons dwell in this second phase of development.

The beauty of human bodies is tied to flesh, and flesh decays. Its transience betrays its lack of reality, and some of us are led to seek a higher manifestation of beauty in things that are more enduring than the physical beauty of objects. The quest is for a vision of the form that makes beautiful things beautiful. The transition here is from an earlier sense of the Greek word *eidos*, the visible physiognomy of a thing or the face it presents, to a later one, the idea or form that allows us to see the thing as what it is. It is by virtue of the eidos or idea of beauty that we can recognize Helen as beautiful. Those who abide in this domain are attracted by ideas rather than things. They are closer to reality because ideas do not pass away as things do, but are more permanent in time.

At this point in the dialogue, Plato writes that Diotima (the wise woman from Mantinea who taught Socrates about love) issues a warning. She tells Socrates that he may not be able to understand what she is about to say. So far, her teaching has remained in the finite realm to which mortals have access, but the true object of love, the ultimate reality, does not change at all. To attain permanent possession of this eternal object, one must become immortal:

> What may we suppose to be the felicity of the man who sees absolute beauty in its essence, pure and unalloyed, who, instead of a beauty tainted by human flesh and color and a mass of perishable rubbish, is able to apprehend divine beauty where it exists apart and alone? . . . Do you not see that in that region alone where he sees beauty with the faculty capable of seeing it, will he be able to bring forth not mere reflected images of goodness but true goodness, because he will be in contact not with a reflection but with the truth? And having brought forth and nurtured true goodness he will have the privilege of being beloved of God, and becoming, if ever a man can, immortal himself.[8]

The end of the quest symbolized by the figure of Eros is immortality, coincidence with immutability or absolute reality, achievement of ultimate transcendence. This requires departure from human flesh, this "mass of perishable rubbish," and entering a realm of pure ideality, pure spirituality—the spirit or mind or psyche being "the faculty capable of seeing" the absolute wherein truth, beauty, and goodness coincide (although it must detach itself from the flesh that tethers it to finitude in order to attain this purity).

As soon as he has articulated this theory, Plato illustrates it in dramatic action. Alcibiades, a golden youth of Athens and an embodiment of physical beauty, bursts into the symposium and confesses his unrequited love for the notoriously ugly Socrates. He tells how he sought to seduce Socrates and win his love, and how he was rejected. Socrates is a philosopher driven by the highest form of Eros to seek ultimate reality and is living his life as a preparation for death, departure from his finite body, and entrance into the realm of pure ideality. He has long since transcended the physical desire that Alcibiades, in his ignorance, is trying to awaken in him. Thus Socrates becomes the symbol of highest development of love, the sublimation or *Aufhebung* of eros into philia.[9]

Where in this Platonic teaching are we to find the germ of romance, that mystification of the quest for transcendence? The short answer is easy to state: the germ of romance lies in the detachment of the idea from the flesh, in the polarization of the two senses of eidos, physiognomy and form, that leads to positing them as mutually exclusive. The Platonic program for human development requires us to take leave of our senses in order to bring our minds to perfection; it requires us to depart from our bodies in order to free our spirits to live in absolute ideality. Here is the thought from which the ideal of romantic love will be generated.

Romantic Love

Romantic love is the desire to appropriate an ideal, to possess perfection, to consummate a union with the beautiful object that betokens sheer pleasure. The object of romantic love can also be defined as love, itself: the romantic lover is in love with love, in love with the ecstatic high that comes in the early phases of a romantic liaison. What the romantic lover seeks is the *experience* of love; the love-object is merely the means of producing this experience. These two definitions coincide: The beautiful object is conceived as such because it produces exquisite pleasure. The contradiction that lies at the heart of the romantic quest is the opposition between the ideality of perfection and the reality of the bodies engaged in the experience. One aspect of this contradiction has already been noted: ideals, especially the ideal of perfection, are held to be timeless and unchanging, but bodies dwell in the domain of transience, and the physical beauty associated with youth is fleeting. Beyond this contradiction, however, there is another which may be even more devastating to the romantic project.

Our bodies are the source of our identity. We come into being when our bodies are conceived or born, and we cease to be when our bodies die.[10] The actions that define our histories, including our speech acts, are bodily actions. Our bodies are not merely vehicles through which some noncorporeal spirit manifests its intentions; our minds—our intelligence, memory, desire, and character—are distributed throughout our flesh and could not function without it. It is a long-standing philosophical mistake to conceive our minds and bodies as disjunct and mutually opposed; they are inextricably intertwined, two aspects of the same reality. The crucial point in the present context is that our bodies are the means by which we enter the social milieu. We recognize each other through our bodily appearance and understand each other through our bodily comportment. We are our bodies, including the traces that other bodies have visited upon ours and the traces our bodies deposit in the world as marks of its passage. It is as bodies that we are and are known. In that broad sense, all our knowledge of each other is carnal knowledge.

Carnal knowledge is usually understood in a narrower sense as sexual intercourse, as the knowing of each other that takes place when we sense each other through the broad spectrum of our body's perceptual capacities. To touch another's body, to feel its flesh and sense its peculiar being, is to encounter another person and learn something of who that person is. Although we can, and sometimes do, attempt to minimize the personal contact in sexual relations, the very means we employ to avoid that contact betrays the fact that carnal knowledge is knowledge. Here lies the contradiction in the heart of romance.

The project of romantic love is to possess an ideal, but bodies are not ideal. Plato knew that. Plato knew that bodies decay and thus could not be perfect. Plato sought perfection and taught us to follow Socrates' example: to eschew the flesh, the "mass of perishable rubbish," and to seek perfection in a realm beyond, a realm of sheer transcendence to be found on the far side of finite human embodiment. Socrates would rather die than embrace the body of Alcibiades. I have spent decades arguing that Socrates made a bad choice, that the ideas and values informing the example left to us by Socrates are misguided and the cause of widespread suffering. Socrates did, indeed, deliberately choose death, and Alcibiades fell from honor into disgrace. I think they would both have led happier, more fulfilled lives, had the wisdom of Socrates reached the third truth of reflection mentioned earlier, the truth that human finitude precludes possession of absolute ideality on this side of the grave, and that on the far side there is nothing.

Nonetheless, there is nobility in the Socratic choice, something that attracts us to it. Similarly, we are attracted to the nobility in the romantic quest. It is the same nobility.[11] Socrates and the romantic lover are both drawn to something higher, something better, than what they see around them. They want—desire—something more. This is the quest for transcendence, born of dissatisfaction and the sense that there is something more to be had. This quest for transcendence marks the point of intersection between the philia that drove Socrates and the eros that drives the romantic lover.

Transcendence. The term is overdetermined; it bears a host of meanings, meanings that generally refer to what is beyond us, but there are as many names for the beyond as there are for divinities both sacred and profane. The goad is need, want, desire, or finitude in general: our sense that we lack something that is required to make us whole or happy or fulfilled. In my view, it is this need that has led us to create our gods and goddesses as symbols of the wholeness, goodness, and perfection we so conspicuously lack. We seek union with godhead as the means of completion and conceive this quest for union as a spiritual quest, that is, as a quest to embrace and embody ideality through the highest aspect of ourselves, the aspect we designate as mind, psyche, spirit, Brahman, atman, soul, and so forth. To succeed in this quest we typically are called upon to go through some self-transforming ordeal, a trial that proves our worth, brings out the best in us, and prepares us for the union. Self-transcendence, going beyond ourselves, is required to reach the transcendence we seek.

Transcendence and self-transcendence: These are the marks of love, be it love for another human being (eros), for wisdom (philia), for humanity as such (agape), or for god (*theosebeia*).[12] Romantic love embodies transcendence and self-transcendence; it participates in that deep truth, but does so in its own unique way.

Romantic love might be viewed in a preliminary way as the deification of the love object. Here is the theme of overestimation (Freud) or crystallization (Stendhal) coupled with the attempt to define and vindicate oneself through the amorous gaze of the fascinated other (Sartre).[13] I attribute perfection to my beloved; my self-dissimulating desire grants to her a perspective that both sees me as I am and affirms me absolutely. If this mystified attribution of perfection is mutual, I find in her eyes the vision of myself that makes me whole and complete. I deify my beloved in order to become the god I must be in order to fulfill my quest for transcendence.

The unfortunate fact that we remain finite poses a problem for all human quests for transcendence, be they religious or amorous in nature. If the transcendence sought is conceived as an absolute, as Plato did, then the problem encountered is the incommensurability of the finite and the infinite, the lack of a common ground on which mortal humans can join with the immortal and unchanging. Different religions offer different solutions that run the gamut from mediation by saints and prophets to mystical union in some form of ecstasy. Christianity, with its doctrine of the Trinity, calls upon the faithful to believe what they cannot understand, the mystery of the coincidence of finite man and infinite god in the figure of Jesus of Nazareth. Romantic love solves this problem in a way that sets it apart from other quests for transcendence and defines its own peculiar character.

Whatever we can reach, touch, understand, or join together with ourselves cannot be transcendent because that contact presupposes that the object is no longer beyond ourselves. Anything a finite human can possess must itself be finite, hence not transcendent. To confer the status of absolute upon a finite object is idolatry. As I have just suggested, romantic love is a form of idolatry, but one with a unique twist—the twist that gives romantic love its identity. In deifying the beloved, the romantic lover at the same time places a barrier between himself and the object of his desire. He keeps his quest alive by strategies designed to preclude the contact with, and carnal knowledge of, his beloved that would reduce her to finite proportions and destroy her transcendence. The beloved, for her part, is complicit in this prohibition and seeks always to remain aloof, elusive, unattainable, mysterious, in any case, unpossessed.[14]

The classical example—upon which I shall not dwell, having treated it extensively in other work—comes to us in the songs of the twelfth-century troubadours in the south of France.[15] They sang of love necessarily unrequited, the prohibition against sexual culmination being the structure that gave romantic love its ethereal ideality. The reality of the time, at least for the aristocracy who adopted this form of love, was governed by Christian values of absolute fidelity in marriage and an economic structure that used marriage as a means of consolidating family wealth. The young bride was given to the older groom, a man of means, in order to unite the families and augment their power. The groom got the girl and her dowry and was not constrained by vows of fidelity as was she. The bride got a man twice her age and economic security. What she did not get was an appropriate lover. It was in this context that the countess of Champagne, delivering a judgment in a court of love convened in 1174, makes the following declaration.

> We say and affirm . . . that love may not extend its rights over two married persons. For lovers grant each other all things mutually and freely without constraint of any motive of necessity, whereas the married are in duty bound reciprocally to submit to the will of the other, and to refuse each other nothing.[16]

Love and marriage are seen as mutually exclusive or at least opposed in principle: Marriage is governed by duty, but love is free, constrained only by the lady's virtue. Her husband has exclusive rights over his young wife's body, but her soul is free to seek the love it desires. She is wooed by troubadours and young men of her own age preparing to seek their fortunes on adventures like the Crusades. She grants them her favors, but the favors granted were fetishes, perhaps a scented handkerchief, that the young men carried next to their hearts as they jousted at home or plundered abroad. The successful ones returned, older and richer, ready now to take young brides of their own.

This is the stuff of which romantic poetry is made. The barrier of conjugal fidelity intensifies the yearning, but beyond this it allows the lovers to create their own fantasies of the love object. One loved the vision of the brave youth or wistful lady that one nurtured in one's dreams. One could do that freely because there could be no body contact, no carnal knowledge of the person involved on the other side of the relationship. And if, by fate or overpowering emotion, the barrier was breached— as it was by Lancelot and Guinevere, Tristan and Isolde, Abelard and Héloïse—disaster and ruin were sure to follow. Furthermore, when Tristan takes Isolde away from her royal husband and off to the Forest of Morrois, when they breach the barriers of her marriage vow and his vow of fealty to the king, they create a new barrier: When King Mark finds them asleep in the forest, they are separated by Tristan's sword, a symbol of chastity. The point is that the intense experience of love they sought could not survive without the barriers that kept their fantasies alive by preventing them from knowing one another.[17]

Here, as in Plato, we see a spiritualized form of love which forsakes the eidos of the fleshly physiognomy for the eidos of the ideal vision. The transcendence of the beloved is preserved by willful ignorance of the flesh-and-blood reality of one's partner. The price is high—romantic love must remain unrequited or fall into ruin—and there is no way to negotiate around these terms: gods that can be touched are no longer godly, but fallen idols. Whence follows the dilemma that devastates romantic love:

> If I possess my love,
> she is not what I long for;
> if I do not possess my love,
> my love is unrequited.

Once one learns to recognize this structure, one finds it cropping up everywhere in the literature of love. For Freud, the primal love object is mother, but the father's prohibition, the taboo against incest, precludes me from possessing her. Hence, for every love object or mother surrogate, if I can have her, she is not the mother figure: My desire is predicated upon her transcendence, her unattainability. For Sartre, the project of love is to possess a freedom as a freedom: For her love to be fulfilling to me, she must give it freely, but what is given freely can also be taken away, and the fear of loss produces anxiety. The lover's quest is to secure through possession the love that is freely given: a manifest impossibility which recapitulates the familiar dilemma. If it is free, it cannot be possessed; if it is not free, it is not what the lover seeks. Postmodern erotic pessimism offers another variant of the same structure: The satisfaction of desire is the death of desire. If you fulfill my desire, I no longer want you; if you do not, I go unfulfilled. One preserves the frisson of desire through strategies of indefinite deferral and unconsummated foreplay or *jouissance*. There are significant differences among these accounts, to be sure, but they remain variations on the same theme, the theme of romantic love: Transcendence attained is transcendence lost.

Beyond Romance

The full spectrum of contemporary erotic malaise cannot be reduced to the dissatisfaction that the structure of romantic love invariably produces. Romantic love is but one of the dead ends to which the demonization of sex leads. Nonetheless, it does explain the ambivalence characteristic of our times, the oscillation from deep cynicism to romantic yearning: We know we cannot have what we want, and that produces cynicism, but we cannot keep ourselves from yearning for it anyway. The ecstasy of new love—the renewal of self in the embellishing eyes of the fresh lover, the familiar stories and gestures and ploys of endearment redeployed before an appreciative other not yet weary of them, the sexual fervor one had almost forgotten—lures us on to cast ourselves into another whirlwind with the forlorn hope that this time it will not just add to the wreckage. We recapitulate the turmoil of adolescent mate selection, but this time with more lives involved. This time a spouse is rejected, not just a former lover, and one's children lose the security of the familiar home as the taken-for-granted horizon of the only lives they have known. One has but one life to live, and one's time and market appeal are running out. One has been duped and disappointed. This is not the way it was supposed to be. There must be more. So we make another desperate grab for transcendence.

The pattern is as dismal as it is prevalent. The promise of true romance sells everything from perfume to vitamin pills. It furnishes the lyrics for operas as well as popular songs and the plots for stage, screen, and novels. *Cosmopolitan* could not exist without it, and neither could *Playboy.* As a culture we are shoveling our lives into a hole that cannot be filled. There has to be another way.

And there is. But we are searching for it in the wrong place. The new wave of thought trickling its way down into popular culture with the promise of something new, different, and better calls itself postmodernism. It is heralded as what comes after the modern times we have found so chaotic, neurotic, and generally unpleasant. From my vantage, however, this new wave is but a back eddy of an ebbing tide, an old form of sophistry refurbished to con a new herd of marks.

Semiological reductionism, the strategy I take to be foundational for postmodern thought, trades on the belief that the meanings we have for ourselves and that others have for us are but symbolic constructs grounded in the cultural forms they, themselves, generate. I will not recapitulate my critique of this movement here, but it is important to see how it intersects with the structure of romantic love.[18] If our identities, yours and mine, are idealities constructed of signifiers, if there is no palpable reality we can reach, then love can only be romance. If I cannot embrace you, I am left to my fantasies, and you provide only the occasion for living them out. If you cannot draw me out of my fantasies and present yourself in the flesh, if you cannot manifest yourself as a reality that transcends my familiar conceptual matrices, then the transcendence I seek in you can be at best only a meaning I project upon you rather than a reality I experience through you, that is, a false transcendence, a mystification.

Love in the postmodern age recapitulates the self-dissemblance of the romantic conceit—the projection of absolute transcendence onto the object of desire—but it proffers a theoretical justification that serves only to compound the mystification. I am condemned to love unrequited because there is no way I can touch or reach or know the object of my love: The way is barred by the web of signifiers through which I construct the meanings that all things, including my beloved, have for me. I cannot perceive you, I have only my perceptions of you. Postmodern lovers hold hands and lament that they cannot really touch one another. This is, of course, half true: I cannot know you, as the Christian god purports to, in your ownmost ipseity, but I am limited to finite apprehensions bounded by space, time, and my own projections. It is, nonetheless, profoundly stupid deliberately to ignore the other half of this truth: I cannot but know you when I see you, feel your anger or your pain, enter the space scented by your breath; your embodied presence obtrudes, it demands recognition and response. I can open myself to the reality you present and attempt to know you, or I can close myself off to protect the ideality I cherish. The first option is love; the second is romance.

Genuine love feeds on the carnal knowledge of the beloved, but this knowledge kills romance by dispelling the fantasy which is the true object of romantic fascination. Fantasies are by nature thin, lacking the rich texture that comes from the complex relationships among worldly things. To begin to know another person is to realize that she outstrips my knowledge, exists in a web of relations that has little to do with me, has a history I have not lived, sees from a perspective that is not my own. The quest for carnal knowledge of another is necessarily endless, since she is ever-changing and becoming. Her identity is emergent and elusive: This grants to love an indefinite span of exploration, capable of filling a lifetime. The poverty of fantasy, however, portends rapid exhaustion; hence boredom is a constant threat to romantic love. My fantasy is a pale reflection of a possible reality, a nexus of thoughts lacking adumbration, an idea that withers if not fed by input from worldly fecundity. Dream lovers are fantastic creatures which cannot transcend the imaginations that created them. And like all dreams, they cannot withstand the light of day: Perceptual reality obtrudes and displaces the image, leaving the romantic lover with a sense of having lost something he can barely re-member, and with nothing left to do but court another vehicle to carry his fantasy.

The *ressentiment* of postmodern love amounts to a pout: The abso-lute is forever out of reach, and nothing less will do. The best response to a pout is a laugh, and there is mirth aplenty to be found here. Postmod-ernism at its best is a prolonged postmortem on the god who, in dying, demonstrated that he never was, except as the projection of an infantile wish. Does one emerge from this investigation with tears of remorse, pouting from the loss of an illusion, having achieved nothing better than a shift from one form of infantility to another? There is no absolute love, therefore there is absolutely no love.[19] The value I demand is an absolute value: Knowing there is no such thing—knowing that the very demand is misconceived—I am *nonetheless* bereft of all value. The laughter is in the nonetheless. And in the kindergarten illogic of the argument contrived in the postmodern rhetoric of baroque virtuosity.

There is no absolute love, but there is finite love.

The absolute is not the measure of love, as Christians and postmoderns believe. Love feeds on desire and lack, that is, on finitude. A loving god is a contradiction in terms. Plato saw that. And then forgot it.[20]

The absolute is peace, serenity, plenitude, stasis, immutability. Absolute transcendence is incapable of self-transcendence: Perfection cannot grow beyond itself; its only movement is to circle narcissistically back into itself.

The categories of love are the categories of becoming: striving, yearning, changing, growing. Love is the force that takes us beyond ourselves toward each other and the selves that emerge through that relation. It is dynamic, restless, questing, and moving always beyond itself to find itself in that very movement.

Plato argued that love as finite desire differs from its object, the permanent possession of the good that constitutes immortality. How can the gap between finite and infinite be bridged? The logic here is inexorable: the fulfillment of desire is the death of desire; the culmination of love is death of the body. This is the thought that will mature through phases of the Christian mysticism of death into the romantic ideal of indefinite deferral culminating in the *Liebestod*. Irony: Derrida's postmodernism recapitulates the same structure that informs the quintessential modernist thinker, Hegel.[21] The mistake that permeates this tradition is the Platonic mistake of conceiving the object of human transcendence in terms of an immutable ideal generated by an infantile rejection of the reality of death. Irony compounds: Death anxiety generates death worship.

In the case of love, to burst the illusion of the absolute is to clear the way toward the reality of human transcendence. The object of finite desire is finite and worldly. The object of finite desire is another person . . . and the other person one grows to be in relation to other persons. It is a movement away from infantility, not a nostalgia for the sense of oneness mistakenly attributed to gestating intrauterine life by Ferenczi and others in fits of idyllic reverie incommensurate with their own scientific knowledge. Even Aristophanes should have known better: It is not the lot of humans to be at one with themselves; the end of life lies on the way to its end, not beyond it. This is a brute fact of temporality and becoming.

Love is primordially tied to ends, ends as goals and ends as terminations. Love is a quest: Desire is a form of goal orientation that is endemic to living organisms. Coming into being and passing away, the life phases of birth-growth-reproduction-decay-death, the body's will to live and its equally implacable will to die, betray a telic structure or purposiveness manifest across the full spectrum of life from the simplest to the most complex of cells. Sexlove is, indeed, the oldest of our gods.

But this aboriginal force is subject to its own self-transforming nature: Love is also our youngest god. A god whose eidos is ever changing, ever renewed in shape and expression. When cells become sufficiently complex, when reflection obtrudes, there arises the possibility of choosing to direct desire in one way rather than another, to pursue this end rather than that. There also arises the awareness that this very project of striving betrays our lack of oneness, perfection, wholeness. To live is to be on the way to another phase, to be incomplete in that way. This is the third truth of reflection, the awareness of which I am seeking to foster here. The youngest god whose physiognomy is forming itself through our awareness of our limits and our possibilities is the one who sees that the transcendence we seek lies in the seeking, that the end of desire is to recognize its own truth.

The quest for transcendence that drives sexlove belongs to the domain of becoming that is definitive of finite reality. It is a philosophical mistake traceable to Plato's Eleaticism, his fascination with the immutable eidos patterned on the ideality of numbers, that leads us to posit permanence and unchange as the criterion of reality. The eidos as idea is parasitic upon the eidos as perceptual physiognomy: to reverse this ordering, as Plato did and postmodernism continues to do, is to get it exactly backward. The quest for transcendence is pointed toward the elusive—more that we sense is there to be found. Pursuit of that something more entails growth and change, development and becoming. This is the reality that is genuinely definitive of human existence, and the longing for stasis, peace, rest, and permanence is just that, a longing, a desiring, a quest tied to becoming and change. It is a misguided quest, this quest for quiescence and death, but it is a quest all the same. Its mistake lies in the contradiction upon which it is founded, the contradiction of seeking a life of peace after a life of turmoil when peace and stasis is exactly what life is not. Whatever form of rest may be beyond the life of becoming is not life because life is becoming.

The something more afforded by life is to be found in the finite realm of worldly reality. The something more that is sought through sexlove is the self that is more than one's own self, the self that will bring me to be more than I am now.

Notes

1. See Calvin O. Schrag, *The Self after Postmodernity* (New Haven, Conn.: Yale University Press, 1997), pp. 148, 144 (hereafter cited as *SP*).

2. Schrag, *SP*, p. 148.

3. "Some argue that Eros, hatched from the world-egg, was the first of the gods since, without him, none of the rest could have been born; they make him coeval with Mother Earth and Tartarus, and deny that he had any father or mother, unless it were Eileithyia, Goddess of Childbirth" [Hesiod, *Theogony* 120]. "Others hold that he was Aphrodite's son by Hermes, or by Ares, or by her own father, Zeus; or the son of Iris by the West Wind" [Alcaeus, quoted in Plutarch, *Amatorius* 20]. Robert Graves, *The Greek Myths* (London: Penguin Books, 1960), 1:58. Plato offers a similar account in the *Symposium,* where Pausanius argues that there are two goddesses of love, heavenly Aphrodite (the primordial figure, a symbol of spiritual love) and earthly Aphrodite (younger and lesser, a symbol of physical love). See Plato, *Symposium,* 180c—81d.

4. "This difference it is that distinguishes Tragedy and Comedy also; the one would make its personages worse, and the other better, than the men of the present day" (Aristotle, *Poetics,* trans. by Ingram Bywater, in *The Essential Works of Aristotle,* ed. Richard McKeon [New York: Random House, 1941 or 71?], 1448a, p. 1456).

5. Gays and lesbians are doubly oppressed—they are vilified not only for being sexual, but for being sexual in a manner contrary to nature—but they have no exclusive claim on the closet. The closet is where we are all supposed to conduct our sexual affairs. Sexual liberation is a task for us all, and gratitude is due to all who take the risk to carry the banner.

6. "Recognizing the need for something that individuates particulars that possess the same form, the ancients and the medievals were motivated to appeal to the human body as the source of individuation. Human beings are similar by virtue of possessing the form of *animal rationale,* they are different because they have different bodies. It is thus the body that functions as the principle of individuation. It does so, however, not in its lived concreteness but somewhat curiously as an abstract *materia signata quantitate.* This 'signate matter,' although amorphous, is not wholly indeterminate. It possesses a propensity to take on form, signifying in each particular individual a resident form of humanity" (Schrag, *SP,* p. 52).

7. The greatest living Plato scholar I know, Harrison J. Pemberton, contends that Socrates "knew" the third truth as well and that he demonstrated that knowledge by conducting himself in accordance with it. To which I reply: maybe. But if he did, he failed to pass it along to his primary pupil and doxographer. Or so I am about to argue. (The failure of teachers to teach what *they* think is most important to their students is endemic to the profession. As this very essay may demonstrate, the students always take away what *they* think is most important.)

8. Plato, *Symposium,* trans. Walter Hamilton (London: Penguin Books, 1951), p. 95 (212a). Hereafter, all references are to the Hamilton edition unless otherwise indicated.

9. "Plato's celebrated tripartite portrait of the human body as a composite of reason, spirit, and appetite was sketched against the backdrop of some profound worries about the uneasy alliance of body and soul. In the end, it is the time-bound and vacillating body, according to Plato, that bears the responsibility for deflecting the vision of the mind as it seeks to prehend the world of eternal and immutable forms. The human body thus figures in the thought of Plato as a metaphysical embarrassment, which explains his reference to the body in the *Phaedo* as the 'prison house' of the soul" (Schrag, *SP*, p. 44).

10. This point is controversial and heavily contested. Jacques Lacan, e.g., has argued that personal identity is a sociolinguistic construct, a *méconnaissance* or mystification driven by the structures of desire and the symbolic forms through which these structures work themselves out. I have addressed the issue of personal identity at length in other work. See Martin C. Dillon, "Desire: Language and Body," in *Postmodernism and Continental Philosophy*, ed. Hugh J. Silverman and Donn Welton (Albany: State University of New York Press, 1988), pp. 34–48, and "Am I a Grammatical Fiction?—The Debate over Ego Psychology," in *Merleau-Ponty's Later Works and Their Practical Implications: The Dehiscence of Responsibility*, ed. Duane H. Davis (Buffalo, N.Y.: Humanity Books, 2001), pp. 309–24.

11. "Nobility" is the English term typically chosen to translate the Greek noun, *to kalon*. It has become a central idea in my thinking about love and is developed in a forthcoming book entitled *Beyond Romance* (Albany: State University of New York Press, 2001). For the moment, suffice it to say that I learned the term from Plato but will follow it along a different path.

12. *Theosebeia* is my transliteration of the Greek θεοσεβεια, the service or fear of god, religiousness.

13. "If the Other loves me then I become the unsurpassable, which means that I must be the absolute end. . . . The object which the Other must make me be is an object-transcendence, an absolute center of reference around which all the instrumental-things of the world are ordered as pure *means*. . . . The beloved can not will to love. Therefore the lover must seduce the beloved, and his love can in no way be distinguished from the enterprise of seduction. . . . To seduce . . . is to risk the danger of *being-seen* in order to . . . appropriate the Other in and by means of my object-ness . . . by means of making myself a *fascinating object*" (Jean-Paul Sartre, *Being and Nothingness*, trans. Hazel Barnes [New York: Washington Square Press, 1966], pp. 481, 484).

14. The gender assignment in this paragraph is deliberate. Historically, the role of the lover is active and, therefore, masculine, whereas the role of the beloved is passive, the object of pursuit, and, therefore, feminine. Assignment of specific roles in human relations based on gender comes close to being a definition of sexism. What follows from this is the truth that romantic love has been defined historically in sexist terms. That may be yet another reason for repudiating it. It should, however, be noted that the literature of the romantic tradition is rife with role reversals, that these role reversals are endemic to romance, hence that the characterizations of masculine and feminine roles do not necessarily coincide with the actual genders of the personae involved. Cleopatra

is portrayed by Shakespeare as the active partner in her relationship with Marc Anthony.

15. Martin C. Dillon, "Toward a Phenomenology of Love and Sexuality," *Soundings* 63, no. 4 (1980): 341–60; "Romantic Love, Enduring Love, and Authentic Love," *Soundings* 66, no. 2 (1983): 133–51; "Desire for All/Love of One: Tomas's Tale in *The Unbearable Lightness of Being*," *Philosophy Today* 33, no. 4 (1989): 347–57.

16. Quoted in an appendix to Stendahl, *Love,* trans. Jean Stewart and B. C. J. G. Knight (Harmondsworth: Penguin Books, 1975), p. 281.

17. "Tristan and Iseult do not love one another. They say they don't, and everything goes to prove it. *What they love is love and being in love.* . . . Tristan loves the awareness that he is loving far more than he loves Iseult the Fair. And Iseult does nothing to hold Tristan. All she needs is her passionate dream. Their need of one another is in order to be aflame, and they do not need one another as they are. What they need is not one another's presence, but one another's absence" (Denis de Rougemont, *Love in the Western World,* trans. Montgomery Belgion [New York: Harper and Row, 1974], pp. 41–42).

18. See M. C. Dillon, *Semiological Reductionism: A Critique of the Deconstructionist Movement in Postmodern Thought* (Albany: State University of New York Press, 1995).

19. Or no justice or no friendship or no truth, etc.

20. Socrates' opening argument in the *Symposium* (200a—4c) characterizes love in the categories of desire as lacking the goodness and beauty it seeks in its object: "Love is in love with what he lacks and does not possess"(201b). But the argument concludes with the lover coming "in contact . . . with the truth . . . and becoming . . . immortal himself" (212a).

21. The relationship between Derridian desire and Hegelian desire is developed in detail in "Ungodly Desire, Unnatural Desire," *Semiological Reductionism,* chap. 6.

PART 4

THE FOURTH CULTURAL VALUE SPHERE

11

Transcendence, Heteronomy, and the Birth of the Responsible Self

Merold Westphal

> The shattered cogito: this could be the emblematic title of a
> tradition, one less continuous perhaps than that of the cogito,
> but one whose virulence culminates with Nietzsche, making him
> the privileged adversary of Descartes.
>
> —*Paul Ricoeur,* Oneself as Another

In his Gifford Lectures Paul Ricoeur makes it clear that he will not
try to put this humpty-dumpty back together again. He seeks rather
to develop a "hermeneutics of the self [that] is placed at an equal
distance from the apology of the cogito and from its overthrow . . . at
an equal distance from the cogito exalted by Descartes and from the
cogito that Nietzsche proclaimed forfeit." The "arduous detours" of this
hermeneutics pass through a series of questions. "Who is speaking of
what? Who does what? About whom and about what does one construct
a narrative? Who is morally responsible for what? These are but so many
different ways in which 'who?' is stated."[1]

It is a similar project that Cal Schrag undertakes in his Ryle Lectures, *The Self after Postmodernity.* He is quite specific about the nature of
the cogito that has had such a great fall. It is "a sovereign and monarchical self, at once self-sufficient and self-assured, finding metaphysical
comfort in a doctrine of an immutable and indivisible self-identity." It is
"a self-identical monad, mute and self-enclosed, changeless and secured
prior to the events of speaking . . . a fixed, underlying substratum . . . a
prelinguistic, zero-point center of consciousness."[2]

Like Ricoeur and Jean-Luc Nancy, Schrag thinks that "a jettisoning
of the self understood in these senses does not entail a jettisoning of
every sense of self . . . a new self emerges, like the phoenix arising from

its ashes."[3] And, like Ricoeur and Nancy, he thinks this new, emergent self, at once more plausible philosophically and more familiar experientially, is best understood in terms of "who" questions rather than of "what" questions, as if the self were a nature or an essence.[4]

Schrag's self is doubly emergent. It emerges theoretically in the aftermath of the critiques that have shattered the cogito. But it emerges experientially as well. The self's identity is not a fact or a given prior to experience but a process worked out in experience.[5] It has a narrative character.[6] Its unity is a matter of convergence without coincidence, or, in Ricoeurean language, it is a matter of ipse identity rather than idem identity.[7] In Rylean language, selfhood is a task word rather than an achievement word.[8]

In speaking of the self "after postmodernity," Schrag might seem to suggest that he simply wants to leave postmodernity behind, that he simply identifies it with Nietzsche's replacement of the cogito with the will to power in its amoral diversity. So we are not surprised to find a critique of Lyotard as giving too extreme an account of the dispersal of the self in the plurality of its language games and of Foucault as reducing ethics to aesthetics.[9] But Schrag finds Derrida to be in important respects an ally and quotes two passages as illuminating his own project. In one of them Derrida says, "I don't destroy the subject. I situate it. That is to say, I believe that at a certain level both of experience and scientific discourse one cannot get along without the notion of the subject. It is a question of knowing where it comes from and how it functions."[10] It is such a view of the self that Schrag articulates in terms of narrative convergence as a task rather than preestablished coincidence, as a guarantee prior to experience.

Derrida affirms the narrative concept of the self as the "common concept" of "autobiographical anamnesis" which "presupposes *identification*. And precisely not identity. No, an identity is never given, received, or attained; only the interminable and indefinitely phantasmatic process of identification endures. Whatever the story of a return to oneself . . . no matter what an odyssey or Bildungsroman it might be . . . it is always *imagined* that the one who writes should know how to say *I*." It is just here that he radicalizes the concept of a narrative self. "It is necessary to know already in what language *I* is expressed, and I *am* expressed. Here we are thinking of the *I think,* as well as the grammatical or linguistical *I,* of the *me* or *us* in their identificatory status as it is sculpted by cultural, symbolic, and sociocultural figures . . . the *I* of the kind of anamnesis called autobiographical . . . is produced and uttered in different ways depending on the language in question. It never precedes them; therefore it is not independent of language in general."[11] This is an example of what Derrida means when he says of the subject, "I situate it."

The second citation is from Derrida's answer to Nancy's question, "Who comes after the subject?" After affirming the significance of the who form of the question, he says, "I would add something that remains required by both the definitions of the classical subject and by these later nonclassical motifs, namely a certain responsibility. The singularity of the 'who' is not the individuality of a thing that would be identical with itself, it is not an atom. It is a singularity that dislocates or divides itself in gathering itself to answer to the other, whose call somehow precedes its own identification with itself."[12]

Here it is not just language in general but the call of the other that precedes the subject. Schrag notes and welcomes this Lévinasian turn in Derrida's thought. It has seemed to many that postmodernism in one or another of its modes has undermined the possibility not only of moral theory in familiar forms but also of the responsible self itself.[13] Among the French poststructuralists, none has sought more assiduously than Derrida to undermine this claim, to show that the shattering of the cogito is not the end of obligation. It is precisely this dimension of Derrida's thought to which Schrag appeals. For all three of the schemes he employs in seeking, with Ricoeur, to locate the self between Descartes and Nietzsche require a responsible self. In his critique of the subordination of ethics to aesthetics he finds in Nietzsche and Foucault, Schrag reaffirms Kierkegaard's three existence spheres: the aesthetic, the ethical, and the religious. Over against Weber and Habermas, who reduce the culture-spheres to science, morality, and art, Schrag reaffirms religion as a culture-sphere.[14] And in asking who the self is, Schrag replies by exploring the four-dimensional self in discourse, in action, in community, and in transcendence. Each of these grids calls for a self who is responsible in relation to the Other. In fact, each one calls for an account of the relation between the religiously responsible self and the morally responsible self. On Schrag's view, some forms of religion and morality may be so tied to the cogito that they perish with its shattering, but not religion or morality as such.

Derrida's reply to Nancy is even more Lévinasian than the reference to "a certain responsibility" reveals. In a long parenthesis immediately preceding it, he speaks of the self's " 'yes, yes' that answers before even being able to formulate a question, that is *responsible without autonomy*."[15] This passage recalls that Derrida issued another very Lévinasian challenge to the autonomous self:

> Language has started without us, in us and before us. This is what theology calls God . . . Having come from the past, language before language, a past that was never present and yet remains unforgettable—this "it is necessary" [to speak] thus seems to beckon toward the event of

an order or of a promise that does not belong to what one currently calls history. . . . Order or promise, this injunction commits (me), in a rigorously asymmetrical manner, even before I have been able to say *I*, to sign such a *provocation* in order to reappropriate it for myself and restore the symmetry. That in no way mitigates my responsibility; on the contrary. There would be no responsibility without this *prior coming* (*prévenance*) of the trace, or if autonomy were first or absolute. Autonomy itself would not be possible, nor would respect for the law (sole "cause" of this respect) in the strictly Kantian meaning of these words.[16]

For Derrida in his Lévinasian mode, heteronomy is prior to autonomy and is the condition for the possibility of whatever autonomy is possible for the self I am. And this autonomy consists, not in self-legislation, but in agreeing with, and thus in appropriating, a saying prior to my own self-consciousness. Whenever I first say "I," it has already been spoken, I have already been laid claim to.

Schrag also challenges the autonomy of the cogito and locates the self as the who of action "*between* autonomy and heteronomy." But because he assimilates this dyad with that of acting/suffering and active voice/passive voice, he can only deny that his emerging self is "a self caught within the constraints of heteronomy, determined by forces acting upon it." He denies both autonomy and heteronomy.[17]

Derrida's is the more radical critique of the autonomy of the "modern" self, for in denying autonomy he affirms a certain heteronomy. For him the question of heteronomy is not that of forces before which the self is passive (though he does not deny these); it is rather the question of a voice before which the self is responsible. It is moral autonomy, rather than ontological autonomy, that needs to be teleologically suspended, *aufgehoben*, recontextualized, relativized in a prior moral heteronomy. It is significant that Derrida makes this point with reference to "what theology calls God," to language that is prior to the who of discourse, the who of action, and the who of community. With (more than) a little help from Lévinas, Derrida brings us to the who of transcendence.

I want to explore this heteronomy as the transcendence that simultaneously shatters the cogito and creates the responsible self. I believe that Schrag needs it to carry out his project and that, while it is not explicit in his discussion of autonomy and heteronomy, it is implicit in the way he draws on both Lévinas and Kierkegaard in developing his own argument.[18]

Accordingly, it is to these two thinkers I turn, first of all to an essay of Lévinas's entitled "No Identity" (1970), which discusses heteronomous transcendence not only in relation to the responsible self but also in relation to the question of the self-identity.[19] It begins with a quotation from the Babylonian Talmud, "If I do not answer for myself, who will answer for me? But if I answer only for myself, am I still myself?" The first question, in agreement with Ricoeur, Derrida, and Schrag, reminds us that the self must remain on the scene and not simply disappear. The second question reminds us that the self is not "a sovereign and monarchical self, at once self-sufficient and self-assured, finding metaphysical comfort in a doctrine of an immutable and indivisible self-identity."[20] I am essentially relative and am myself only in and through my relation to an Other to whom or for whom I am answerable. But in that answerability I am myself. So we know from the outset that the title, "No Identity," does not signify the simple disappearance of the self. It is not the denial of any identity whatever, but of the monadic, atomic identity that is prior to relation.

Lévinas's point of departure is the "end of humanism" and "death of man" slogans of structuralist human sciences, "the apocalyptic ideas or slogans of intellectual high society" that "impose themselves with the tyranny of the last word, but become available to anyone and cheapened." This charge of dogmatic fadishness does not sound especially friendly, but Lévinas does not wish to dismiss these ideas. He rather affirms the "methodological" truth of human sciences "distrustful of an ego that hearkens to itself and feels itself but remains defenseless against the illusions of its class or the phantasms of its latent neurosis." We cannot escape the insights of Marx and Freud. They lead to what we might call a political rather than a purely epistemic critique of "the legislative sovereignty of the transcendental consciousness":

> Do not the contradictions that rend the rational world, allegedly issued from transcendental legislation, ruin the identity of the subjective? That an action could be obstructed by the technology destined to render it efficacious and easy . . . that a politics and an administration guided by the humanist ideal maintain the exploitation of man by man and war—these are singular inversions of rational projects, disqualifying human causality, and thus transcendental subjectivity understood as spontaneity and act also. Everything comes to pass as though the ego, the identity par excellence from which every identifiable identity would derive, were wanting with regard to itself, did not succeed in coinciding with itself.[21]

So ringing is Lévinas's endorsement of the apocalyptic slogans of structuralism that he favorably quotes Blanchot's antihumanism: "To speak nobly of the human in man, to conceive the humanity in man, is to quickly come to a discourse that is untenable and undeniably more repugnant than all the nihilist vulgarities."[22] At this point Lévinas sounds like the assistant professor who has just assumed the self-appointed role as campus terrorist.

Having paid attention to the opening talmudic quotation, we are not surprised by the "yet" with which Lévinas signals that he does not swallow the end of humanism hook, line, and Saussure, or, if you prefer, Lévi-Strauss, Lacan, and Foucault. In their structuralist mode, the human sciences are "the preemption of certain significations." Appropriately suspicious, with Marx and Freud, of a putative rationality blind to its own blindnesses, they are blind to their own positivist prejudices in seeking to imitate the objectivism of mathematical physics. Thus they eliminate the subject and inwardness (a very Kierkegaardian term to which Lévinas is not at all allergic) altogether. As Lévinas notes, "The inwardness of the self-identical ego is dissolved into the totality which is without recesses or secrets. The whole of the human is outside. That can pass for a very firm formulation of materialism."[23]

With this last remark Lévinas calls our attention to the affinities between the philosophical behaviorism and eliminative materialism of Anglo-American philosophy of mind and French-structuralist antihumanism.[24] Lévinas agrees with all these materialisms when they say, "Identity seems to be not strictly inward. *I is an other.*" But he refuses to draw the conclusion they draw, that meaning "would have to be sought in a world that does not bear human traces."[25]

Ceding to its critics the self-sufficient ego always able to return to itself enriched in its idem-identity by the loot it brings back from its excursions into the world, Lévinas nevertheless seeks to retain a certain inwardness, an "impossible inwardness . . . an impossibility we learn of neither from metaphysics nor from the end of metaphysics. There is a divergency between the ego and the self, an impossible recurrence, and impossible identity. No one can remain in himself: the humanity of man, subjectivity, is a responsibility for the others, an extreme vulnerability. The return to the self becomes an interminable detour."[26] In this inwardness we have what Schrag is looking for, a self that has not disappeared before the assaults of Nietzsche and Heidegger, structuralism and poststructuralism, behaviorism and eliminative materialism but which, on the other hand, is not yet there either. It is emerging, becoming, a process or rather a task not yet completed. It is "an ego ceaselessly missing itself."[27]

How does Lévinas argue for this inwardness, this ipse-identity, this "non-coincidence of the identical"? He does this by denying primacy and ultimacy to questions about free action in the causal sphere, about "making the best of a bad situation." There are three presuppositions to such freedom. First, reference to a bad situation implies that there are forces which oppose me or impose themselves on me. I can affirm myself only by seeking to overcome, or at least to manage, these. The other two presuppositions concern that by which the will, as practical reason, is guided as it seeks to make the best of a bad situation. One of these is its own interests, its *conatus essendi,* in whose service it seeks to overcome, or at least to manage, the opposing and imposing forces. The other is that by which the will is guided in seeking its own ends, its representations. The self in question here "delivers itself over to freedom, which is always correlative with an intentionality."[28]

Lévinas does not deny this dimension of our lives, nor offer us a new theory of how it works. His description blends together Aristotle's theory of practical reason with Heidegger's analysis of the link between representation and the will to power. Rather, Lévinas relativizes free action by recontextualizing it in a horizon whose fundamental fact it is not. That fundamental fact he here calls "vulnerability," and it is in terms of this concept that he makes his signature gesture, the teleological suspension of freedom in responsibility.

It is obvious that this vulnerability cannot signify our weakness in the face of causal forces, whether external or internal.[29] For the purpose of this notion is to decenter the stage on which the battles of freedom in that sense are fought. Lévinas asks rhetorically, "Does human causality correspond with the meaning of subjectivity . . . does free action answer to subjectivity's vocation?" In a phrase Lévinas never tires of using, he calls this vulnerability a passivity "more passive than every passivity." The paradox of this phrase can be eliminated by speaking of a passivity more passive than every causal passivity, for Lévinas is explicit that he is not speaking about the causal "openness of every object to all others" as described in Kant's third analogy of experience. This openness "cannot be interpreted as a simple exposedness to being affected by causes. . . . The impotency or humility of [this] 'suffering' is on the hither side of the passivity of undergoing. . . . In vulnerability there lies a *relationship with the other* which causality does not exhaust."[30]

We are fully prepared for Lévinas to develop this transcausal vulnerability in terms of inwardness, especially after he reminds us of the *Aufhebung* of freedom in responsibility by saying that "where the other is from the first under my responsibility, 'something' has overflowed my freely taken decisions, has slipped into me, *unbeknownst to me,* thus alienating my identity."[31] But we are not at all prepared to hear the openness of vulnerability described as "the denuding of the skin exposed to wounds and outrage . . . the aptitude, which every being in its 'natural pride' would be ashamed to admit, 'to be beaten,' 'to receive blows.' 'He offered his cheek to the smiters and was filled with shame,' says, admirably, a prophetic text."[32] Lévinas describes this all-too-physical vulnerability all too literally as nakedness. In *Totality and Infinity* it was the face of the Other that was naked as its gaze made me a responsible self.[33] Now it is I who am naked in the vulnerability that constitutes my responsibility.

But where is the inwardness in all this? How does getting beaten take us to "the hither side of the passivity of undergoing"? The first clue is in the nature of the relationship to the Other. Because the vulnerable self is "being *for another* . . . [because] the subject is *for the other*," the suffering is "suffering for the suffering of the other" rather than simply suffering from the other.[34] Lévinas describes the relation as a certain sensibility, which we could express in the familiar words, "I feel your pain." But his very physical descriptions make it clear that it goes beyond "I feel your pain" to "I share your pain," becoming victim myself.

Whether we are speaking of empathy or an even more radical sharing of the Other's suffering, the second and crucial factor is the quasi-voluntary nature of the sensibility, to which I can easily enough become desensitized. Speaking of the prophetic text he has just quoted, Lévinas writes, "Without introducing a deliberate searching for suffering or humiliation (turning the other cheek), it suggests, in the *primary suffering*, in *suffering as such*, an unendurable and harsh *consent* that animates the passivity and does so strangely despite itself." This consent is what takes us to "the hither side of the passivity of undergoing."[35] We must speak its quasi-voluntary nature, because it is prior to the realm of free action and the voluntary in the usual sense. We could also call it "quasi-transcendental," "transcendental" because it is prior to experience and choice and "quasi-" because it does not originate in the meaning-constituting subject of intentionality but in the preexperiential answering to a preexperiential call or accusation.

Lévinas proceeds to spell out this "passivity more passive than every passivity" in terms familiar to readers of *Otherwise than Being*: obsession, substitution, expiation, election, hostage, and persecution. Similarly, he speaks of "being implicated prior to my freedom," of "the accusation prior to any fault," of being "responsible even for their responsibility," of a saying that has "a meaning prior to the truth it discloses," that is, of "the saying that precedes the said," and of "the surplus of meaning over the being that bears it."[36]

This is not the place to explore these crucial themes but only to note their intimate connection, in Lévinas's mind, with the question of self-identity, on which we must keep focused.[37] The consent which takes us beyond the realm of causal forces is the uncoerced abdication of the "self-enclosed," "self-sufficient," "self-assured," monadic self, secure in its "immutable and indivisible self-identity."[38] Whenever I would say "I," intend the world, take a position, or decide whether to love or hate my neighbor, I find that my neighbor has already intruded into the inner sanctum of myself and has become a dimension of myself in a way to which I have already consented.[39] The "deportation or drifting of identity," the "strange defeat or defection of identity," of which Lévinas speaks, has always already happened. And it is a good thing. For this "difference that opens between the ego and itself, the *non-coincidence* of the identical, is a fundamental *non-indifference* with regard to men."[40]

In other words, having "no identity," in the sense carefully delineated in this essay, is a condition for the possibility of being a responsible self. Kant said, "I have therefore found it necessary to deny *knowledge,* in order to make room for *faith.*"[41] As we have seen, Lévinas says, "I have found it necessary to deny freedom, in order to make room for responsibility." Now he reformulates that to read, "I have found it necessary to deny identity, in order to make room for responsibility." In the case of freedom, of course, he does not deny it but rather displaces it, making it subsequent and subordinate. But in the case of identity, however, he does flatly deny that a certain kind of identity is to be found anywhere other than in the fantasies of those who, whether philosophically sophisticated or not, make their own *conatus essendi* primary and essential and the rights and needs of the Other secondary and accidental. So far is the shattering of the cogito from taking us beyond good and evil into cynical nihilism or arrogant aestheticism, it is rather the repentance that responsibility requires.

At least it can be. But if one sets up a simple either/or between the self as an ontologically guaranteed self-identity prior to experience and relation on the one hand and "a world that does not bear human traces" on the other hand, the end of humanism and the death of man could signify the demise of responsibility as well.[42] If, however, the self survives the death of its false pretensions, the story could be quite different, and it is clearly such a story Lévinas wants to tell.

That is why there is nuance in his denial of identity. The self does not simply disappear into causal nexus like a stone in a pond whose ripples last but a moment. Where Ricoeur speaks of ipse-identity and Schrag of the emerging narrative self, Lévinas speaks of "the uniqueness of the irreplaceable."[43] I am uniquely irreplaceable just by virtue of a responsibility for the Other than I cannot transfer to anyone else. This is my identity. It is mutable, because my responsibilities change, and divisible because I have it by virtue of the vulnerability by which the Other becomes essential to who I am. "If I answer only for myself, am I still myself?" the Talmud asks. No, Lévinas replies, but when you answer for another as one who has been elected to be for the Other, you become for the first time yourself.[44]

In this way "a defense of man understood as a defense of the man other than me, presides over what in our day is called the critique of humanism." In spite of structuralist scientism, "man has not ceased to count for man," and in Paris during the year 1968 this, precisely, is the meaning of youth. As Lévinas suggests, "Able to find responsibilities again under the thick stratum of literature that undo [sic] them . . . youth ceased to be the age of transition and passage . . . and is shown to be man's humanity."[45]

This new humanism after the end of humanism could also be called the self after postmodernity. It enables Lévinas to nuance the theme of alienation he introduced earlier, when he said that in responsibility the Other "has slipped into me . . . thus alienating my identity." But no sooner does he say this than he puts it into question. I am alienated from a certain identity, to be sure. At the same time this thought gives rises to the following remark:

> Is it then certain that in the deportation or drifting of identity, caught sight of in the inversion of human projects, the subject would not signify with all the dash of its youth? Is it certain that Rimbaud's formula "I is an other" only means alteration, alienation, betrayal of oneself, foreignness with regard to oneself and subjection to this foreigner? Is it certain that already the most humble experience of him who *puts himself in another's place*, that is, accuses himself for another's distress or pain, is not animated with the most eminent meaning of this "I is an other"?[46]

Three times Lévinas asks, Is it certain? Someone should do a study of his rhetorical questions, designed to cut against the grain. Are they not his best arguments? He uses still another question to point in still another way to the possibility of an "eminent," nonalienating meaning to "I is an other": "Or shall the strange defeat or defection of identity confirm the human election—my own, to serve, but that of the other for himself?"[47] Election is a central theme in both Jewish and Christian theology. It means to be chosen of God for salvation and to be a light to the nations. To be sure, for Lévinas the concept is intimately intertwined with such severe notions of obligation as hostage, substitution, and expiation, just as for Jewish theology election and the law are inseparable. In this context, where Lévinas evokes the Bible, by which "we Westerners are nourished . . . but in a way that owes nothing to the certainty of the *cogito*," he twice makes reference to Psalm 119. The longest chapter in the Bible, it is a hymn of praise for the gift of the law and a plea for help in living up to it. The law is light and wisdom, not oppression and slavery.

Yet we cannot, and should not, downplay the fact that responsibility comes as heteronomy. Theologically, in the biblical traditions, the law comes from a radically transcendent God, not from the self-legislation of human reason. Philosophically, on the Lévinasian analysis, responsibility is born with the incursion of the Other into my very identity as the saying that demands my nonindifference.[48] The command of the Other, and the consent I find myself already to have given, keep this from being the causal heteronomy of those subjected to forces they cannot control. But the consent is already a reply and not a legislation. It is not constitutive of the meanings that confound it even as it confirms them. The responsible self is not autonomous. The astonishing claim of Lévinas is threefold: The responsible self is born from transcendence, transcendence means heteronomy, but heteronomy does not mean alienation. For "no one is enslaved to the Good."[49]

No one doubts that the God of Kierkegaard's *Fear and Trembling* is a heteronomous transcendence. Is this God also the shattering of the cogito and the birth of the responsible self?

When Schrag first turns to Kierkegaard it is to *Either/Or*—more specifically, to Judge William's admonition to the young aesthete to choose himself. This conversion to the ethical sphere from the aesthetic would be an existential paradigm shift of truly revolutionary import. Perhaps it would be, as Judge William clearly thinks, the birth of the responsible self. If so, it would not be necessary to proceed to *Fear and Trembling*. We could stay with the highly user-friendly God of whom the judge speaks so often and so glibly, the God who confirms but never challenges his bourgeois complacency; we would not need to proceed to the "terrifying" and "repelling" God of Abraham, whom one can only approach with a "shudder" and a "*horror religiosus*."[50] But since Schrag evokes *Either/Or* in developing the self in action and not the self in transcendence, and since we expect Kierkegaard, like Lévinas, to seek the birth of the responsible self in transcendence, this hope may be premature. Let us see.

The choice Judge William urges on his young friend is not the choice of good over evil in a particular situation, which is secondary, but the choice of good and evil rather than aesthetic categories as those of highest importance for shaping and evaluating his life. It is the decision to enter the ethical sphere, to play a different game with different goals and different rules.[51]

The Sartrean overtones of the notion of self-choice are undermined when Judge William equates choosing oneself with receiving oneself and with becoming oneself: "When the soul comes to be alone in the whole world, then before one there appears, not an extraordinary human being, but the eternal power itself, then the heavens seem to open and the I chooses itself, or, more correctly, receives itself . . . He does not become someone other than he was before, but he becomes himself."[52]

This choice is the decision to be a responsible self. After a person "has found himself, has chosen himself absolutely, has repented of himself, he then has himself as his *task* under an eternal *responsibility*. . . . But since he has not created himself but has chosen himself, *duty* is the expression of his absolute dependence and his absolute freedom in their identity with each other."[53] Just because Judge William presupposes what Sartre denies, namely, that the self is created by God, self-choice can never signify an absolute autonomy. By choosing myself, I accept responsibility to One who has chosen me. There is a hint of heteronomy here.

For Lévinas, too, self-choice always presupposes the Other's prior presence as one to whom, and for whom, I am responsible. But in Lévinas's terms, the self-choice of which Judge William speaks would be an empirical, voluntary ratification of the quasi-transcendental consent that has always already been given. Moreover, the content of this choice, as presented by the judge, would be the moral order of a certain society, what Lévinas would call an order of justice trying to take into account the presence of the third. But the birth of the responsible self takes place between two, before the third appears on the scene. So while this choice might signify the responsible self learning to walk, it cannot be the birth of that self.

Nor can Judge William's account of the transition from the aesthetic sphere to the ethical be an adequate account of the birth of the responsible self for Kierkegaard. First, while he talks a lot about God and, in the passage just cited, speaks of being alone before "the eternal power itself," he does not analyze the God-relation, nor does he explore what it might mean to be alone before God, what it might mean for the birth of the responsible self to take place between two, before the third appears on the scene. Second, and as a consequence, the religious is for him no more than a cultural sphere. Judge William is never alone before God but is always surrounded by, immersed in—and in a very real sense indistinguishable from—respectable, Danish, bourgeois, Lutheran society. Hegel could only be proud of one who embodied his concept of *Sittlichkeit* so well. The institution of marriage which the judge commends so highly to the young aesthete—whom he no doubt suspects of "living in sin"—is precisely the social practice that Hegel makes basic to his account of *Sittlichkeit* in the *Philosophy of Right*.[54]

But Kierkegaard cannot rest here. As Schrag notes with appreciation, Kierkegaard wants to articulate a transcendence that can critique and relativize all the culture-spheres, not only science, ethics, and art, but even religion. So we will have to proceed to *Fear and Trembling* after all. Silentio's Abraham is Kierkegaard's analysis of what it means to be alone before God, and in its teleological suspension "the ethical is reduced to the relative."[55] It is not just a secular humanism, if you like, that is marginalized to make way for the religious. In context it is perfectly clear that the ethical sphere is that of both Hegel and Judge William, which already includes, in both cases, religion as a cultural sphere. Kierkegaard will eventually call it Christendom. We must go beyond such an ethical to find the self in transcendence; and it is only there—for Kierkegaard as well as for Lévinas—that we will find the birth of the responsible self.

Abraham is alone. We see this most dramatically in Problem 3, which explores Abraham's silence before his wife Sarah, his son Isaac, and his servant Eliezer.[56] The tragic hero—Agamemnon or Jephthah or Brutus—can explain himself when called upon to sacrifice a child. For while he does a terrible and painful thing, it is justified by the universal, not just by the needs of the society of which he is a member but by the ethical standards they share (*Sittlichkeit*). Everyone can be expected to understand that he is doing the right thing. They can weep together. The knight of faith has no such support. He cannot expect even his family to understand and approve. They cannot weep with him but only shrink back in horror.

Largely on the basis of the loneliness of Abraham, Kierkegaard is often presented as having an atomic or monadic theory of the self. Thus, for example, Mark Taylor writes, "While Hegel is the genius whose vision inspires recent forms of socialism, Kierkegaard remains the greatest theoretician of contemporary individualism."[57] Nothing could be further from the truth. Abraham is alone only to secular or pantheistic eyes for which the only actual Other is a human person. But Abraham is alone— before God. *Coram Deo* means that the knight of faith is never alone. In a variety of texts and in his appeal to "that single individual" whom he hopes to find as his reader, Kierkegaard regularly seeks to isolate the individual, to help reflect the individual, not out of every relation, but out of every finite relation, to be freed for the infinite relation, alone, like Abraham, before God.

This is an important difference between Lévinas and Kierkegaard. For Lévinas, the Other is in the first instance the human Other, the widow, the orphan, the stranger, in short, the neighbor. For Kierkegaard, all such relations are secondary to the primary relation to God.[58]

But there is also a deep agreement here. The self is always already in relation, and a hierarchical, asymmetrical relation at that. Prior to experience, prior to the choice of an aesthetic, ethical, or religious "lifestyle," the transcendental trauma has already occurred. An Other has already slipped into me, unbeknownst, depriving me of any possibility of a self-enclosed identity. The invasion of my innermost identity by this Other is the birth of the responsible self. Whatever responsibilities I may incur in whatever culture spheres into which I enter are relativized by an absolute duty, prior and higher. That this absolute duty is to God, and not to my family or to my society, is the thrust of the three Problems that make up the bulk of *Fear and Trembling*.

There is another difference between Lévinas and Kierkegaard, but I believe this one to be only apparent. Paradoxical as it may seem, given his sustained critique of ontology, Lévinas's account is ontological, at least as we usually use the term; it concerns the very being of the self. To be sure, the traditional ontologies he challenges affirm the identity of the self in some quite strong sense, while he insists, "no identity." But this is not so much to abandon ontology as to give a different account of the being of the self, and, in the process, of being itself. He begins with a "negative ontology," invoking traditional categories such as identity but under a negative sign, and he proceeds to new, affirmative, ethical categories, such as vulnerability and so forth.[59] Lévinas nicely expresses the primacy of his ethical categories by identifying the self's horizon as "not a world but a kingdom . . . the kingdom of the Good." Accordingly, philosophy is "the wisdom of love" rather than the love of wisdom.[60]

Similarly, Kierkegaard's positive account of the self is in ethical terms, for example, the absolute duty to God with which Silentio explicates the teleological suspension of *Sittlichkeit* and Christendom. But the contrast for him is more often a "negative epistemology" than a "negative ontology." He does not use the ontological language in which I have just interpreted his account of the incursion of God into the self. He shatters the cogito, not so much in terms of its self-identity as of its performance, by challenging the ultimacy of its knowledge claims. Thus for Silentio the sign of transcendence is "the paradox" and "the absurd."[61] (Similarly, Climacus will go on to challenge the cogito as recollection in *Philosophical Fragments* and as speculation in *Concluding Unscientific Postscript*.)

In a variety of writings, not least in *Fear and Trembling*, Kierkegaard sets faith against reason. But we should not take this to be a Promethean defiance of faith before Reason as some cosmo-ontological first principle. It is precisely to protest against the identification of the cogito with such a principle that Kierkegaard pits faith against reason, which is always human reason in its finitude and fallenness. Thus, Abraham has faith "by virtue of the absurd" which is absurd not in the light of divine reason but of "human calculation." To find oneself alone with God is to lose confidence in the absoluteness of "one's own understanding" along with "everything finite, for which it is the stockbroker."[62] Just as the amnion must break if the baby is to be born and the shell must be cracked if the chick is to be born, so the cogito must be shattered at the birth of the responsible self.

That Kierkegaard uses epistemic terms rather than the language of self-identity strikes me as a superficial difference for two reasons. First, a self that loses its (presumed) epistemic and moral autonomy at the same time is a self whose self-enclosed self-identity has been dramatically compromised, even if one does not use such language to express the trauma. Second, Lévinas's own critique of "ontology" is largely epistemic. Hence his sustained critique of intentionality, thematization, representation, transcendental apperception, and so forth. There is an essential interchangeability of ontological and epistemological categories. As Catherine Pickstock puts it, "an ontology separated from theology is reducible to an epistemology."[63] Apart from transcendence, being becomes convertible, not with intelligibility in itself, but with intelligibility *for us*. Being is that which gives itself to be fully comprehended by *human understanding*. Thus, speaking of the simple natures on which the entire edifice of our knowledge is founded, Descartes assures us that they "are known *per se* and are wholly free from falsity. . . . Whence it is evident that we are in error if we judge that any one of these simple natures is not completely known by us. For if our mind attains to the least acquaintance with it . . . this fact alone makes us infer that we know it completely."[64]

Whenever the soul or the cogito or the transcendental ego represents this kind of epistemic hubris, it becomes the unbirthing of the responsible self or, perhaps, the birth of the irresponsible self. For the responsible self, as presented by Lévinas and Kierkegaard, is triply heteronomous before transcendence. In terms of its being, its knowing, and its doing, it is essentially given over to an Other. It is not the self-identical, self-contained, and self-sufficient self in which "modernity" placed its hopes. Postmodernity is the boy who shouts, "The emperor has no clothes!"—the investigative journalism that exposes the Wizard of Oz for the sham he is. To rediscover the self "after postmodernity" is to discover a radical, heteronomous responsibility; and this is to resist the cynicism of disillusionment.

Schrag seeks the birth of the responsible self beyond modernity, beyond cynical, nihilistic postmodernity, and—briefly, at the conclusion of his argument—beyond classical theism, by claiming that "the classical metaphysics of theism comes up lame in locating the source and dynamics of transcendence."[65] I believe that Schrag is mistaken on this point and that, whatever its weaknesses, one of the greatest strengths of classical theism is its articulation of divine transcendence.

By "classical theism" I mean belief in a personal Creator and Redeemer who is not only infinite and eternal but, above all, loving. Such a view of God is the widely shared core of Jewish, Christian, and Muslim monotheism. In the Christian context, it is shared not only by those most classical of classical theists, Augustine and Aquinas, but also by two other groups: on the one hand, by theologians like Luther, Calvin, and Barth, who seek—in various ways and degrees—to pull Jerusalem away from Athens and the Platonic or Aristotelian frameworks so important to Augustine and Aquinas; and, on the other hand, by lay believers who neither read nor write academic theology.

Classical theism presupposes and presents a triple transcendence. First, there is cosmological transcendence. God is "outside" or "above" or "beyond" the world. This is not to deny that God is intimately present to the world and to every creature in it. It is rather to affirm a crucial existential asymmetry. The world cannot exist without God, but God can exist without the world. This is the meaning of creation. God is not a world soul which is actual only in union with the world as its body. Nor is God the source from which the world emanates as heat and light from a fire. For while there cannot be the heat and light without the fire, so there cannot be the fire without the heat and light that radiate from it. This asymmetry distinguishes classical theism from every emanationist and pantheistic way of thinking.

Cosmological transcendence is first, not as the axiom of a deductive system, but in a Hegelian sense. It is the thinnest, most abstract, least adequate, but nevertheless necessary, way of thinking of God's transcendence. At first glance it does not appear to be a shattering of the cogito or the birth of the responsible self. In fact, it could all too easily become a theory which, like a trophy bride or other forms of conspicuous consumption, serves as a sign of our superiority, placing us at the center rather than decentering us: "Lord, I thank Thee that I am not a pantheist."

But as classical theism thinks through the meaning of creation more concretely, two further forms of divine transcendence emerge. The first of these is epistemic transcendence, and this comes in two forms. To begin with, the need for special revelation is affirmed. On a spectrum that finds Aquinas at or near one end and Karl Barth at or near the other end, classical theists disagree about the nature and extent of the knowledge of God available to us by unaided human reason. They do agree, however, that whatever knowledge, if any, we have in this way, it is not enough. God needs to provide us, by grace and beyond our own natural powers, with knowledge that corrects and supplements our "natural" thinking about God. Thus, for example, we have Augustine telling us what he did not find in the books of the Platonists but only in the Bible and complaining about the "presumption" of the Platonists who are content with the results of philosophical speculation.[66] And the Sunday school child, who has never heard of Augustine, knows the same thing. Jesus loves me. This I know, for the Bible tells me so.

This is indeed a dangerous supplement, for it is the shattering of the cogito. Truth is defined as the *adaequatio rei et intellectus,* while classical theism tells us that our best efforts never achieve adequation but rather stand in need of both correction and supplementation. What clearly and distinctly seems to me to be the case, even with the help of methodological carefulness, is not the measure of being. If I knew how things really were, I would need to be tutored by the God without whom I could not exist but who can exist without me. Thus the epistemic corollary: I cannot truly know without God's help; but God's knowledge, which simply is the truth, does not need my assistance.

The second moment of epistemic transcendence intensifies the first. It comes in the affirmation of the incomprehensibility of God. God is "wholly other," not just ontologically as the only uncreated being, but epistemically as well. Even with the help of divine revelation, God remains mysterious and exceeds our conceptual grasp. Thus, for example, Aquinas regularly insists that, in this life, even with the help of divine revelation, our intellect never sees the divine essence, which "surpasses our intelligence and is unknown to us: wherefore *man reaches the highest point of his knowledge about God when he knows that he knows him not,* inasmuch as he knows that that which is God transcends whatsoever he conceives of him."[67] Our knowledge never achieves adequation. Strictly speaking, it is never true.

Even in a state of rapture or in the life to come, when the blessed apprehend the divine essence, they do not comprehend God. For when "the thing known exceeds its grasp, then the knowing power falls short of comprehension."[68] Only a cogito that no longer sees this humbling as humiliation can be happy in heaven.

This epistemic transcendence casts a different light on two points at which Schrag's critique of classical theism seems to have Aquinas especially in mind. The God of Kierkegaard's religiousness B, Schrag says, "is not a metaphysical entity, as proposed by the proponents of classical theism. One finds no alleged proofs for the existence of a supernatural being in the writings of Kierkegaard . . . because the very project of a metaphysics of theism becomes problematized, deconstructed, if you will, through the dynamics of 'existential faith.' "[69]

Though some of my best friends are Thomists, I am not. In fact, my sympathies lie more with Kierkegaard than with the *doctor angelicus.*

However, it seems unnecessary to me to use Kierkegaard to deconstruct Aquinas's "metaphysics of theism" for the sake of divine transcendence. The proofs of God's existence can seem to be a quintessentially onto-theological gesture, the positing of a Highest Being who is not only (1) the key to the meaning of the whole of being but also (2) the means by which the whole of being becomes fully intelligible to human under-standing.[70] Epistemic transcendence would be lost. The proofs are clearly one way of making the first gesture. But then, whoever affirms God as Creator makes this move, whatever the epistemic basis for the affirma-tion. Aquinas would be making the second, crucial gesture, however, only if it were assumed that God, the key to the meaning of the whole of being, were fully intelligible to us. And that Aquinas repeatedly and emphatically denies. For him it is just the opposite. The affirmation of God as creator is the acknowledgment that neither God nor the world can be fully intelligible to us.[71] Where God remains mysterious, metaphysics in its onto-theological constitution is already overcome. When Aquinas says that full intelligibility is available to the divine but not to any created intellect, he is paraphrasing Kierkegaard, whose Climacus writes, "Exis-tence itself is a system—for God, but it cannot be a system for any existing spirit."[72]

Schrag also says that Kierkegaardian transcendence "focuses atten-tion away from the categorial constraints of a theo-metaphysics that is destined to construe transcendence as a quasi-scientific cosmological principle."[73] Once again, this suggests Aquinas, for whom God is surely a cosmological principle. But then God is a cosmological principle for anyone who affirms God as Creator. But it does not follow that God is nothing but a cosmological principle. For classical theism, cosmological transcendence is only the abstract beginning; we have already seen it spill over into epistemic transcendence and will shortly see ethical transcen-dence emerge as well.

Before turning to that theme, however, we should look briefly at the "quasi-scientific" character of God as cosmological principle. Aquinas comes to mind again because he treats theology as a "quasi-scientific" dis-cipline. But the "quasi" is utterly important. For Aquinas *scientia* requires insight into the essence of the entities dealt with by a particular science.[74] In the case of God, that is precisely what we do not have. Just as our knowledge of God is by analogy rather than by adequation, so theology has the form of science while lacking the *Wesensschau* that is its essential ingredient.[75] It is only "quasi-scientific." Aquinas's "theo-metaphysics" de-constructs itself precisely to preserve the transcendence of God. In the process the cogito is dethroned. It is no longer the czar of cognition, the king of knowledge. As long as transcendence is the issue, I see no need to drive a wedge between Kierkegaard and the likes of Aquinas, nor to turn to Tillich's project of "transcending theism" in search of the "God beyond God."[76] Along that path it just might be transcendence itself that gets transcended.

God is my highest good. A final question. Is the shattering of the cogito represented by classical theism also the birth of the responsible self? This brings us to the question of ethical transcendence, which brings cosmological and epistemic transcendence to their most concrete, or, if you prefer, most existential completion. For purposes of convenience we can stick with Aquinas, whose treatise on law signifies a triple heteronomy of the self in whom responsibility is born from the Other.

He begins teleologically and eudaemonistically. But the telos whose achievement is my happiness is properly defined by the eternal law which is both ontologically and epistemologically transcendent. My being, and hence its perfection, arise from participation (here Aquinas is more Platonic than Aristotelian), from my limited engagement with, and imperfect orientation to, a being whose being, as the identity of essence and existence, is radically different from my own. My being has its ground, not just causally but teleologically, outside itself. Hence the strange claim that God is my highest good.

Just as human being participates in divine being, so the human intellect participates in the divine intellect. Grounded ontologically in the very being of God, my perfection is known primarily in the knowledge of God (subjective genitive); this is what Aquinas calls the eternal law, the principle of my perfection and happiness as known by God. By participation, and thus secondarily and imperfectly, the truth of my perfection and happiness is known by my own understanding; this is the natural law (the moral equivalent of natural theology). But here epistemic transcendence reemerges. Human reason's apprehension of the eternal law is important to Aquinas; it is not nothing. But because of both human finitude and fallenness, it requires supplementation, which Aquinas calls the divine law. It consists of the law given by grace as part of special revelation beyond and apart from the natural workings of human reason.

At this point teleological ethics becomes deontological, for the divine law is the commands issued to me from an Other. With Kierkegaard, as distinct from Lévinas, this Other is, in the first instance, God. This completes the triple heteronomy of Thomistic ethics. There is ontological heteronomy in that my being is not just derived from, but is also ordered toward, the being of an Other. There is epistemic heteronomy in that reason is incapable of being a fully adequate guide and needs the supplement of revelation. And there is moral heteronomy in that I find myself obliged by a law that does not depend on my understanding or my consent for its legitimacy. The divine law is anything but self-legislation, whether of monological reason, as in Kant, or of dialogical reason, as in Habermas. Just to the degree that I understand the divine law, and just to the degree that I consent to it, I find myself acknowledging an obligation that is essentially prior to my own acts of understanding and consent.

It is not clear that either Lévinas or Kierkegaard is able to articulate a more potent sense of transcendence. In their own ways Descartes and Kant tried to unite the concept of God as Creator with radical human autonomy at the epistemic and ethical levels. By doing so, they opened the door to the loss of transcendence in Spinoza and Hegel. Instead of fixing a great gulf between Lévinas and Kierkegaard on the one hand and classical theism on the other, we might see the former pair as seeking to restore the sense of transcendence that comes to us from the radical monotheism we sometimes call classical theism. It is the original home of that shattering of the cogito that is the birth of the responsible self.

Notes

1. Paul Ricoeur, *Oneself as Another,* trans. Kathleen Blamey (Chicago: University of Chicago Press, 1992), pp. 4, 23, 19.

2. Calvin O. Schrag, *The Self after Postmodernity* (New Haven, Conn.: Yale University Press, 1997), pp. 27, 33 (hereafter cited as *SP*).

3. Ibid., p. 9. See Eduardo Cadava, Peter Connor, and Jean-Luc Nancy, eds., introduction to *Who Comes after the Subject?* (New York: Routledge, 1991).

4. Schrag, *SP,* pp. 4, 12–13.

5. Ibid., pp. 26, 37.

6. Ibid., pp. 19–28.

7. Ibid., pp. 33–35.

8. See Gilbert Ryle, *The Concept of Mind* (New York: Barnes and Noble, 1949). In her interpretation of the *Phaedrus,* Catherine Pickstock finds "a suggestion that a person's identity is defined and performed . . . by a kind of journeying, an 'identity' which is always *in medias res*." She calls this a "doxological identity" because of Socrates' insistence on praising the god and, ultimately, the Good and the Beautiful. "I" am not just *unterwegs* but turned outside of myself to that which is greater than myself and which calls me to its infinity rather than serving my finite projects. This is the "doxological dispossession" (pp. 170, 177, 194, 250) of a premodern version of the "self after postmodernity."

9. Schrag, *SP,* pp. 28 ff., 68 ff.

10. See Richard Macksey and Eugenio Donato, eds., *The Languages of Criticism and the Sciences of Man: The Structuralist Controversy* (Baltimore: Johns Hopkins University Press, 1970), p. 271, quotation on p. 14, n. 3.

11. See Jacques Derrida, *Monolingualism of the Other or The Prosthesis of Origin*, trans. Patrick Mensah (Stanford, Calif.: Stanford University Press, 1998), pp. 28–29. The question, Who speaks? becomes the sharper question, Who speaks in what language? This would be the one-sided triumph of plurality over unity, of which Schrag accuses Lyotard, only if language games had the kind of monadic self-enclosure which Derrida regularly sees as the denial of difference. John Milbank makes a similar point when he writes, "Objects and subjects are [for postmodernity] as they are narrated in a story. Outside a plot, which has its own unique, unfounded reasons, one cannot conceive how objects and subjects would be, nor even that they would be at all." See John Milbank, "Postmodern Critical Augustinianism: A Short *Summa* in Forty-Two Responses to Unasked Questions," in *The Postmodern God*, ed. Graham Ward (Oxford: Blackwell, 1997), p. 265. Such narratives include not only the stories of individuals but also the meganarratives, the larger, communal stories which constitute the languages in which the individual stories are told.

12. Cadava, Connor, and Nancy, eds., *Who Comes after the Subject?* p. 100, quotation on p. 14. Quote is by Schrag, SP, on p. 14 from *Who Comes*, p. 100.

13. See John D. Caputo, *Against Ethics* (Bloomington: Indiana University Press, 1993); Edith Wyschogrod, *Saints and Postmodernism* (Chicago: University of Chicago Press, 1990). Both Caputo and Wyschogrod draw a sharp distinction between these two questions.

14. On this point see Schrag's splendid essay, "The Kierkegaard-Effect in the Shaping of the Contours of Modernity," in *Kierkegaard in Post/Modernity*, ed. Martin Matuštík and Merold Westphal (Bloomington: Indiana University Press, 1995), pp. 1–17.

15. Cadava, Connor, and Nancy, eds., *Who Comes after the Subject?* p. 100 (emphasis added).

16. Schrag, *SP,* p. 59.

17. See Jacques Derrida, "How to Avoid Speaking: Denials," in *Derrida and Negative Theology*, ed. Harold Coward and Toby Foshay (Albany: State University of New York Press, 1992), p. 99.

18. Lévinas closely links heteronomy and transcendence when he suggests that they are what is lost when Buber presents the I-Thou relation with too much of a focus on reciprocity, "as a harmonious co-presence, and an eye to eye," which Lévinas takes to be different from the face-to-face. See Emmanuel Lévinas, "Dialogue," in *Of God Who Comes to Mind*, trans. Bettina Bergo (Stanford, Calif.: Stanford University Press, 1998), p. 150.

19. Emmanuel Lévinas, "No Identity," in *Collected Philosophical Papers*, trans. Alphonso Lingis (Dordrecht: Martinus Nijhoff, 1987), p. 141.

20. Nor is it "a self-identical monad, mute and self-enclosed, changeless and secured prior to the events of speaking." These are Schrag's definitions of the presumptuous modern cogito. See Schrag, *SP,* pp. 27, 33.

21. Lévinas, "No Identity," pp. 141, 142.

22. Ibid., pp. 141–42.

23. Ibid., p. 142.

24. Lévinas also associates Heidegger with these philosophies insofar as human beings are but mouthpieces of being (Lévinas, "No Identity," pp. 143–44). As Lévinas writes, "But for Heidegger the subject has nothing inward to express" (Lévinas, "No Identity," p. 144, n.4).

25. Ibid., p. 143.

26. Ibid., p. 149. Lévinas does not distinguish idem identity from ipse identity. Thus he describes the transcendental I beyond which the Other takes us as "the identity of an *I* that from the start, without objectifying reflection, is a *self,* the identity of an *ipseity.*" See Emmanuel Lévinas, *Outside the Subject,* trans. Michael B. Smith (Stanford, Calif.: Stanford University Press, 1994), p. 1.

27. Ibid.

28. Ibid., pp. 149, 145. Compare Emmanuel Lévinas, "Is Ontology Fundamental," in *Emmanuel Lévinas: Basic Philosophical Writings,* ed. Adriaan T. Peperzak, Simon Critchley, and Robert Bernasconi (Bloomington: Indiana University Press, 1996), pp. 7–10, where Lévinas seeks to break from the knowledge-is-power tradition. Lévinas's sustained critique of intentionality is found in Emmanuel Lévinas, *Discovering Existence with Husserl,* trans. Richard A. Cohen and Michael B. Smith (Evanston, Ill.: Northwestern University Press, 1998), and in "Beyond Intentionality," in *Philosophy in France Today,* ed. Alan Montefiore (Cambridge: Cambridge University Press, 1983), pp. 100–15.

29. With reference to the id, Freud cites Georg Groddeck's claim that "we are 'lived' by unknown and uncontrollable forces." See Sigmund Freud, *The Ego and the Id,* chap. 2, from *The Standard Edition of the Complete Psychological Works of Sigmund Freud,* ed. and trans. James Strachey (London: Hogarth, 1953–74).

30. Lévinas, "No Identity," pp. 145, 146.

31. Ibid., p. 145. Compare Emmanuel Lévinas, *Otherwise than Being or Beyond Essence,* trans. Alphonso Lingis (Dordrecht: Kluwer Academic Publishers, 1991), p. 150. Catherine Pickstock, in arguing against Derrida's interpretation of the *Phaedrus,* presents Socratic eros as the priority of the Good and the Beautiful over the soul. Because of this transcendence, the philosophical gaze is reverent rather than violent and "The erotic gaze is therefore neither totalizing nor rationalizing . . . The erotic gaze institutes an ontologically constitutive loss of self." See Catherine Pickstock, *After Writing: On the Liturgical Consummation of Philosophy* (Oxford: Blackwell, 1998), pp. 32–33.

32. Lévinas, "No Identity," p. 146. The biblical text is Lam. 3:30. Compare Isa. 50:6, which Handel set to music in *Messiah.*

33. I understand this nakedness both literally, signifying the poverty of the widow, orphan, and stranger who above all are the Other, and symbolically, signifying that the Other comes shorn of anything that would make her attractive or useful to me. No beauty. No bribes.

34. Lévinas, "No Identity," pp. 146–47.

35. Ibid., p. 146 (emphasis added).

36. Ibid., pp. 146, 147–51.

37. See, e.g., Lévinas, *Otherwise than Being,* pp. 13–15, for the close link between the concept of substitution and that of the self's identity.

38. These phrases, cited at the beginning of this essay, were used by Schrag to describe the cogito whose shattering he applauds.

39. In *Otherwise than Being* Lévinas speaks of "the other in the same" (p. 25), of vulnerability and exposure as "one-penetrated-by-the-other" (p. 49), of the passivity of proximity as "having-the-other-in-one's-skin" (p.115).

40. Lévinas, "No Identity, pp. 145, 148, 149 (emphasis added).

41. Kant, *Critique of Pure Reason*, trans. Norman Kemp Smith (London: Macmillan, 1961).

42. Lévinas, "No Identity," p. 143.

43. Ibid., p. 150.

44. In Lévinas, *Otherwise than Being*, because "I exist through the other and for the other," it is for that reason that "I am 'in myself' through the others" (pp. 114, 112). Compare Augustine, *Confessions* 7.11, "If I do not remain in Him, I shall not be able to remain in myself" (trans. Rex Warner).

45. Lévinas, "No Identity," p. 151.

46. Ibid., p. 145. It is because George Steiner sees only the first meaning to Rimbaud's *Je est un autre* that he sees postmodernism only as a danger to be overcome. See George Steiner, *Real Presences* (Chicago: University of Chicago Press, 1989), pp. 94–110. Lévinas repeatedly insists that the intrusion of the Other into the self is not inherently an alienation. See Lévinas, *Otherwise than Being*, pp. 105, 112, 118.

47. Lévinas, "No Identity," p. 148.

48. Responsibility as nonindifference Lévinas also calls "agape," or love without concupiscence. See Emmanuel Lévinas, *Entre Nous: On Thinking-of-the-Other*, trans. Michael B. Smith and Barbara Harshav (New York: Columbia University Press, 1998), pp. 103, 113, 131, 149, 169, 186, 194, 216, 227, and 228.

49. Lévinas, *Otherwise than Being*, p. 11; cf. pp. 15, 43, 105.

50. Søren Kierkegaard, *Fear and Trembling/Repetition*, trans. Howard V. Hong and Edna H. Hong (Princeton, N.J.: Princeton University Press, 1983), pp. 9, 33, 61.

51. Søren Kierkegaard, *Either/Or*, 2 vols., trans. Howard V. Hong and Edna H. Hong (Princeton, N.J.: Princeton University Press, 1987), 2:166–69.

52. Ibid., 2:177. See Edward F. Mooney, "Kierkegaard on Self-Choice and Self-Reception: Judge William's Admonition," in *International Kierkegaard Commentary: Either/Or, Part II*, ed. Robert L. Perkins (Macon: Mercer University Press, 1995), pp. 5–31.

53. Kierkegaard, *Either/Or*, 2:270 (emphasis added).

54. I have spelled this out in detail in my "Hegel's Radical Idealism: Family and State as Ethical Communities," in *Hegel, Freedom, and Modernity* (Albany: State University of New York Press, 1992).

55. Schrag, *SP*, pp. 118–25; Kierkegaard, *Fear and Trembling/Repetition*, p. 70. We cannot identify Kierkegaard with Johannes de Silentio, the pseudonym of *Fear and Trembling*, any more than we can identify him with Judge William. What I am attributing to "Kierkegaard" is a view that emerges from reading the pseudonymous and nonpseudonymous writings in relation to each other, and not stopping

with *Concluding Unscientific Postscript.* See my "Kierkegaard's Teleological Suspension of Religiousness B," in *Foundations of Kierkegaard's Vision of Community,* ed. George B. Connell and C. Stephen Evans (Atlantic Highlands, N.J.: Humanities Press, 1992), pp. 110–29.

56. But Abraham's silence has been anticipated all along. See Kierkegaard, *Fear and Trembling,* pp. 21, 60, 67, 71, 76, 79–80. Actually, neither Sarah nor Eliezer is mentioned in the Gen. 22 story, but it is clear that Isaac does not know what his father is up to.

57. Mark C. Taylor, *Journey's to Selfhood: Hegel and Kierkegaard* (Berkeley and Los Angeles: University of California Press, 1980), p. 10.

58. I have discussed this difference in "The Transparent Shadow: Kierkegaard and Lévinas in Dialogue," in *Kierkegaard in Post/Modernity,* pp. 265–81, and in "Lévinas' Teleological Suspension of the Religious," in *Ethics as First Philosophy: The Significance of Lévinas for Philosophy, Literature, and Religion,* ed. Adriaan T. Peperzak (New York: Routledge, 1995), pp. 151–60.

59. The inescapability of ontological language is a central thesis of Derrida in "Violence and Metaphysics," *Writing and Difference,* trans. Alan Bass (Chicago: University of Chicago Press, 1978). That Lévinas does not so much simply abandon ontology as offer an alternative ontology is argued by Adriaan Peperzak in *Beyond: The Philosophy of Emmanuel Lévinas* (Evanston, Ill.: Northwestern University Press, 1997). Like Derrida, Lévinas recognizes the affinity of his thought for negative theology, though he denies their identity. See Lévinas, *Otherwise than Being,* pp. 44, 147, esp. 150–51.

60. Lévinas, *Otherwise than Being,* pp. 52, 162.

61. For "paradox," see Kierkegaard, *Fear and Trembling,* pp. 33, 48–53, 55–56, 62–66, 85, 88. For "the absurd," see pp. 34–37, 40, 46–51, 56, 59.

62. Kierkegaard, *Fear and Trembling,* pp. 35–36. I have discussed this theme in relation to Johannes Climacus in *Becoming a Self: A Reading of Kierkegaard's* Concluding Unscientific Postscript (West Lafayette, Ind.: Purdue University Press, 1996), pp. 123–26, 180–84.

63. Pickstock, *After Writing,* p. 62. By contrast, the self engaged with transcendence, in her case, Socrates, has an "'identity' which is always *in media res.* . . . The person who gives praise [to the Good] is not estranged, yet neither can he lay claim to a fixed or completed identity" (p. 45).

64. From Rule 12 in Descartes's *Rules for the Direction of the Mind,* in *The Philosophical Writings of Descartes,* trans. John Cottingham, Robert Stoothoff, and Dugald Murdoch (Cambridge: Cambridge University Press, 1985). Pickstock cites part of this passage in her analysis of the collapse of ontology into epistemology. See Pickstock, *After Writing,* p. 64.

65. Schrag, *SP,* p. 138.

66. See Augustine, *Confessions* 7.20

67. Aquinas, *De Potentia Dei* 7.5.14. For a helpful summary of this theme, see John F. Wippel, "Quidditative Knowledge of God," in *Metaphysical Themes in Thomas Aquinas* (Washington, D.C.: Catholic University of America Press, 1984).

68. Aquinas, *De Veritate* 8.2. Compare Aquinas *Summa Theologiae* 1.12.1.3 and 1.12.7.

69. Schrag, *SP,* p. 135.

70. I have argued that the intelligibility thesis is an essential part of Heidegger's critique of onto-theology. I do not commit onto-theology merely by affirming a Highest Being who is the key to the meaning of the whole of being. See my "Overcoming Onto-Theology," in *God, the Gift, and Postmodernism,* ed. John D. Caputo and Michael J. Scanlon (Bloomington: Indiana University Press, 1999), pp. 146–69.

71. That Aquinas's doctrine of creation implies that we cannot fully understand even created beings is argued skillfully by Joseph Pieper in *The Silence of St. Thomas,* trans. John Murray, S.J., and Daniel O'Connor (Chicago: Henry Regnery, 1965), pp. 45–71.

72. Søren Kierkegaard, *Concluding Unscientific Postscript,* trans. Howard V. Hong and Edna H. Hong (Princeton, N.J.: Princeton University Press, 1992), 1.118.

73. Schrag, *SP,* p. 134.

74. For a lucid and succinct account of Aquinas's concept of science, see Scott MacDonald, "Theory of Knowledge," in *The Cambridge Companion to Aquinas,* ed. Norman Kretzmann and Eleonore Stump (New York: Cambridge University Press, 1993), pp. 160–95.

75. Kierkegaard's Climacus might well agree. For subjectivity is not presented as the abolition of objectivity but as its dangerous supplement.

76. Schrag, *SP,* p. 136.

12

In Search of a Sacred Anarchy: An Experiment in Danish Deconstruction

John D. Caputo

L ike Heidegger, like many of us, Calvin Schrag has had a theological
point of departure. His earliest work, *Existence and Freedom,* published some forty years ago, undertook one of the first important
confrontations of Heidegger and Kierkegaard in English.[1] Schrag understood that a great deal of continental philosophy originated in the decision made by Kierkegaard to expose philosophy to biblical categories,
on the premise that if the categories of Greek philosophy are all we have,
then the poor existing individual is lost. It was in no small part from
that decision that Heidegger's *Being and Time* emerged, and with that
book, much of contemporary continental thought. Kierkegaard's was the
first "deconstruction" of speculative metaphysics, and it has remained
paradigmatic for continental philosophy to this day. Does this mean, I
wonder, that we are to include the achievement of Cal Schrag—like that
of Kierkegaard, Heidegger, Ricoeur, and Lévinas (it is difficult to know
where to do the line here)—among those whose work amounts to what
Jacques Derrida calls a nondogmatic repetition of religion, "a *thinking*
that 'repeats' the possibility of religion without religion"?[2] I simply pose
that as a question, for him, for myself, for his readers.

In tribute to the remarkable contribution Calvin Schrag has made
to philosophical thinking in America, in gratitude for the lead he has
given us in showing us how to think in America within a continentalist
framework, and in the spirit of Schrag's first book, his early *Auseinan-
dersetzung* of Kierkegaard and Heidegger, I would like to conduct a little experiment in what I will call Danish deconstruction. By this lovely

little alliteration, Danish deconstruction, I have in mind the concept of deconstruction with constant reference to Kierkegaard. My idea is to put the names of Derrida and Kierkegaard to work in order—to speak oxymoronically—to set forth the plans and stake out the borders of what I will call here a "sacred anarchy," the whole idea for which turns on a hypothesis that I will spell out below, about the communication between God, philosophy's most famous protagonist, and *différance*, philosophy's most famous misspelling.

A Kingdom of *Différance*

I begin with the misspelling, with *différance*. *Différance* is a secular word coined for a secular philosophical world by a philosopher who says of himself "I quite rightly pass for an atheist."[3] Still, for whatever reasons, God and *différance* keep up what must seem to some an unholy communication with each other, with which Derrida has constantly to deal.[4]

Some years ago, in his famous essay *"Différance,"* Derrida said that *différance* "everywhere comes to solicit, in the sense that *sollicitare,* in old Latin, means to shake as a whole, to make tremble in entirety." For that reason, he went on to say that *différance* should not be construed as some sort of *primum ens* sent into the world to set things straight, some principle of order and governance:

> It governs nothing, reigns over nothing, and nowhere exercises any
> authority. It is not announced by any capital letter. Not only is there no
> kingdom of *différance,* but *différance* instigates the subversion of every
> kingdom. Which makes it obviously threatening and infallibly dreaded by
> everything within us that desires a kingdom, the past or future presence
> of a kingdom. And it is always in the name of a kingdom that one may
> reproach *différance* with wishing to reign, believing that one sees it
> aggrandize itself with a capital letter.[5]

In other words, although many of its admirers have come to expect quite a lot of it, *différance* is not God, and it does not set up court in something like a kingdom of God. Indeed, far from having the status of God or of any sort of arche, divine or otherwise, far from being a principium or prince which orders and stabilizes, *différance* is downright subversive of such orderliness. Its "natural" tendency, if it had a nature, is to destabilize the stable, to shake the firm, resolutely to oppose every kingdom, every ordered totality. Not only is there no *royaume de différance,* the very idea of *différance,* if it is an idea, is the idea of no more reigning, no more kingdoms, not now, not ever, the idea of subverting kingdoms wherever they appear.

Unless of course, in the best spirit of deconstruction, one might speak, in all perversity, of the possibility of a kingdom of the kingdom-less, a kingdom of those who do not reign and have no power, an un-kingly, an-archic kingdom. That is the possibility that interests me, in the spirit of a certain deconstruction, and also in the spirit of what Derrida now calls the "democracy to come" which also suggests a slightly anarchi-cal arche.[6]

Derrida does not mean to say that *différance* breeds outright chaos. He does not favor a simpleminded anarchy that would let lawlessness sweep over the land, although that is just what his most simpleminded and anxious critics take him to say. For that would amount to nothing more than a counterkingdom, a kingdom of lawlessness, where lawless-ness rules, where a still greater violence holds sway. Like a simple totali-tarianism, a simple anarchy would break the tension between the arche and the anarche; pure life would spell death. That is why, twenty years later, in "Force of Law," and in his more recent writings generally, Derrida has made it plain that deconstruction is not a matter of leveling laws in order to produce a lawless society, but of deconstructing laws in order to produce a just society.[7] To deconstruct the law means to hold the con-structedness of the law plainly and constantly in view so as to subject the law to relentless analysis, revision, and repeal, to rewriting and review, and this in view of the fact that there is a structural and necessary gap between the law, which is constructed, and justice, which is undeconstructible, a fundamental tension that must never be relaxed. *Lex mala, lex nulla:* A bad law is no law at all, not if the law is meant to serve justice. Decon-struction resists the closure of the law in the name of what laws close off and exclude, namely, the singularity of the poor existing individual. Deconstruction, which situates itself in that gap, breeds justice, even as it is born and bred of justice; indeed, to invoke one of Derrida's most startling formulations, "deconstruction is justice." That is not an act of self-congratulation but the name of a task. Deconstructing the law means to hold the law in question, to solicit the law, to make the law tremble, while always letting oneself be solicited and troubled by justice, by the need for justice, by the need to let justice come, to let justice flow like water over the land, to let justice rule.

But if justice "rules," then is there not a "kingdom of justice," not in the sense of some locality where justice is to be found, but in the sense of the summons that justice issues, of a call to let justice reign, a demand to stay steadily open to the call of justice, tuned to justice's address? After all, there are kingdoms and there are kingdoms, and "kingdom" is not a "bad name," not evil in itself.[8] Indeed, "kingdom" is nothing in itself, apart from the economy in which it is made to operate.

Could we not say that the rule of justice, the reign or kingdom of justice, constitutes a world or social order in which the sails of the law are trimmed close to the winds of justice? Could there not be a kingdom of *différance* after all, contrary to Derrida's most literal claim, albeit a very strange sort of kingdom, one governed not by a powerful and overarching arche, a positive, princely principium which holds all things mightily in its sway, but, almost the opposite, a kingdom organized around the power of the powerless, by a sustained sense for the exceptional and singular, the different and the left out, the foreigner and the immigrant, to which the arche is systematically blind? Would this not be something of an an-archic kingdom, a kingdom whose ear is cocked for the different, whose *Stimmung* is tuned to those who stand outside the law? Could there not be a kingdom, not of law but of justice, not of unbending rule but of the holding sway of the outlaws and the losers, the left-out and the lost, which keeps an ear and eye out for poor existing individuals?

In that sense, *différance* would have the effect of subverting every "kingdom of law," every archical kingdom, every rigorous and unbending rule of law, precisely in the name of another kingdom, a "kingdom of justice." The kingdom of justice is (dis)organized around everything singular and outlawed, everything marginal and dispossessed, everything that is null and void before the law, and this just in order to let justice reign. This kingdom of *différance* would constitute an anarchic kingdom of cast-offs and cast-outs, of the ill-born and lowborn, of everyone unroyal and unkingly, uncourtly and disreputable, a kingdom of everyone who amounts to nothing or who is nobody from the point of view of worldly power, a "kingdom of nuisances and nobodies," as John Dominic Crossan puts it.[9] In this very odd kingdom, everything odd and out of step would enjoy special favor, would capture justice's anarchic eye, watched over in the watch that justice keeps for the anarchical who slip beneath the radar of the arche and the law. If the law is blind, then deconstruction takes its stand with the glance that the eye of justice casts upon the singularity to which the law blinds itself, which we might call, in the language of Danish deconstruction, the *Augen-blick* of justice.

Now if we take a "prophet" in the biblical sense, not as one who tries to the see the future, which is what the blind Greek prophet and seer has in mind, but as one who speaks for (*pro-phetes*) justice, then the kingdom of justice would have a *prophetic* quality about it. The kingdom of justice calls to us and puts "us" in the accusative, on the spot, called on the carpet about the privileges "we" currently enjoy under the law and in the present order. In prophetic grammar, the "we" is always part of the problem, and the idea behind the prophetic is to reconstitute the "we" as an "us" which recognizes itself as under accusation, *me voici:* here I am, here we are, on the receiving end of a call. That would mean that the present order, which certainly includes the "euphoria of liberal democracy" and of the "new world order," is the very kingdom for which deconstruction is designed to make trouble.[10] In Danish deconstruction, what Kierkegaard called the "present age," the age of presence and the present, is always under the "revolutionary" gun.[11] A prophet is a troublemaker who speaks for justice now, in the present, which is why he usually ends up getting killed, which is another thing that distinguishes Jewish prophets from Greek ones. A prophet is not someone who sees the future but someone who comes to deliver the word that "we" in the present do not want to hear, to tell us what is urgently demanded of us, now, in the present—justice deferred is justice denied.[12] The prophet lets us know what we do not want to know, troubles and solicits us, makes us tremble, decentering the "I," the arche/self, which has a tendency to organize everything around itself and to ensure that everything returns to itself. Like *différance,* the prophetic is an operation of solicitation. It is because of their common commitment to *sollicitare,* to disturbing the peace, to troubling the tranquillity of the present order, of the present age, that Derrida can say that deconstruction is "produced in a space where the prophets are not far away."[13] The "present age" is not a fixed date in calendar time, but a floating structure of human existence, like a Heideggerian "existentiale," a structure that, like the poor, you always have with you, that is always already in place, wherever two or three are gathered together. The present age is the structure of the authority of presence and of the prestige of the present, for which there is a standing need of solicitation, that is, of deconstruction, for Danish deconstruction is always the deconstruction of presence, of the power and prestige of the present age.

Divine Subversion and Danish Deconstruction

Now I turn to God (a lifelong task), and to my hypothesis.

Suppose we grant all this business about disturbing the prestige of the present. What has any of this to do with God or with a kingdom of God? Does not *différance* spell trouble for God? Does not *différance* spell the end of religion and the death of God? *Différance* steadfastly resists becoming a "master word or master concept" and accordingly "blocks every relationship to theology," since the discourse on God is a discourse on the master-word *par excellence,* the Lord and master of the universe.[14] Is not God the dream of plenitude, "of being as presence, as Parousia, as life without *différance,*" and is not "theology" the very name, the very model, of the logocentric love of presence and the effacement of the trace?[15] Can one imagine a more powerful presence or a more prestigious Parousia, a more permanently present presence than the "God" around which religious power groups itself? Can one imagine anything more supportive of the established order, anything more top-down, more entrenched in the status quo, anything more immobilized, contented, and *nunc stans* than religion and religion's "God"? *Pro deo et patria:* Is that not literally a call to arms in whose ungodly name more blood has been spilled than just about anything else we can imagine? What has founded and grounded top-down orders of power more firmly than such a "God"? How often has the "reign of God" (a very theocratic idea!) meant a reign of terror? What has been more violent than theocracy? What more patriarchal, more hierarchical? What more authoritarian, inquisitorial, misogynistic, colonialist, militaristic, terroristic?

But suppose—and this is our working hypothesis in this experiment in Danish deconstruction—as a regular reader of essays like *"différance"* and "The Present Age," we raise the possibility of a "God" who belongs not to the order of presence but to the (dis)order of the deconstruction of presence? Suppose God does not belong to the order of manifestation and presence, and hence even of truth, whether truth is taken as *aletheia* or *adequatio rei et intellectus,* but rather withdraws from the world in order to station himself or herself (Godself is the gender-neutral word) with everything that the world despises?[16] Suppose our thought of God is not swept away by ecstatic visions of the supereminent power of the supreme creator of heaven and earth, its arche and telos, but takes its lead from the most powerless remnants and marginalized nobodies, the little *me onta,* the obscure pockets and folds and hovels of the world? Suppose God most especially hovers and makes a home among the homeless, so that God would be the last one to speak *"pro deo et patria"?*

Suppose further that "religion" tends systematically, structurally, regularly to forget this, to such an extent that religion, which is our doing, not God's, and religion's God, might almost be defined by its oblivion of "God" so that the first step that would be required, as Meister Eckhart said, is to pray "God" to rid us of God? To which we might add, "I pray 'God' to rid us of religion," since, according to Isaiah (Isa.1:11–17), Amos (Amos 5:21–24), and Hosea (Hos.6:6), God is not interested in religion, in cultic sacrifice and ritual, but in justice.[17] Suppose we add the prophets to the list that Derrida composes of those who advocate a religion without religion? Suppose, indeed, that "God" is stationed not on the side of arche and the principium, or of timeless being and unchanging presence, of the true, the good, and the beautiful, but on the side of the an-archic and subversive, as the driving force—the *agens movens*—of a divine subversion? Suppose "God" is situated not inside the churches on the high altars, but among the beggars with outstretched hands on the church steps? Suppose "God" is not to be conceived as the overarching governor of the *ordo universi*, of the kosmos, but as what disorders such orders, deworlds such worlds, and subverts such universes? Suppose "God" is not conceived theo-cratically and onto-theo-logically, as the rock solid ground upon which the onto-theo-political edifice is erected, but systematically associated with the different, the marginal, the outsider, the left-out, the least among us, the poor existing individuals, the destitute, the *anawim*, those who are plundered and ground under (Amos 8:4)—and hence as subversive and "revolutionary"? Suppose "God" is to be found at the heart of a revolutionary age, not as the stabilizing center of the present age?

Suppose "God" is not identified with infinite power, *omnipotens deus*, but with the powerless? Suppose the sense of "God" is to interrupt and disrupt, to confound, contradict, and confront the established human order, the human, all-too-human way of doing business, the authority of man over man—and over women, animals, and the earth itself—human possessiveness and dominion, to pose, in short, the contradiction of the "world"? Suppose the idea behind the "rule of God" is not to back up human authority but to break it up, to turn the eye of the law to the widow, the orphan, and the stranger, which is the *Augen-blick* of justice? Suppose the idea behind calling God a father is not to set up an oppressive patriarchal model but to establish a relativization of worldly power: "Do not call any man on earth father, for you have one Father, and he is in heaven . . . the greatest among you must be your servant" (Matt. 23:8–12).[18] Then repeat that with a difference, a sexual difference, and say that you have one Mother in heaven, and for the same reason.

Suppose we associate God with disseminating tongues and deconstructing towering edifices, with confusion and profusion, the way he interrupted the plans of the Shemites (Gen. 11:1–9), who wanted to build the tower of Babel and who disseminated their language into a profusion of unintelligible tongues so that they could no longer build up a consensus, no longer communicate, and no longer build their transcendental tower?[19]

Suppose we stop thinking about God onto-theo-logically as *prima causa*, as some sort of ontological power source, and onto-theo-politically as the foundation of value and good order, "one nation under God," the backup for the established order, and begin to think of "God" in terms of what is left out and ground under by the whole "economy" of nations, causes, values, orders, and what groans for freedom. Suppose "God" stands for everything that confounds, confuses, contradicts, and scandalizes this economy, these crusts of power and privilege, this order of presence, *not*, I hasten to add, in order to throw us to the wolves but in order to let the lamb lie down with the wolf (Isa. 11:6), not in order to level institutions and civilizations but precisely in order to keep them just, to let justice reign? Suppose, as Jean-Luc Marion suggests, we cross out the name of "God," which parallels Heidegger's crossing out of the name of Being, as well as the deforming *a* in *différance*, in order to save the name of God from *religion*'s God, which is an idol, a graven image, an instrument of institutional power, moral melancholy, and confessional divisiveness?[20]

What then?

Then the "kingdom of God" would begin to look a little like this so-called anarchic kingdom of *différance*, and we would find ourselves with a certain analogy which helps get something like Danish deconstruction off the ground: that the kingdom of God threatens and subverts the "world" (kosmos) just the way the kingdom of *différance* threatens and subverts the order of presence. For the world is the kingdom of this world, the holding sway of the present age, of the *aion*, in the Jewish and Christian scriptures, where the world stands for the business as usual of the powerful and privileged, the oppressive system that builds wealth on the backs of the poor and the outcast, that builds privilege on the backs of the despised and the different.

In Danish deconstruction *différance*, a defaced and misspelled word, would not lack a certain analogy to the effects produced by crossing out the name of God as suggested by Jean-Luc Marion (who is following Heidegger's crossing out of Being, which Marion then brilliantly crosses with the Cross).[21] Then this kingdom of *différance*, this anarchic kingdom, if there is such a thing, would serve as a certain *reminder* to religion of the kingdom of God (*basileia tou theou*), the repression of which allows religion to sit down to table with the world and thus constitutes religious power.

I hasten to add that I am not saying that the deconstructor occupies God's point of view. I am not trying surreptitiously to insinuate the divinity of *différance*, surreptitiously to claim that *différance* is to be raised up to the status and stature of the divine or of God (even as I do not say that God can be reduced to *différance*). Derrida has been plain about this. Although the "detours, locutions, and syntax in which I will often have to take recourse will resemble negative theology," still it must be insisted:

JOHN D. CAPUTO

> *Différance is not,* does not exist, is not a present-being (*on*) in any form. . . .
> It derives from no category of being, whether present or absent. And yet
> those aspects of *différance* which are thereby delineated are not theological,
> not even in the order of the most negative of negative theologies, which
> are always concerned with disengaging a superessentiality beyond the
> finite categories of essence and existence, that is, of presence, and always
> hastening to recall that God is refused the predicate of existence, only in
> order to acknowledge his superior, inconceivable, and ineffable mode of
> being.[22]

There are "syntactical" similarities between the God of negative theology
and *différance,* similarities in the rhetorical resources needed to name
something which, in each case, *mutatis mutandis,* does not exist, which is
not a being, not an entity, not one more thing, not even if it is the highest
thing. When Crossan asked, "Why, then, are the syntactics so similar if
the semantics are so different?" Hart rightly responded by saying that
this has to do with the difference between the ineffability of God's utter "transcendence" and the ineffability of a "transcendental," or better,
quasi-transcendental called *différance.*[23] No one should at this late date be
tempted to confuse the God of negative theology with *différance.*

The Task of Justice: The Impossible

On this hypothesis, God is not only the *hyperousia* of negative theology,
the *puritas essendi* beyond being, not only the God of eminence and su-
pereminence, but the one who stands with nullity and insignificance, the
one who stands steadfastly with the nobodies of the world. The prophetic
God is not to be found high above in the realm of Neoplatonic *hyperousia* but down below in the bowels of the earthly kingdom of the *me
onta.* The question of confusing *différance* with God, which is resolved by
showing that *différance* is not a *hyperousios,* was a characteristic problem
of Derrida's early writings. But in Derrida's later writings the effect of
différance is not only to prevent closure in the work of *naming* God—the
basic resource upon which negative theology draws, which is why negative
theology needs deconstruction—but also to address the closures effected
by power, to address ethico-political closures. Hitherto the question of
deconstruction and theology has been a little too preoccupied with the
question of negative theology, while I am proposing here, on my more
Danish hypothesis, that this is only half the story. For over and beyond
the question of how to speak, or of how not to speak, of God (*comment*

ne pas parler), of what we are to call God, there lies the question of what God calls us, what God calls upon us, to do.

In Danish deconstruction, that is to say, in the sphere of poor existing individuals, the name of God is not a name to speculate about, as Johannes Climacus insists, but the name of a *task* which is infinitely difficult to carry out.[24] And that is the rest of this little hypothesis: If the name of God is the name of a disruptive, deconstructive force, then the name of God is the name of a *task* or a *deed*.

The name of "justice" must be added to the list of tasks enumerated by Johannes Climacus, where the simplest things become exceedingly difficult, more difficult even than astronomy and veterinary science, indeed impossible (*the* impossible), once they become a deed, a matter for doing, not speculating.[25] Just like father Abraham, deconstruction would become great not by doing the possible or the necessary but by doing *the* impossible. Deconstruction turns on what Climacus calls "subjective truth," which means that truth is something to do, not to think, which is what Augustine means by *facere veritatem*, one of Derrida's favorite Augustinian lines.[26] In Danish deconstruction justice is indeed a deed, not a matter for speculation; it is a demand to do *the* impossible, to pursue the impossible justice which contradicts the prevailing order of presence, which calls for something else, for something different, something to come. Justice is the stuff from which the hope of something to come is woven. For justice is not *différance*, but justice is the moral life of *différance*, for *différance* means nonclosure and justice is the obligation that is imposed upon us by the different, the marginalized, the excluded, or closed-off. Derrida's "justice" functions not theo-logically or onto-theo-logically, which would mean serving as a backup for the order of presence, but *prophetically*, with a touch of what he nowadays calls the "messianic," which serves to threaten and subvert the order of presence.[27] Indeed, is not the "prophetic imagination," as Walter Brueggeman says, a "subversive imagination," a way of imagining differently, whose aim is the reconfiguration of the present world, the role of the prophets being to "fund" the present with "materials for subversion"?[28] As long as there is God or "justice," there is a "beyond," a higher court of appeal to challenge the present order, the "age" or the "law." Derrida's "justice" occupies the same "place" as God, the place of the displaced, addressing a call from the margins to the centers of power, and it belongs to the same "time," coming from the future, calling for what is to come, *à venir*, for a justice to come, for a kingdom to come. Let the kingdom come.

If justice and God are nonnames, impossible names, names for *the* impossible, so that we do not know what we ask for when we call for the rule of God, or for justice's rule, then is justice God or is God justice? That of course is what the prophets have always thought. But from that identification Derrida will always keep a respectful distance. He does not speak or think with the authority of a prophet, or with any authority, and it is an important part of what he says to insist that he does not know, determinately and decisively, what he is saying when he says "justice" or from where the call of justice originates. He will never say, "Hitherto you have been told to do this, but *I tell you* do that," or that he himself has been *sent* to tell us this or that, which are central parts of the prophetic style. Perhaps this Derridean modesty is all the propheticism of which we postmoderns, or late, very late, moderns, are capable. Or perhaps this is the condition of contemporary intellectuals, for while the present age has not been without prophetic voices, from Ghandi to Martin Luther King to Nelson Mandela, they have not been the holders of endowed chairs.

We are all held captive by the "secret," which makes it impossible to resolve the translatability of these sacred names, to translate one into the other, or both into some metalanguage which adjudicates between the two. We are all alike, Danish and non-Danish, deconstructors or not, caught up in the flux of *différance,* the flux of these names, which name what we love and desire, but whose speculative cognitive contours we cannot quite make out. For seeing is not what they are all about. God and justice are matters for doing, not seeing, in the spirit in which Augustine speaks of "doing the truth," *facere veritatem.*

Sacred Anarchy

On my little Danish hypothesis, that the name of God is the name of a disruption and a deed, of a disruptive deed, it follows that the decon-struction of religion releases religion's prophetic side. I do not say its prophetic *roots,* for who can claim to know roots and origins, *Ursprung* and arche, the *Ur*-spring from which all things spring, and who knows if things have a root, a single root, one deep root, let alone whether there is just one thing called "religion"? To avoid this foundationalist discourse, let us just say that *différance* keeps religion on its prophetic toes. With a little dash of *différance,* religion can be made to recall that God stands for difference, stands with the differend, which implies the outcast and outsider, and that the name of God is the name of something to do. That has the effect of displacing the notion of a "hierarchy," of a sacred order, a divinely organized order of rank which keeps each thing in its divinely "appointed place" in the "present age," all of which would be from a prophetic point of view an extremely ungodly and unholy idea. In its place we put the notion of a hier-anarchy, or let us say, a sacred an-archy.

If the idea of God commits us to the notion that something is sacred, and not just to saying it but to doing it, then I am arguing that what is sacred is not the arche but the an-arche, so that if there is anything sacred in deconstruction, it would have to be part of a sacred anarchy, of a blessed rage for a (certain) disorder, pace David Tracy, a disorder in which the last will be first and the first last. Now it is often lamented in these "postmodern times," this "epoch of *différance*," that nothing is sacred. That is true enough, in the sense that our egalitarian sensibilities have led us rightly to distrust sacred cows of any sort and to suspect their privileges, and in that sense the loss of the sacred is not bad news. But the good news delivered to religion by *différance,* one might even say its kerygma, the call it constantly proclaims, is to recall religion to a different sense of the sacred, to the old prophetic sense where the sacred means precisely what is left out of every hierarchical order, what is systemically forgotten, repressed, excluded, ground under. The good that deconstruction can do for religion is to dislodge it from its corporate headquarters, to get it back in the streets and the alleyways of life, to make the order of presence suspect, and to put God on the side of the remnants and leftovers so that the effect of invoking the name of God would be to set off a sacred anarchy.

If one were willing to surrender the deliciously disruptive effect of "sacred anarchy" (*hier-an-arche*), one might, on strictly Lévinasian grounds, prefer to speak instead of a "holy" anarchy (which has the advantage, in American English, of sounding a little like "(raising) *holy* hell." Lévinas distinguishes the holy (*saint*) from the sacred (*sacré*), as the separate or transcendent from the immanent, where the world or the earth, a mountain or a homeland, is "sacred." He is trying to make trouble for Heidegger, trying to call him a "pagan." Lévinas is more or less right about this, I think, and Heidegger deserves what he is getting from Lévinas, because in Heidegger this Hölderlinian economy of gods and mortals, heavens and earth, is all put in the service of poetizing a dangerous Greco-German homeland of Being. But that should not blind us to the power of the "sacred"—the power, say, of Native American reverence for the earth, which is a counter to a destructive violence of the technological will to power that Heidegger understands extremely well and Lévinas ignores (nothing is simple). The "holy," on the other hand, in Lévinas's scheme, is the power of the transcendent, of the other, of the wholly other, and here the paradigm is not Native American religion but the God of Israel, the transcendent Jahweh, whose unnameable Name is/means "I am who I am and choose to be" (and you, Moses, should mind your own business) (Exod. 2:14).

That paradigm of difference, of the "wholly other," of the one who always eludes the order of presence, has to do with the *saint,* not with the *sacré,* and that is what is behind the present experiment. The crucial thing, however, is not to take this transcendence onto-theo-logically or onto-theo-politically and to make of this transcendence something grandly ousiological, some superbeing that outknows and outdoes and outexists everything here below, and not to mythicize this being into a higher entity, a hyperpresence dwelling in a higher world. The crucial thing is to see that all of the resources of this transcendence are deployed on behalf of the different and with the aim, not of supporting presence with a hyperpresence, but of disturbing presence. On this scheme, and this is the anarcho-prophetico-deconstructive point, in the religion of a deconstructionist, "God" stands not above being as a hyperpresence, but *in* the middle of being, by identifying with everything the world casts out and leaves out. Indeed, rather than speaking of God's transcendence, it would be better to speak of God's "insistence," in the sense of God's withdrawal from the worldliness of the world, from the world's order of presence, into those pockets or recesses which are formed in the world by the little ones, the nothings and nobodies of the world, what Paul calls *ta me onta,* where God pitches his or her tent.

When, in accordance with our hypothesis we hold the name of God in tandem with *différance,* the name of God falls like a blow upon the order of presence and crosses it out, shocking the powers that be, displacing the complacent, disturbing the established order, putting business as usual into question. The prophetic name of God is subversive and threatening, "infallibly dreaded" (which is the only sense of infallibility I accept), above all by religions and lovers of infallibility. The name, or nonname, of *différance* is a "formal indication," to use the language of the young Heidegger, a syntactical and semantic rule or nonrule, of which the name, or nonname, "God," is a certain deformalization, organizing a specific semantic and practical field in which the effectiveness of *différance* itself is organized, its energies harnessed and deployed, its powers potentiated, the infinite range of its potential effects defined, focused, and unleashed, given a certain finite form. The God of prophetic religion, and the talk and practice that God engenders, communicates with *différance* along the most internal and vital lines. God and *différance* belong together in the most interesting and productive ways, and they need each other. Far from being antagonists, God crossed out and *différance* are collaborators, coconspirators, fellow subversives, and defaced inscriptions.

For after all, *différance* in itself, if there is such a thing, does not exist, is not a thing somewhere that will come to save us, and the kingdom of *différance,* even if there is one, is not a place we can actually go.[29] There is no *différance.* God is one of the ways that *différance* enters the world, by entering the interstices and back alleys of the world, a way of giving it flesh and bones, historical and linguistic actuality, institutional life. It is not by deconstructive analysis, or a new core curriculum, however important both may be, that prophetic transformations are effected, that things are really moved, that hearts are changed (metanoia), but by Martin Luther King or Nelson Mandela, by grassroots movements which are shoots coming out of the stump of Jesse (Isa.11:10). Movement is prophetic movement. If it makes Heidegger happy to think that language is the house Being, by which he mainly means Greco-German poetry, the prophetic is the house of *différance,* or rather the name of its homelessness. That is why *différance* needs God; in order to exist, or to impinge upon the order of existence, even as God needs *différance,* in order to slip free of the order of presence and to protect religion against itself. *Différance,* which does not exist, is a condition, a quasi-transcendental condition, without life or substance, actuality or vitality, except insofar as it comes about in traditions and institutions, languages and literatures, practices and programs, one of which—there are many, I am not trying to tie up *différance* or corner the market on *différance*—is prophetic religion.

The Kingdom of God

I am not, nor is deconstruction, in the business of inventing a private religion. If anything, I have been speaking like Johannes Climacus in *Philosophical Fragments* about the communication of deconstruction and "the god," without giving it any historical garb. So now I must, like Climacus, here "call the matter by its proper name and cloth the issue in its historical costume."[30] For I have been speaking all along of a determinate, biblical religion, however far from that ideal "Christendom," as Kierkegaard liked to call it, or the churches generally, or Islamic or Jewish fundamentalism, may have drifted. My references to *ta me onta* were perfectly transparent allusions to Paul's First Letter to the Corinthians, where Paul flaunts the scandal and the anarchy of the ones who are favored in God's kingdom, the ones upon whom God has set his eye and his favor. God chose everything foolish (*moria,* moronic), Paul says, to solicit the wisdom (sophia) of the wise, which, according to Isaiah (Isa. 29:14), God means to "destroy" (*apolo*), to confound and scandalize. When human rule is displaced, which is what it means to say that God rules, then foolishness is favored over the sophia and philosophia of the present age (*aion*) (1 Cor.1:18–20). Those whom God calls upon, Paul says, are not wise, not powerful, not well born (*eugeneis*):

> God chose what is weak in the world to shame the strong; God chose what is low and despised (*ta agene*) in the world, things that are not (*ta me onta*), to reduce to nothing things that are (*ta onta*). (1 Cor. 1:27–28)

God chose the "outsiders," the people deprived of power, wealth, education, high birth, high culture. Theirs is a "royalty" of outcasts so that, from the point of view of the *aion*, the age or the world, the word "kingdom" is being used ironically, almost mockingly, to refer to those pockets of the lowly and despised that infect and infest the world.[31] For this is a Kingdom of the low-down and despised, the "excluded," the very people who, it could be shown with the right socioeconomic structural analysis, are precisely the victims of the worldly kingdom.

First Corinthians, then, which proceeds from a heightened sense of God, is the almost perfect "inversion" (Nietzsche would say, with a Greco-German sneer, the *Umwertung*) of Greek sophia or *phronesis,* subverting, soliciting, threatening the world's wisdom, making it tremble. In contrast to the smart, moderate man who knows what is best for himself and for the polis generally, to Aristotle's virtuous gentlemanly man of reason, Paul says that God chose people who are fools from the world's point of the view, people who do not act in their own best interest, who are of "no account," no Logos, a-Logos. In the kingdom, things turn on what Paul calls the "*Logos tou staurou*" (1 Cor. 1:18), the mad logic, word, or message of the Cross which crosses out the world and in the process gets done in by the world, taking a hit from the world, as opposed to the Aristotelian *Logos,* which means staying on top of what is going on around you and knowing how to hit the mark (and hoping to get lucky).

The Aristotelian comparison is especially instructive. Aristotle wanted to cultivate the virtues of the mind, of the intellect or reason (nous, Logos). His *phronimos* "sees" something, has "insight" into the particularities of the case, whereas the Corinthians are to be bowed over, overcome, touched by the needs of one another, which is what should rule in their hearts. That means that the "rule of God" is associated with the rule of that part of the soul that Aristotle called the "a-Logos," whereas for Aristotle the Logos is the divine part and should rule, not the a-Logos, which is the part that should be ruled.

When Paul says that the kingdom is populated with "*ta me onta*" (1 Cor. 1:28) he is almost taunting the Greeks, flaunting one of the most honorable words in Greek philosophy. Being (*to on,* ousia), the central concept of Greek philosophy, has the sense of what really and truly is, what is enduringly and permanently present, as opposed to all that is fleeting and apparent and superficial. Rhetorically, even conceptually, associated with sun, light, and gleaming manifestation, the essence of Greek wisdom is to bend all one's efforts to ascend to the element of Being and to avoid getting caught up in non-Being. The wise man is wired up to Being, knows his way around what is, can sort through what is and what is not, and can always hit the mark of what is. But the Kingdom of God is populated with shadowy semibeings, with half-real nobodies of no worldly account. By choosing "what is not" (*ta me onta*), God can "cross out," again following Jean-Luc Marion, the difference the Greeks make between Being and non-Being, between wisdom and foolishness. God crosses one sort of "kingdom," a worldly kingdom, a kingdom in the "straight" sense, with another, paradoxical, even ironical kingdom, in which the rule of everything human-all-too-human has been shattered.

I would add still one more gloss to this remarkable passage. Paul cites Isaiah, who says, as we saw above, that God "will destroy" (*apolo;* 1 Cor. 1:19) the wisdom of the wise. In Latin, *apollumi* is *destruere, destructio.* John Van Buren has suggested that Heidegger's *"Destruktion"*—of which, of course, Derrida's *"déconstruction"* is a paraphrase and translation— derives from Luther, who spoke of the need for a *destructio* (in Latin) of medieval scholasticism, and Van Buren suggests that Luther may possibly have had this citation of Isaiah from First Corinthians in mind.[32] One could then, by a certain interesting retrojection, render this text of Isaiah, "I will deconstruct the wisdom of the wise," or, more freely, "I will deconstruct the metaphysics of the onto-theo-logians, sayeth the Lord God." The Kingdom of God, then, is the deconstruction of kingdom in the ordinary sense; the Kingdom of God is what things look like when the business as usual of human power is displaced, disordered, disarrayed, anarchized, inverted, crossed out.

The "kingdom of God" meant a certain style or way to be—a certain structure of existence, a certain existentiale—in which the rule of everything human that was all too human had been broken, a way to be in which human power and authoritarianism are shaken, solicited, broken, displaced, deconstructed. In the kingdom of God, the *aion* is subjected to another, uncanny, unusual rule, a rule of displacement, in which the oddest things eventuated, in which the oddest results obtained. In the business of the kingdom of God, God means no more business as usual.

You know you have to do with God and the "kingdom of God" just when something unreasonable from the world's point of view is demanded of us, just when we are expected to forgo our own interests, just when our most natural tendencies and desires to have things our own way are contradicted and we are told to look like a fool for the kingdom of God. The "kingdom of God" lands like a blow to the head, contradicting the world and its wisdom, confronting the kosmos, the ways of this world, the "system."

The "system" was for Jesus as for Jeremiah (Jer.7:4) embodied in the "temple," and when Jesus attacked the temple, he was quickly killed. As Daniel Maguire writes:

> He [Jesus] was fussing with the system, and scholars now think he may have been killed within hours of his attack on the temple. Jesus was attacking the law and order that preserves unjust privileges and exploitative social arrangements. Had he and Jeremiah contented themselves with urging private charity and a depoliticized piety, they could have died in their beds at a ripe old age. Neither did, because they were prophets of Israel and agents of the subversive reign of God.[33]

The "kingdom of God" is the contradiction of the "world" (kosmos), which is the order of power and privilege, of greed and self-interest, of the business as usual of the most powerful. Kierkegaard could not have been more biblical and more prophetic when he insisted that Christianity stands in permanent, structural opposition to this world, to the kingdom of this world, and that it is a sign of decadence in Christianity to have sat down to table with the world, to have made peace with that kosmos upon which it is called to make war. He also said that the way to refute Christendom was simply to walk through the streets holding the New Testament over one's head for all to read.

The kingdom of God is a kingdom of base, ill-born, powerless, despised outsiders, a kingdom of nobodies who are null and void in the eyes of the world, dropouts measured by the world's arche and the world's *aion*, and yet precisely for that reason favored by God, precisely the ones whom God called (*kletos*) and set apart, whom God chose, favored, singling them out for all their singularity and exceptionality. The call that God makes, what God calls for, is justice, *sedaqah*, breaking the rule of power and privilege, which is what the prophets announced when they call for the rule of God, a call that often costs the prophets their life.

Cynicism and Philosophy

To see just how far we are carried by this hypothesis of a sacred anarchy, let us pursue a point made by John Dominic Crossan. Crossan's research into the apocryphal and noncanonical gospels, into lost, outlawed texts that have been marginalized and silenced by the institutionally sanctioned canon, has proven to be itself quite a nuisance to the powers that be. Crossan has been deliciously disturbing the academic and ecclesiastical peace for some time now by telling us a remarkable story about just such a "kingdom of God," just such a sacred anarchy, as we have begun to sketch here. Crossan has been carefully, even tediously, reconstructing a surprisingly best-selling portrait of a historical Jesus as all-at-once Mediterranean, thoroughly Jewish, and a peasant, indeed, "an illiterate peasant, but with an oral brilliance that few of those trained in literate and scribal disciplines can ever attain," about whom these same institutional and right-wing political powers that be do not want to hear, one that situates Jesus squarely on the prophetic side—and so, by my perverse accounting, deconstruction on Jesus' side—which situates the church and the right wing you know where.[34] The church, after all, as a religious and legal institution, is something to be deconstructed, something which demands the most regular, rhythmic, systematic deconstruction, in order to save it from itself, while justice and God are not deconstructible.

According to Crossan, Jesus included in the "kingdom" just about everybody whom the Greco-Roman world excluded from power and prestige, whoever is "a nothing, a nobody, a nonperson." Jesus waged a "savage attack on family values," which will not bring the sanctimonious Christian right wing much comfort, in which patriarchal power and domestic peace is displaced—"whoever does not hate father and mother"—by the radical egalitarianism and open-endedness "equally accessible to all under God" that defines the kingdom of God. Jesus said that it is the poor who are blessed and who especially deserve the kingdom of God. When Matthew (the tax collector) redacts this saying, among the most authentic according to most scholars, to poor "in spirit," he removes the sting of *ptochos,* which means "destitute" rather than merely "poor" (*penes*), and diverts it from economic to interior poverty, whereas Jesus seems to have been saying, in contemporary terms, blessed are the homeless and the street people. Crossan comments:

> In any situation of oppression, especially in those oblique, indirect,
> and systemic ones where injustice wears a mask of normalcy or even of
> necessity, the only ones who are innocent or blessed are those squeezed
> out deliberately as human junk from the system's own evil operations.[35]

So then Jesus is saying, blessed are the junk, the rubbish, those whom society excretes, its detritus and excretions and so—I am citing a citation in

Glas—its "shit," which provides an opportunity for a still more irreverent use of "holy" than "holy hell" or "holy anarchy."[36]

The parables of "open commensality," in which a master commands his servants to go out on the streets and bring in anyone they can find, "both bad and good" (Matt. 22:10), to his banquet, are particularly suggestive of the open-endedness and inclusiveness of the kingdom. The invitation is indiscriminate—male or female, free or slave, highborn or lowborn, ritually pure or impure. The "hospitality," as Derrida would say, is "unconditional." Adds Crossan:

> Think, for a moment, if beggars came to your door, of the difference between giving them some food to go, of inviting them into your kitchen for a meal, of bringing them into the dining room to eat in the evening with your family, or of having them come back on Saturday night for supper with a group of your friends.[37]

If, as has been argued, table fellowship is a miniature of the larger social network in which the system of socialization is writ small, then this parable of "egalitarian commensality" would have been viewed as particularly threatening. If Jesus dined nondiscriminately, then he would be accused of consorting with "tax collectors and sinners," and if women were present, of eating with "whores." The kingdom was structured around radical, disturbing, and extreme egalitarian practices which completely unhinge the binary social scheme of honor and shame upon which Greco-Roman societies turn, destroying the wisdom of the wise. Jesus then would have had nothing to do with the fraternalism and phallocentrism of the "Christian" conception of philia—something that Derrida discusses in *The Politics of Friendship*—but he would have practiced a "discipleship of equals," which is what would be left of friendship if one withdrew it from this phallocentric scheme of philia.

Crossan's Jesus thus is a revolutionary, not an armed revolutionary, to be sure, but one whose practices of eating and healing hovered on the "borderline between the covert and overt arts of resistance." After his death a revolutionary "movement" formed, not of armed insurgents and zealots conducting a guerilla war, but of migrant disciples, traveling in pairs, with no provisions:[38]

> Go, look, I send you out as lambs among wolves. Do not carry money, or bag, or sandals; and do not greet anyone on the road. . . . Whatever house you enter, say, "Peace be to this house." And if a child of peace is there, your greeting will be received. But if not, let your peace return to you.

And stay in the same house, eating and drinking whatever they provide, for the worker deserves his wages. Do not go from house to house. . . . Pay attention to the sick and say to them, "God's kingdom has come near to you." (Luke 10:2–11)

These texts, says Crossan, among the oldest we have, closely connecting eating and healing, are not to be confused with Paul's dramatic missionary campaigns to major urban centers in the Greco-Roman world. The disciples move from peasant village to peasant village within Galilee, taking up as guests in a house, accepting no payments beyond food and lodging, in a spirit of egalitarian sharing. They were radical missionaries who traveled without provisions and who strike many scholars today as Jewish Cynics, Jewish versions of those ancient "philosophers" who flaunted common standards of propriety and decency.

The Cynics are not gentlemen but, as Aristotle (who seems to be repeating a familiar epithet) called them, dogs (*kyon, canes*), whence the name by which they are known to us today. They are Greek philosophers—the word sticks in Aristotelian throats—who repudiate the aristocratic and hierarchical system of the polis and who do so by leading a countercultural life which flaunts the model of the urbane and gentlemanly *phronimos*. On this point, the Cynics were not unlike those eccentrics, the prophets themselves, who, from Isaiah to John the Baptist, showed a shocking penchant for nudity, for howling and wailing, for life in the wilderness and bizarre diets of locusts and honey.[39]

The Cynics followed "nature," the rule of the gods, of the divine, not "culture" (polis), which is man made. They lived in the city, but they did so as if they were living in the wild. The rule (*basileia*) of nature, of God, for them is the rule of freedom, that is, freedom from culture, other people, social standing, income, prestige, power, from all the things that Aristotle called "external goods," which formed for Aristotle a "necessary supplement" to arete. They carried only a cloak, a staff, a satchel; they wore uncut hair and bare feet, and lived itinerant, mendicant lives. Their physical poverty constituted a spiritual freedom (HJ, 78–79); they believed that poverty provides freedom, which constitutes the true royalty (Kingdom).[40]

Cynicism overlaps with "Stoicism" as an internal attitude of mind, but it differs radically from Stoicism in externals. The Stoic says, "I have but do not care," while the Cynic says, "I do not have but do not care." Marcus Aurelius could be a Roman Emperor and Stoic, and Seneca could be millionaire and a Stoic, but they could hardly be Cynics. Comments Crossan:

> Cynicism is the Greco-Roman form of that universal philosophy of eschatology or world-negation, one of the great and fundamental options of the human spirit. For wherever there is culture and civilization there can also be counterculture and anticivilization.[41]

Now the Cynics bear a striking resemblance to the earliest followers of Jesus, the so-called "Q"-community—something we can say without knowing what Jesus knew of the Cynics, whether he was "just reinventing the Cynic wheel all by himself," or whether he might have encountered Cynics, say, in the nearby town of Sepphoris, and taken a page from their book.[42] Like the Cynics, the disciples too were itinerants who lived like the birds of the air, who scolded society for its falsity, who said outrageous things to shock the establishment, and who set out on journeys with the barest of provisions. But the singular difference between the Cynics and the followers of Jesus—apart from the fact that the Cynics inhabited the cities and the disciples were rural—was that the Cynics went nowhere without their knapsack, which contained a little food and the few things necessary for life. The Cynics stressed their independence, their self-sufficiency, which they achieved by reducing their needs to the minimal point at which they could provide for themselves; they needed nothing because they wanted nothing that they could not provide for themselves. The followers of Jesus, however, took not even a knapsack for the day's food, not to show their independence, but because they trusted that their needs would be provided for by those who would receive them in the next town, by the brethren, which means by God's rule. For the very hospitality with which the brethren receive one another, the agape and caritas, means that there God's rule holds sway. The kingdom has drawn near; it is not off in a distant place. It reigns here, now, in this hospitality, and its mark is agape.[43]

Conclusion

I have undertaken this experiment in Danish deconstruction not because I am sick of philosophy (or cynical about it) and have turned to religion, but in order to jolt philosophy off dead center and give it a new start, which is pretty much what I think Kierkegaard did when he decided to shock the categories of Greek philosophy with biblical categories on behalf of poor existing individuals everywhere. I agree with Derrida, and with the poststructuralists generally, that disciplinary borders need to be crossed and new objects of study invented, the difference being that for most postmodern writers, such crossings generally mean crossing over to the turf of art and literature, not of religion, religious poetry, and sacred literature. Derrida himself will tell us, however, that "the original, heterogeneous elements of Judaism and Christianity," before they were assimilated by Greek philosophy, belong to the "other" of Greek philosophy and Western civilization, an other that "haunts" the philosophical tradition, "threatening and unsettling the assured 'identities' of Western philosophy."[44] As Kevin Hart says, Judaism and Christianity—before they are assimilated by Greek philosophy—are part of the process of deconstruction, not part of deconstruction's prey.[45]

The idea behind this experiment in sketching the lines of a sacred anarchy is to expose philosophy to its other, to another of its others, to some other other than *dichtendes Denken,* to the more scandalous other of the prophetic, messianic, and eschatological lines of force that run through the Kingdom. The idea is to let ourselves be solicited by the scandal of what must seem to some an ungodly communication between God and *différance,* which means to let religion's God, and the God of the philosophers, be crossed out by God, where the name of God is the name of a task and a disruption.

The idea is not all that different than the one Calvin Schrag had some forty years ago when he first sketched the lines of communication between existence and freedom.

Notes

1. Calvin O. Schrag, *Existence and Freedom: Towards an Ontology of Human Finitude* (Evanston: Northwestern University Press, 1961).

2. See Jacques Derrida, *The Gift of Death,* trans. David Wills (Chicago: University of Chicago Press, 1995), p. 49 (hereafter cited as *GD*).

3. See Jacques Derrida, *Circumfession: Fifty-Nine Periods and Periphrases,* in *Jacques Derrida,* ed. Geoffrey Bennington and Jacques Derrida (Chicago: University of Chicago Press, 1993), p. 155 (hereafter cited as *Circum*). That is not true, however, of *écriture,* a word which means both "writing" and "Scripture," and the constant rendering of it as "writing" by Derrida's translators tends to efface its theological sense. Most deconstructors are not interested in making deconstruction a study of Scripture, although that is a sense that the theologically tuned will hear. See Kevin Hart, *The Trespass of the Sign* (Cambridge: Cambridge University Press, 1989), pp. 49 ff., who suggests that this oscillation in *écriture* is like the oscillation in *pharmakon* and "*supplément,*" and hence that *écriture* is an undecidable. Whatever Derrida's authorial intentions, "Derrida's text cannot help but signify both 'writing' and 'scripture' " (p. 61).

248

4. I have examined the question of Derrida and religion in more detail in two books: *The Prayers and Tears of Jacques Derrida: Religion without Religion,* Indiana Series in the Philosophy of Religion (Bloomington: Indiana University Press, 1997); and *Deconstruction in a Nutshell: A Conversation with Jacques Derrida,* edited with a commentary by John D. Caputo (New York: Fordham University Press, 1997).

5. See Jacques Derrida, *Margins of Philosophy,* trans. Alan Bass (Chicago: University of Chicago Press, 1982), p. 22 (hereafter cited as *MP*).

6. See Jacques Derrida, *Specters of Marx: The State of the Debt, the Work of Mourning, and the New International,* trans. Peggy Kamuf (New York: Routledge, 1994), pp. 64–65 (hereafter cited as *SoM*).

7. See Jacques Derrida, "The Force of Law: 'The Mystical Foundation of Authority,'" trans. Mary Quaintance, in *Destruction and the Possibility of Justice,* ed. Drucilla Cornell et al. (New York: Routledge, 1992), pp. 68–91, pp. 14–15 (hereafter cited as *FL*).

8. See Jacques Derrida, *Of Grammatology,* trans. Gayatri Spivak (Baltimore: Johns Hopkins University Press, 1974), p. 42 (hereafter cited as *OG*).

9. John Dominic Crossan, *Jesus: A Revolutionary Biography* (New York: Harper-Collins, 1994), pp. 54 ff. (hereafter cited as *J*).

10. Derrida, *SoM,* p. 56.

11. Søren Kierkegaard, *Kierkegaard's Works,* vol. 14, *Two Ages: The Age of Revolution and the Present Age,* ed. and trans. H. Hong and E. Hong (Princeton, N.J.: Princeton University Press, 1978).

12. Derrida, *FL,* p. 26.

13. When Augustine defined "peace" as the tranquillity of order, he reflected a world in which Christianity had made its peace with political power and had begun to devise a theory of just war. Christian life after Constantine soon lost its prophetic spirit, which distrusts the tranquillity of the prevailing order and is bent on disturbing the peace, and this in the name of *shalom. Shalom* is the peace that comes from "justice" (*seqadah*) for the poor and the outcast, the peace which comes of God's rule, not the highly hierarchical domestic tranquillity prized by the religious and political right wing. By devising a theory of just war, Christianity had unfortunately lost the prophetic spirit that was alive and well in the sayings of Jesus, in Jesus' prophetic discourse on the "kingdom of God." See Richard Kearney, ed., *Dialogues with Contemporary Thinkers* (Manchester: Manchester University Press, 1984), p. 119.

14. Jacques Derrida, *Positions,* trans. Alan Bass (Chicago: University of Chicago Press, 1981), p. 40.

15. Derrida, *OG,* p. 71.

16. Commenting on Hegel who is commenting on Moses Mendelssohn, Derrida writes, "Since God does not manifest himself, he is not truth for the Jews, total presence or parousia. He gives orders without appearing" (Jacques Derrida, *Glas,* trans. Richard Rand and John Leavey [Lincoln: University of Nebraska Press, 1986], p. 51a, cited by Hart, *Trespass of the Sign,* p. 62). Yahweh then would be what is "essentially other than truth," not Heideggerian lethe, which is the very

heart of truth, pace John Sallis, "Deformatives: Essentially Other than Truth," in *Double Truth* (Albany: State University of New York Press, 1995).

17. Daniel Maguire, *The Moral Core of Judaism and Christianity* (Minneapolis: Fortress Press, 1993), pp. 189–90.

18. Ibid., pp. 264–65.

19. See Hart, *Trespass of the Sign*, pp. 107 ff.; Derrida, "Des tours de Babel," trans. Joseph Graham, in *Difference in Translation* (Ithaca, N.Y.: Cornell University Press, 1985), pp. 209 ff.

20. Jean-Luc Marion, *God without Being: Hors-Texte*, trans. Thomas A. Carlson (Chicago: University of Chicago Press, 1991), pp. 70 ff.

21. Ibid., pp. 70 ff.

22. Derrida, *MP*, p. 6.

23. See John Dominic Crossan "Difference and Divinity," *Semeia* 23 (1982): p. 39; Hart, *Trespass of the Sign*, p. 186.

24. Søren Kierkegaard, *Kierkegaard's Works*, vol. 12, bk. 1, *Concluding Unscientific Postscript to Philosophical Fragments*, ed. and trans. H. Hong and E. Hong (Princeton, N.J.: Princeton University Press, 1992), pp. 165 ff.

25. Derrida, *GT*, p. 6.

26. Derrida, *Circum*, pp. 47–48.

27. Derrida, *SoM*, pp. 167–69.

28. Walter Brueggemann, *Texts under Negotiation: The Bible and the Postmodern Imagination* (Minneapolis: Fortress Press, 1994), pp. 90–91. Indeed, Yahweh himself is not above lying (or advising Samuel to lie) in order to plot a coup against Saul's rule, and so Yahweh too subscribes to Nietzsche's famous description of truth as fiction, as a mobile army of metaphors and metonymies (79–83).

29. Derrida, *MP*, p. 6.

30. Søren Kierkegaard, *Kierkegaard's Works*, vol. 7, *Philosophical Fragments*, ed. and trans. H. Hong and E. Hong (Princeton, N.J.: Princeton University Press, 1985), p. 109.

31. A little like Heidegger, who, in a comment on Heraclitus's saying that the *basileia* is in the hands of a child (*paidos*), speaks of a child king, a kingdom in the hands of a child at play, of an-archic arche. See *Der Satz vom Grund, 3. Aufl.* (Pfullingen: Verlag Gunther Neske, 1965), p. 188. Hereafter cited as *SG*.

32. John Van Buren, *The Young Heidegger* (Bloomington: Indiana University Press, 1994), p. 167.

33. Maguire, *Moral Code*, pp. 159–60.

34. Crossan, *J*, p. 58.

35. Ibid., pp. 64, 60, 62.

36. Derrida, *Glas*, p. 1a.

37. Crossan, *J*, p. 68.

38. Ibid., p. 105. Translation of Luke 10:2–11 is from Crossan.

39. Maguire, *Moral Code*, pp. 183–86.

40. John Dominic Crossan, *The Historical Jesus: The Life of a Mediterranean Jewish Peasant* (San Francisco: Harper), pp. 78–79. Hereafter cited as *HJ*.

41. Ibid., p. 117.

42. This hypothesis on the connection between the Cynics and the Q-community is argued by F. Gerald Downing, *Christ and the Cynics: Jesus and Other Radical Preachers in First-Century Tradition* (Sheffield: Sheffield University Press, 1988); John Kloppenborg, *The Formation of Q: Trajectories in Ancient Wisdom Collections* (Philadelphia: Fortress Press, 1987); and Leif E. Vaage, *Galilean Upstarts: Jesus's First Followers according to Q* (Valley Forge, Pa.: Trinity Press, 1994). For an overview of both sides of this debate, see Hans Dieter Betz, "Jesus and the Cynics: Survey and Analysis of a Hypothesis," *Journal of Religion* 74 (October 1994): 453–75. See also Crossan, *J*, p. 122.

43. Crossan, *J*, pp. 117–22.

44. Kearney, ed., *Dialogues,* pp. 116–17.

45. Hart, *Trespass of the Sign,* p. 93.

PART 5

COMMUNICATIVE PRAXIS

13

The Interruptive Nature of the Call of Conscience: Rethinking Heidegger on the Question of Rhetoric

Michael J. Hyde

I have been a student of Calvin Schrag for more than twenty years. In his graduate seminars on existentialism, phenomenology, and hermeneutics, he first introduced me to such influential thinkers as Kierkegaard, Nietzsche, Sartre, Jaspers, Heidegger, Gadamer, Ricoeur, and Derrida. Although he seemed to have had his favorites, as evidenced in his early works *Existence and Freedom* and *Experience and Being*, Professor Schrag's ability to appreciate, and to critically assess, these and other philosophers was, to say the least, awe-inspiring. We students wondered: How could anyone be this good, and so caring, too? Professor Schrag once told me how Jaspers treated him as a student: "He would sit with you in his office and not let you leave until he was sure that you understood the matter at hand. He practiced what he preached: the 'loving struggle' of authentic communication." Professor Schrag did the same. Sure, there were times in seminars when he would run his hand through his hair, thus giving a clear indication that he was not "comfortable" with what some student was arguing. If he repeated this movement before one was done talking, it literally became a hair-raising experience for all concerned. The well-known and highly respected scholar and teacher was about to take you to task. It could be a very humbling experience, especially since Professor Schrag was such a master at making you realize that, despite what he termed "the possible error in your thinking" (a.k.a.: stupidity), you still warranted respect as a member of the class. One feared being "wrong" in Professor Schrag's presence because it felt so bad when you thought you were disappointing him. He is one of those special people who helps others cultivate their conscience; he is a model for learning how to say "Here I am!" to those in need of acknowledgment, guidance, and friendship; he is, without a doubt, a very gifted soul.

I speak of Professor Schrag in terms that will be emphasized throughout this chapter: conscience, acknowledgment, and gift. These terms, among many others, are crucial to Professor Schrag's award-winning and ongoing work on the nature and function of human "communicative praxis" and the way in which "rhetoric" informs both the manipulative and ethical aspects of this phenomenon.[1] Like many of his students who learned to appreciate seeing his hand move through his hair, I also have experienced the joy of seeing how certain of my scholarly contributions have had some positive influence on his work. In this chapter I will try again to return my teacher's gift of acknowledgment by suggesting how Heidegger's assessment of "the call of conscience," as developed in his *Being and Time,* allows for an understanding of rhetoric that, to the best of my knowledge, has yet to be formulated by scholars interested in these and related topics. Rhetoric, I argue, appears on the scene as soon as the call of conscience, which in its most essential way of being is not a human creation, first shows itself as a primordial "interrruption" of everyday existence. The interruptive nature of the call of conscience is a "given" and hence a "gift." With this gift before us, we are always situated in the world so as to be responsible for answering a question of conscience—Where art thou?—that challenges us to acknowledge others in a caring way.

My project unfolds in three parts. As a way of further orienting the reader to the position being developed here, I first offer a brief discussion of previous research that helps one begin thinking about how the call of conscience and rhetoric are related. I next examine in some detail Heidegger's understanding of the interruptive nature of the call of conscience. Finally, I suggest how this phenomenon may itself be seen as a rhetorical happening. Heidegger never saw the matter in this way. Such an oversight, I argue, is due to an underdeveloped, and thus unclear, understanding on his part of how the call of conscience makes itself known as an interruption.

On the Relationship between Conscience and Rhetoric

Philosophers and rhetoricians have for some time been writing about how Heidegger's philosophical investigations of Being can be used to further an understanding of the ontological nature of rhetoric. The most common argument supporting the possibility of such a project can be summarized as follows. With his reading of Aristotle, Heidegger realized that rhetoric, despite its possible shortcomings, is nevertheless an essential ingredient in the ethical functioning of humankind's sociopolitical existence. That is, rhetoric is essentially an art of evocation: Before it is transformed into "an art of persuasion," rhetoric functions *to call* our attention to things such that we might, especially by way of collaborative deliberation, form an "authentic" understanding of their essential nature. Rhetoric thus has a crucial role to play in what Heidegger saw as one of philosophy's primary tasks—that of awakening people from their ontological slumber in everyday existence such that they might be more appreciative of what it means *to be*. It thus might be said that the "the call of philosophy" that Heidegger continually answered and sounded in his investigations of the meaning and truth of Being has something basically rhetorical about it. Philosophy needs rhetoric in order to construct what Schrag describes as a "fitting response" to life's circumstances, a response that can open and move people toward an appreciation of how to think, judge, and act in responsible ways.[2]

Although Heidegger never explicitly aligned his vocation with the practice of rhetoric, I do not believe that the above reading of Heidegger is misleading. The descriptive and interpretive intent of phenomenology is certainly seen by Heidegger as being primarily directed toward the advancement of discourse that operates as a "showing-forth" (*epideixis*) of what is. Heidegger, to be sure, helped influence the course of twentieth-century philosophy with his epideictic, evocative, and thus rhetorical discourse—a discourse that also has been described as being "downright homiletical."[3]

There are, of course, other readings of Heidegger's discourse that do not see matters this way. Those like Paul R. Falzer, for example, contend that, rather than being a supporter of the rhetorical enterprise, Heidegger conceives of the orator's art as being primarily a tool for bringing about mindless conformism and thus inauthenticity.[4] One might read Heidegger this way because, as seen in *Being and Time*, rhetoric is associated with the utilization and production of "moods" or emotional orientations that sustain our "publicness"—the world of common sense and common praxis that too often inhibits critical reflection and thereby conditions us to be herdlike creatures who are merely content to just go along with the crowd, or what Heidegger describes as abiding by the "dictatorship" of the "they." Yet, in making this point, Heidegger is not necessarily dismissing rhetoric's potential for doing good.

Look at what Heidegger has to say about the matter: "Publicness . . . not only has in general its own way of having a mood, but needs moods and 'makes' them for itself. It is into such a mood and out of such a mood that the orator speaks. He must understand the possibilities of moods in order to rouse them and guide them aright."[5] I take this last sentence to be especially important. The original German reads: "Er Bedarf des Verständnisses der Möglichkeiten der Stimmung, um sie in der rechten Weise zu wecken und zu lenken."[6] John Macquarrie and Edward Robinson translate "*in der rechten Weise*" as "aright." In her more recent translation of *Sein und Zeit,* Joan Stambaugh translates the phrase as "in the right way."[7] Keeping in mind, however, that the German *recht* carries with it a moral sense (as when, e.g., one says "*es is nicht recht von dir*"—"it's wrong [or unfair] of you"), a still less condensed translation is possible. The orator "must understand the possibilities of moods in order to rouse them and guide them in a right and just manner."[8] With this translation, I believe, one sees Heidegger explicitly acknowledging something good about the practice of rhetoric, something that enables it to be more than a vehicle for generating mindless conformism. Like rhetorical theorists dating back at least to Aristotle, Heidegger thinks of rhetoric as something that can "move" (*emovere*), and thereby advance, the moral consciousness and conduct of people. Rhetoric plays a crucial role in the articulation of civic virture and morality: it is evocative; it calls.

In *Being and Time* this specific linguistic act is associated with a person taking on the responsibility of becoming a voice of conscience for others and thus a voice that has a role to play in the establishing of "authentic community": a way of being-with-and-for others that respects and remains open to their differences and that encourages them to make use of their own authenticity by assuming the ethical responsibility of affirming their freedom through resolute choice. Heidegger identifies "considerateness" (*Rücksicht*) and "forbearance" (*Nachsicht*) as the two interpersonal orientations that inform this community-building process.[9] With these two ways of being toward others, the self maintains an open-minded and patient stance in "communicating" and "struggling" with them about matters of possible contention. Considerateness and forbearance also promote the crucial practice of attentive listening. According to Heidegger, it is essential that the self listen carefully to the discourse of others, for "listening to . . . is Dasein's existential way of Being-open as Being-with for Others."[10] Being open to others, listening to and taking seriously what they have to say, is how the self counters the egotistic and selfish tendency of becoming so engrossed in figuring out what it wants to express and maintain that it misses, dismisses, or forgets what others are trying to say. Authentic community is not built on egoism but rather on an openness to, and a collaborative deliberation with, others.

This is not to say, however, that the self owes it to others to capitulate completely to their interpretations of the issues at hand. Heidegger speaks to us of a self whose communicative struggle with others is essentially a "struggle for unconcealment," a struggle devoted to disclosing the "truth" of some matter of importance. Others must be treated with considerateness and forbearance so that they can engage in a codisclosing of the matter and thereby possibly display a degree of rhetorical competence that is capable of moving the thought and behavior of people "in a right and just manner." For the evocative art of rhetoric, this, to be sure, is a moral thing to do. Rhetoric is capable of sounding a call of conscience.

The Interruptive Nature of the Call

As is well known, Heidegger exhibited horrendous political judgment in 1933 when he added his voice to a movement whose rhetoric was the epitome of inauthenticity in that it displayed no considerateness and forbearance toward anyone who was other than the Aryans who concocted it. Hence, one might say that the philosophy of rhetoric that can be drawn from the pages of *Being and Time* exposes a contradiction between what Heidegger preached here and what he practiced when speaking of "the inner truth and greatness" of National Socialism.[11] Had Heidegger been true to what he said about the orator's art and its relationship to conscience and the ways of authentic community, he would have had to speak a rhetoric that interrupted, and thereby called into question, the movement's noxious and close-minded outlook. When rhetoric functions this way, it is most in tune with what Heidegger identifies as the ontological workings of the call of conscience.

Heidegger's phenomenological assessment of the call is directed primarily toward a description of how it makes itself known in everyday experience. As structured in the workings of some moral system (e.g., institutionalized religion), the call of conscience is typically heard as a "voice" that commands: "Thou shall" do this! "Thou shall not" do that! The prescriptions advanced by this voice call for concerned thought and the "appropriate" behavior to go with it. A moral system's call of conscience is action-oriented. Even when it tells us *not* to do something, it still is telling us not *to do* something. There is, therefore, a "challenge-response" logic at work when conscience calls. No moral system could exist without it.

For Heidegger, however, this logic defines an operation that originates in something greater (and thus *other*) than the system's specific ethical prescriptions and prohibitions. The operation shows itself originally in the way our temporal existence is itself a challenge calling for a response: We are creatures who are always caught up in the play of time, always on the way toward understanding what can or will be in our lives but is not yet, and thus always confronted with the task of trying to make sense of, and to do something with, our lives. Human being (Dasein) is its own evocation and provocation; it calls for the responsiveness of concerned thought and action, for that which enables us, even in the most distressful situations, to take charge of our lives as we assume the ethical responsibility of affirming our freedom through resolute choice and thereby become personally involved in the creation of a meaningful existence. This is how systems of morality come into being in the first place. The language of morality is the language of responsiveness and responsibility; the challenge-response logic at work in a moral system's call of conscience is always already operating in the very being of our temporal existence.[12]

The call of conscience discloses itself first and foremost as the "giving-to-understand" of our ownmost "potentiality-for-Being." For Heidegger, it thus makes perfect sense to speak of the "call" or "voice" of conscience when describing the ontological workings of the phenomenon, for conscience does indeed function discursively: It has the formal structure of "discourse" (*Rede*), which is a mode of "disclosure" in which something is said, pointed out, revealed, and shared. The call of conscience is human existence disclosing itself to the one who is living it. This is what is "talked about" when conscience calls: the givenness, "the bare 'that it is,' " of one's Being. Or, as Heidegger also puts it: "In conscience Dasein calls itself."[13]

This way of stating the matter alerts us to the fact that the call of conscience is not something that comes first and foremost from you, or from me, or from any other individual. Dasein is not a person; rather, it is the Being of a person's temporal existence—that which we live every day but that which we did not create, that which warrants a response but that which we "have neither planned nor prepared for nor voluntarily performed." The givenness of the call of conscience is an unrequested gift that comes to us from something other than the traditional ways of life that constitute and define the "I," the ego, of one's subjectivity. Hence, as he writes about conscience Heidegger emphasizes that " 'it' calls" and that it does this "against our expectations and even against our will."[14]

Human existence brings with it a challenge-response logic, a most primordial call of conscience that has both a *constructive* and *deconstructive* ring to it: The future is constantly calling us to acknowledge our authenticity and thus to shoulder the responsibility of making thoughtful decisions about how to construct, and live, a meaningful life. Heidegger notes, however, that if we are to remain authentic while living the commitment of our decisions, we must be prepared and willing at any moment to question the supposed correctness of what we are thinking and doing as a result of having made these decisions. The constancy of the call demands as much, for it speaks to us of the certainty of uncertainty. The future orientation of existence is forever opening us to the possibility of change, of things being otherwise than usual, of how what is yet to come in our lives may require us, for truth's sake, to rethink and revise what we currently hold to be correct about our ongoing commitments, involvements, and interpretive practices. From the heart of existence comes a constructive call for concerned thought and decisive action, a call of conscience. But this call, related as it is to the future, also has a deconstructive ring to it, for it repeatedly calls into question our desire for certainty and stability—a desire that manifests itself whenever we assume the personal and ethical responsibility of affirming our freedom through resolute choice in an effort to bring meaning and order to our everyday existence. In short, listening to the call of conscience we are constantly told of the importance of being both decisive and open-minded. Owing to the changing circumstances of our lives, what appears to be "right" now may be "wrong" later. Our everyday way of inhabiting the world is always open to question, always being challenged by something other than itself. The call of conscience speaks to us of (discloses) this fact of life.

Attending to the moment when this revelation actually happens in our everyday lives, Heidegger emphasizes that the call of conscience functions to "interrupt" the way in which we are currently "losing" ourselves "in the publicness and the idle talk of the 'they.' "[15] What thus "gets broken by the call" are our conditioned and typical involvements with things and with others, especially as these involvements admit little more than a complacent and conformist allegiance to those values, standards, and conventions that govern and normalize the perceptions, thoughts, and practices of our everyday existence. Heidegger is rather vague, however, when discussing how this interruption initially occurs. We are only told that it manifests itself as an "abrupt arousal." One might therefore read Heidegger as suggesting that the call is its own catalyst; the abrupt arousal of its interruption is all that is needed to make us aware of how we are losing ourselves in the world of the "they" and thus how we must assume the responsibility of making a resolute choice if we are to reverse the process.

What was said above about the deconstructive nature of the call's future orientation does lend some support to this reading: The call of conscience is human existence disclosing itself to the one who is living it. The call thus speaks to us of how our temporal Being is forever opening us to what is not yet in our lives and to the uncertainty and possibility of change that are concomitant with this way of being toward the future. The call thereby makes us aware of how our everyday understanding of the world is always open to question. Recall also that the call is not something that is "voluntarily performed." Rather, it happens "against our expectations and even against our will"; it reveals itself as something other than that which it calls for (concerned thought and decisive action) as it interrupts our lives. The call of conscience is always already at work before these capacities are put to use. It may therefore be said that, in the way that it functions, the call of conscience is its own catalyst of change, its own interruption, which is constantly occurring, constantly calling and challenging us to be more than a "they-self," whether we realize it or not. The call raises a question of personal responsibility: "Where art thou?" It is left to us to acknowledge this question and to commit ourselves to answering it: "Here I am!"[16]

Is it the case, however, that the call's ongoing interruption, in and of itself, is enough to make us aware of how we are faring in this everyday realm of thought and practice such that we can reform its influence by assuming the responsibility for our own acts as we respond to the call? The process, I submit, is not that simple. The call of conscience does sound a constant interruption, but its "abrupt arousal" is not perceived until something happens to disturb or break down our conditioned and typical ways of understanding the world and of becoming involved with things and with others. Although Heidegger fails to clarify this point while attending to the workings of the call of conscience, he does prepare us to understand its significance when, earlier in *Being and Time,* he discusses the process by which human awareness arises out of human activity. This discussion, as is well known, centers on what Heidegger discovers to be taking place when a tool that we are skillfully using to accomplish a certain task suddenly breaks in our hands.[17] A brief consideration of this matter should therefore prove helpful in advancing our understanding of a specific concern that remains unclear in Heidegger's ontological assessment of the call of conscience.

When using a tool to accomplish a given task, we find ourselves firmly situated in the practically oriented world of circumspective concern, demonstrating a competence for knowing-how to deal with the immediacy of some goal-directed activity. Our successful involvement with what we are doing here is conditioned by the tool's transparency, by how well it goes unnoticed as it is being used, by how efficiently it facilitates an endeavor by not getting in our way, by not drawing attention to itself, by enabling us to forget its presence. The tool must remain inconspicuous if we are to maintain our preoccupation with the situation at hand.

At the moment the tool breaks, however, all of this changes. The tool now obtrudes on our awareness, revealing itself as a *factum brutum*, a "thing" divested of its practical significance. This thing gets in the way and impedes our progress. In so doing, it also give us pause for thought: What is going on here, and what can be done about it? We ask these questions as beings who can step back from, contemplate, and theorize about our daily preoccupations such that we might understand them better and perhaps improve on their performance. The defective tool forces us to become engaged in this reflective process to some degree; it thereby brings about a modification of our circumspective and instrumental way of being situated in the world. That is, when the tool breaks, loses its transparency, and becomes an all-too-noticeable thing, we are abruptly dislocated from a preoccupation, from work in progress, and situated in a more theoretically oriented position to understand the environment. For when the tool breaks, its status as a well-designed, "ready-to-hand" piece of equipment discloses itself differently, more fully and explicitly, and thus in a way which was not possible so long as the work was flowing smoothly. The tool's being—what it is and does—is no longer absent and forgettable but is instead quite present, memorable, and remarkable. The broken tool opens itself for inspection as it "announces itself afresh."[18]

What we are thereby given to see more vividly when this happens is not, however, restricted to a single piece of equipment. For the tool's "unusability" not only calls attention to the tool itself, but it also makes us more mindful of other pieces of equipment whose functions are connected to what the tool is supposed to do. For example, when a computer malfunctions and becomes conspicuous and thus questionable, it also calls into question the usefulness of the desk, printer, paper, workstation, and well-lit room that once supported its operation. The everyday world of know-how marks out an instrumental matrix whose infrastructure entails the interconnectivity of equipment.[19] The broken tool gives notice of this; it discloses a "truth" (about itself and related things) that warrants thought, especially if we are to figure out and fix what went wrong such that we can get back to being preoccupied with the task at hand and thus back to a world of practice where "all is well" once again.

Could something as simple as a tool that abruptly breaks in our hands alert us to the call of conscience? It is possible. For example, a malfunctioning computer might arouse its user not only to become more aware of what it takes to perform and complete a given task (e.g., working on a manuscript) but also to give thought to how a sustained preoccupation with this task is leading this person to become too neglectful of others (e.g., family members) who deserve to be treated in a more caring and respectful way. In this case, the question brought about by the defective tool—What is going on here and what can be done about it?—is no longer merely restricted to knowing how to remedy a technological breakdown. A certain realization has made the situation more complicated than that. Another option for action is now apparent—one that, if taken, will further delay the person's preoccupation with completing a task as he or she attends instead to other pressing concerns. Hence, in this situation the person is necessarily confronted with the personal responsibility of explicitly choosing a course of action that is oriented toward reinstating a sense of order in the person's life. The call of conscience, in other words, has caught the person's attention ("Where art thou?") and awaits a response.

Heidegger tells us that the call of conscience "makes itself known as a Fact only with factical existence and in it."[20] The above example offers a concrete illustration of how this is so. We are alerted to the call by way of an occurrence that so disrupts our conditioned and typical ways of understanding and inhabiting the world that we are thereby brought face-to-face with the ever-present challenge of owning up to our own existence, our own "authentic potentiality-for-Being." Heidegger speaks of the "unshakable joy" that we should feel when this happens; for then we find ourselves in the awe-inspiring situation where the moment has come for us to be more than a conformist, more than a "they-self," more than what others simply tell us to be.[21] The dictatorship of the "they" is an impediment to the "individual Dasein" struggling to live out an authentic existence by hearing and responding to the call of conscience, to that which is "other" than others even though it is part of their "own" existence. Owing to the temporal structure of their Being and to their capacity to care about the meaningfulness of their lives, human beings are fated to experience a primordial call that is there to interrupt their lives at any time of the day or night.

The Rhetorical Function of the Call of Conscience

Because he is so taken with the otherness of the call, and because the issue he makes of it entails a rather critical assessment of another source of otherness in our lives (i.e., other people), Heidegger is open to the charge of offering a theory of conscience that ends up disparaging the social nature of human being. The charge is especially chilling when made by those who see a connection between Heidegger's political involvements in the 1930s and all that he had to say about authentic Dasein in *Being and Time.*[22] As suggested above, however, I believe this charge misses the mark. The story of authentic Dasein is intimately tied to the building of an ethical and moral community, a being-with-and-*for others.* Dasein has a responsibility to be a voice of conscience to others and thereby to involve them in collaborative deliberation so that they, too, can have a say in registering the truth of matters of importance. Here is where the evocative function of rhetoric comes into play. The orator must employ this function "in a right and just manner" in order to move people to ideas and ideas to people. The call of conscience, the practice of rhetoric, and the cultivation of a community's moral ecology go hand in hand; they work together to promote a process that operates in both a constructive and a deconstructive way, that is directed toward the ascertaining of truth, and that would therefore have people acknowledge, and remain open to, the differing perspectives of others. A system of meaning (e.g., National Socialism) that has been constructed in such a way so as to silence any critical, deconstructive impulses is not a system that lends itself to the ways of authentic Dasein.

Heidegger should have listened more carefully to what he wrote in *Being and Time;* he should have interrupted his ongoing thinking on the meaning and truth of Being and, *in no uncertain terms,* apologized for his tragic error of not speaking out against and interrupting the worldview of a murderous regime. Heidegger emphasizes the "courage" it takes to perform such a conscientious and rhetorically noble deed. To be sure, a well-formulated and appropriate rhetorical interruption oftentimes requires not only artistic skill but also the bravery that comes with the cultivation of this virtuous way of being-with-and-*for others.* Offering a genuine response to the call of conscience is not an activity for the weak at heart.[23]

The call of conscience calls for, among other things, rhetorical interruptions. In his discussion of the latter phenomenon, Thomas B. Farrell writes: "Rhetoric, despite its traditional and quite justifiable association with the preservation of cultural truisms, may also perform an act of *critical interruption* where the taken-for-granted practices of culture are concerned. . . . The phenomenon of rhetorical interruption juxtaposes the assumptions, norms, and practices of a people so as to prompt a reappraisal of where they are culturally, what they are doing, and where they are going."[24] What Farrell fails to realize, however, is that this phenomenon is always already at work before the orator steps in with his or her discourse. It is how the call of conscience embedded in the temporal structure of human existence calls us into question: "Where art thou?" One might therefore say that the call of conscience is a rhetorical interruption in its purest form—an interruption that assumes more concrete detail whenever people get caught up, for example, in controversies like the euthanasia debate. As seen in this debate, rhetorical interruptions are constantly at work as people invent ways of acknowledging others and getting them to see exactly what life, death, medical science and technology, and morality are supposedly all about.[25]

Heidegger never speaks of the call of conscience as a "rhetorical" interruption. Perhaps he would have if he had given more thought to how the interruptive nature of the call, as suggested above, makes itself known by way of breakdowns in our lives. Just like a tool that abruptly breaks in our hands (or even a hand that moves through one's hair), the practice of rhetoric can interrupt our habits of thinking and living and thereby encourage us to rethink the wisdom of our everyday behavior. Rhetorical interruptions awaken us from our ontological slumber and, if only for the moment, open us to existential possibilities that, for one reason or another, are no longer, or have never been, an important factor in our lives. Rhetorical interruptions are evocative. Raphael Demos offers a perceptive description of the process at work here. "Evocation," he writes,

> is the process by which vividness is conveyed; it is the presentation of a viewpoint in such a manner that it becomes real for the public. It is said that argument is a way by which an individual experience is made common property; in fact, an argument has much less persuasive force than the vivid evocation of an experience. The enumeration of all the relevant points in favor of a theory and against its opposite can never be completed; far more effective is it to state a viewpoint in all its concreteness and in all its significant implication, and then stop; the arguments become relevant only after this stage has been concluded.[26]

The process of evocation is a "showing-forth" (*epideixis*) of what is. The call of conscience involves us in this process; it speaks a truly epideictic discourse, the first there is. Clearly, something fundamentally rhetorical is going on here, something "designed" to move us toward the realization of who and how we are and where we are going. Because of what it is and how it functions, the call of conscience inspires moral consciousness by way of an ancient art.

Like others before me, I am, of course, putting words in Heidegger's mouth by speaking about how his philosophy adds both ontological and moral weight to the practice of rhetoric. My particular way of doing this has been to center on an all-important topic in *Being and Time:* the interruptive nature of the call of conscience. When this topic is carefully attended to and clarified, one can further his or her appreciation of just how fundamental rhetoric is to our Being. "In conscience Dasein calls itself." To be sure, we *are* creatures of rhetoric.

With this point and some recent work of Professor Schrag's in mind, I think it would be fair to say that rhetoric is the "communicative praxis that first provides the space for a genealogy of the ethical subject and the delineation of moral imperatives."[27] Put another way: It all begins with a rhetorical interruption—a primordial saying (the call of conscience) that lies at the heart of existence and that speaks against attitudes and outlooks that are close-minded, egotistical, brutally selective when it comes to caring for others, and unapologizing for this tragic lack of considerateness and forbearance, compassion and wisdom. In the Judeo-Christian tradition this saying is aligned with the "Word of God"—a Word that was heard by Adam, Moses, Abraham, and others as a question ("Where art thou?") that evoked both anxiety and joy as it commanded personal acknowledgment ("Here I am!"). Heidegger would have us wonder about this Word in a certain way: "Only from the truth of Being can the essence of the holy be thought. Only from the essence of the holy is the essence of divinity to be thought. Only in light of the essence of divinity can it be thought or said what the word 'God' is to signify." He thereby asks: "How can man at the present state of world history ask at all seriously and rigorously whether the god nears or withdraws, when he has above all neglected to think into the dimension in which alone that question can be asked."[28]

Heidegger has a point. If we want to understand the genuine meaning of the call of conscience, we have to pay careful attention to the Being of human being, which is "other" than a mere human creation. Heidegger's mistake in performing this task was not paying careful enough attention to how the otherness of others, and the call of conscience that comes with it (especially when others are in need of help), allows the "dimension" in question to be appreciated for what it is. Conscience is a gift that calls on us to acknowledge not only ourselves but also other selves and things that can break before our eyes and interrupt our daily preoccupations.[29] Persons known and respected for their high moral character (*ethos*) embody this gift: When they are among us, their "simple" presence is enough to remind us of how important it is to think and act "in a right and just manner." This chapter is written to acknowledge such a person.

Notes

1. See, e.g., Calvin O. Schrag, *Communicative Praxis and the Space of Subjectivity* (Bloomington: Indiana University Press, 1986) (hereafter cited as *CPSS*), and *The Self after Postmodernity* (New Haven, Conn.: Yale University Press, 1997) (hereafter cited as *SP*).

266

MICHAEL J. HYDE

2. Schrag, *CPSS,* pp. 179–214. Also see Henry W. Johnstone, Jr., "Rhetoric and Communication in Philosophy," in *Validity and Rhetoric in Philosophical Argument: An Outlook in Transition* (University Park, Pa.: Dialogue Press of *Man & World*), pp. 62–72; and Michael J. Hyde and Craig R. Smith, "Hermeneutics and Rhetoric: A Seen but Unobserved Relationship," *Quarterly Journal of Speech* 65 (1979): 347–63.

3. Johnstone, "Rhetoric and Communication," p. 68. For other excellent works that emphasize how Heidegger's discourse admits a "religious" calling, see Robert Mugerauer, *Heidegger's Language and Thinking* (Atlantic Highlands, N.J.: Humanities Press International, 1988); Craig R. Smith, "Martin Heidegger and the Dialogue with Being," *Central States Speech Journal* 36 (1985): 239–53; Michael P. Sipira, "Heidegger and Epeideictic Discourse: The Rhetorical Performance of Meditative Thinking," *Philosophy Today* (fall 1991): 239–53; and Allen Scult, "Hermes' Rhetorical Problem: The Dilemma of the Sacred in Philosophical Hermeneutics," in *Rhetoric and Hermeneutics in Our Time,* ed. Walter Jost and Michael J. Hyde (New Haven, Conn.: Yale University Press, 1997), pp. 290–309.

4. Paul R. Falzer, "On Behalf of Skeptical Rhetoric," *Philosophy and Rhetoric* 24 (1991): 238–54.

5. Martin Heidegger, *Being and Time,* trans. John Macquarrie and Edward Robinson (New York: Harper and Row, 1962), p. 178 (hereafter cited as *BT*).

6. Martin Heidegger, *Sein und Zeit* (Tübingen: Niemeyer, 1979), pp. 138–39.

7. Martin Heidegger, *Being and Time,* trans. Joan Stambaugh (Albany: State University of New York Press, 1996), p. 130.

8. Michael J. Hyde, "The Call of Conscience: Heidegger and the Question of Rhetoric," *Philosophy and Rhetoric* 27 (1994): 375.

9. Heidegger, *BT,* p. 159.

10. Ibid., p. 206. I would emphasize the phrase "Being *for Others,*" because Heidegger is commonly criticized by those such as Emmanuel Lévinas, e.g., for not recognizing how the interpersonal orientation it signifies is essential to humankind's communal well-being. The recognition clearly is there, although, as I will suggest later in this chapter, what Heidegger recognizes in *Being and Time* about one's being for others is not something that is well developed in his work.

11. This phrase, as is well known, is used in Heidegger's *An Introduction to Metaphysics* (1959), when he writes: "The works that are being peddled about nowadays [summer 1935] as the philosophy of National Socialism but have nothing whatever to do with the inner truth and greatness of this movement (namely the encounter between global technology and modern man)—have all been written by men fishing in the troubled waters of 'values' and 'totalities' " (p. 199). This specific conception of the movement was not articulated in 1935 when Heidegger first gave the lecture. He appended the parenthetic explanation to the 1953 German edition of his book so to clarify how, in his personal opinion, "the inner truth and greatness" of National Socialism was far different than the fascist rhetoric that claimed to know what this truth and greatness actually were.

12. Schrag, *CPSS*, p. 204; Theodore Kisiel, *The Genesis of Heidegger's "Being and Time"* (Berkeley and Los Angeles: University of California Press, 1993), pp. 433–36.

13. Heidegger, *BT*, pp. 320–21.

14. Ibid., p. 320. In his later works Heidegger extends his thinking on the call of conscience, associates this call with "the call of Being," and speaks of the givenness of this call as a "gift." See, e.g., Martin Heidegger, *What Is Called Thinking?* trans. Fred D. Wieck and J. Glenn Gray (New York: Harper and Row, 1968), pp. 113–37. When Schrag considers the workings of the call of conscience (see Schrag, *SP*, pp. 93–97), he does not employ the term "gift," although his thinking on the nature of "the gift" certainly supports my use of the term to describe the call: "To acknowledge the gift as gift, both in its being given and its being received, is to attest to an alterity that transcends both the categories of ownership and moral intent. In this regard, the gift is without origin—at least without origin in the realm of our mundane socio-cultural existence" (Calvin O. Schrag, "On the Ethics of the Gift: Acknowledgement and Response," pp. 4–5). Consider, too, how Schrag in the same essay writes of the "fitting response" to the gift: "A fitting response has its moment of origination in the voice and the face of alterity. It is elicited via the incursions of exteriority rather than through legislations of law within a recessed interiority" (p. 23). Schrag's essay is scheduled for publication in a collection honoring the philosopher Gary B. Madison.

15. Heidegger, *BT*, pp. 315–16.

16. This specific way of speaking about the call of conscience is adapted from the philosophy of Emmanuel Lévinas, who is well known for taking issue with Heidegger's ontology. See, e.g., Emmanuel Lévinas, *Totality and Infinity*, trans. A. Lingis (Pittsburgh: Duquesne University Press, 1969). According to Lévinas, it is not the case that the call of conscience is rooted in "the temporality of Being," in that which is other than a human creation. Rather, the call comes from another source of otherness or "alterity": the presence of others who "face" us everyday and, in so doing, give expression to a call that can be "traced" back to a source more "mysterious" than the Being of Dasein: the Almighty. Lévinas describes the expression given here as a "primordial saying" that is capable of touching us even before it is transformed into everyday discourse. The "face speaks," writes Lévinas, and this "first saying" commands acknowledgment, the responsible response of interpersonal and communal commitment whereby one says "Here I am!" to all those who are in need of help. With this saying the face arouses a person's "goodness" as it speaks for justice and civic virtue, for "the miracle of moving out of oneself," out of egoism and know-it-all attitudes, both of which close us off to others, to their differences, to the alterity of their otherness. The saying of the face is a "showing-forth" of a most fundamental truth, an "epiphany" that "interrupts" the complacency of self-satisfaction as it discloses the "vulnerability" of the human body and thereby sounds a call of conscience. Hence, although both Heidegger and Lévinas understand the call of conscience as something that is rooted in otherness, Lévinas's thinking on the

matter is much more explicit when it comes to appreciating how the otherness of other human beings is a source of the call. As I will indicate later in this essay, however, Heidegger's theory does not preclude an understanding of how others can inspire a hearing of the call of conscience. I believe it is therefore legitimate to speak of this theory in terms of the question/answer: "Where art thou? Here I am!" For a more detailed analysis of the similarities and differences between these two philosophers' theories of conscience, see my *The Call of Conscience: Heidegger and Lévinas, Rhetoric and the Euthanasia Debate* (Columbia: University of South Carolina Press, 2001).

17. Heidegger, *BT*, pp. 95–106.

18. Ibid., p. 105.

19. For a more detailed discussion of this point, esp. as it applies to the world of media technology, see my "Human Being and the Call of Technology," in *Toward the Twenty-First Century: The Future of Speech Communication,* ed. Julia T. Wood and Richard B. Gregg (Cresskill, N.J.: Hampton Press, 1995), pp. 47–79.

20. Heidegger, *BT*, p. 313.

21. Ibid., p. 358.

22. After *Being and Time* Heidegger no longer speaks of the call of conscience, but emphasizes instead how this call is essentially the "call of Being." For a critique of Heidegger and how his political involvements supposedly are associated with his answering the call, see Richard Wolin, *The Politics of Being: The Political Thought of Martin Heidegger* (New York: Columbia University Press, 1990). For a more comprehensive and balanced account, see Michael E. Zimmerman, *Heidegger's Confrontation with Modernity: Technology, Politics, and Art* (Bloomington: Indiana University Press, 1990). For an excellent collection of documents, letters, memoirs, testimonials, lectures, interviews, and statements by Heidegger himself and by many other intellectuals who commented on his philosophy and politics, see Gunther Neske and Emil Kettering, eds., *Martin Heidegger and National Socialism: Questions and Answers,* trans. Lisa Harries and Joachim Neugroschel (New York: Paragon House, 1990).

23. Heidegger, *SP*, pp. 298, 310–11. Employing Heidegger's own language, one might therefore accuse him of being a "coward" (*BT*, p. 311), as he continued throughout his life to avoid offering a clear-cut rhetorical interruption that clarified his lack of judgment (*phronesis*) in the 1930s. For an excellent discussion of the "silence" that went on here, see Jean-François Lyotard, *Heidegger and "the jews,"* trans. Andreas Michel and Mark Roberts (Minneapolis: University of Minnesota Press, 1990).

24. Thomas B. Farrell, *Norms of Rhetorical Culture* (New Haven, Conn.: Yale University Press, 1993), p. 298.

25. For a case study that illustrates the point being made here, see my "Medicine, Rhetoric, and Euthanasia: A Case Study in the Workings of a Postmodern Discourse," *Quarterly Journal of Speech* 79 (1993): 201–24. Additional case studies can also be found in my *Call of Conscience.* In this debate, of course, people are more concerned with "broken" bodies than with broken tools. Such bodies sound a powerful call of conscience.

26. Raphael Demos, "On Persuasion," *Journal of Philosophy* 29 (1932): 229.

27. Calvin O. Schrag, "Ethics of the Gift," p. 9.

28. Martin Heidegger, "Letter on Humanism," trans. Frank A. Capuzzi in collaboration with J. Glenn Gray, in *Basic Writings: From* Being and Time *(1927) to* The Task of Thinking *(1964)*, ed. David Farrell Krell (New York: Harper and Row, 1977), p. 230.

29. As suggested at n. 16 above, it is Emmanuel Lévinas, more than Heidegger, who would have us pay particular attention to how the call of conscience is made known by the presence of others. Still, however, as Jacques Derrida emphasizes, it is the Being of human being that must first be attended to if one is to grasp the genuine meaning of the other's call. He notes, e.g., that the "thought of Being" is essential to Lévinas's entire philosophy: "Thought—or at least the precomprehension of Being—*conditions* . . . the *recognition* of the essence of the existent (for example someone, existent *as* other, *as* other self, etc.). It conditions the respect for the other as what it is: other. Without this acknowledgement . . . no ethics would be possible." See Jacques Derrida, "Violence and Metaphysics," in *Writing and Difference,* trans. Alan Bass (Chicago: University of Chicago Press, 1978), pp. 137–38.

14

Structure, Deconstruction, and the Future of Meaning

David Crownfield

This chapter traces a line of thought generated by juxtaposing two seminal essays of the early 1970s, Paul Ricoeur's "Structure, Word, Event" and Jacques Derrida's "Signature Event Context."[1] Ricoeur's articulation of the role of structure in discourse, together with Derrida's deconstructive critique, poses a critical challenge to the whole process of objective determination of meaning and thus to the public accountability of utterance. It is therefore a pivotal moment in the postmodern challenge.

I first became directly engaged with these issues at a summer National Endowment for the Humanities institute at Purdue University, on the topic "the linguistic turn in recent continental philosophy," directed by Calvin Schrag. As I have worked further with these issues, in the classroom and in the library, that involvement has been greatly enriched by Schrag's own recent publications. His recent works have all directly addressed the question of how to sustain together the fruitfulness of postmodern insights and the public accountability that is appealed to by the rational tradition. He articulates three issues that seem particularly central to me. One, developed especially in *Communicative Praxis and the Space of Subjectivity,* is that of "texture," meaning a system of semiotic differences (in a broad sense) in which linguistic signs and structures are interwoven with a diversity of practices and with patterns of difference in the world, in a multiform configuration of meaning, a kind of multimedia structuralism.[2] This notion of texture preserves the structuralist project of determining sense through a system of differences, while at the same time it exceeds in principle the structuralist constraint, of restricting language to a set of elements that must be finite, arbitrary, in principle enumerable. At the same time the notion of texture integrates the structuralist reliance on a system of differences with a phenomenological focus on the act of speaking and a social and pragmatic attention to shared practices. The question of the efficacy of this fusion opens a crucial issue as to whether an open-ended semiotics can be intelligible and can sustain accountable discourse.

A second and related theme in Schrag's recent work is the notion, developed in *The Resources of Rationality* and deployed also in *The Self after Postmodernity*, of "transversal rationality."[3] Schrag does not offer a simple formal definition of this notion, which he has adapted especially from Félix Guattari. Transversal rationality is not governed by hierarchy, nor by an atomic and linear logic, nor by a totalizing dialectic. It develops in social practice, in engagement with a multivariant, polydimensional interplay of differences and problems. Transversal rationality is constructed, shared, provisional, transitional. It is controlled not by a normative logic but by practical shared utility for this time, place, and situation. Accountability is thus not to formal and conceptual correctness but to a shared aim of interpersonal and practical utility.

The third related issue I want to attend to is that of the self. Self is for Schrag not a subject, a substance, but practice, performance, communicative self-implicature. He shares with Sartre (and Heidegger) this attention to the task of enacting, rather than being able to presuppose, the unity of self. But Schrag sees the unifying enactment of consciousness as response to "the entwined discourse and action of the other"[4] rather than seeing it as an original self-construction in the sense often attributed to the early Sartre. Self, for Schrag, is a responsive integration of, and assumption of responsibility for, a social process of recognition and interaction, in a contexture of discourse and practice. It is thus a temporal venture of transversality, gathering a largely shared having-been toward a largely shared horizon of possibility, within a transitional community of practical engagement with a world textured by interwoven relevances and aims.

The possibility as well as the significance of this sort of move beyond postmodernity depends on the assessment of the postmodern challenge itself. Some critics of postmodern thought hold that it leads either to sheer relativism or to the total collapse of rationality. Schrag does not accept these alternatives, but appeals to communicative textures of shared practice, to social enactments of transversal rationality, to responsive assumption of selfhood in community. I argue that the rationality of structural semiotics and phenomenological hermeneutics, which are fused in some of the work of Ricoeur, leads directly to the deconstructive impasse enacted by Derrida and that that impasse results not in the collapse of meaning and community but precisely in the focusing of the need for a shared engagement in textures of communicative practice, relying on a transversal rationality, as responsive selves.

Ricoeur: Phenomenology beyond Structuralism

Ricoeur's "Structure, Word, Event" discusses the nature and limits of the efficacy of structuralism as a formalization of meaning. Not unaware of Lévi-Strauss, Barthes, and others, who apply structural analysis to cultural areas beyond the field of linguistics, he deliberately confines himself to an analysis of linguistic structuralism. At the same time his critique clearly intends the whole breadth of the structuralist approach. Some of the issues he raises might, with appropriate adjustments, be applicable to any formalist theory of meaning, whether structural, logistic, or whatever.

In Ricoeur's account, intelligibility is for structuralism a function of a closed system, consisting of an inventory of elements, oppositional relations between them, and a combinatory system among them. To make linguistics an object of an empirical science, structuralism postulates an ideal and formal systematicity (in good Galilean fashion).[5] The basic object of structural linguistics is a synchronic structure; the diachronic history of linguistic development is seen as a study of the sequence of states of the formal system. Within the synchronic structure there are no independent terms, but only relationships of opposition (and of synonymy) between terms. It is thus a closed system of internal relations. Signs are specifiable in terms of their external differences from each other and in terms of their internal distinction between signifier (mark, sound) and signified (concept, function, location relative to the other terms). The system is in actuality never totally present, never totally static; but it is in principle comprehensively present as the determinant of every occurrence of its elements.

As a result of its idealization and formalization, Ricoeur says, structuralism cannot deal with free and novel combination, and it does not attend to the basic act of someone saying something to someone about something. It determines an ideal, semiotic "meaning," but it is unable to engage what is external to the system, which is what every ordinary saying is about. The science fixes language as an object for study, while language in use mediates relations in the real, and aims to disappear in the content it indicates and invokes.

Discourse in operation—linguistic utterance—is an act, is a temporal engagement, a venture and exposure. It articulates possibilities and
calls for choices. It generates new combinations: of words, of meanings,
of sense and context, of relations of coexistence. The very externality
excluded by the structuralist system is what language is about, in use.
It is in use that language can have not only sense but reference: not a
controlled, formally idealized reference, but an aim, a venture of advancing toward reference, toward fulfillment of the intention by the world.
In speech, Ricoeur says, "Effects of meaning are offered to the bite of
the real."[6] The connection between speaking and the world has three
dimensions: the referent, the addressee, and the speaker. These are all
extralinguistic realities from, for, and about which anybody says anything
in the first place.

To move beyond this antithesis between the structural system and
the speaking act, Ricoeur addresses two sorts of approach. One is through
grammar: Chomsky's generative grammar that formalizes the combinatory principles for a potential infinity of (unprecedented) well-formed
sentences, and Gustave Guillaume's analyses of parts of speech and of
tenses, which function to articulate the principles for any actualization of
linguistic structures in time and space. In both respects, Ricoeur says, the
science of discourse is understood as a science of operations, of "struc-
tur*ing*" rather than of a "structured inventory." The other sort of approach Ricoeur addresses is semantic. A "word" in his usage is a linguistic
sign "in speech position."[7] It functions as a "trader" between system and
act, structure and event. Used in a sentence, in a context, in the world, the
word subsequently returns again to the system, displaced, recontextualized. Such returns and displacements construct the history of the system.

Words are characteristically polysemic: They have, in the same state
of the system, more than one sense. In enactment and return, they participate in a *process* of meaning. Metaphor is one component of this
process, involving the innovative exploitation of intersections, analogies,
and tensions between multiple meanings, which are generated as words
that are deployed in unique contexts. By this and other means, meaning
is cumulative and shifting. Every such cumulation and shifting alters the
whole background fabric of differences, contrasts, and oppositions which
participate in constituting meaning in each instance and so continually
recontextualizes and modifies all meanings.

In the shifting interplay between polysemy and recontextualization,
terms are always in motion, generating convergence, surcharge of meaning, novelty, changing alliances, and oppositions. The internal relations
among the other elements of the system tend to limit and attenuate

each innovation. The process thus generates a multiplicity, but not an infinity, of meaning. The inertial effect of the already established fabric within which each novelty enters the system works toward an equilibrium between expansion and limitation of meanings.

A functioning degree of univocity, sufficient to make signification work, is achieved in most instances by context. The tendencies toward consistency and toward coherence with a specific frame of reference serve together to effect an "isotopy" of sense that overcomes, for the moment, the polysemy of terms. In poetic and other deliberately polysemic discourse, two or more distinct frames of reference may be coherently sustainable at the same time, and their conjunction may effect a fruitful mutuality (a sort of metametaphor).

The word brings to speech its place in the necessary overall structural order. In the same act, however, it brings contingency, disequilibrium, and novelty into the system. For Ricoeur, the word thus mediates the antitheses of system and act and of semiotics and semantics. Moving beyond structuralism in Ricoeur's way means understanding the thesis (system), sharply and rigorously posing the antithesis (act of speaking), and finding in the word-in-act the reconciliation in which the dialectical opposites are overcome and surpassed.

Derrida: Deconstruction beyond Formalism

Derrida's "Signature Event Context" was presented at a conference of francophone philosophers in Montreal in 1971, for which the announced topic was "communication" and the keynote speaker was Paul Ricoeur. Derrida's essay addresses Ricoeur's themes, but its explicit references are to Condillac (and to J. L. Austin). He begins by questioning the univocity of the title word, "communication." The key issue, he says, is one "of polysemia and communication, of dissemination—which I will oppose to polysemia—and communication."[8] If (as Ricoeur holds) polysemy is reduced by context, then context must become the issue. Is there a rigorous concept of context? It is, says Derrida, never absolutely (or adequately) determinable, never certain, never saturated. (All that indefiniteness—both of extent and of relevance—which Saussure wished to exclude in formalizing the object of linguistics [so as to make it a science] is reintroduced by the impossibility of specifying a delimited "context.")

A classic view (represented by Condillac) says that writing is an instrument of communication, extending the reach of speaking. It merely carries already-understandable communication "louder," farther, longer, without having any effect on its meaning. According to this view, we write to communicate thought, ideas, and representations. We already do communicate: Writing is communication "to absent persons," a supplement, without effect on content. Writing is conceived of as developing from picture, pictograph, representation, imitation; it is a sign of an idea. It operates in the absence of the addressee (and the sender). Absence here attenuates, delays, displaces presence. Not a pure negation, it is treated as a remotion and modification of presence. In expressing, representing, and so forth, writing is a trace, a retracing, of an idea, which traces/represents a thing. Writing is said to be a species of the genus "communication": Its specific difference is "absence."

But *any* sign, qua sign, is not what it signifies: It supposes absence. Is the absence that defines writing specifically different? If it is not, then writing is (perhaps) not a *species* of communication. The absence by which writing is explained might then be proper to *every* sign, spoken or otherwise. The hierarchy by which speech is said to be more basic than writing would thus be undermined.

Writing is, (perhaps) inherently, communication in conditions of absence, distance, delay. It is legible in the absence of the addressee. It is thus structured by its iterability, which has for Derrida a dual sense: both its repeatability and its alterity. Structurally legible in the absence of both its addressee and its author, it is "a trace of death," the implicit erasure of authorial intention.[9]

Writing is thus disconnected from the authority of consciousness. It cannot be adequately understood as communication of consciousness. It functions in displacement from any original semantic and hermeneutic horizon. The appeal to context to reduce its polysemy thus does not suffice to control the effects of an utterance's dissemination (its drifting recontextualization). The notion (held by Ricoeur) that language can acquire its determination in use from the interaction between its (original) real and linguistic contexts is thus disengaged.

These problems of writing, Derrida says, are generalizable to all language (and beyond). Every instance requires a mark (spoken or written or . . .) that can be construed beyond the presence of its being inscribed, and beyond the presence of its subject of origin or of address. A mark is essentially decontextualizing, indefinitely recontextualizable. It requires, in order to be a mark in a code, a (migratory) legibility apart from intent and context. Its recombination, resituation, recontextualizing are essential to its occurrence. And the constitution of a mark requires the possibility of its extraction, of its displacement from the site of the indexicality by which it is originally connected to the real. Its material dissemination necessarily and continuingly effects this displacement.

A code, and a mark, thus themselves effect dislocation, decontextualization and recontextualization, a differing brought about through the changes of the differences within which they function. A sign is as such dependent on absence, on its separability from intention and ostensive reference (and so even from original sense). Second imposition, empty reference, misdirection, absence of intent, even absence of "sense" are intrinsic possibilities of any sign as such. Signs are inherently citable, therefore infinitely recontextualizable, resiteable. Meaning, then, cannot be adequately determined by the formal structure of a sign system.

It is this set of issues that leads up to Derrida's discussion of the question of performatives, of J. L. Austin's *How to Do Things with Words,* which provoked a much-discussed reply by John Searle. Derrida finds difficulties in Austin's discussion, which result, he holds, from the failure to understand the "graphematic" character of locution: its essential reliance on iterable, disseminable, counterfeitable, citable forms. Austin idealizes the context, offering a theoretical model of the defining conditions of legitimacy, or force, of a performative. In so doing he erases from consideration the intrinsic and irreducible uncertainty that is essential to the constitution of any iterable mark.[10]

The presence of the conscious and genuine intention of the speaking subject is not a determinable condition, but without it the conditions of adequacy of a performative cannot be controlled. The attempt to specify such conditions—through conventionalizing the formulae, through rules for correctness of execution, and through a formally delimitable and determinable completeness of the act—necessarily fails. It fails because the ritualized words, the standardized forms of execution, and the defining conditions of completeness are essentially constituted by iterability, dissemination, and so forth. These are not accidental variations, in Derrida's account, but are intrinsic to the ability of marks to function as signs at all. The exposure of signs to risk of misuse is inherently unavoidable, and so the adequacy of a performative is always underdetermined.

The *conventionality* of locution in general is absolutely essential to its possibility, and therefore so is its exposure to failure and falsification. Citability, which entails the possibility of mimicry, counterfeit, quotation, dramatization, hypocrisy, . . . is requisite for any signification whatever. (A Galilean idealization of the conditions of performative utterance thus shares with Saussure's Galilean idealization of linguistic structure a disengagement from the ongoing, changing, ambiguous, unstable world of people and acts. Such idealization is much more a feature of Searle than of Austin; Austin does it, but appears to be aiming primarily at opening up the differences between sorts of speaking rather than at the formalization of a normative performative.)

In a Derridean analysis of general iterability, intention remains a component of the situation, but it does not govern, and it is neither adequately determinable nor present *in* the utterance. Spacing—absence, displacement, the disruption of "presence" in the iterable mark—is inherent in writing, and in utterance in general. Austin thus, Derrida says, reaches an impasse every time his analysis seeks to determine any specific criterion that must be "present" for an effective performative. Austin also focuses on first-person utterance as a kind of (indexical) "presence-uttering" or "signature," but signature, too, requires iterability, and so the possibility of forgery, of illegitimacy: thus an intrinsic (potential) absence.

In the course of his concluding generalizations, Derrida appeals to his well-known critique of the tacit value hierarchies that tend to be concealed in the oppositional determination of terms. Deconstruction, he indicates, cannot settle for a simple neutralization of these oppositions but must provisionally practice a reversal of the hierarchy and a general displacement of the system. This disruption is at the same time a noncompliance with that disposition of nondiscursive forces which is supported by the tacit hierarchy of oppositive signs (i.e., hierarchies of gender, wealth, race, imperialism, hegemony of various kinds).

In general, the attempt to deal with communication as though we have an adequate understanding of consciousness, of meaning, of intention, and can view utterance as simply instrumental to it, proves unsustainable. The duplicity and disruption of signs participates in our thinking and intending as well as in our uttering. At best, the attempt to master language through formalization, systematization, and the like (whether structuralist, logistic, transcendental, or whatever) only postpones rather than dispels the root difficulties.

After Deconstruction: Shared Discourse, with No One in Control of Its Meaning

To begin with, let us review where we are left by Ricoeur and Derrida. Ricoeur's essay establishes that meaning cannot be adequately determined by an ideal linguistic structure. First, this is so because a structural model does not deal with the discursive act, in which the language exceeds itself to the real by effecting a relation of the speaker and addressee to one another and to the world of which they speak. Second, a system of terms must be operative in relation to a partially dissimilar range of situations and addressed to unanticipated configurations of likeness and difference. Polysemy is thus inherent in the system and must be controlled by context (both by the discursive context and by the local world-context). Ricoeur notes also that linguistic innovation plays back into the system and so continually effects a shift in the differential web that constructs meaning. This is damped by the resistance of the system, but it is always operative, always reconstructing meanings, as the history of the language.

Derrida radicalizes the critique. The formal signifying effect of an utterance is disseminated into contexts beyond the anticipation and control of the speaker or writer, and the web of differences on which signification depends is continually subject to change beyond the control and purview of an author. The indexical, locative, and temporal signature that is to tie an utterance to its "proper" context is subject to mimicry, dissimulation, forgery, and the like as an unavoidable effect of the very linguistic forms and rules of propriety that make it intelligible.

Derrida's argument implies, typically, that if this interplay of singularity and system is a dialectic, it is something like a Kierkegaardian one, where the existing individual is located in the extremity of the antithesis and must invent and enact the reconciliation. At the same time it is a social dialectic, in which differences within the community of practice themselves solicit a contingent and singular resolution. Such conflicts are temporal, always in transition, so meaning cannot be controlled at the point of utterance.

How, then, is any communication possible? Do these impasses paralyze, or propose to paralyze, all discourse? Yes, unless . . . Unless the notion of the *presence* of meaning in utterance is abandoned. Unless the normative project of defining whether other people have a right to say or think what they do say or think, or demanding that they produce "warrants" or "justifications," is renounced. Unless the attempt to *control* meaning, to enforce a system of what can mean or what can be real, is given up. Unless the hierarchies implicit in lexical differences are brought into the open and we learn to speak locally, from where we are, acknowledging that it is *not* a universal position.

The language available for critique of language is the language in need of critique. To go on requires a discourse that unmasks its own contingency, its hierarchy, its misfit to its context. It requires the kind of performative contradiction that declares the universal principle that there is no universal principle.[11] Going on requires allowing the fiction of presence to keep breaking down over absence, allowing the structural frame always to topple into the future, and sustaining an endless interactive practice of trial and error.

Caught between the closedness and duplicity of the structure on the one hand and the relativity and unavoidable dissemination (the un-controllable recontextualization) of the act of utterance on the other, we must rely on what we cannot control in order to effectuate our acts of meaning. Not authorial intention, not the terms of the code, not the conditions of legitimacy, but the future human efficacy of the dissemi-nated and reconfigured discourse constructs the determinative context of meaning and truth. That efficacy is not controllable in advance by the speaker, and it is not determinable by the application of normative criteria. Going on, together, in the space opened in our reading of each other's utterance, we may appropriate and enact a truth in it over which we have no definitive control. We can risk, hope, trust, try and try again, and certainly listen and work as well as write and speak; but we cannot accomplish determinate, meaningful, justifiable utterances at the point of issue. Only later, only contingently, only in unforeseeable contexts and senses, do effects of meaning occur.

But if the meaning of an utterance occurs only afterward, in a context unpredictable at the point of origin, then how is communication possible at all? Only through the venture of offering utterance to the bite of the other and of the future, and through attentively and inven-tively construing the other's utterance in return. In practical interaction with one another and the world we may construct together a texture of significance and efficacy (in Schrag's sense of texture). The emergent and inherently incomplete commonality of understanding that is thus constructed functions for the time being as a transversal rationality—a shared practical and provisional intelligibility—which is more oper-ative than it is formally specifiable. And in venture and commitment, and in fidelity to the words whose meanings we could not quite under-stand in the uttering, we enact a performative and transversal selfhood that has no foundation but accepts, in advance, a founding corespon-sibility.

Ricoeur's dialectic of structure and act, and Derrida's deconstruc-tion of presence, of context, and of hierarchy, taken together, exhibit the radicality of the postmodern challenge to the accountability of public discourse. Schrag's themes of texture, of transversal rationality, and of re-sponsive selfhood, taken together, expand the implicit appeal of Ricoeur and Derrida to the primacy of the human act and human community. They thus indicate a way forward from the postmodern impasse, relying on the futural, creative, shared character of meaning. In dialogue with these studies of communicative practice, of transversal rationality, and of responsive selfhood, we may together move beyond the impasse mapped by Ricoeur and Derrida to construct and enact an aim toward meaning and a practice of responsible and responsive sensemaking.

Notes

1. Paul Ricoeur, "Structure, Word, Event," in *The Conflict of Interpretations: Essays in Hermeneutics,* Northwestern University Studies in Phenomenology and Existential Philosophy, ed. Don Ihde (Evanston, Ill.: Northwestern University Press, 1974), pp. 79–96; Jacques Derrida, "Signature Event Context," in *Margins of Philosophy,* trans. Alan Bass (Chicago: University of Chicago Press), 1982, pp. 307–30.

2. Calvin O. Schrag, *Communicative Praxis and the Space of Subjectivity* (Bloomington: Indiana University Press, 1986), pp. 23–24.

3. Calvin O. Schrag, *The Resources of Rationality* (Bloomington: Indiana University Press, 1992), pp. 148–79, and *The Self after Postmodernity* (New Haven, Conn.: Yale University Press, 1997), pp. 131–34 (hereafter cited as *SP*).

4. Schrag, *SP,* p. 84.

5. The reference here is, of course, to Galileo, not to Galilee.

6. Ricoeur, "Structure, Word, Event," p. 84.

7. Guillaume, p. XX (emphasis added); Ricouer, "Structure, Word, Event," p. 84.

8. Derrida, "Signature, Event, Context," p. 310.

9. Ibid., p. 316.

10. J. L. Austin, *How to Do Things with Words,* ed. J. O. Urmson and Marina Sbisà, 2d ed. (Cambridge, Mass.: Harvard University Press, 1975).

11. Deconstructive critique appears to entail that performative contradiction is covertly inherent in the nature of discourse. This view, so outrageous to critics, contradicts itself precisely by making its contradiction overt. Perhaps the point is that trying to make shared sense of life is not at all the same thing as issuing nonparadoxical utterances.

15

In Defense of Poiesis:
The Performance of Self
in Communicative Praxis

Lenore Langsdorf

> If the deconstruction of the subject is an announcement of the
> first revolution in current philosophical and scientific thinking,
> the recovery and restoration of the subject within the folds of
> the space of communicative praxis sets in motion the second
> revolution [which] . . . will make possible the recognition of the
> subject in the hermeneutical self-implicature of the speaker and
> actor within a form of life as decentered subjectivity, and will
> provide the directions for detailing its genealogy and its patterns
> of individual and social formation.
>
> —*Calvin O. Schrag,* Communicative Praxis and the Space of Subjectivity

G ranted, communicative praxis weaves a space for subjectivity; but
just how does the weaver come to be, within that space? Does the
space dictate a particular sort of subject, or do subjects config-
ure their spaces, or is there a reciprocal interaction between the always
mysterious (and currently much-maligned) subject and the space within
which it dwells? I want to argue here for that reciprocal relation, by extending Schrag's concept of communicative praxis as an "interweaving"
or "amalgam of discourse and action."[1] "Discourse and action are *about*
something, *by* someone, and *for* someone," he holds.[2] "Communicative
praxis [he continues] thus displays a referential moment (about a world
of human concerns and social practices), a moment of self-implicature
(by a speaker, author, or actor), and a rhetorical moment (directedness
to the other)."[3] It is interest in the "genealogy" of the second facet of

that display—the "self-implicature" of a speaker, author, or actor—in relation to the third—the "rhetorical moment"—that leads me to defend poiesis as a performative, as well as a productive, process that typically is overshadowed by praxis. In what follows, I sketch Schrag's conception of communicative praxis and its implicated subject in order to thematize this performative aspect.

Schrag's analysis, as it develops in *Communicative Praxis and the Space of Subjectivity* (1986) and in *The Self after Postmodernity* (1997), leads to his discerning a dimension of "transcendence" that is made present as a supervenient aspect of the doings that comprise discourse, action, and community. This presence is a matter of our making, rather than our doing, and so I turn to the classical notion of poiesis, in contrast to (but always also, as a moment within) praxis. I sketch Plato's and Aristotle's conceptions of poiesis, praxis, and *theoria*, in order to propose that Plato's denigration of poiesis instigated an emphasis (beginning with Aristotle) on the formulaic sense of techne as technique, at the expense of the innovative sense that is manifest in artistic production and that often is associated with crafts in contrast to manufacture. I characterize this neglected mode of making as performative, in contrast to productive. On the basis of these two senses of making, I argue for two dimensions within poiesis. One dimension is the making of things—spatiotemporally existent entities—which are the intrinsic product of poiesis. The second is the constituting of self in performances that may also produce things. The subjectivity that comes into being in the space of communicative praxis is the extrinsic, or transcendent, result of poiesis.

Communicative Praxis as Production and Performance

> One has discourse only in the performance of a saying, in which the act of speaking and the system of language conspire as a unitary event. It is in and through this unitary event that the speaking subject is implicated. Here the question "Who is speaking?" is not only permissible—it is unavoidable. . . . The "I" and the "you" are, as it were, coconstituted, sharing a common, intersubjective space. . . . The "I" and the "you" thus need to be seen as coemergents within a more encompassing intentional fabric of intersubjectivity. No "I" is an island, entire of itself; every subject is a piece of the continent of other subjects, a part of the main of intersubjectivity.
>
> —*Calvin O. Schrag,* Communicative Praxis and the Space of Subjectivity

Speaking, which for Schrag always includes "the deployment of gestural meaning and articulations through bodily motility," rather than being limited to verbal behavior, is one element of the "multifaceted event" that is discourse. The activity of speaking certainly is a productive one, and Schrag is more interested in *how* its products are formed than in *what* those products are: "The reality of praxis as a form resides in the forming process itself, which proceeds by way of an appropriation of established patterns of custom and habit and a distanciation and critical disengagement wherewith the established patterns are redescribed, modified, or straightway displaced." Analysis of this "forming process" is one that must begin in the middle, for we—who are the subjects (analysts) who do analysis as well as its objects (subject matter)—"never stand at a beginning but are always somehow already begun, held within a web of delivered discourse, social practices, professional requirements, and the daily decisions of everyday life."[4]

To the extent that this web is a tightly fused one (so to speak), it seems that a subject's forming process has little room for innovation, because appropriation is constrained to reproduce what that web provides for the subject-in-formation's experience. In that case the "space of communicative praxis" would be more aptly characterized as an amalgam than as an interweaving, intertwining, or interplay. Schrag uses all of these metaphors in the course of explicating the texture of communicative praxis, although the cluster of "inter-" terms predominates as his inquiry proceeds.[5] Yet an "amalgam" is a fused and stable mixture of diverse components, such as the substance used to fill dental cavities, while "interweaving," "intertwining, and "interplay" connote an entwining of components that remain distinct and available for refiguration. This difference suggests an ambiguity within Schrag's analysis that threatens his claim that what is appropriated may be "redescribed, modified, or straightway displaced." This is an instructive ambiguity in that it encourages closer examination of our mundane assumptions about the genesis of self and instigates criticism of social scientific constructs—rooted in those assumptions—which encourage conceiving of subjectivity as closer to a fusion than to a woven textile or basket.

A metaphor that suggests malleable reticulation, such as "interweaving," supports Schrag's conviction that neither "the social doctrine" that "defines the self as simply an ensemble and product of societal relations" nor the "individualist perspective" that "argues for a self-constituting individuality that proceeds independently of relations with others" is an "acceptable" alternative "for elucidating the portrait of the self as a human subject."[6] Both "sociologism" and "egologism" provide explanations of how selves are produced from materials that are supplied either externally or internally. Both models incline toward the "amal-gam" metaphor, insofar as they understand the formation of self as a fusion of tendencies or characteristics that are provided by a particular environment. Schrag rejects both sociologism and egologism because they do not enable us to understand how the "struggles of embodied agents seeking liberation and recognition in a concrete lifeworld of con-frontation and participation" may succeed in not simply reproducing that life-world in their actions, but in making present, through their per-formances, selves who transcend those life-worlds.[7] We need to consider, then, how "the forming process itself," as it appropriates an environment, enables the emergence of selves within processes that range across a spec-trum from reproductive to innovative. Both lived experience and textual reflection are relevant to that consideration, although phenomenologi-cal analysis privileges the former.

Observation of actual self-formation processes suggests that this ap-propriation is not a matter of simply importing, or being inscribed in and even determined by, the past. When we inquire into the genesis of any process of self-implicature, we can identify possibilities for appropriation that remain distantiated from the self-in-formation—perhaps as a matter of literal or cultural distance from the immediate context of a "forming process"; perhaps as a result of choice, causal relations, or happenstance that disengages those possibilities from a particular process. Reflection upon the upbringing of children within environments that appear to be the same for several children who mature into dramatically different social beings persuades me that the "web of delivered discourse" and "so-cial practices" informing communicative praxis as it develops a space for subjectivity is not a matter of simply incorporating what is available. My own experience of child raising is expanded by folk wisdom stories of sib-lings who grow up to be judges and criminals, or nurturing parents and abusive parents, or advocates of country living and convinced urbanites. One way of accounting for the emergence of those individuals from (so to speak) a common pool of possibilities is to posit biological causes and genetic dispositions that respond to "why" questions. Given the scarcity of longitudinal microanalytic studies of child development, responses that invoke causal relations and/or happenstance have a certain plausibility.

Another way of understanding the emergence of self through ap-propriation of an environment is to recognize that self-implicature within communicative praxis is a creative process in which an emergent self performs in ways that actualize some, but not all, possibilities for becom-ing. One source of evidence for this mode of explanation comes from reflection upon the common experience of "turning over a new leaf." Here again folk wisdom adds to my own experience of persons who have been troubled by a variety of threats to their visions of the good life (such as alcoholism, compulsive gambling, and eating disorders) and were able to construe a changed vision of their relationship to those threats in the course of communicative activity generated in Alcoholics Anonymous or similar twelve-step programs. Their telling of that process typically includes mentioning that there was no new information transmitted in that communicative activity. Rather, engaging in specific new performances (e.g., participating in meetings, having conversations with their sponsors, disrupting entrenched daily schedules with periods for meditation) enabled them to reconfigure their situations with alternative meanings that arose from those innovative performances. These meanings were not given *to* them, however. Rather, close analysis of their communicative praxis reveals a rhetorical dimension that broadens Schrag's characterization of discourse and action as always "*by* someone and *for* someone," as well as "*about* something": There is a rhetorical force in their innovative performances that makes communication both by, and for, the participant who is engaged in reconfiguring his or her situation. This efficacy broadens Schrag's recognition of the rhetorical moment as being a "directedness to the other" to include its efficacy for (as well as by) the emergent self-as-other.[8] That is, engaging in these performances enables an emergent self to appropriate alternate meanings that were created in his or her own communicative praxis, rather than reproduced from others' experience or produced for a discourse partner's consumption. The emergent self comes to know itself as capable of more than—and even, as other than—its own history.

We can now add textual reflection to these examples of lived-experiential evidence for innovative, in contrast to reproductive, doing and knowing. Schrag's discussion offers this textual clue for understanding self-emergence as a performative creation from elements that interweave to form the space of subjectivity:

> In a manner reminiscent of Kant, we can say that knowledge of the other self *begins* with experience, but then we must quickly add . . . that our knowledge of the other self does not *arise out* of experience. Knowledge of the other as other arises out of exterior and supervenient forces that impinge or intrude on our experience—forces issuing from visages, voices, and actions always already extant. This is most poignantly the case when these visages, voices, and actions are signals and cries of discontent, oppression, and suffering.[9]

This remark's reference to "the other self" can be extended to include the emergent self, which is already somewhat "other" than the self from which it begins (given the intrinsic changes necessitated by the flux of temporality and sedimentation). It suggests that self-emergence is a matter of a particular sort of praxis that arises from the emergent self's performances, but draws upon "supervenient forces" that transcend the experience from which that emergent self begins. These can constitute "a way of dwelling" that Schrag calls "responsibility" in contrast to a reproductive form of praxis that he calls "responsivity": "Responsivity functions basically as a descriptive term; responsibility [in contrast] connotes . . . an ethical stance, an ethos, a way of dwelling in a social world that gives rise to human goals and purposes."[10] Insofar as I am "responding to prior discourse and prior action," Schrag goes on to say, "the parameters for any socialization of the self have already been marked out. Within those parameters the self never begins itself; it finds itself to be always already begun . . . by virtue of its responsivity to the speech and action of others."[11] Responsibility, however, involves going beyond those always-already-set parameters into "a way of dwelling in a social world" that accomplishes self-implicature in performances that engage those "supervenient forces" in innovative rather than reproductive ways. In everyday terms, we come to know things otherwise than we had known them, and so "*make* something of the situation," rather than merely continue "*doing* business as usual."

We can fill in something of the nature of this difference—which I want to elaborate upon as the presence of poiesis (innovative making) within praxis (mundane doing), and more particularly, as the efficacy of performance in poiesis—through Schrag's characterization of the "economy of discourse." With reference to his earlier articulation of self-implicature (in *Communicative Praxis and the Space of Subjectivity*), Schrag sets out, in *The Self after Postmodernity*, to "examine the formation process of the self as a who that is implicated in the economy of discourse . . . [which] involves a production and consumption, a distribution and exchange, of speech and language."[12] Although the "production" part of this economy is clear, the "consumption" part gives one pause. Is the self consumed, as well as produced, in this speaking and/or use of language? Is the self, in other words, taken up into (consumed by) its discursive practices, so that it is nothing but those practices? Or does it transcend—even though it is formed within—those practices?

Schrag chooses the latter conception of the self as implicated in, although not consumed by, its communicative praxis. The self "at the crossroads of speech and language," he recognizes, "understands itself as a self that has already spoken, is now speaking, and has the power yet to speak."[13] Speaking "already" and speaking "now" certainly are understandable as producing discourse, and there is a sense in which we could say that those productions are "consumed" as materials for the forming process of the self who speaks. Yet the "power yet to speak" is a potential for production, rather than a production. As such, it is not available for consumption. It stands precariously outside of the "economy of discourse" insofar as it does not simply reproduce what has been spoken and so has already been traded about within that economy, but carries an innovative potential; a promise of creating a self who can "make something" of its situation, rather than merely continuing to "do business" within the (past and present) economy of discourse. This is a self who transcends the specificity of its situation, in much the same way as "language transcends every particular speech act," as action is "a going over to that which is not yet," and as the "totality of received social practices" that constitutes a community "exceeds its particular hold on the world"—that is, cannot be equated with the particular way those practices are manifest at any moment.[14] This potential for transcendence allows Schrag to speak of such a self as being "*in* history but not *of* history."[15]

A certain double-sidedness to the space of subjectivity is suggested by Schrag's development of the theme of transcendence. It moves us farther from conceptualizing self as constrained by an amalgam fused from extant ways of being a self, and so only able to reproduce those ways. Possibilities that transcend those existent ways, if realized by innovative performances, serve as materials for continual, and even novel, reweaving of the space of subjectivity. Instead of merely "making do," the emergent self's praxis can realize those possibilities and thereby engage in the *making* of self, rather than continuing to *do* what the self of past experience did. More generally speaking, the emergent self can be understood as continuing to do what has been done—to reproduce extant patterns—or its *doing* can be in the service of *making* a self from possibilities discerned as "residing on the other side of the economies of human experience."[16] The latter path, I want to propose, is one of poiesis, rather than praxis. We need now to examine the history of these concepts, in order to consider the cogency of that claim and to assess the value of understanding the self as a result of poiesis occurring within communicative praxis.

Poiesis as Performance and Production

> The Greek term "praxis" . . . is usually rendered as "practice."
> It could also be translated as "action," "performance," or

"accomplishment." . . . Praxis displays a different sort of knowing than the knowing appropriate to *theoria.*

On the heels of this distinction, however, there follows rather closely another, which plays on the difference between praxis and poiesis. Poiesis as artifactual production is distinguished both from the sphere of human action and from theoretical philosophizing. That which guides this artifactual production is *techne,* which is assigned a role distinct from those of *episteme* and *phronesis.* . . . Poiesis as artifactual production is an activity that produces an object that lies beyond the dynamics of the activity itself. . . . Now a measure of technique is involved in calculation of the results of such an activity as well as in the mapping of means, such as rules and procedures, to attain the end. . . . Nonetheless, this programming of technique is not of the essence of *techne.*

—*Calvin O. Schrag,* Communicative Praxis and the Space of Subjectivity

Edward P. J. Corbett notes (in his introduction to *The Rhetoric and Poetics of Aristotle*) that "the *Poetics* has been unquestionably the most influential and the most discussed document of literary criticism in the Western world."[17] This influence extends beyond literary criticism, however, for Aristotle's conceptions of *theoria,* poiesis, and praxis continue to dominate our scholarly and everyday understanding of the differences among art, ethics, politics, and science. It will be useful to sketch his taxonomy of those domains before focusing on the differences he proposes between poiesis and praxis and their correlative kinds of knowing.

Theoria requires the kind of knowing called episteme, in contrast to doxa (opinion). At its best (and especially in the Platonic scheme that Aristotle inherited), this is sophia (wisdom, the province of philosophy). It also includes physics, the science of material things (which are subject to change), and mathematics, the science of mathematical entities (which are immutable and can be studied independently of their material conditions), as well as metaphysics, the science of being (whether material or nonmaterial being). In all of these domains, episteme concerns itself with what is necessarily so. Theoretical knowing is at its best when it reveals the nature of a science's subject matter through demonstrative reasoning (inference from certain premises) that traces the being of any subject matter to the principles (causes, in Aristotle's sense) of its being as it is.

From the perspective of our current interest in praxis and poiesis, the most salient point to be made about *theoria* is that, in a profound sense, it is not practical and also not productive. In other words, it differs from both praxis and poiesis in that it is concerned with general knowledge, without regard for either its applicability to acting (doing) in particular circumstances or to fabricating (making) particular products. *Theoria* may well inform our knowledge of particular things; but it does not entail any particular knowledge claim or produce its subject matter.

Praxis requires the kind of knowing called *phronesis*. Without question, it is as much practical as *theoria* is impractical, for its subject matter is the actions by which humans go about their everyday lives as members of communities—whether that be the Aristotelian polis or contemporary political or professional communities. Correlative to *theoria*'s strict concern with thinking, praxis is concerned with acting as it is informed by thinking. This "informing" is a matter of tracing action to its principles (causes)—of using cognitive procedures intrinsic to *theoria*—but now in relation to very different subject matter. The growth of an acorn into an oak tree is a topic for *theoria* (specifically, physical science) because, once it is determined that the "final cause" of an acorn is to be an oak, its developmental stages can be accurately known, and both hindrances and deviations can be (theoretically, at least) predicted and controlled.

Aristotle posits a correlative "final cause" for human beings: to live the good life, which includes seeking both knowledge and happiness. Although humans are material things, we are also rational things. Thus Aristotle recognizes that humans (unlike acorns) make a multiplicity of choices toward that end, and we make them in highly complex ways—given that we do so in the context of historical and present communities. Choices can collide; thus, their implications and consequences cannot be known with any certainty. In other words, humans are intrinsically interactive with their environments, whereas acorns are acted on by their environments but do not act on them in significant ways. Since the development of humans toward their goals (i.e., the accomplishing of deeds that we hope, or expect, will work toward our "final cause" of living the good life) is quite a different matter from the process that takes acorns toward their ends, (physical) science will give us only partial knowledge of human action. However, lack of scientific knowledge (in the sense of *theoria;* i.e., certain knowledge gained through demonstrative reasoning) does not mean that we act without any knowledge at all. Rather, we use practical reason to arrive at contingent knowledge of the practices appropriate to particular situations and their immediate goals. Given the complexity involved in choosing and using practices, *phronesis* as a mode of reasoning focuses on process rather than product; on human doing and the deeds that intrinsically develop in our doing.

Poiesis requires a different kind of knowing called techne. If we were to arrange these three modes of knowing along a continuum from certain to contingent, techne would occupy the middle position. It almost seems as though techne is the object of a pulling and tugging from both episteme and praxis: now toward certainty, insofar as techne can be reduced to the sort of replicable methods that characterize science; now toward contingency, insofar as it does not allow of strictly codified methods. Correlatively, poiesis seems pulled at times toward episteme, and at other times toward praxis. (I will return to this point.) Unlike "*theoria*" and "praxis," the term "poiesis" resists comfortable transfer into English. We transfer "*theoria*" as "science" because two of Aristotle's kinds of *theoria* (physics and mathematics, although not metaphysics) fall within what we now typically understand as science. "Praxis," perhaps because of Marx's use of the term, at least connotes something of everyday "practice"—despite the undoubted differences in Marx's and Aristotle's usages. "Poiesis" has an auditory closeness to "poetic" which is both furthered and confounded by Aristotle's explication in the *Poetics, Nicomachean Ethics,* and *Metaphysics.* I want now to look at those discussions in order to propose that poiesis includes two distinct kinds of making. The defense of poiesis which I develop here depends on recognizing that one of these modes, which typically is not distinguished from the other, is the kind of making that constitutes human subjects within the space of communicative praxis.

The *Poetics* is a book about how to write (make) plays. Aristotle here uses the same general pattern of cognition in relation to that subject matter as he does elsewhere (e.g., in discussing how to organize a government in the *Politics*). First, develop a taxonomy that reveals different species within the genus, in hierarchical arrangement. Then, determine the principles that make the genus and each species that which it is— and, in particular, determine the relevant final cause of each. Finally, when analysis reveals that the genus is one that must be made, figure out the general method that will organize the appropriate material, efficient, and formal causes, so that the product will be made in accord with its final cause. This process is described in Aristotle's detailed discussion in book 6 of the *Nicomachean Ethics,* where he refers to techne as the mode of reasoning used in making things. Not all "things" are made; for example, mathematical objects are simply accessible to thinking, and natural things such as acorns generate themselves.[18] The things which humans make are initiated in the same sort of thinking that results in action.[19] But making (poiesis) differs from acting (praxis) by virtue of its ends. Unlike action, which is intrinsically connected to its end, making results in a "qualified" or relative end as well as an ultimate end, both of which are "other than itself."[20] For instance, the end of the "particular operation" which is the carpenter's making of a chair is the chair itself. But its ultimate end (final cause) is enabling bodies to be seated above the ground. Thus, the excellence of the carpenter's productivity can be judged by how comfortable and durable the chair is when used toward that end.

In the *Poetics*, Aristotle determines that the making of poetry (what we would today call literary art, including prose), as well as of other arts (such as painting, dance, and music), imitates actual life. That is, production begins with ends that already exist (e.g., already-made chairs, dances, and poems) and uses those as patterns for the making of other instances. The influence of Plato's analysis of production is clear here. Richard McKeon summarizes that position as "a constant relation between something which is and something made like it":

> The imitator is defined as a maker of images and is contrasted to the maker of realities; unlike the latter he has no knowledge of being but only of appearances. Both varieties of maker, moreover, stand in contrast to an eternal reality. Like the painter who paints the picture of a couch, the imitator makes a product at three removes from nature, for he imitates not that which is but that which seems to be. . . . All the arts are imitative . . . All verbal accounts . . . are imitations. . . . The universe is distinguishable into three fundamental forms: the model form, the imitation of the model, and the Space or Receptacle in which Becoming takes place.[21]

He goes on to note that for Plato the "productive arts" are "divided into those which produce things and those which produce images." But in Plato's understanding, all production imitates eternal ideas, whether directly (e.g., the chair made by a skilled woodworker) or indirectly (e.g., the chair painted, say, in van Gogh's *Portrait of the Artist's Room*).

McKeon finds a radical difference between Plato's and Aristotle's conception of imitation. He writes, "For Aristotle imitation is not . . . of ideas . . . nor is it . . . of appearances [which are] themselves imitations"; nor is it "of an idea in the mind of the artist. . . . Rather, imitation is of particular things; the object of imitation, according to the statement of the *Poetics* which seems to be intended to apply to all the fine arts, is the actions of men."[22] We have here (in *Poetics* 2) the impetus for a more nuanced analysis of production (poiesis) as differentiated by virtue of whether imitation is of things or of actions. Before taking up that impetus, we need to look more closely at Plato's concept of imitation in order to emphasize the contrast between his and Aristotle's conceptions of production.

When ideas are the prototypes for production, as in Plato's analysis, there is no reason to understand the productive process of things that have intrinsic use value (such as chairs and buildings) as essentially different from that of "images" that imitate actions (such as visual, verbal, and kinetic works of art; e.g., paintings, poems, dances). For Plato, the only difference is that of being two, rather than three, removes from the object (idea) imitated.[23] Plato maintains the superiority of being only two removes from the idea in one's production, and thus he assumes that "craftsmen" (whose imitation of ideas gives us things of evident use value) are superior to "artists" (whose imitation of actions gives us images without intrinsic use value). In other words, he does not differentiate productive processes on the basis of what and how they produce. Rather, Plato understands any making as an imitation of its correlative idea ("model form"), regardless of whether the product is a "thing" (a chair in which sitting can occur) or an "image" (a painting of a chair; a dance that evokes a chair within particular movements). His orientation is toward the one idea that both the carpenter's chair and the painter's chair imitate.

This focus upon immutable ideas (ideal Forms) deflects analysis away from actual productive processes, their results, and the extent to which those results further the "final cause" of living well for participants in the productive processes. In terms of Aristotle's four causes (or principles): for Plato, the formal, rather than final, cause is paramount. Thus, attention is turned from the particularity of various productive processes, the need to adapt to changing circumstances, the kind of knowing that develops in *phronesis* (rather than in episteme), and how participants in particular productive processes accomplish the "final cause" of living the good life. Plato's attention remains fixed upon discerning a unified method for grasping the Form that in a sense produces, and certainly transcends, both the producing and its product.

In contrast, Aristotle's analysis focuses attention on how a productive process achieves its (final) end. Thus when Aristotle focuses on poetry—which we may take as exemplary of verbal, visual, and kinetic art—he finds that tragedy, which imitates the actions comprising certain kinds of plots, is its highest species.[24] He proposes that tragedy's final cause—the end toward which the poet aims—is the pleasure an audience takes from learning about the actions that comprise it. The poet's central concern in producing tragedy, then, is how to organize its principles (material, efficient, and formal causes) and its parts (plot, character, thought, diction, melody, and spectacle) appropriately, in order to make images of actions that contribute to accomplishing that final cause. Obviously, a thing is made in this process—a play, a musical composition, and a painting—have tangible manifestations that allow attention to them apart from the actions that produce them, much as a chair, building, or pair of shoes can be attended to in themselves. Both paintings and buildings are things situated in time and space; they are intrinsic results of their producers' actions, and their excellence is judged in relation to other such things which instantiate a particular Form. Yet productive processes also have extrinsic ends. The play evokes images of actions for those who participate in it, whether as producer (playwright, painter, dancer, etc.) or as consumer (audience member). This second kind of product leads Aristotle to distinguish production (poiesis) from action (praxis): "Production has an end other than itself, but action does not; good action is itself an end."[25]

I suggested, when noting that the making of a chair is prototypical for understanding production, that Plato's conception of the craftsman's production of things has dominated our conception of making (poiesis). This prototype constrains our understanding of production by emphasizing closeness of fit between two different kinds of reality: the intrinsic product (the physical chair, etc.) and the idea (Form) of the chair. The carpenter is supposed to produce a physical copy of the nonphysical Form. The particular contingencies of production—such as availability of materials and various kinds of seating needs (e.g., classroom in contrast to living-room furnishings)—and the creativity exercised in accommodating those contingencies are ignored in favor of whether the producer succeeds in instantiating what is judged (by the craftsman, as instructed by the philosopher) as the essence of the relevant Form. In effect, thinking is privileged over acting, and as a result, our understanding of production inclines toward *theoria* that delivers a proper method (technique) for making things, rather than toward praxis that enables performance in accord with the "final cause" of both the human and artifactual participants in production.

Aristotle's conception of poiesis clearly is rooted in Plato's, yet he focuses on performing actions to be imitated, rather than on imitating ideas in the making of things. This enables Aristotle to notice a close connection between becoming a particular kind of self and performing particular kinds of action: "Men become builders by building houses, and harpists by playing the harp."[26] In both these examples, making on the basis of techne is not simply doing (building the house; playing the harp). Rather, it is a two-dimensional affair: It produces both intrinsic and extrinsic ends. One dimension produces an intrinsic thing (the house or music) by systematically using particular materials in particular ways to make an object quite distinct from those materials and methods. Aristotle makes this point clear in relation to his second model for making, medicine, for he emphasizes that the art of medicine transcends piece-meal connection of means (e.g., medications; surgery) to ends (e.g., cure; health): "Men of experience discern the fact 'that' but not the reason 'why,' whereas experts know the . . . explanation."[27] Medicine as an art systematically produces health by assessing an individual situation on the basis of what is generally the case for a category of situations and then applying that generalization to a particular instance of that illness: "To have art is to grasp that all members of the group of those who are ill of this disease have been helped by this medicine."[28] This syematic-ity reemphasizes the focus on method that inclines poiesis so strongly toward *theoria* in Plato's understanding. But Aristotle's explication in terms of imitating (recreating) *actions,* rather than instantiating ideas, brings poiesis into a balance of *theoria* and praxis; thinking and doing. In other words, it balances the first dimension (intrinsic production of things) with a second: extrinsic production of the *makers* of those things as particular kinds of selves, by virtue of their performative imitation of particular kinds of actions. The "end other than itself," which, for Aristotle, characterizes poiesis in contrast to praxis, is the emergent self that is implicated in productive activities.

We can now relate this multifaceted understanding of poiesis to Schrag's analysis of self-emergence within communicative praxis.

Communicative Poiesis

> In our society, art has become something that is related only to objects and not to individuals or to life. That art is something which is specialized or done by experts who are artists. But couldn't everyone's life become a work of art? Why should the lamp or the house be an art object but not our life? . . . From the idea that the self is not given to us, I think there is only one practical consequence: we have to create ourselves as a work of art.
>
> —*Michel Foucault,* Ethics: Subjectivity and Truth

The importance of this second dimension of extrinsic production of selves in relation to Schrag's explication of the work of communicative praxis in constructing the space of subjectivity may best be indicated by referring to McKeon's remark (quoted earlier) on Aristotle's cosmol-ogy: "The universe is distinguishable into three fundamental forms: the model form, the imitation of the model, and the space or receptacle in which becoming takes place."[29] Subjectivity becomes (takes place) in the space of communicative praxis; but it is not equivalent to that space. Rather, communicative praxis enables the formation of selves—particular instances of subjectivity—through imitation of actions that occurs within that praxis. Once we acknowledge that "imitation" is not always (although it can be) a matter of producing a mirror image, nor of instantiating an ideal form, we can seek out imitative processes that use possibilities as their "model."

Any productive activity takes retentions of already achieved actions as possible models, yet when we attend to an actual process of production, we discern that the producer works at a different place, in a different time, with materials that differ in their particularity (even if not by virtue of the kind of thing they are) from other materials, and is engaged in performances that result in a product that is at least minimally (spatiotemporally) different from those which resulted from the models provided by retention. Thus any making of an object implies the intrinsic end of its activity—products such as chairs and lamps, as well as sentences and paintings—even as it implicates the emergent self who is performing that productive activity. This is to say that forming the intrinsic product out of actual (real) materials simultaneously generates the extrinsic, transcendent self out of possibilities for performing. In both cases, we have "an open-textured gathering of expanding possibilities" for making both the object and the self.[30] The complexity and contingency of possible consequences for the making of the self, however, means that the "technique" sense of techne can extend, at most, to knowing how to perform, not to how to create the self which is made in those performances. "The who of discourse," Schrag reminds us, "is an achievement, an accomplishment, a performance, whose presence to itself is admittedly fragile, subject to forgetfulness and semantic ambiguities."[31] When we respond to Foucault's question by turning our attention from its usual focus on the things we make to the performances that are a condition for that making, we may recognize that we are always performing ourselves as the subjects of poiesis, even as we are producing its objects.

Notes

1. Calvin O. Schrag, *Communicative Praxis and the Space of Subjectivity* (Bloomington: Indiana University Press, 1986), pp. 31, 33 (hereafter cited as *CPSS*).

2. Ibid., p. viii, cf. p. 179.

3. Ibid., p. viii.

4. Ibid., pp. 34, 33, 63, 4.

5. Ibid., pp. 11, 33, 34, 37, 46, 47 (for use of "amalgam"), pp. 31, 34, 102, 121, 204 (for use of "interweaving," "intertwining," and "interplay"), pp. 23, 30, 37, 40, 43, 46, 47, 63, 144, 170 (for use of "texture").

6. Calvin O. Schrag, *The Self after Postmodernity* (New Haven, Conn.: Yale University Press, 1997), pp. 79–80 (hereafter cited as *SP*).

7. Ibid., p. 81.

8. Schrag, *CPSS*, p. viii.

9. Schrag, *SP*, p. 85.

10. Ibid., p. 91.

11. Ibid.

12. Ibid., p. 16.

13. Ibid., p. 17.

14. Ibid., p. 111.

15. Ibid., p. 109.

16. Ibid., p. 114.

17. Edward P. J. Corbett, *The Rhetoric and Poetics of Aristotle* (New York: Modern Library, 1954), p. xx.

18. Aristotle, *Nichomachean Ethics* 6.1140a13–16 (hereafter cited as *NE*). Translations are from Aristotle, *Nichomachean Ethics*, trans. Martin Ostwald (Indianapolis: Bobbs-Merrill Company, 1962).

19. *NE* 6.1139b1–2.

20. *NE* 6.1140b6.

21. R. McKeon, "Literary Criticism and the Concept of Imitation in Antiquity," *Modern Philology* 34 (Aug.—Dec. 1936), pp. 1–35; reprinted in R. S. Crane et al., eds., *Critics and Criticism, Ancient and Modern* (Chicago: University of Chicago Press, 1952), pp. 152–54.

22. Ibid., pp. 161, 161–62.

23. Plato, *Republic* 10.597e. Translations are from Plato, *The Republic*, trans. G. M. A. Grube (Indianapolis: Hackett Publishing, 1974).

24. Aristotle, *Poetics* 26. Translations are from Aristotle, *Poetics*, trans. Edward P. J. Corbett, in his *Rhetoric and Poetics of Aristotle*.

25. Aristotle, *Metaphysics* 6.4.1140b5–7; cf. 6.4.1140a2–3. Translations are from Aristotle, *Metaphysics*, trans. Richard Hope (Ann Arbor: University of Michigan Press, 1960).

26. Aristotle, *NE* 2.1102a34–35.

27. Aristotle, *Metaphysics* 1.981a28–31.

28. *Metaphysics* 1.981a10–12.

29. McKeon, "Literary Criticism," p. 154.

30. Schrag, *SP*, p. 129.

31. Ibid., p. 33.

16

The Professions, the Humanities, and Transfiguration

Victor Kestenbaum

An examination of Cal Schrag's writings yields an interesting finding, one which I shall, rather boldly, turn into a recommendation for his future work, or at least some of his future work. The finding is this: In his books and articles, Cal says very little, indeed almost nothing, about the professions and the humanities, or about education in the professions and the humanities. One might imagine him responding by saying that the professions and the humanities are "practices" which involve experience, communication, reason, and the self; hence, everything he has written is relevant to some aspect of professional and humanistic practices. I think Cal would want to go further, deeper, than this, and in this chapter I urge him to do so.

There is one small, but notable, exception to the silence regarding the professions and the humanities in his work, and even this is only indirectly related to them. The exception is found in his article entitled "Liberal Learning in the Postmodern World," which was published in the *Key Reporter*. With the remarkable combination of verve and understatement that we have come to identify with him, Cal says: "The Phi Beta Kappa ideal remains intact, although it will need to be deconstructed and decentralized as an overarching principle of unification. It needs to be transfigured and articulated in a new way, but it should not be cast aside."[1] These two sentences set the context for this chapter and provide a succinct set of terms in which its aim can be stated. Cal's work in phenomenology, existentialism, hermeneutics, deconstructionism, and critical theory has taken its proper place as one of the more distinguished contributions to philosophy in the second half of the twentieth century.

What I should like to ask Cal is that he draw out some aspects of his thinking with particular reference to the ideals customarily associated with the professions and the humanities. What ideals are embodied in the professions and in the humanities? Are these ideals intact as we open a new century? Must these ideals be deconstructed? How does one concretely go about transfiguring and articulating ideals in a new way without, in some measure, casting them aside? What is left of the ideals which have historically shaped the professions and the humanities? Indeed, what is left of ideality?

Entangled with the notion of transfiguring as a change of concept and practice is the potential, if not the promise, of spiritual change, of spiritual transcendence. What have the professions and the humanities to do with transcendence? In *The Self after Postmodernity*, Cal defines transcendence as "a robust alterity." He then continues: "Responding to the beckoning of this otherness of transcendence, the wayfaring self struggles for a self-understanding and a self-constitution within the constraints of an irremovable finitude."[2] Transcendence as "robust alterity" is good as far as it goes, but does it go as far as it should . . . and could? Can the professions and the humanities quicken in us a responsiveness to something more than our finitude? Think here of Whitehead's assertion that "importance is derived from the immanence of infinitude in the finite."[3] Is it possible that the professions occasionally, and the humanities more frequently, do remove our finitude, for very short yet sublime moments? I turn to Cal for help with these questions, not because there is insufficient talk about the professions and the humanities, but for precisely the opposite reason. So much that is said is shallow, narrow, irrelevant, and unimportant. Cal can be counted on to improve this situation. In what follows, I suggest some starting points for Cal and some specific points where his work-to-date and the work-to-be-done intersect.

The Professions

Professions, professionals, and professionalization have been studied from such disciplinary perspectives as sociology, psychology, education, and to a lesser extent, what may be called philosophy of higher education. Mention should also be made of the philosophical study of professional ethics. Each of these vantage points focuses on certain problems or sets of problems. Sociological analysis typically attends to such matters as professional socialization (a large area including role theory, preservice images of the profession, student and practitioner characteristics, transmission of professional cultures, etc.), organizational settings, power, and control. Psychology considers issues related to career choice, career paths, self-concept and professional satisfaction, personality traits, and admissions criteria. Education concerns itself with instructional and curricula questions, professional growth and in-service programs, training functions.

Philosophy has both an older and a more recent voice in the discussion of the professions. Since the Greeks the value and proper place of the practical arts (need) and the theoretical arts (eros), the technical and the liberal, have always been the subject of dispute. Some of these issues received classic formulation in John Henry Cardinal Newman's work, *The Idea of the University,* particularly in the address entitled "Knowledge Viewed in Relation to Professional Skill."[4] Finally, in the past two decades, philosophers have become keenly interested in the ethical problems of the professions. Issues such as truth telling, responsibility, equity, confidentiality, and many others have stimulated philosophy to take a more "applied" turn, at least with respect to the professions.

These issues, along with the disciplines that address them, demonstrate considerable overlap. The current conversation about the professions is fairly extensive, diverse, and in many respects, important, but it is also relatively unphilosophical. Except for the specialized areas of philosophy of higher education and of professional ethics, we do not encounter much thinking about the professional and the professions which can be called philosophical.[5] Here I am referring not to individual professions but rather to philosophical discussion that takes professional activity as a distinct class of phenomena, just as philosophy of art, science, or religion approaches its objects of study. On its own, education has one of the longest histories of systematic philosophical self-examination, while some of the "newer" professions have, understandably, almost no history of such reflection.[6] Philosophical reflection in one profession is almost certain to have no effect on the philosophical reflections of other professions.

The specificity of a profession's practical concerns tends to be partially reproduced by, and through, the profession's philosophical concerns. This became clear to me during the three years that I edited *The Humanity of the Ill: Phenomenological Perspectives,* a volume to which Cal contributed a superb article, "Being in Pain."[7] At that time I was concerned with the culture of medicine and health care and with the ways in which these cultures think about the experience of illness. It seemed to me that there was an abundance of philosophical questions, not only about the phenomenology of illness, but also about the professionalization of illness. These questions involved professional knowledge, judgment, and practice. They involved beauty, evil, character, authority, time, expression, and interpretation, as well as the human condition

and human nature. In short, these questions involved humanistic concerns which might prompt, and promote, greater wisdom in connection
with illness, suffering, and pain but which were virtually absent from the
discourse—philosophical and otherwise—of the medical and the health
professions. There were many exceptions, but not enough to change my
belief that most of the philosophical questions under scrutiny served
either to clarify technologically induced problems or simply to get the
jaded health-care practitioner to be more "thoughtful" about the com-
plexities of health care through an occasional weekend workshop on
"Ethical Dilemmas of Nurses" (or physicians, or administrators) or on
"The Health Care Professional's Responsibility to Dying Patients." Neither of these roles is unimportant to philosophy, but neither seemed
destined to fully realize what Ernest Gellner has called the "cognitive
potential" of the humanistic disciplines, a concept that I would wish to
extend to the professional disciplines.

This realization is not solely dependent on philosophical work being done in, or to, the professions. It certainly will not occur, however,
until we have seen some of the philosophical, and broader, intellectual
issues involved in the concept and conduct of the professions in a broader
frame of reference than has been suggested (and required) by the traditions and practices of individual professions. I should like to note that for
some years I have been collecting material for a book entitled "A True
Professional: Philosophical Considerations." My interest in this area is
not unselfish: I live in the two environments roughly designated "liberal"
(college of arts and sciences) and "professional" (school of education).
Perhaps because it is a topic of such importance to me, I am a little
restrictive when it comes to imagining with whom I would wish to col-
laborate on such a project. This is an open invitation to Cal to join me in
thinking about the following issues and questions. I shall simply list them
in fragmentary form, capturing, I am afraid, the fragmentary status of my
thinking on them and revealing why I need Cal.

1. Since professionalism is a state of mind and a habit, what happens to the
   mind when it becomes professional? What happens to the professional
   mind when it becomes "experienced"? These questions require
   rethinking ideas about learning and socialization and about other
   traditional explanations for the endurance or "lastingness" of meaning.
   Few philosophers today are better positioned than Cal Schrag to deepen
   our understanding of the genesis of meaning in professional practice.

2. Let us consider the question that Donald Schon raises in his book, *The
   Reflective Practitioner: How Professionals Think in Action:* "How is professional
   knowing like and unlike the kinds of knowledge presented in academic
   textbooks, scientific papers, and learned journals?"[8] Donald's book is one

of the very few by a philosopher on the subject that I refer to as the philosophy of the professions. In his examination of the work of five professions—engineering, architecture, management, psychotherapy, and town planning—Schon finds plenty of work for a philosopher like Cal Schrag. Cal would have ample opportunity to mull over what it is to have something "in mind" (idea, plan, goal, intention, rule, image) and whether having something in mind is necessary for knowledgeable action (think here of Aristotle, James, Dewey, Heidegger, Merleau-Ponty, Wittgenstein). What does one expect a surgeon to have in mind, in hand, in language? A lawyer? A teacher?

3. What is the basis of professional judgment? What regulates the relationship between abstract idea and particular circumstance? Really, how far can *phronesis* take you? These questions consider judgment to be the play of presence and absence; of actuality and possibility.

4. The next questions concern the professional as natural pragmatist, the tension between the professional's search for epistemic authority and the deconstruction of the quest for epistemic foundations, and Rorty's position on epistemological grounding and the search for foundations. What is the nature of groundless professional authority? What sort of Schragian "communicative praxis" do we need?

5. The next questions concern Hannah Arendt's discussion of "thinking." How do practitioners respond to what she calls "reason's need to think beyond the limits of what can be known"? Why is thinking not decision making? What can be said regarding what she calls the "clash between thinking and willing"? Cal would offer considerable help in figuring out what to make of the following comment by Arendt in the context of the professions: "Will always wills to *do* something and thus implicitly holds in contempt sheer thinking, whose whole activity depends on 'doing nothing.' " Is this the source of the practitioner's frequent contempt for theory?

6. Let us finally consider the everyday life of the professional: the routinization of trouble, difficulty, and challenge versus the wonder of it all; the professional's stance toward unanswerable questions; how wonder approaches its objects; idealistic/realistic professionals and their relationship to wonder; immanence and transcendence and the ideal of professional growth.

Over the years I have made progress in thinking about such matters. Perhaps Cal will now have a little more time to join me in thinking about what Arendt calls "the tonality of mental activities" which is characteristic of a certain kind of mind, the professional mind. I am not unaware of the fact that Cal probably would spend four or five months simply on the phrase "professional mind."

The Humanities

John Dewey wrote in *Democracy and Education* (1916) that "education is the laboratory in which philosophic distinctions become concrete and are tested."[9] Today this is no less true, but as I have suggested above, the rise of the professions has created a new laboratory within which philosophical distinctions, problems, and issues take on contemporary definition and meaning. "Professional" has come to represent the embodiment of an ideal for the mind's development. More concretely, professional excellence has come to define the standards by which we judge the excellence of the mind's activities—in business, industry, health, art, and education. I want to make a few comments regarding education in the humanities and the effect of professionalization on humanist ideals. I will once again provide some indications where I think Cal has a great deal of work to do.

In "The Crisis in the Humanities and the Mainstream of Philosophy," Ernest Gellner writes:

> Philosophy provides or services the basic conceptual equipment of humanist thought. If some anxiety is felt throughout the humanist culture, it is echoed with enormously magnified forces in the secondary industry, philosophy. The crisis of philosophy is the accentuated echo of the "humanist" crisis.[10]

Since the publication of Gellner's essay in the 1970s, things have changed. If there is a crisis in the humanities, it probably is not the one Gellner had in mind. We are postmodern, Gellner was modern. His view of the crisis strikes us now as somewhat quaint, evoking in us a sort of nostalgia for *that* kind of crisis, one which antedates the politicization of the humanities, the culture wars, the canon wars, the deconstruction of hierarchies, and the resultant demotion of truth. The crisis for Gellner is that the humanist—the monk, the clerk, the man and woman of letters and sensibility, the all-purpose intellectual—has "lost much of his standing now as a source of *knowledge* about the world. The educated public in developed countries turns to the scientific specialist when it wants information about some facet of the world."[11] I do not believe Gellner was simply recycling C. P. Snow's concern about "two cultures." It goes deeper. We nervously, or haughtily, reassure ourselves that as humanists we have a reason for being which is almost unchallengeable: We ask the big questions, consider first and last things, reflect on the "why's" of existence and not just the "how's." How could such a central activity of mind, such an ultimate and basic activity, lose standing?

Before turning to Cal Schrag, I turn to Hannah Arendt. According to Arendt:

> Man has an inclination and, unless pressed by more urgent needs of living, even a need (Kant's "need of reason") to think beyond the limitations of knowledge, to do more with his intellectual abilities, his brain power, than to use them as an instrument for knowing and doing. Our desire to know, whether arising out of practical necessities, theoretical perplexities, or sheer curiosity can be fulfilled by reaching its intended goal; and while our thirst for knowledge may be unquenchable because of the immensity of the unknown, so that every region of knowledge opens up further horizons of knowables, the activity itself leaves behind a growing treasure of knowledge that is retained and kept in store by every civilization as part and parcel of its world. The activity of knowing is no less a world-building activity than the building of houses. The inclination or the need to think, on the contrary, even if aroused by none of the time-honored metaphysical, unanswerable "ultimate questions," leaves nothing so tangible behind, nor can it be stilled by allegedly definite insights of "wise men." The need to think can be satisfied only through thinking, and the thoughts which I had yesterday will be satisfying this need today only to the extent that I can think them anew.[12]

Arendt's distinction between thinking and knowing, between reason and intellect or cognition, is perhaps overly simplified, not as novel as she may have thought, and generally not as illuminating as it initially sounds. It nevertheless contains a basic insight into humanist culture and into the crisis which Gellner believed was facing humanist culture.

It is uncertain that practitioners in fields other than the humanities are "pressed" by "urgent needs of living" more than their humanist colleagues. It is also uncertain that they typically use their brainpower as "an instrument of knowing and doing" more than humanists do. Humanists are inspired by goals and tasks, and the "knowables" of existence enable them to get there, a condition which characterizes the work of nonhumanists as well. In addition, both humanists and nonhumanists desire to leave behind a record of successful practices; what is more, they desire to leave behind a "a growing treasure of knowledge." In the university we call that treasure "research" or "scholarship." What, then, is the difference between the professional in the humanities and in the nonhumanities?

The professional practitioner in a nonhumanities field is commonly regarded as one who can *act* expertly on the basis of superior *knowledge*. The professional in a nonhumanities field may think in order to know, but to profess in that field one must know and not merely think. The questions put to experience by fields other than the humanities should, ideally, be answerable, should lead to limitless "horizons of knowables." "Knowables," however, in or about *Moby Dick* or *Daisy Miller: A Study* or Plato's dialogues are not the principal substance, effect, or good of these works. The humanities have not one but three subject matters: experience, knowledge relevant to the experience, and thought about the experience. Thus, knowledge is not rejected by the humanistic fields. However, I think we should entertain the idea that the humanities teach us "to think beyond the limitations of knowledge" and that they do not find their fulfillment in knowing or a special kind of knowing as somehow unique to the humanities. That dimension of the life of the mind—and soul—which is inspired and sustained by the humanities depends for its life on tangibles such as books, paintings, performances of compositions, and plays. But our experience of such tangibles may not occur through a "knowable" and, sometimes, not even through a thinkable. We do, however, think *about* the experience, and often we press thought to imitate knowledge, to yield conclusions, even though thought "leaves nothing so tangible behind."

This is where I would like to hear from Cal. In his article "The Idea of the University and the Communication of Knowledge in a Technological Age," he says:

As we confront this threat of an overextension of the model of cybernetics we urge a recovery of the practice of maieutics. Indeed, a reclamation of the maieutic artistry of the Athenian Socrates may be the most urgent requirement of our time. This would make it possible for us to reestablish learning as an adventure in the pursuit of knowledge. It would enable us again to approach communication as a creative process of dialogue and dialectics and thus restore both language and thought to their deserved eminence in the life of the university. In the end it is language and thought that suffer the fate of displacement in a fully formalized cybernetic world. In restoring language and thought we at the same time restore those who teach and those who are taught in their full existential posture as inquiring minds, pursuing basic questions, capable of wonder in the face of the world. Maieutics, as the dialectic art of eliciting and educing, encourages the student to engage in that most difficult but also most rewarding forgotten achievement of the human mind—the adventure of thinking. Correspondingly, it challenges the teacher to fulfill what is assuredly one of the most demanding tasks in the odyssey of the human spirit—to allow and nurture this adventure of thinking.[13]

There is little disjunction here, which has *very* large implications and consequences for liberal and humanistic education, both in the university and in our K–12 classrooms across the country. Learning, Cal says, is "an adventure in the pursuit of knowledge." But, he says, the most rewarding—and forgotten—achievement of the mind is "the adventure of thinking." These two adventures are not necessarily antagonistic or incompatible, but if Arendt is right, neither are they identical or equivalent. Thinking ventures beyond the limitations, not simply of what is presently known, but "beyond the limitations of knowledge." Arendt sees two adventures. How many adventures does Cal see?

Schrag's essay, first presented at a conference in 1980, was published in 1982; since then, a great deal has changed in the humanities and in Cal's thinking about knowledge, experience, reason. With the publication of *Communicative Praxis and the Space of Subjectivity* (1986), *The Resources of Rationality* (1992), and *The Self after Postmodernity* (1997), Cal has the means to deepen our critical discussion of knowing and thinking in the humanities. Here are a few questions, comments, and observations which he might consider along the way:

1. One wonders about the relationship between what Cal calls "communicative praxis as expression" in *Communicative Praxis* and his assertion that learning is "an adventure in the pursuit of knowledge." He says:

> Expressive action should thus not be restricted to the deliverance of meaning through conscious motivation and reflective, deliberative acts. The sources of human motivation, and the layers of meaning that encircle them, are drawn from a wider context and a wider space, in which acquired habits, established customs, and historical trends mix and mingle.[14]

A student's hand goes up in response to the professor's question or remark or perhaps in response to that of another student. It may be a class in English literature, philosophy, music, classics, or religion. Should the professor restrict his or her response to the "deliverance of meaning" which is accessible through analysis and argumentation, that is, the communication of knowables? Are there "layers of meaning" which are essential to the humanities but which are not—cannot—be pursued as knowledge? How are such meanings to be communicated in a class? In other words, what praxis befits the professor of humanities who recognizes a difference between thinking and knowing?

2. The humanities are commonly thought to be among our major cultural resources for ennoblement. They benefit us through their

visions of human weakness and greatness; ultimately, through their portrayal of ideals that transcend circumstance and context. As we know, though, temporality and historicity matter to Cal. So we are not surprised when he says: "We are looking for that window on the world from which we might get a glimpse of ideality from the side of the temporality and historicity that envelop every speech performance."[15] Cal is not terribly happy with a "transcendental region of ideality," and Habermas comes in for criticism as a result of his disposition in favor of such a region. Even what Cal calls "Heidegger's existentialized version" of the transcendental viewpoint is not acceptable. So what does Cal want? He says:

> The ideals which guide self-actualization, as well as those that direct the course of society, are "forms of praxis." As forms of praxis they answer neither to a Platonic requirement, in which the becoming of praxis is a moving image of some transcendent idea, nor to a transcendental requirement, in which form is an *a priori condition* for action. The reality of praxis as a form resides in the forming process itself, which proceeds by way of an appropriation of established patterns of custom and habit and a distanciation and critical disengagement wherewith the established patterns are redescribed, modified, or straightway displaced.[16]

A high school student reads *The Old Man and the Sea* or a college student reads the poetry of Anne Sexton. These open, may open, for these students a region, realm, or field of ideality. Are these works thereby forms of praxis? What is won and lost when a novel or a poem is interpreted and experienced as a form of praxis? And suppose a student is moved just that much closer to self-understanding and self-actualization by the region of ideality offered in a poem, short story, play, or essay. Is that movement not at least partly inspired by "a moving image of some transcendent idea," say, love, friendship, spiritual peace, physical transformation, death?

    3. Points 1 and 2 above refer to Cal's arguments in *The Resources of Rationality*, where he has taken the transversal turn and the rationality or praxis is his target or destination. He says:

> Reason remains transversal to the various forms of our personal and social forms of life. It lies across them diagonally; it is neither vertically transcendent to them nor horizontally immanent within them. It operates "between" them in such a manner that it is able to critique, articulate, and disclose them without achieving a coincidence with any other particular form of discourse, thought, or action. The integrity of otherness—other forms of thought and other social practices—is maintained, accomplishing at once a better understanding of that which

is one's own and a recognition of the need to make accommodations and adjustments in the response to the presence of that which is other.[17]

"At once"? This is hopeful. Rather more common than an "at once" revision of the habitual structure of my being is the lurching, halting, erratic movement of what I am, what I know of what I am (or think I am), and so forth. It would be good to have much more from Cal not only on the suddenness of self-understanding but also more on the otherness afforded by the humanities. Transversal reason may not, as Cal says, achieve "a coincidence with any particular form of discourse, thought, or action." But what of the transversal human reasoner in our humanities courses? If Kant or Sophocles or T. S. Eliot or Beethoven speaks for the student, lifts up the student, is the student's coincidence with that inspiring soul to be rejected? Cal and I both like the idea of vigilance, and it helps a little to say that the student must be encouraged and helped to remain vigilant, to be wary of totalizations, to think *more*. But when we are stirred on the level of our habitual being by a poem, an idea, or a symphony, we simultaneously coincide with, and transcend, the world. The coincidence and transcendence may be sublime. It may be agony. Such coincidence may not be lasting or eternal, nor may transcendence, thereby permitting and even inviting what is other. But is the importance of the experience in its other, in its codicil?

4. I have been suggesting that as humanists we are moved by what Arendt beautifully calls "reason's need to think beyond the limits of what can be known."[18] This is not encouragement to be inattentive to knowables. It does encourage the realization that compared to the practical importance of knowers and knowables, humanist intimations of the unknowable and unresolvable are going to look pale, derivative, and almost irresponsible. In other words, thinking is fine, but then what? What do you do with it? What praxis follows from it? These are, one might say, natural questions, and they lead to this startling remark from Arendt: "Thinking, the quest for meaning—rather than the scientist's thirst for knowledge for its own sake—can be felt to be 'unnatural,' as though men, when they begin to think, engage in some activity contrary to the human condition."[19] Notice that Arendt is restrained. Thinking is not unnatural; it "can be felt" to be unnatural. Thinking is not contrary to the human condition; it is "as though" it were contrary to the human condition. Yet, even with such restraint and qualification, it is evident that Arendt's notion of thinking unsettles a great deal, including the priority which Cal gives to praxis.

In *The Self after Postmodernity,* Cal argues that disputes with regard to relativism contra absolutism, historicism contra universalism, and nihilism contra a priori values are generated "by the requirement of theory to lay out criteria of justification in advance of the specific practices to which such criteria might apply." He further suggests: "Let us suppose that the either/or that provides the occasion for both personal and social morality is not of a theoretical sort at all."[20] Cal is on the way to something big, and his arrival, while not unexpected, is nonetheless surprising:

> Against the backdrop of these suppositions one would do well to recommend a shift from theory to praxis, from antecedent rule-governed criteria to context-informed criteria, to an either/or that no longer stands in wait of a theory to swoop down from on high but instead is firmly ensconced within the everyday communicative practices where life's decisions take place.[21]

It would be a fine thing indeed to have more from Cal on this "shift from theory to praxis." I am not suggesting that this is a sudden shift, appearing only in the last couple of years of his work. The shift was there in his first book, *Existence and Freedom* (1961).[22] What I do suggest is that "reason's need to think beyond the limits of what can be known" may require, certainly allows, rationality to spread its wings beyond the knowables of context-conditioned praxis. The student who has been moved and enlightened by the poetry of Emily Dickinson or the short stories of John Updike may see the world differently, may make decisions that are different in character from those they made before reading these writers—decisions that may be different in any number of respects. Such decisions may reflect differences in habit or differences in habits of mind and may find expression in what Cal calls "communalized existence," in rather subtle, darting, insubstantial ways. These are the ways thinking shows itself in experience and then withdraws. That the humanities have practical value, I do not doubt. That they can withstand "a shift from theory to praxis" I have rather more doubt.

5. It seems to me that Cal is in an almost unique position to shed light on some of the questions which, on a deep level, trouble the humanities today. Take for example, the following from Allan Bloom:

> The natural sciences are able to assert that they are pursuing the important truth, and the humanities are not able to make any such assertion. That is always the critical point. Without this, no study can remain alive. Vague insistence that without the humanities we will no longer be civilized rings very hollow when no one can say what "civilized" means, when there are said to be many civilizations that are all equal. The claim of "the classic" loses all legitimacy when the classic cannot be believed to tell the truth.

The truth question is most pressing and acutely embarrassing for those who deal with the philosophic texts, but also creates problems for those treating purely literary works. There is an enormous difference between saying, as teachers once did, "You must learn to see the world as Homer and Shakespeare did," and saying, as teachers now do, "Homer and Shakespeare had some of the same concerns you do and can enrich your vision of the world." In the former approach students are challenged to discover new experiences and reassess old; in the latter, they are free to use the books in any way they please.[23]

Cal's distinction between "context-conditioned" and "context-determined" applies some much-needed philosophical pressure to Bloom's formulation of the "truth question." But Bloom applies considerable pressure on Cal's contextualism. Does Shakespeare tell the truth? Bloom apparently thought so, and he would have cited as evidence of the deterioration of the humanities Cal's rejection of "a foundationalist universality and necessity." For Bloom, Schrag's discussion about the communalized self "*in* history but not *of* history"[24] is a perfect example of a theoretical either/or which undermines humanistic study while seemingly embracing only a limited contextuality. For Schrag, Bloom's discussion about telling "the truth" is a perfect example of a theoretical either/or which undermines humanistic study by embracing a contextless universalism.

If the humanities speak to the human condition, how do they do so in light of Cal's books and articles? That is not a particularly elegant question, or at least not an elegant formulation of the question, but it puts the full force of the issue before us. Rather than multiply the questions soliciting Cal's attention, think of some of the chapter titles from a recent collection of essays, *What's Happened to the Humanities?* and the opportunties they afford for Schragian reflection. We have: "The Practice of Reading" by Denis Donoghue; "The Pursuit of Metaphor" by Christopher Ricks; "The Demise of Disciplinary Authority" by Louis Menand; and "Scholarship as Social Action" by David Bromwich. Or, consider some of chapter titles in a book by John M. Ellis, *Literature Lost: Social Agendas and the Corruption of the Humanities.* We have: "Activism and Knowledge," "Power, Objectivity, and PC Logic," and "Is Theory to Blame?"[25] Again, I would like to know Cal's thinking on such matters. I would like to know how he aligns praxis and the humanities in ways which respect their sometimes intersecting and sometimes divergent interests.

Most humanists are aware that they always have sought ways to naturalize their unnatural proclivity to "think beyond the limits of what can be known." Some have simply disavowed any interest in what cannot be known, confining their interest to methods and manners which at least look as though they are adding to our "treasure of knowledge." Another tactic is to accept knowing and doing as the primary, most natural motives in human beings and then try to dress them up by humanizing them. In this case, the humanist grudgingly accepts the student's intent to be a certified knower, that is, a professional in something or other. Naturally, the grudge factor is distinctly less if it happens to be one's own humanistic field in which the student is professionally interested.

I hope that it has become clearer why I began this brief reflection on Cal's work with some comments on the professionalization of consciousness. Professionals in virtually every undertaking other than the humanities stand in an acting relationship to their world. They know—and think—in order to act, to decide, to intervene. The resources of rationality are brought to bear on a matter that needs attention, not merely invites it. The urgencies of such needs are sometimes dramatic, other times more indirect and disguised. If the viability of humanist culture has become even more tenuous than it was twenty or thirty years ago, it is not principally because the deconstructionists, relativists, historicists, antifoundationalists, and multiculturalists have weakened an otherwise ongoing concern. The foundations and values of the humanities have been uncertain, growing uncertain, for a good while longer than this.

I agree with Ernest Gellner: "The problem is serious and must be faced, and it is sociological as well philosophical: It concerns 'cultures' and their styles of thought and life, their cognitive potential so to speak."[26] If the "cognitive potential" of humanist culture is thinning and weakening, it is not because humanists are losing ground to technologists and scientists, for after all humanists have long held their own against, and sometimes in alliance with, techno-scientific culture. Nor do I think that postmodernity has caused, or signaled, the demise of the humanities as we know them. The severest challenge to the "cognitive potential" of the humanities is probably not offered by Rorty, Derrida, Foucault, or Lyotard. Rather, I believe a view of professionalism which asserts that intelligibility is governed more by the knowable than the thinkable is probably the deeper challenge to the "cognitive potential" of the humanities. I believe it is in the culture of the professions where the ideals of "*humanitas*" and "paideia" will have their most interesting and consequential test. It is in this third culture of professionalism where humanist culture will reestablish its vision. This is the vision that the thinkable extends much farther than the knowable, and unless it is firmly reestablished, humanist culture could be consigned to adjunct status in a world of professionalized knowers.

So where does this leave us? Where does Cal leave us? As usual, he leaves us thinking. In the article I mentioned earlier, "Liberal Learning in the Postmodern World," Cal says:

> A goal of liberal learning is to foster and develop a critical mind. In academe, no professed theories, no alleged facts, and no established procedures are sacrosanct. There are no absolutes: all theories, alleged facts, and procedures are subject to possible revision. Every assertion or claim requires the qualifier "until further notice."[27]

This vision of the ideals of liberal learning obviously is not one greeted with universal acclaim. For some, this is a vision which leads to cultural decline, spiritual decline, intellectual decline, moral decline. In this vision, all manner of things are entertained as possible, but few, if any, are lasting, deep, soulful. We live without absolutes and until further notice. Transversal movement displaces and erases what is genuinely sacred, even sacrosanct. The query, "Is nothing sacred?" is not without point or force.

Cal could avoid, and possibly counter, such a criticism by a simple move. He could attach the addendum "including this one" onto the last sentence of the above quotation. That is, he might say there are no absolutes . . . at the moment. The space is kept open for absolutes, the room is ready, it is just that there are no registrants. This, however, is not the path, or the only path, Cal could take. I think Cal would remind us of a sentence from the Arendt quotation I cited earlier: "The need to think can be satisfied only through thinking, and the thoughts which I had yesterday will be satisfying this need today only to the extent that I can think them anew."[28] To "think them anew" is not new advice, originating either with Arendt or Cal. This was Socrates' practice, and he embedded it firmly, and fatally, in a transmissible social reality.

Having hinted at a comparison of Socrates and Cal, I shall take it a bit further with the help of my friend and former colleague, Bill Arrowsmith. In his essay "Turbulence in the Humanities," Bill says the following about Socrates:

> Knowledge in the humanities is a way of *being* or it is nothing. Socrates was what he *knew;* it was because he lived greatly everything that he knew—and he knew a great deal despite his disclaimer—that he has so profoundly influenced conduct for two millennia. Not everyone, of course, is given the chance to seal his knowledge with his life, but for Socrates dying was merely a way of remaining loyal to his life. In some sense he had always

laid his life on the line. But despite the universal admiration for Socrates, and such Socratic men as the Emersonian scholar or the Nietzschean "Destroyer," the Socratic scholar has now no emulators, imitators, or exponents.[29]

In neither Arendt nor in Cal is there a diminution of the importance of knowledge, of knowing. But if the humanities are to be humanly significant, their knowledge must, as Bill says, constitute a "way of *being* or it is nothing." I have known very few teacher-scholars whose knowing and thinking have been so integrated, on so high a level, as that of Cal Schrag. To make a point, Bill Arrowsmith was known to exaggerate, and of course he did exaggerate when he said that the Socratic scholar at present has no emulator. There are many such Socratic exponents. In Cal Schrag we have a philosopher, a professional, and a humanist who *lives* what he knows and thinks. By embodiment and example, Cal reminds us that even after postmodernity it is still possible to live greatly what one knows. Through such an exemplary "way of *being*" as Cal's, the professions and the humanities find a basis for an intimation of transfiguration.

Notes

1. Calvin O. Schrag, "Liberal Learning in the Postmodern World," *Key Reporter* 54, no. 1 (autumn 1988): 1–4.

2. Calvin O. Schrag, *The Self after Postmodernity* (New Haven: Yale University Press, 1997), p. 148 (hereafter cited as *SP*).

3. A. N. Whitehead, *Modes of Thought* (New York: Capricorn Books, 1938), p. 28.

4. John Henry Cardinal Newman, *The Idea of the University* (Notre Dame, Ind.: University of Notre Dame Press, 1982), pp. 114–35.

5. The exceptions include a number of important contributions to the study of the profession of philosophy. See, e.g., Albert William Levi, "Contemporary Philosophy: The Age of the Professional, G. E. Moore," in *Philosophy as Social Expression* (Chicago: University of Chicago Press, 1974); Richard Rorty, "Professionalized Philosophy and Transcendentalist Culture," in *Consequences of Pragmatism* (Minneapolis: University of Minnesota Press, 1982); F. E. Sparshott, *Looking for Philosophy* (Montreal: McGill-Queens University Press, 1972); Daniel J. Wilson, "Professionalization and Organized Discussion in the American Philosophical Association, 1900–1922," *Journal of the History of Philosophy* 17, no. 1 (January 1979): 53–69.

6. For an example of the attempt of a "young," "new," or "aspiring" profession to reflect on its general philosophical foundations through attention to ethical considerations, see the special issue on ethics, *Therapeutic Recreation Journal* 29,

no. 4 (1985). My article, "Professions, Ethics and Unity," addresses the tension between unity as an epistemological or ontological value and unity as an ethical value (pp. 41–50). See also my introductionary article "Leisure and the 'Perfection of Importance,'" in *Leisure and Ethics: Reflections on the Philosophy of Leisure*, ed. Gerald S. Fain and Kimberly A. Gillespie (Reston, Va.: American Association for Leisure and Recreation, 1991), pp. 1–5.

7. Calvin O. Schrag, "Being in Pain," in *The Humanity of the Ill: Phenomenological Perspectives*, ed. Victor Kestenbaum (Knoxville: University of Tennessee Press, 1982), pp. 101–24.

8. Donald Schon, *The Reflective Practitioner: How Professionals Think in Action* (New York: Basic Books, 1983), p. viii.

9. John Dewey, *Democracy and Education: An Introduction to the Philosophy of Education* (New York: The Free Press, 1916), p. 329.

10. Ernst Gellner, "The Crisis in the Humanities and the Mainstream of Philosophy," in *The Devil in Modern Philosophy* (Boston: Routledge and Kegan Paul, 1974), p. 26.

11. Ibid., p. 27.

12. Hannah Arendt, "Thinking and Moral Considerations: A Lecture," *Social Research* 38 (autumn 1971): 421–22.

13. Calvin O. Schrag, "The Idea of the University and the Communication of Knowledge in a Technological Age," in *Communication Philosophy and the Technological Age*, ed. Michael J. Hyde (Tuscaloosa: University of Alabama Press, 1982), pp. 112–13.

14. Calvin O. Schrag, *Communicative Praxis and the Space of Subjectivity* (Bloomington: Indiana University Press, 1986), p. 39.

15. Ibid., p. 60.

16. Ibid., p. 63.

17. Calvin O. Schrag, *The Resources of Rationality: A Response to the Postmodern Challenge* (Bloomington: Indiana University Press, 1992), p. 158.

18. Hannah Arendt, *Thinking*, vol. 1 of *The Life of the Mind* (New York: Harcourt Brace Jovanovich, 1978), p. 14.

19. Arendt, "Thinking and Moral Considerations," p. 424.

20. Schrag, *SP*, p. 103.

21. Ibid., p. 104.

22. Calvin O. Schrag, *Existence and Freedom: Towards an Ontology of Human Finitude* (Evanston, Ill.: Northwestern University Press, 1961).

23. Allan Bloom, *The Closing of the American Mind: How Higher Education Has Failed Democracy and Impoverished the Souls of Today's Students* (New York: Simon and Schuster, 1987), pp. 373–74.

24. Schrag, *SP*, pp. 108, 109.

25. See Alvin Kernan, ed., *What Happened to the Humanities?* (Princeton, N.J.: Princeton University Press, 1997); John M. Ellis, *Literature Lost: Social Agendas and the Corruption of the Humanities* (New Haven, Conn.: Yale University Press, 1997). Ricks shows that the theoretical, heavily philosophical, pursuit of metaphor has yielded little in the way of sustainable truth claims. Surveying the fortunes of

metaphor in "theory's empire," Ricks asks the metatheoretical question: "Why, or when, is it proper to desist from further elaborating of the argument, from further philosophizing? How, in reply to this, would one make the case that pursuit of the theoretical elaborations may be intrinsically misguided, and therefore, though, onerous, idle?" (p. 181). My agreements and disagreements with Ricks, practical and theoretical, always have been stimulating, always surprising.

26. Gellner, *Devil in Modern Philosophy,* p. 32.

27. Schrag, "Liberal Learning," p. 4.

28. Arendt, "Thinking and Moral Considerations," p. 422.

29. William Arrowsmith, "Turbulence in the Humanities," *Arion: A Journal of Humanities and the Classics,* 3d ser. 2.2, 3 (spring and fall 1992/93): 207.

17

Response to Contributors

Calvin O. Schrag

I have been asked to respond to the fine essays in this volume. Unfortunately, there is no canon of academic etiquette that provides guidelines for fashioning a response to Festschrift contributions. Given that this is my first charge within this literary genre, I must confess a measure of uncertainty in regard to my task, calling to mind poor Barnabas, the messenger assigned to the central character in Franz Kafka's novel *The Castle*. Barnabas, you may recall, remains unsuccessful in establishing any significant communication with the officials in the castle because he suffers from a profound ambiguity regarding his designated function.

There appears to be a mind-set in the academic community that the requirement for a colleague who has the good fortune of having his works discussed by collegial critics is to finesse a burden of proof that defends his/her consummate authorship. Now if this indeed were to be my task, I would take a page from Martin Luther's celebrated defense before the inquisition of Archbishop Eck at the Council of Worms. Countering the archbishop's charge that his writings were heretical, Luther boldly announced that he was prepared to defend them all—and he would do so on the basis of *reason* and *Scripture*. And that is how I would define my strategy: first use reason, and if that proves to be unsuccessful, appeal to Scripture!

That a formal response to the oft-intricate analysis and critique in the presented essays has intrinsic merit, and might indeed be expected, is surely not in question. However, given the large number of contributions and the consequent restriction of allotted space, such would not be feasible for the current project. This would be a task for another day. Instead, I will define my current function as that of offering a brief narrative, a

315

petit récit, at times anecdotal and nostalgic, of the role that each of the contributors has played in my professional journeying along life's way, explicating the contributions of each in light of the main focus of the volume, *The Task of Philosophy after Postmodernity.*

My association with some of the contributors is long-standing. Other associations are more recent. The story of these associations could be told in a chronological order, proceeding from the earlier to the later. But the specific occasions for earlier and later encounters quickly become blurred. Hence, I have opted to proceed alphabetically rather than chronologically.

I have followed Sandra Bartky's professional career over the years with a great deal of interest and admiration. She is well known on both the local and the national level for her contributions to gender studies, which are always informed by careful research and sensitive political awareness. What is often overlooked, however, is that she was one of the first American philosophers to address the later philosophy of Heidegger—a task that is not particularly suited for the philosophically faint of heart!

Her contribution to the current volume is of particular significance for helping us define the task of philosophy for the new millennium as we assess the advantages and disadvantages of postmodernism. Her central argument is that the jettisoning of the repressive hypothesis by Foucault in his *History of Sexuality* is too hurried. She is of the mind that more attention needs to be given to the accounts of the repressive hypothesis as theorized by the likes of Freud, Reich, and Marcuse. The lesson to be learned from Bartky's project is that on this issue, as well as on many others, the postmodern should not be so facilely severed from the modern. The modern remains ensconced in the postmodern as the postmodern continues to open up new avenues for an understanding of the modern. This helps us set the agenda for the task of philosophy after postmodernity. The reclamation of the tradition remains a pressing requirement for our future philosophical investigations. To be sure, this is not a reclamation of the traditions as a set of finished and finalized truths but rather as a continuing field of possibilities yet to be explored.

Linda Bell was a participant in my 1982 National Endowment for the Humanities Seminar for College Teachers, selected from a pool of nationwide applicants. Linda quickly became a pivotal contributor to the daily discussions, utilizing her expertise on the philosophy of Jean-Paul Sartre. She instructed us well on the highways and byways of Sartre interpretation. Her book, *Sartre's Ethics of Authenticity,* which appeared shortly thereafter, made an immediate impact on the secondary literature. In it she silenced many of the Sartre critics by defending the claim that if one digs deep enough one will find a coherent ethical stance in Sartre's writings.

In her contribution to the Festschrift she picks up on the theme of my interrogation of the "who" of discourse, action, community, and transcendence that provided the format for my book, *The Self after Postmodernity*, and raises some important critical questions. She has some concerns about my concept of self-identity, arguing that it is too rigid, evoking an abiding permanence that occludes the realities of change and the continuing revision of projects. She recommends a concept of self more mobile, mutable, and variable, clearly reminiscent of Sartre's notion of the *pour soi* as fluid, vacuous, open-ended, perpetually in process of becoming that which it is not yet. In continuing my conversation with her on this point, I would make an effort to respond positively to her portrait of the self as a self always in process while at the same time moderating Sartre's heavy dose of nothingness at the heart of being-for-itself. We need to investigate the possibility of splitting the difference between the metaphysical take on self-identity as a rigid being-in-itself and a facile rejection of self-identity in the life of human consciousness as being-for-itself. Such a splitting of the difference would enable a self-understanding in which the self continues to recognize itself in its dynamic becoming.

Jack Caputo and I have traveled common stretches of the philosophical road for some time. As he remarks in his essay, we have shared interests both philosophical and theological, interests which at times have undergone the serendipity of becoming *anti*-philosophical and *anti*-theological. His "experiment in Danish deconstruction," designed as a search for a "sacred anarchy," illustrates our converging explorations, making explicit our common commitments to Kierkegaardian ruminations. Both of us, throughout our philosophical careers, have urged our colleagues to approach Kierkegaard's writings with the proper Kierkegaardian earnestness and seriousness. And here I am able to recall the provocative demand presented by one of my Heidelberg University professors, who opened his lecture course on Kierkegaard with the challenge to either take Kierkegaard "merely historically" (*nehmen sie ihn bloss historisch*) or "earnestly" (*nehmen sie ihn ernst*)!

There are no major problems for our collegial journeying against the backdrop of Caputo's Danish hypothesis that *différance* can stand in for the Deity, accentuating the divine as a disruption and a deed, at once anarchical and sacred, reclaiming and intensifying the prophetic role of religion. What is missing, however, and what would make our journeying even more collegial, is an incorporation of Kierkegaard's *Works of Love* into Caputo's Danish experiment. It is love as deed on the heels of disruption that provides the crowning transvalued virtue in any

CALVIN O. SCHRAG

Kierkegaardian journeying along the stages of life's way. And this is a love of a quite distinctive sort—not the human-all-too-human love that always expects to be paid well in the end, but rather an unconditional love, without desire for recompense or reward. A truly difficult art of loving to be sure, but one that is able to stand in for the Deity along with *différance.* I have some confidence that Caputo would accept my suggested expansion of his experiment. In any case, the consummate contribution of Caputo's essay condenses into a call for an examination of how we are to talk about God after postmodernity.

It was during my tenure as visiting professor at Northwestern University in the early 1960s that I met Ed Casey. My recollection is that we first met at Professor Bill Earle's apartment during one of his impromptu, existential, spirit-enhanced gatherings for philosophical enlightenment. All philosophical problems were solved that evening. It is a pity that by morning we had forgotten what the solutions were! Ed was completing his doctoral studies at the time, and he was part of a very vibrant graduate program in philosophy at Northwestern that was exceptionally strong in twentieth-century Continental thought. This initial meeting marked the beginning of a long collegial friendship throughout the years, from which I have benefited immensely. The philosophical world has long known of Ed Casey's incisive and oft-revolutionary phenomenological analyses of perceiving, imagining, and remembering. More recently, he has given his attention to a phenomenological understanding of the structure and dynamics of place and space. While many of us in the profession busy ourselves with *talking about* phenomenology, Casey is one of the few practitioners in the field who veritably *does* phenomenology.

His contribution to the current volume is no exception to his continuing professional development. In his essay on "The Ethics of the Glance," he provides the reader with a carefully crafted interpretive analysis of the envelopment of ethical practice and embodied comportment. It was of course Maurice Merleau-Ponty who called the world's attention to the role of embodiment in philosophy of perception. Casey continues the legacy of Merleau-Ponty by providing us with a veritable clinic on how the corporeality of our embodiment and the ethical are entwined. What we can take from this is that any philosophy of the future will need to return time and again to the seminal insights and descriptions within the phenomenological tradition, and particularly to its requirement for a continuing interpretive analysis of the way that we live our bodies.

Among the contributors it is David Crownfield who was the first of my philosophical acquaintances. We were graduate students at Harvard during the mid-1950s, and we shared concerns about the prevailing winds of neopositivism. There was much ado about protocol statements and sense data by certain members of the faculty. The writings of Bertrand Russell and Alfred J. Ayer were standard fare in many of the courses. So David and I sought out mentors that were devoted to stemming the tide of latter-day positivism. These included John Wild, Raphael Demos, Harry A. Wolfson, and Paul Tillich. I had decided to enroll at Harvard principally to continue my undergraduate interests in the philosophy of Alfred North Whitehead, who spent the latter years of his career at Harvard and who had bequeathed his legacy to one of his most brilliant students, Raphael Demos. Demos later joined the Harvard faculty and took Whitehead's celebrated one-liner, "The history of Western philosophy is but a series of footnotes to Plato," with utmost seriousness and chose to devote his professional career to a mastery of the main text rather than to the footnotes! Demos became one of America's leading Plato scholars, and I benefited much from his tutelage.

It was John Wild, however, who became my principal mentor on matters philosophical, introducing me to Heidegger's *Sein und Zeit,* of which he and some of his former students had made a paraphrase translation. And then Paul Tilllich joined the Harvard faculty as Distinguished University Professor, adding strengths in recent Continental philosophy and theology. Crownfield and I relished this counterthrust by Wild and Tillich to the aggressive neopositivism that pervaded much of the faculty. As a teaching fellow assigned to assist Tillich in his undergraduate course "The Interpretation of History," I recall some firsthand experiences in dealing with the disparagement of anything that strayed from positivistic vocabulary. An undergraduate philosophy student had enrolled in Tillich's course and asked me if he would be able to count the course toward his the major. Insofar as the course was a quite standard course in the philosophy of history, I told the student that there ought not be a problem but that he had better check with the current chairperson of the philosophy department on the matter. The student shortly returned and, in a state of utter befuddlement, told me that the chairperson informed him that the course could not count toward his major because Tillich was *not* a philosopher—he was a *thinker!* Somehow word soon spread across campus that one needs to carefully distinguish nonphilosophical thinkers from nonthinking philosophers!

In his contributed essay Crownfield explicates the task of philosophy after postmodernity against the backdrop of Derrida's radicalization of Ricoeur's amalgam of structure and event, system and context, as the underbelly for the determination of sense and reference. Crownfield is of the mind that Derrida's project of radicalization leads to an impasse in which the search for meaning is constrained by the vagaries of structure and system on the one hand and a recalcitrant dissemination and uncontrollable recontextualization on the other hand. The requirement for philosophy in the present age, according to Crownfield, is to proceed beyond this impasse by excising the presupposition that meaning is controlled by universalizable signification—precisely the presupposition that produces the Derridean semantic impasse. In the aftermath of expunging this presupposition, we will still be able to talk of meaning and of rationality, but this will need to be a meaning more praxial than theoretical and a rationality more transversal than universal.

My collegial relationship with Fred Dallmayr goes back to the late 1960s, at which time Fred joined the faculty of the political science department at Purdue University. We in the philosophy department always considered Fred to be a "displaced philosopher" who, by the misfortune of fate, was destined to be in the wrong department! Happily, however, the relations between the philosophy and political science departments were always uncommonly cordial, which fostered productive interdisciplinary collaboration. Fred played an important role in securing Jürgen Habermas and Karl-Otto Apel for visiting appointments at Purdue. Among other things this provided the historic occasion for Habermas to jettison the transcendental standpoint—at least momentarily! This auspicious event occurred at a specific time and place, following a Habermas/Apel graduate seminar, as we were on the way to lunch at the Purdue Memorial Union. En route, the late professor Richard Grabau and I somewhat playfully suggested the substitution of a pragmatic for a transcendental vocabulary. Evincing some exasperation, Habermas stopped in the middle of the street, turned to his colleague, and said, "Karl, you know, when we discuss philosophy with Americans we might well avoid invoking the transcendental." It is not surprising that Apel was not particularly receptive to Habermas's suggestion, fearing that it would undermine any compelling claims for universality in his own transcendental pragmatics!

Dallmayr's critical concerns in his essay are right on target. He worries about the ethical implications of my friendliness toward Lévinas's heavy accent on exteriority, alterity, and asymmetry. If the likes of such are to guide our philosophical ruminations, what becomes of the ethical requirement for reciprocity, equality, and distributive justice? Yes, there is a quite legitimate concern here that needs to be pursued in some depth and detail. In continuing the conversation with Fred on this issue, I would recommend consideration of the very suggestive notion of a possible "asymmetrical reciprocity"—a notion that has been sketched and developed by Iris Young and Patricia Huntington. The central point at issue is that asymmetry does not ipso facto displace reciprocity. Alterity does not in itself preclude the requirement for response. Asymmetry and alterity may indeed provide the first moment. But this moment achieves fulfillment only through the reciprocity of a fitting response.

Bernard Dauenhauer and I have had, for some time now, a critical exchange on the status and role of human agency, which happens also to be the topic of his contributed essay. He is of the mind that I need a more robust notion of the agent as actor and initiator so as to keep my portrait of the self from becoming simply "the product of antecedent causal processes." Now plainly enough, I do not want that to happen. Hence, his friendly critique challenges me to pick up the gauntlet and provide a more nuanced defense of my position. Clearly, more than my allotted space would be needed to fashion a thoroughgoing response to the important critical questions that he raises. At this juncture I am able only to point out the direction that such a response might take.

In my response I would argue for the need of a shift in standpoint, a kind of paradigm switch if you will, and an experimentation with a new grammar for addressing the old issues of human agency, free will, the voluntary versus the involuntary, determinism versus indeterminism, heteronomy versus autonomy, and so forth. I am more optimistic than is Bernard about moving beyond the metaphysically loaded categories of substance and attribute, cause and effect, actuality and potentiality, activity and passivity, which traditionally have been employed to solve the issues of human agency. We need to probe the meaning of cause, among other things distinguishing it from motive, and we need to find a space between activity and passivity, between the nomos that is one's own (autonomy) and the nomos that is superimposed from the outside (heteronomy). This is the space of a middle voice, not yet either active or passive, and the space of a praxis that antedates the nomos, the law of the human economy, construed either subjectively or objectively. It is this middle voice and this originative space of praxis that is older than the categorial schemes of cause and effect, actuality and potentiality, activity and passivity. In exploring this space, one might be able to elicit some help both from Heidegger's notion of *Gelassenheit* and Derrida's notion of *différance*.

Martin Dillon, like Dallmayr and Dauenhauer, has been a demanding and helpful critic of my work over the years. Tenacious in his argumentation and rigorous in his critique of concepts, he leaves no stones unturned. In his current essay he raises some troubling questions about my interpretive analysis of love against the backdrop of gift giving, explicating love as a gift that is given without any expectation of return. And he is particularly nervous about my endorsement of Kierkegaard's *Works of Love*, in which the Christian version of love as *agapē*, unconditional and freed from all desire for recompense and reward, is made central. Dillon finds such a modality of love to be quite impossible. Maybe no quid pro quo, he is willing to concede, but nonetheless some sort of desire for recompense, he argues, remains in every loving relationship.

There remains much to be discussed on this matter. At issue is the quite complex story of "gift exchange" within the economy of human societies from times past to the present. When gift giving becomes institutionalized as a social practice within market-oriented societies, it is difficult to keep the giving of gifts outside the web of commodity exchange, both material and symbolic. However, when gift giving becomes gift exchange, in which there is an expectation, or indeed a requirement, to return something in kind, the very meaning of "gift" suffers disfiguration. For a gift to be genuinely a gift, it needs to be *aneconomic*, freely given, without any strings attached, issuing from a resource and measure for giving that transcends the economy of repayment of debts and solicitations of rewards. But is the giving of such a gift indeed possible? And in thusly defining the gift, do we not gravitate into an aporia in which a gift is annihilated in the moment that it is given?

Given the human-all-too-human predilections of our embodied existence, such may indeed appear to be the case. Gift giving, unable to override the desires that all human flesh is heir to, would seem destined to remain an impossibility. And it is this that appears to underlie Dillon's argument against the notion of love as *agapē,* freed from all expectations of return. Certainly one needs to acknowledge the difficulty and ambiguity of such Kierkegaardian "works of love," but difficulty and ambiguity do not necessarily translate into impossibility. What is required, we suggest, is a dislodging of the tacit presupposition that love is necessarily centripetal, destined to return to the center. Let us suppose that love, in its most untrammeled expression, can also be centrifugal, always transitive, moving outward to the "other," to the neighbor within our environs, and beyond. As teachers we offer the gift of knowledge to our students not with the expectation that they will repay us by returning that which they have been given. Rather, the hope is that they will continue to give the gift to others. Such is the centrifugal dynamics of gift giving, and specifically in its exemplification of an art of loving that transcends the economy of production and exchange, possession and dispossession, recompense and reward.

Michael Hyde's contribution to the philosophical task for the new millennium is that of effecting a convergence of philosophy and rhetorical theory. Throughout his writings he has furrowed new conceptual territory across the boundaries of these fields of investigation. With a veritable mastery of the original sources in both the philosophical and rhetorical disciplines, Michael provides us with a fresh, imaginative, and provocative read of Heidegger's understanding of the call of conscience vis-à-vis its rhetorical function. The rhetorical function is that of an "interruption." In this rhetorical function the call of conscience plays itself out as an interruption of the flattened, anonymous, and depersonalized world of *das man*, calling Dasein to the truth of authentic existence. Rhetoric is thus seen as a moment of philosophical discourse itself, an intrinsic part of the very fabric of communicative praxis.

The important wider lesson that we learn from Michael's project is the need for a recollection of the medieval trivium (in which logic, language, and rhetoric were taught as sister disciplines) as he marks out new strategies for addressing the public and its problems. As at once philosopher and rhetorician, Michael teaches us how to combine theory and practice, thought and action, reminiscent of the Socratic task of philosophy that was always geared to an achievement of self-knowledge within a polis of public concerns.

When Hwa Yol Jung came to Purdue as Visiting Professor at the invitation of Fred Dallmayr, I was surprised to learn that we had had a common mentor, John Wild. It is apparent that John Wild had much to do with Hwa Yol's interest in Continental philosophy, which then set him on the path to explore a possible meeting of East and West on matters philosophical. In his fine volume, *The Crisis of Political Understanding*, Hwa Yol has a dedication inscription that reads: "To John Wild, who introduced me to the Tao of phenomenology." Wild, as we all know, had a profound influence on a whole postwar generation of scholars working in the areas of existentialism and phenomenology. He was single-handedly responsible for the founding of the Society for Phenomenology and Existential Philosophy, and I would venture to say that he played a significant role in shaping the professional futures of many of the contributors to the current volume. Indeed, if I were to select one person to whom one might dedicate the assembled essays in this volume it would be John Wild.

In his essay Hwa Yol continues the explorations that he had launched in some of his previous publications. I am thinking particularly of his very fine article, "The Tao of Transversality as a Global Approach to Truth," in which he shows how the concepts of transversal rationality and transversal communication play themselves out in the arena of comparative cultural studies, bridging the chasm between Eastern and Western thought. In his current essay he elaborates the thematic of transversality and extends the trajectory of his investigations into the realm of geophilosophy, providing us with instruction on how to deal with the pressing concerns in an age of globalization. What we are offered here is a veritable cosmopolitan philosophy that has some profound specific implications for political theory and practical politics. It is thus that we learn from Hwa Yol that the task of philosophy after postmodernity will include interdisciplinary explorations across the terrains of philosophy and political science.

Victor Kestenbaum further widens the scope of a philosophy of the future by setting the agenda for reclaiming the legacy of American pragmatism. Ever since the publication of his extraordinarily fine book, *The Phenomenological Sense of John Dewey,* his credentials for original scholarship in the philosophy of John Dewey, and American philosophy more generally, have become visible both at home and abroad. In this work Kestenbaum rescues Dewey's notions of habit and meaning from the clutches of reductive naturalism by demonstrating that Dewey's strategy is more like that of a *phenomenological* reduction. In one fell swoop, as it were, Victor is able to provide a fresh interpretation of Dewey's philosophy and invites us to search for phenomenological roots in indigenous American philosophy more generally.

In his Festschrift contribution Victor becomes a spokesperson for the role of the humanities in the postmodern university. He has some concerns about my emphasis on the constraints of finitude for the philosophical task, and he suggests that the humanities may indeed have resources for opening up vistas of the sublime in which finitude is overcome. Coupled with this concern is his worry that my concept of transcendence is too lame for enabling such vistas of sublimity.

In continuing my conversation with Victor, I would make an effort to show that there may well be more agreement than disagreement on the matter at hand. Although finitude itself cannot be removed, it can be robustly transformed and transfigured through transcendence toward the sublime. The sublime indeed has the resources to liberate us from *estranged* finitude; although finitude itself cannot be left behind. As Kierkegaard has shown in his book, *The Sickness Unto Death,* the self that seeks to constitute itself as infinite loses itself as a dialectical unity of finitude and infinitude. Much of the matter here turns on the distinction between finitude and estrangement. Estrangement is not a necessary implication of finitude. One of my continuing criticisms of Heidegger has been that he tended to blur the distinction between finitude and estrangement with his notion of guilt as an ontological structure of human existence. On this point Kierkegaard (from whom Heidegger did indeed borrow much) was more perceptive than was Heidegger, insisting on a distinction with a difference between human finitude and existential estrangement. Existential estrangement can be overcome through the resources of transcendence.

Lenore Langsdorf, in her essay "In Defense of Poiesis," points out a lacuna in my concept and project of communicative praxis, understood as an amalgam of discourse and action. Illustrating her strategy of gentle yet probing critique, for which she has become known, she makes a case for a need to find a place for the poetic posture within the space of communicative praxis. It is her critical assessment that in privileging discourse and action, speaking and doing, as that which informs the text and texture of communicative praxis, I tend to neglect the role of making, a role whose acknowledgment goes all the way back to the Greek concept of *poiesis*. The thrust of her argument is that the function and role of the poetic, as making and originative creativity, need to be grafted on to my notion of communicative praxis so as to expand the horizons of our communicative engagements. She is of course quite right about this. There are times when one must simply accept the critical suggestions of a colleague, take the suggestions to heart, and then move in a collaborative effort to further the discussion of the issue at hand. And this is how I must respond to the essay by Lenore. Suffice it to say that had I had the benefit of Lenore's counsel on this issue before the final draft of my *Communicative Praxis and the Space of Subjectivity* was sent to press, her critical suggestions would have been appropriated with a significant measure of gratitude.

Gary Madison has been a long-standing mentor of mine, providing inspiration and direction along the highways and byways of French philosophy, and particularly the philosophies of Merleau-Ponty and Paul Ricoeur. More recently I have learned much from his book *The Political Economy of Civil Society and Human Rights*, which is a splendid work on the subject of social and political philosophy. Throughout the years we have shared common philosophical commitments on numerous issues. He has highlighted these in his lead essay for the Festschrift. They include the following themes and critical concerns: (1) certain trouble spots in French deconstructionist thought and specifically its recurring tendencies to a species of pantextualism; (2) Habermas's overdetermination of rationality in his doctrine of validity claims; (3) the poverty of metaphysical concepts of self and society, and particularly those of an essentialist sort; and (4) an interest in keeping the legacy of phenomenological philosophy alive, albeit not in an uncritical manner. We are in particular agreement that the philosophy of Merleau-Ponty still has a great deal to offer and that any philosophy of the future will in particular need to give attention to the issues that he raised in his discussions of embodiment.

Acknowledging our indebtedness to Merleau-Ponty, Gary and I have made common cause for a refiguration of subjectivity as concretely embodied. On this point we find ourselves in disagreement with our postmodernist colleagues, some of whom have proposed a deletion of "subject" and "subjectivity" from the philosophical lexicon. We are in solid agreement on the importance of the role of rhetoric in philosophical discourse. All of these common concerns come to the fore in Gary's essay, apprising the readers that, in our extended philosophical journey over the years, we have found it difficult to quarrel with each other on the task and scope of philosophy.

Robert Scharff was a student both during my visiting appointment at the University of Illinois and later at Northwestern University. He was an undergraduate at Illinois and a graduate student at Northwestern. Our association at the University of Illinois took place during the era of Chief Illini Analytical Philosophy! This meant that faculty and students alike who were interested in Continental philosophy would need to read their Husserl, Heidegger, Sartre, and Merleau-Ponty with their window blinds securely shut! But Bob, who already at that time was interested in the philosophy of Heidegger, persevered and after graduation matriculated in the philosophy program at Northwestern University. This was during the early 1960s, at which time Northwestern had the premier philosophy department specializing in Continental philosophy. Bob completed his graduate studies at Northwestern with a defense of a dissertation on the philosophy of Wilhelm Dilthey, in which he dispelled some of the common misconceptions of Dilthey's contribution. More recently we have all become familiar with his book on the philosophy of Auguste Comte, a work in which he rescues Comte from doctrinaire positivism.

Scharff's Festschrift contribution proceeds along the lines of a critical trajectory similar to the one that he fashioned in his historical study of Comte. In his essay he selects Descartes as the subject of inquiry and succeeds in rescuing Descartes from Cartesianism as in his earlier work he rescued Comte from positivism. The lesson to be learned from Scharff's critical studies for the philosophy of the future is that the great thinkers of the tradition need to be delivered time and again from the sedimentation of their legacies.

Merold Westphal has played a decisive role in my more recent return to Kierkegaard. Readers of my work may have noticed increasing references to the philosophy of Kierkegaard. Merold, along with my current colleague at Purdue, Martin J. B. Matuštík, is principally responsible for this "return." I speak of this as a return because it was with an investigation of the thought of Kierkegaard (and Heidegger) that I began my professional career. My first book, *Existence and Freedom: Towards an Ontology of Human Finitude,* developed the thesis that Heidegger's analytic of Dasein can be explicated as a secularization and ontologization of Kierkegaard's concrete, ethico-religious dialectic of the self, both in terms of its general format as well as in some of its details. I am still of the mind that this thesis, first developed in my doctoral dissertation of 1957, is basically correct. However, I am no longer as enthusiastic about the merits of such a secularization and ontologization on the part of Heidegger. Indeed, it may be that much was lost in such a move, and the time for the recovering of what was lost may well be long overdue. It was basically Matuštík and Westphal's edited book of essays, *Kierkegaard in Post/Modernity*, which set the agenda for any future Kierkegaard studies, rekindled my interest in the thought of Kierkegaard, and offered an opportunity to rethink the contribution of Kierkegaard as a possible resource for responding to the postmodern challenge.

Some of Merold's concerns about my interpretation of the religious significance of Kierkegaard's thought come to the fore in his contributed essay for the present volume. Much turns on our read of Kierkegaard vis-à-vis the "theism" issue. Merold has more sympathies with the tradition of classical theism than do I, and he reads Kierkegaard as providing support for these sympathies. I, however, read Kierkegaard as moving us beyond the theism-versus-atheism problematic itself, beyond the use of metaphysical schema and categories (essence and existence, substance and attribute, actuality and potentiality, causality and dependence) to shore up the truth of religion as an existence sphere. According to Merold, my nontheistic, or better, "otherwise than theistic" read of Kierkegaard ends up being soft on the notion of transcendence, which certainly appears to play a very important role in Kierkegaard's thought, and particularly in his detailing of "religousness B" in the *Postscript*.

Much of course turns on the meaning that one ascribes to transcendence. The transcendence that I find in Kierkegaard is not a *metaphysical* transcendence. We are told quite explicitly in Kierkegaard's book *Repetition* that it is on the category of repetition that all metaphysics founders. What is at issue here is not the metaphysical transcendence that has been so dear to the hearts of classical theists, whose projects have been basically those of a *metaphysics* of theism. But it is a transcendence nonetheless. Let us call it a protoethical transcendence that finds its chief exemplification in the robust transcendence of a love of neighbor that expects no recompense. And this does strike me as being very much the take on transcendence offered by Kierkegaard in his unparalleled *Works of Love*.

Bruce Wilshire is a former colleague of mine from earlier times. During the 1960s he was on the faculty at the Purdue University regional campus in Indianapolis. This was the beginning of a collegial collaboration on a wide range of topics that we have discussed and rediscussed over the years. It is difficult to overstate the importance of Bruce's role in the discovery of the sources of an indigenous American phenomenology. His book, *William James and Phenomenology*, landed on the scene as a veritable blockbuster, reverberating through the citadels of research on the thought of William James, making known to the world that there is a rich tradition of phenomenological inquiry on American soil.

Wilshire's contribution to the task of philosophy after postmodernity, which is the centralizing topic for the collected essays that make up the Festschrift, details a provocative application of the concept of transversality to genocide. Genocide is the systematic persecution of a designated group because the members of the group are viewed as "other." The ethical task in combating the unspeakable horrors of genocide, Bruce argues, is that of transversal understanding and transversal communication across the terrain of otherness. Such understanding and communication enables one to accept differences of race, gender, and cultural practices while acknowledging the integrity of that which is other. As we move into the new millennium, with its increasing globalization of thought and institutional practices, the transversal and cosmopolitan ethics of the stripe suggested by Wilshire will become an increasingly urgent requirement.

In conclusion, I wish to thank each and every one of the contributors for their thoughtful and skillfully crafted essays. Given the limitation of space in a volume of this sort, my responses to each had to be very much abridged. Yet, I hope that I have had some success in pointing out the directions that an extended discussion of the several critical issues that each of the contributors raised would take. Such continuing discussion, we surely can agree, is a pressing requirement as we face the challenge of reinventing the task of philosophy after postmodernity.

Publications of Calvin O. Schrag

Books (Sole Authorship)

Schrag, Calvin O. *Communicative Praxis and the Space of Subjectivity.* Bloomington: Indiana University Press, 1986. (*Choice* selection for Outstanding Academic Book List for 1987.)

———. *Existence and Freedom: Towards an Ontology of Human Finitude.* Evanston, Ill.: Northwestern University Press, 1961.

———. *Experience and Being: Prolegomena to a Future Ontology.* Evanston, Ill.: Northwestern University Press, 1969. (Cited in the new *Oxford English Dictionary* as one of the textual contributions to the definition of "phenomenology," Supplement, p. 759.)

———. *Philosophical Papers: Betwixt and Between.* Albany: State University of New York Press, 1994.

———. *Radical Reflection and the Origin of the Human Sciences.* West Lafayette, Ind.: Purdue University Press, 1980. (*Choice* selection for Outstanding Academic Book List of 1980.) Korean trans. Chong Pok Moon. Seoul: Hyung Sol Publishing Co., 1998.

———. *The Resources of Rationality: A Response to the Postmodern Challenge.* Bloomington: Indiana University Press, 1992.

———. *The Self after Postmodernity.* New Haven, Conn.: Yale University Press, 1997. Korean trans. Chong Pok Moon and Yeung Phil Kim. Seoul: Ulsan University Press, 1999.

Monographs

Schrag, Calvin O. *Communicative Rhetoric and the Claims of Reason.* Evanston, Ill.: Northwestern University School of Speech, 1989.

Books (Multiple Authorship)
Contributed Essays

Schrag, Calvin O. "Authorial Reflections." In *American Phenomenology: Origins and Developments,* edited by Eugene Kaelin and Calvin O. Schrag. Dordrecht, The Netherlands: Kluwer Academic Publishers, 1989.

————. "Being in Pain." In *The Humanity of the Ill: Phenomenological Perspectives*, edited by Victor Kestenbaum. Knoxville: University of Tennessee Press, 1982.

————. "The Challenge of Philosophical Anthropology." In *The Phenomenology of Man and of the Human Condition*, edited by A.-T. Tymieniecka. Dordrecht, The Netherlands: D. Reidel Publishing Company, 1983.

————. "The Concrete Dialectic of Self-with-Society." In *Experience Forms: Their Cultural and Individual Place and Function*, edited by George G. Haydu. The Hague, The Netherlands: Mouton, 1979.

————. "Explanation and Understanding in the Science of Human Behavior." In *Reconsidering Psychology*, edited by James E. Faulconer and Richard H. Williams. Pittsburgh: Duquesne University Press, 1990.

————. "From Experience to Judgment in the Aftermath of the Postmodern Critique." In *Analecta Husserliana*, edited by A.-T. Tymieniecka. Dordrecht, The Netherlands: Kluwer Academic Publishers, 1998.

————. "Hermeneutical Circles, Rhetorical Triangles and Transversal Diagnonals." In *Rhetoric and Hermeneutics in our Time*, edited by Michael Hyde and Walter Jost. New Haven, Conn.: Yale University Press, 1997.

————. "Husserl's Legacy in the Postmodern World." In *Husserl's Legacy in Phenomenological Philosophies*, edited by A.-T. Tymieniecka. Dordrecht, The Netherlands: Kluwer Academic Publishers, 1991.

————. "The Idea of the University and the Communication of Knowledge in a Technological Age." In *Communication Philosophy and the Technological Age*, edited Michael J. Hyde. Tuscaloosa: University of Alabama Press, 1982.

————. "The Kierkegaard-Effect in the Shaping of the Contours of Modernity." In *Kierkegaard in Post/Modernity*, edited by Martin J. Matuštík and Merold Westphal. Bloomington: Indiana University Press, 1995.

————. "La récupération du sujet phénoménologique." In *Analecta Husserliana*, vol. L, edited by A.-T. Tymieniecka. Dordrecht, The Netherlands: Kluwer Academic Publishers, 1997.

————. "The Life-World and Its Historical Horizon." In *Patterns of the Life World*, edited by James Edie, Francis Parker, and Calvin O. Schrag. Evanston, Ill.: Northwestern University Press, 1970.

————. "My Dialogue with Twentieth Century Continental Philosophy." In *Portraits of American Continental Philosophers*, edited by James Watson. Bloomington: Indiana University Press, 1999.

————. "Phenomenology and the Consequences of Postmodernity." In *Reason, Life, Culture: Phenomenology in the Baltics*, edited by A.-T. Tymieniecka. Dordrecht, The Netherlands: Kluwer Academic Publishers, 1993.

————. "Philosophical Anthropology as an Analytic of Mortality." In *Transparencies: Philosophical Essays in Honor of Jose Ferrater Mora*, edited P. N. Cohn. Atlantic Highlands, N.J.: Humanities Press, 1982.

————. "The Question of the Unity of the Human Sciences Revisited." In *The Phenomenology of Man and of the Human Condition*, edited by A.-T. Tymieniecka. Dordrecht, The Netherlands: D. Reidel Publishing Company, 1983.

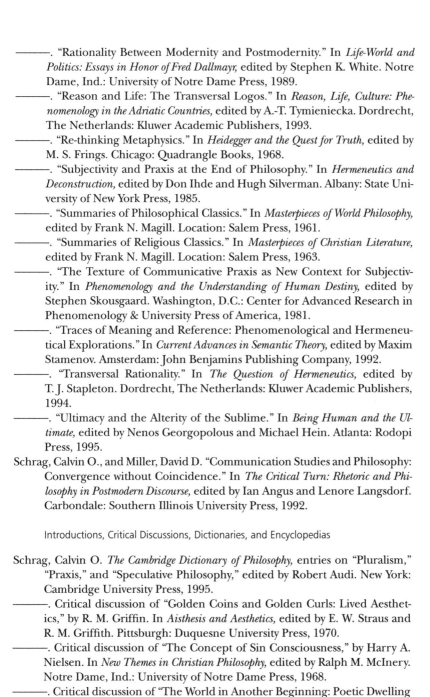

———. "Rationality Between Modernity and Postmodernity." In *Life-World and Politics: Essays in Honor of Fred Dallmayr*, edited by Stephen K. White. Notre Dame, Ind.: University of Notre Dame Press, 1989.

———. "Reason and Life: The Transversal Logos." In *Reason, Life, Culture: Phenomenology in the Adriatic Countries*, edited by A.-T. Tymieniecka. Dordrecht, The Netherlands: Kluwer Academic Publishers, 1993.

———. "Re-thinking Metaphysics." In *Heidegger and the Quest for Truth*, edited by M. S. Frings. Chicago: Quadrangle Books, 1968.

———. "Subjectivity and Praxis at the End of Philosophy." In *Hermeneutics and Deconstruction*, edited by Don Ihde and Hugh Silverman. Albany: State University of New York Press, 1985.

———. "Summaries of Philosophical Classics." In *Masterpieces of World Philosophy*, edited by Frank N. Magill. Location: Salem Press, 1961.

———. "Summaries of Religious Classics." In *Masterpieces of Christian Literature*, edited by Frank N. Magill. Location: Salem Press, 1963.

———. "The Texture of Communicative Praxis as New Context for Subjectivity." In *Phenomenology and the Understanding of Human Destiny*, edited by Stephen Skousgaard. Washington, D.C.: Center for Advanced Research in Phenomenology & University Press of America, 1981.

———. "Traces of Meaning and Reference: Phenomenological and Hermeneutical Explorations." In *Current Advances in Semantic Theory*, edited by Maxim Stamenov. Amsterdam: John Benjamins Publishing Company, 1992.

———. "Transversal Rationality." In *The Question of Hermeneutics*, edited by T. J. Stapleton. Dordrecht, The Netherlands: Kluwer Academic Publishers, 1994.

———. "Ultimacy and the Alterity of the Sublime." In *Being Human and the Ultimate*, edited by Nenos Georgopolous and Michael Hein. Atlanta: Rodopi Press, 1995.

Schrag, Calvin O., and Miller, David D. "Communication Studies and Philosophy: Convergence without Coincidence." In *The Critical Turn: Rhetoric and Philosophy in Postmodern Discourse*, edited by Ian Angus and Lenore Langsdorf. Carbondale: Southern Illinois University Press, 1992.

Introductions, Critical Discussions, Dictionaries, and Encyclopedias

Schrag, Calvin O. *The Cambridge Dictionary of Philosophy*, entries on "Pluralism," "Praxis," and "Speculative Philosophy," edited by Robert Audi. New York: Cambridge University Press, 1995.

———. Critical discussion of "Golden Coins and Golden Curls: Lived Aesthetics," by R. M. Griffin. In *Aisthesis and Aesthetics*, edited by E. W. Straus and R. M. Griffith. Pittsburgh: Duquesne University Press, 1970.

———. Critical discussion of "The Concept of Sin Consciousness," by Harry A. Nielsen. In *New Themes in Christian Philosophy*, edited by Ralph M. McInery. Notre Dame, Ind.: University of Notre Dame Press, 1968.

———. Critical discussion of "The World in Another Beginning: Poetic Dwelling and the Role of the Poet," by Werner Marx. In *On Heidegger and Language*, edited by Joseph J. Kockelmans. Evanston, Ill.: Northwestern University Press, 1972.

———. Foreword to *The Long Path to Nearness,* by Ramsey Eric Ramsey. Atlantic Highlands, N.J: Humanities Press, 1997.

———. Introduction to English translation of Edmund Husserl, *The Phenomenology of Internal Time-Consciousness,* trans. J. S. Churchill. Bloomington: Indiana University Press, 1964.

———. Introduction to Korean translation of *Radical Reflection and the Origin of the Human Sciences,* by Chong Pok Moon. Seoul: Hyung Sol Publishing Co., 1998.

———. Introduction to *The Crisis of Political Understanding: A Phenomenological Perspective in the Conduct of Political Inquiry,* by Hwa Yol Jung. Pittsburgh: Duquesne University Press, 1979.

———. Symposium contribution in *Phenomenology of Memory,* edited by E. W. Straus and R. M. Griffith. Pittsburgh: Duquesne University Press, 1970.

Schrag, Calvin O., and John T. Kirby. Reading list for "Philosophy of Aesthetics." In *The Comparative Reader.* New Haven, Conn.: Chancery Press, 1998.

Schrag, Calvin O., L. Embree, J. Edie, D. Ihde, and J. Kockelmans.. *Encyclopedia of Phenomenology,* entry on "United States." Dordrecht, The Netherlands: Kluwer Academic Publishers, 1997.

Edited Volumes

Schrag, Calvin O., and Eugene F. Kaelin. *Phenomenology in America: Origins and Developments.* Dordrecht, The Netherlands: Kluwer Academic Publishers, 1989.

Schrag, Calvin O., and Edith M. Kersey. *Women Philosophers: A Bio-Critical Source Book.* Westport, Conn.: Greenwood Press, 1989.

Schrag, Calvin O., and William L. McBride. *Phenomenology in a Pluralistic Context (Selected Studies in Phenomenology and Existential Philosophy).* Albany: State University of New York Press, 1983.

Schrag, Calvin O., and A.-T. Tymieniecka. *Foundations of Morality, Human Rights and the Human Sciences.* Dordrecht, The Netherlands: D. Reidel Publishing Co., 1983.

Schrag, Calvin O., James Edie, and Francis Parker. *Patterns of the Life-World.* Evanston, Ill.: Northwestern University Press, 1970.

Journal Articles

Schrag, Calvin O. "Appendix to Professor Spiegelberg's 'Reflections on the Phenomenological Movement,' " *Journal of the British Society for Phenomenology* II (1980): 280–81.

———. "At the Crossroads of Hermeneutics, Rhetoric, and Ethics," *Man and Ideas: The Journal of the Yeungam Center for Research in Eastern and Western Philosophy* 10 (1997).

———. "Communication in the Context of Cultural Diversity," *Phenomenological Inquiry* 16 (1990): 111–17.

————. "The Crisis of the Human Sciences," *Man and World* 8 (1975): 131–35.

————. "Decentered Subjectivity and the New Humanism," *Alaska, Quarterly Review* 2 (1984): 115–29.

————. "Existence and History," *Review of Metaphysics* 13 (1959): 28–44.

————. "Existentialism and Democracy," *Pacific Philosophy Forum* 2 (1964): 95–100.

————. "The Fabric of Fact: Beyond Epistemology," *Eros* 7 (1980): 83–97.

————. "Faith, Existence and Culture," *Journal of Religious Thought* 18 (1961–62): 83–91.

————. "Heidegger and Cassirer on Kant," *Kant-studien* 58 (1967): 87–100.

————. "Heidegger on Repetition and Historical Understanding," *Philosophy East and West* 20 (1970): 287–95.

————. "The Historical as a Feature of Experience," *University of Dayton Review* 8 (1971): 7–16.

————. "Husserl's Legacy in the Postmodern World," *Phenomenological Inquiry* 12 (1988): 125–33.

————. "Interpretation, Narrative, and Rationality," *Research in Phenomenology* XXI (1991): 98–115.

————. "John Wild on Contemporary Philosophy," *Journal of Philosophy and Phenomenological Research* 22 (1962): 409–11.

————. "Kierkegaard's Existential Reflections on Time," *The Personalist* 42 (1961): 149–64.

————. "Kierkegaard's Teleological Suspension of the Ethical," *Ethics* 70 (1959): 66–68.

————. "La Philosophie à la Fin du XX-Siècle avec un Commentaire sur Lucian Blaga," *Revista de Filosofía* 43 (1996).

————. "Liberal Learning in the Postmodern World," *The Key Reporter* 54 (1988): 1–4.

————. "The Lived Body as a Phenomenological Datum," *The Modern Schoolman* 39 (1962): 203–18.

————. "The Meaning of History," *Review of Metaphysics* 17 (1963): 703–17.

————. "Method and Phenomenological Research: Humility and Commitment in Interpretation," with Ramsey Eric Ramsey, *Human Studies* 131–37.

————. "Ontology and the Possibility of Religious Knowledge," *Journal of Religion* 42 (1962): 87–95.

————. "Phases of Phenomenological Philosophy in the United States," Japanese trans. Shoji Myochin, *Journal of Ideas* (Japanese) 5 (1972): 71–78.

————. "A Phenomenological Perspective on Communication," *Resources in Education,* the ERIC index, Nov. 1979 (microfiche).

————. "The Phenomenological Sociology of George Psathas: Appraisal and Critique," *Phenomenology and the Human Sciences* 16 (1991): 1–16.

————. "Phenomenology, Ontology and History in the Philosophy of Heidegger," *Revue Internationale de Philosophie* 44 (1958): 2–16.

————. "The Phenomenon of Embodied Speech," *The Philosophy Forum* 7 (1969): 3–27.

————. "Philosophical Anthropology in Contemporary Thought," *Philosophy East and West* 20 (1970): 83–89.

————. "Praxis and Structure: Conflicting Models in the Science of Man," *Journal of the British Society for Phenomenology* 6 (1975): 23–31.

————. "The Problem of Being and the Question about God," *International Journal for Philosophy of Religion*.

————. "Professor Seigfried on Descriptive Phenomenology and Constructivism," *Philosophy and Phenomenological Research* 40 (1980): 411–14.

————. "Reconstructing Reason in the Aftermath of Deconstruction," *Critical Review* 5 (1991): 247–60.

————. "The Recovery of the Phenomenological Subject: In Conversation with Derrida, Ricoeur, and Levinas," *Journal of the British Society for Phenomenology* 28 (1997).

————. "A Response to 'A Response to *Radical Reflection,*' " *Reflections: Essays in Phenomenology* (Winter 1981): 40–45,

————. "A Response to My Critics: Professors O'Neill and Mays," *Journal of the British Society for Phenomenology* 14 (1983): 40–49.

————. "Reminiscences on Paul Tillich: The Man and His Works," *North American Paul Tillich Society Newsletter* XXI (1995): 3–8.

————. "Rhetoric Resituated at the End of Philosoophy," *Quarterly Journal of Speech* 71 (1985): 164–74.

————. "The Story of the Human Subject in the Aftermath of Postmodern Critique," *Revue Roumaine de Philosophie* 1–2 (1996).

————. "The Structure of Moral Experience: A Phenomenological and Existential Analysis," *Ethics* 73 (1963): 225–65.

————. "Struktur der Erfahrung in der Philosophie von James and Whitehead," *Zeitschrift für Philosophische Forschung* 23 (1969): 479–94.

————. "Substance, Subject and *Existenz,*" *Proceedings of the American Catholic Philosophical Association* 42 (1969):175–82.

————. "The Topology of Hope," *Humanitas* XIII (19977): 269–81.

————. "Towards a Phenomenology of Guilt," *Journal of Existential Psychiatry* 3 (1963): 333–42.

————. "The Transvaluation of Aesthetics and the Work of Art," *Southwestern Journal of Philosophy* 4 (1973): 109–24.

————. "Twentieth Century Philosophy at the Crossroads with a Note on Lucian Blaga," *Romanian Review* 51 (1996).

————. "Whitehead and Heidegger: Process Philosophy and Existential Philosophy," *Dialectica* 13 (1959): 42–56.

Schrag, Calvin O., and Chong-Mun Kim. "On the Hermeneutics of Gadamer and Habermas," *Korean Journal of Philosophy* 12–13 (1996): 135–48.

Articles Reprinted in Anthologies

Schrag, Calvin O. "Communicative Rhetoric and the Claims of Reason," reprinted in *Man and Ideas* 2 (1990).

————. "Husserl's Legacy in the Postmodern World," reprinted in *Man and Ideas:*

The Journal of the Yeungnam Center for Research in Eastern and Western Philosophy 1 (1989).

———. "The Lived Body as a Phenomenological Datum," reprinted in *Sport and the Body: A Philosophical Symposium,* edited by Ellen Gerber. Philadelphia: Lea & Febiger, 1972 (2nd ed. 1979).

———. "Ontology and the Possibility of Religious Knowledge," reprinted in *Religious Language and the Problem of Religious Knowledge,* edited by Ronald E. Santoni. Bloomington: Indiana University Press, 1968.

———. "Phenomenology, Ontology, and History in the Philosophy of Heidegger," reprinted in *Phenomenology: The Philosophy of Edmund Husserl and Its Interpretation,* edited by Joseph J. Kockelmans. New York: Doubleday & Company, 1967,

———. "The Transvaluation of Aesthetics and the Work of Art," reprinted in *Thinking About Being: Aspects of Heidegger's Thought,* edited by Robert Shahan and J. N. Mohanty. Norman: University of Oklahoma Press, 1984.

———. "Whitehead and Heidegger: Process Philosophy and Existential Philosophy," reprinted in *Philosophy Today* (Spring 1960).

Translations

Schrag, Calvin O. "Christian Root-Terms: Kerygma, Mysterium, Kairos, Oikonomia," by Erich Przywara. German trans. *Religion and Culture: Essays in Honor of Paul Tillich,* edited by Walter Leibrecht. New York: Harper & Brothers, 1959.

Notes on Contributors

Sandra Bartky is a professor of philosophy and gender and women's studies at the University of Illinois at Chicago. She is the author of *Femininity and Domination: Studies in the Phenomenology of Oppression* and *"Sympathy and Solidarity" and Other Essays*.

Linda Bell, a professor of philosophy and the director of the Women's Studies Institute at Georgia State University, teaches and publishes in the areas of existentialism, ethics, and feminist theory. Her publications include *Sartre's Ethics of Authenticity, Rethinking Ethics in the Midst of Violence: A Feminist Approach to Freedom, Visions of Women* (editor), and *Overcoming Racism and Sexism* (coeditor).

John D. Caputo holds the David R. Cook Chair of Philosophy at Villanova University. His most recent publications are *On Religion; More Radical Hermeneutics: On Not Knowing Who We Are; Blackwell Readings in Continental Philosophy: The Religious* (editor); *Questioning God* (coeditor); *God, the Gift, and Postmodernism* (coeditor); *The Prayers and Tears of Jacques Derrida: Religion without Religion;* and *Deconstruction in a Nutshell: A Conversation with Jacques Derrida*. A former executive codirector of the Society for Phenomenology and Existential Philosophy, he edits the Fordham University Press series Perspectives in Continental Philosophy.

Edward S. Casey is Leading Professor of Philosophy at SUNY, Stony Brook, where he was chair of the philosophy department for most of the 1990s. He is the author of *The Fate of Place, Representing Places in Landscape Paintings and Maps*, and *Earth-Mapping*. His contribution to this volume is connected with his book project *The World at a Glance*.

David Crownfield is professor emeritus of religion and philosophy at the University of Northern Iowa and the owner-operator of a used-book store in Cedar Falls, Iowa. He is a member of both the Society for Phenomenology and Existential Philosophy and of the American Academy of Religion, of which he has chaired the Philosophy of Religion Section. He is also past president of the Midwest Division of the American Theological Society and editor of *Body/Text in Julia Kristeva* and coeditor of *Lacan and Theological Discourse*.

Fred Dallmayr is Packey J. Dee Professor in the Departments of Government and Philosophy at the University of Notre Dame. He specializes in recent Continental philosophy and also in comparative philosophy. Among his books are *Alternative*

Visions: Paths in the Global Village, Border Crossings, and *Achieving Our World: Toward a Global and Plural Democracy.*

Bernard P. Dauenhauer is a professor emeritus of philosophy at the University of Georgia. His most recent book is *Paul Ricoeur: The Promise and Risk of Politics.*

Martin C. Dillon is Distinguished Teaching Professor of Philosophy at Binghamton University. His publications include *Merleau-Ponty's Ontology, Semiological Reductionism: A Critique of the Deconstructionist Movement in Postmodern Thought, Beyond Romance,* and more than fifty journal articles.

Michael J. Hyde is University Distinguished Professor of Communication Ethics, Wake Forest University. His most recent book is *The Call of Conscience: Heidegger and Levinas, Rhetoric and the Euthanasia Debate.*

Hwa Yol Jung is a professor of political science at Moravian College in Bethlehem, Pennsylvania. He studied existential phenomenology under the guidance of the late John Wild at Northwestern and Yale and was a visiting professor at Purdue in the spring of 1975. He has published numerous articles and books in the areas of systematic political philosophy, philosophy of the social sciences, comparative philosophy, literary theory, environmental philosophy, philosophy of technology, and body politics.

Victor Kestenbaum is an associate professor of philosophy and education at Boston University. His principal areas of interest include pragmatism, phenomenology, philosophy and literature, and philosophy and the professions. He is the author of *The Grace and the Severity of the Ideal: John Dewey and the Transcendent.*

Lenore Langsdorf is a professor at Southern Illinois University, Carbondale. Her research and teaching are focused on the philosophy of communication, using resources from both the phenomenological (Husserl, Gadamer, Ricoeur) and American pragmatic (Dewey, Mead) traditions. Her current work is directed toward a phenomenology of communicative action; a recent publication that develops aspects of that project is "The Real Conditions for the Possibility of Communicative Action," in *Perspectives on Habermas.*

Gary B. Madison is an emeritus professor of philosophy at McMaster University in Canada. The author of numerous books and dozens of articles on contemporary Continental philosophy, he also has written on political and economic thought, including, most recently, *The Politics of Postmodernity: Essays in Applied Hermeneutics.*

Martin Beck Matuštík is a professor of philosophy at Purdue University. He is the author of *Jürgen Habermas: A Philosophical-Political Profile.*

William L. McBride is Arthur G. Hansen Distinguished Professor of Philosophy at Purdue University. He is a former executive cosecretary, with Calvin O. Schrag, of the Society for Phenomenology and Existential Philosophy. His most recent book is *From Yugoslav Praxis to Global Pathos: Anti-Hegemonic Post-Post-Marxist Essays.*

Robert C. Scharff is a professor of philosophy at the University of New Hampshire. He writes on nineteenth- and twentieth-century Continental philosophy (especially Dilthey, Heidegger, and the hermeneutics of science), the history of positivism, and the philosophy of technology. He is the author of *Comte after Positivism* and coeditor (with Val Dusek) of *Philosophy of Technology: The Technological Condition, a Reader.* Since 1995 he has been the editor of *Continental Philosophy Review* (formerly *Man and World*).

Merold Westphal is Distinguished Professor of Philosophy at Fordham University. In addition to books on Hegel and Kierkegaard, he is the author of *God, Guilt, and Death, Suspicion and Faith,* and *Overcoming Onto-Theology.*

Bruce Wilshire is a senior professor of philosophy at Rutgers University. He is the author of *William James and Phenomenology: A Study of "The Principles of Psychology"; Role Playing and Identity: The Limits of Theatre as Metaphor; The Moral Collapse of the University: Professionalism, Purity, and Alienation; Wild Hunger: The Primal Roots of Modern Addiction; The Primal Roots of American Philosophy: Pragmatism, Phenomenology, and Native American Thought; Nihilistic Consequences of Analytic Philosophy;* and a manuscript on genocide—a hypothesis about its precipitating factors.